Yale Historical Publications, Miscellany, 130

Abigail Scott Duniway signing the woman suffrage proclamation, 30 November 1912, in presence of Governor Oswald West and Mrs. Henry Waldo Coe, president of the Oregon State Woman Suffrage Association

REBEL FOR RIGHTS
ABIGAIL SCOTT DUNIWAY

Ruth Barnes Moynihan

Yale University Press

New Haven and London

In order to keep this title in print, this edition was produced using digital printing technology in a relatively short print run. This would not have been attainable using traditional printing methods. Although the reproduction of this copy may not appear the same as in the original edition, the text remains the same and all materials and methods used still conform to the highest book-making standards.

Designed by Nancy Ovedovitz and set in VIP Baskerville type. Printed in the United States of America by Lightning Source.

Library of Congress Cataloging in Publication Data
Moynihan, Ruth Barnes.
  Rebel for Rights, Abigail Scott Duniway
  (Yale historical publications. Miscellany ; 130)
  Based on the author's thesis (Ph.D.)—Yale University.
  Bibliography: p.
  Includes index.
    1. Duniway, Abigail Scott, 1834–1915. 2. Suffragettes—United States—Biography. 3. Women's rights—United States—History—19th century. 4. Women—Suffrage—United States—History—19th century. 5. Women—Suffrage—Oregon—History—19th century.
I. Title. II. Series.
HQ1413.D86M69 1983   324.6'23'0924 [B]   83-1142
ISBN 0–300–02952–7
ISBN 0–300–03478–4 pbk. ISBN-978-0-300-03478-4 (pbk)

For my children—Robert, Elaine, Edward, Neil, Susan, Richard, and Benjamin

CONTENTS

ILLUSTRATIONS

Frontispiece: Abigail Scott Duniway signing the woman suffrage proclamation, 30 November 1912, in presence of Governor Oswald West
and Mrs. Henry Waldo Coe, president of the Oregon State Woman
Suffrage Association. By permission of David Duniway

following page 106

Sectional map of Tazewell County, Illinois. From *History of Tazewell
County, Illinois* (1879).

James Scott (1779–1860) of Pleasant Grove, Illinois. By permission of
David Duniway

John Tucker Scott (1809–80), ca. 1870. By permission of David
Duniway

Ann Roelofson Scott (1811–52) from *Oregon Historical Quarterly* 14 (June
1913): opp. p. 104. By permission of Oregon Historical Society

Harvey Scott, 29 August 1857. From tintype reproduced in Harvey
Scott, *History of the Oregon Country*, vol. 1, opp. p. 90

Abigail Scott Duniway as teacher, ca. 1862. By permission of David
Duniway

Abigail Scott Duniway, editor of *New Northwest*, 1871. By permission of
David Duniway

Duniway home in Albany, Oregon. Snapshot by Mabel Cronner, May
1919. By permission of David Duniway

Ben and Abigail Duniway with children in Albany, Oregon, 1868. Standing: Hubert, Willis, Clara, and Wilkie; in Ben's lap: Clyde; added:
Ralph. By permission of David Duniway

Abigail Scott Duniway reading from a copy of her book *David and Anna
Matson*, 1876. By permission of David Duniway

Ben C. Duniway, 1876. Davidson Bros. photographers, Portland,
Oregon. By permission of David Duniway

Duniway home at 5th and Clay streets, Portland, Oregon. By permission
of David Duniway

Abigail Scott Duniway, with spirit of Colonel E. D. Baker, ca. 1886. D. H.
Hendee, photographer, East Portland, Oregon (Alfred C. Jones pho-
tocopy). By permission of David Duniway

Abigail Scott Duniway, 4 October 1895. Trover-Cronise Collection
#A-2980b. By permission of Oregon Historical Society

Abigail Scott Duniway at the polls. By permission of the Oregon Historical Society, #ORE 4599

Abigail Scott Duniway voting. By permission of the Oregon Historical Society, #ORE 4601

ACKNOWLEDGMENTS

To explore Abigail Scott Duniway's long and productive life (1834–1915) is to explore many of the most significant events and issues of nineteenth-century America. Her life provides a remarkable focus for that exploration, as well as for understanding the private reality of frontier women and family life. Thus, my greatest debt is to Abigail Duniway herself, and to the generosity of spirit which made her so available to her own and future generations.

I must also acknowledge my debt to David Cushing Duniway of Salem, Oregon, retired state archivist and grandson of Abigail Duniway. His careful preservation of the Scott and Duniway Papers and the letters to Clyde Duniway, plus his own extensive genealogical research, is an important resource for all scholars. David's hospitality to me when I was in Oregon and his cooperation and encouragement have been invaluable. He has continued to be helpful even through occasional disagreements on some of my interpretations. I cannot thank him enough.

Particular thanks are also due to Professor Jean Ward of Lewis and Clark College in Portland. Betty Book of the Oregon State Library and Louise Gerity of the Lewis and Clark Library facilitated my first reading and photostating of the Duniway Papers. The Oregon Historical Society has been most cooperative. Librarians at Smith College and at Yale made it feasible for me to tackle the mountainous task of reading the *New Northwest* on microfilm. Joy and Edwin Browne let me read the Scott letters in their possession at their home in Independence, Missouri. I am especially grateful to Mildred (Billie) Durfee and her husband, Dr. Raphael Durfee, for their unexpected and generous hospitality to this "wandering scholar," a stranger, during my first trip to Portland. Not only did their accommodations enable me to develop a permanent nostalgia for Abigail Duniway's home city; they also nursed me through a bad case of flu!

Professor Howard Lamar of Yale University, who was my thesis advisor, has been both a fine critic and an encouraging friend. His never-failing kindness, availability, and astute suggestions contributed immeasurably to the progress and completion of this work. I must also thank my other Yale history department advisors, Professors Jonathan Spence (who encouraged my study of women's history before there were any graduate courses on the subject), Cynthia Russett, David Brion Davis, and Edmund S. Morgan. Many other scholars and colleagues have also provided information or useful advice.

Florence Thomas, Jean Hankins, and Mary Whitney have been cheerful and efficient typists at all stages of this work. Thanks also are due for the careful and perceptive work of my editors, Charles Grench and Lawrence Kenney.

The Danforth Foundation gave me a Graduate Fellowship for Women from 1973 to 1977. Combined with a Yale University Fellowship, it made my Ph.D. studies possible. In dissertation form, this book received the Beinecke Prize in Western History from Yale University in 1979. An American Council of Learned Societies (ACLS) Grant-in-Aid in 1980 enabled me to do the revision for publication.

The good-humored responsibility, independence, loyalty, and patience of my family during these years of research and writing cannot be sufficiently praised.

INTRODUCTION

"When woman's true history shall have been written," said Abigail Scott Duniway in the words of one of her self-revealing fictional characters, "her part in the upbuilding of this nation will astound the world."[1] This book reveals Abigail Duniway's own "true history," forgotten or misunderstood by many, important to all Americans.

I discovered Abigail Scott Duniway in Eleanor Flexner's *Century of Struggle*, where she is described as "the hardiest and most tireless suffrage worker the western states produced." But Flexner, following the *History of Woman Suffrage* account, also accused Duniway of "unbridled vanity," "errors in judgment," egotism, and unjustifiable bitterness during her later years.[2] I was intrigued. Was there another side to the story? Why did Duniway have such conflicts with some other suffragists? Why was she so vehemently opposed to prohibition in contrast to the growing Women's Christian Temperance Union? Was she uniquely independent or was she typical of nineteenth-century frontier women? What could her life experience reveal about the nature and potential of American women?

The title of Duniway's autobiography, *Path Breaking*, was a conscious expression of the self-image which shaped and motivated her life. The paradigm of the pioneer, a breaker of new paths in a frontier wilderness, was her heritage from generations of pioneers within her own family. The image as well as the experience provided justification for her personal self-definition, encouraged by the loyalty and admiration of her father and a network of sisters and other relatives. Abigail Duniway was not unique in nineteenth-century America, only uniquely gifted by circumstance and talent.

Jenny Scott, as she was called during her youth, was essentially self-taught. Her "formal" education totalled less than twelve months in school, though she and her family were all readers, thinkers, and people of "deep convictions." Her intellectual development is evident in her own writing, from the dialectical speech forms and spelling in her overland journal of 1852 and her early letters (purposely retained in this book) to the passionate colloquialism and references to her reading in later letters and speeches. Her novels and journalistic style are documents of the pragmatic, oral–auditory culture of nineteenth-century rural and western society. What Mrs. Duniway said and how she said it became increasingly unacceptable to the "refined," educated easterners and urbanites who later joined the woman's movement. But her straight-forward iconoclasm could never be stifled.

Abigail Scott Duniway's philosophy represents the continuing vitality of the Jeffersonian tradition in political and social thought. Like most first-generation suffragists, she based her equal rights arguments on the principles of justice enunciated in the Declaration of Independence—no taxation without representation, no aristocracy of sex. Her demand for the vote was a logical extension of America's continuing democratiza-tion—a process that had been underway since the eighteenth century and that culminated in suffrage for all citizens (except women) without regard for "race, color, or previous condition of servitude" as granted in the Fifteenth Amendment. Her insistence on individual financial auton-omy for women paralleled her commitment to personal independence for all human beings and her concern for the progress and development of the West. She believed in entrepreneurial ambition and small-scale, cooperative capitalism, an ideology widely shared in mid-nineteenth-century America and by no means limited to westerners. Her insistence upon the priority of personal moral reform rather than imposed prohi-bition of alcohol was based on opposition to governmental or religious coercion, a major tradition in American history. For the same reason she opposed big business, monopoly finance, and the pretensions of the elite—both male and female.[3]

These issues were the crux of her problems with a new generation of upper-middle-class, Christian temperance suffragists. They were also the reason why Gilded Age politicians and capitalists opposed, harassed, and frequently defeated her work. Urbanization, industrialization, com-mercialism, immigration, and related problems changed the political and social hegemony after the Civil War and profoundly affected the behavior and treatment of American women. We can see those changes occurring in the life story of Abigail Scott Duniway.

When Oregon became the seventh state in the nation to approve votes for women in 1912 (eight years before the national constitutional amendment), it was a close race and a major victory for the indomitable Mrs. Duniway. Though opponents questioned her tactics, their argu-ments seem unconvincing and their enmity divisive and vindictive. Abigail Duniway could be difficult, but she had earned her position of leadership, and she had many intelligent, dedicated followers. Further-more, she was entirely correct about prohibition; it did cause the delay of woman suffrage by mobilizing opposition, and it did prove an unen-forceable disaster as a law.

Abigail Scott Duniway's greatest achievement was her lifelong exam-ple and the never-ending publicity she gave to the cause of women's rights. Her personal energy and determined action made her an inspiration to thousands. She kept the subject of the right to vote and the right to one's own autonomy constantly present in the consciousness of Oregonians, making herself a symbol which could not be ignored, even by her opponents. One can never fully assess such influence, but one can guess from much testimony like that of Governor Oswald West. He remembered standing as a small boy at the edge of a crowd on Salem's town square listening to Mrs. Duniway. When she argued that mothers had as much right to vote as "saloon bums," he agreed, and did not forget. More than thirty years later he asked Abigail Scott Duniway to write the official Woman Suffrage Proclamation before he signed it into law.[4]

In Portland, Oregon, there is a park named for Abigail Scott Duniway. A public school in East Portland bears her name. She is included on the League of Women Voters plaque at the League's Washington headquarters. In 1944 the Oregon Shipbuilding Company named a new Liberty Ship the *Abigail S. Duniway*. (It was later sold to a Panamanian concern and renamed the *Virago*.) And in 1981 the Oregon legislature nominated her unanimously as Oregon's representative in the newly established National Woman's Hall of Fame.

Through her words Duniway's influence continues. Most of her arguments are as relevant today as they were one hundred years ago. And the frankness of her expression is as refreshing. I have striven to do justice to the ambiguities of her career and to the complexity of her personality without imposing any methodological or ideological structure upon her own reality. That reality, however, places Abigail Duniway in the first rank of American feminists. She was a woman who would not, and should not, be ignored.

CHAPTER 1

A Frontier Childhood

"Poor baby! A woman's life is so hard!"

Abigail Jane Scott was born in a log cabin at seven in the morning on her parents' fourth wedding anniversary, 22 October 1834. She was the second daughter and third child of Ann Roelofson and John Tucker Scott. Their first child, a boy, had died before he was four months old. Her father stormed and her mother wept at Abigail's birth because she was a girl. Their sorrow, her mother later told her, "was almost too grievous to be borne."[1]

Jenny Scott, as she was nicknamed, quickly established herself within her family as the wild and difficult daughter. Nine more children, six girls and three boys, followed Abigail Jane into life in the harsh conditions of newly settled Tazewell County, Illinois. She was seventeen months younger than dutiful Mary Frances (Fanny) and two years older than pious Margaret Ann (Maggie). Jenny was "dreamy, untaught and imaginative," hot-tempered, and frequently ill. Though she could be a compulsive worker, she hated domesticity and came to fear the hell-fire camp-meeting rhetoric of her Cumberland Presbyterian relatives. Younger sister Catherine called Jenny Scott "the burden bearer of our childhood."[2]

During Abigail Jane's first year of life, the spring and summer of 1835, Illinois experienced destructive rain and flooding, followed by one of the worst droughts in its history. Crops were destroyed and disease was widespread. Superabundant flies and mosquitos spread the endemic malaria. Farm families had to rely for income even more heavily than usual on the wife's production of eggs, butter, and woven "jeans." There was no time for pampering or cuddling. Jenny Scott spent her first summer, like many other frontier babies, sitting on the floor "complaining and neglected, soothed only by a piece of bacon, attached by a string to a bed-post, or a loom stanchion, until [she] would fall asleep from exhaustion, a prey to numerous houseflies."[3]

Not that the Scotts were any poorer than most of their neighbors. In fact, John Tucker Scott and grandfather James Scott were leading citizens of the small town of Groveland, just six miles east of Fort Peoria on the Illinois River in central Illinois. Tucker Scott was postmaster and manager of a sawmill—two of the most essential services in a new community. His father had the government contract for hauling mail twice a week from the riverboat dock at Pekin eight miles away. James Scott was also road and school commissioner, tax collector, and Tazewell County sheriff until 1835. He had staked his claim and built his cabin in the timbered wilderness of Groveland Township in 1824, preparing the way for his family and numerous other relatives to join him from Kentucky. The only other settlers so far north in Illinois were a blacksmith to the local Indians, a noted hunter on the United States surveying team, a family from Ohio, and James's younger brother Peter Scott. (Chicago was not founded until 1830.) Grandmother Frankie Scott named their location Pleasant Grove and gave a hen and chicks to each new settler.[4]

John Tucker Scott met Ann Roelofson when she came to a neighboring farm to help her sister Esther Johnson with a first baby. Neill Johnson was an idealistic circuit-riding preacher for the Cumberland Presbyterians. He had come to the Groveland vicinity shortly after the Scotts and bought the land adjoining James Scott's claim. When Ann and Tucker Scott married, they moved into a cabin on section 25, just before the winter of the Great Snow—the worst in living memory according to the local Pottowatomies, whose campground and tribal burial ground were nearby. Famine, death, and wolves stalked the prairie frontier that winter. For all the transplanted Kentuckians it was only one of many hardships to follow.[5]

In this preindustrial agricultural era, farm mothers were working women. Farm fathers had equally essential chores. Adults tended to believe "that no child was in danger of injury from overwork," Abigail Duniway later wrote, calling this "an almost fatal misconception . . . in my case, as the resodding of a blue grass lawn at the age of nine . . . gave me a chronic weakness of the spine." The pains of rheumatoid arthritis continued all her life and made her a cripple in her final years.

Jenny Scott had many other childhood duties:

> My first task . . . was washing dishes while standing on a chair to reach the table; my next was a seemingly overwhelming job of paring, quartering, coring and stringing apples, in long festoons for drying. Then followed the sleep-urging monotony of picking wool by hand; and after this came the spinning wheel.

She had to milk cows morning and evening, make butter, plant and hoe the corn and potatoes, and help her brother Harvey gather and chop wood. At an early age she and Harvey (three and a half years younger) were designated to plant a ten-acre field of corn. They "grew so tired that we skipped an entire 'land' in the middle of the field to shorten the job; but we realized our mistake when the fraud was discovered, almost too late to correct it."[6]

Danger, too, stalked the lives of children, contributing to the sense of responsibility in a sensitive older child. Of the few specific incidents which Abigail Duniway recalled in the mere eight pages on childhood in her autobiography, two involved rescuing younger siblings from the fire. Once it was Harvey. Later it was Catherine, who "toppled forward from her chair and fell into the fire" as the others screamed "and brought our agonized mother to the scene." Fanny and Jenny "always felt that we ought to have known enough to have kept her away from the fire."[7]

Jenny Scott found her childhood tasks onerous, both in fact and in memory, because she was always being pushed to the limits of her ability. The pattern was established so early that it became part of her psyche; she had to be busy, to be working, to be striving with all her energy—yet always simultaneously longing for rest, for time to write and think, for protection from the stresses of her life. As she later wrote, "I was never a strong or healthy child, my numerous ailments resulting, as I afterwards learned, from often self-imposed stints of heavy overwork in my first decade of existence from which I am still a sufferer." The words "often" and "heavy" were inserted in the handwritten sentence, while "self-imposed" implies the attempt to gain attention and approval by means of willful commitment to work even in her childhood. Work was also a means of identification with her mother, who "had worn . . . herself to a frazzle with just such drudgery" throughout her marriage.[8]

The task Jenny Scott hated most involved the "many hot Summer days, of seemingly interminable length, when we were kept busy at picking wool by hand," and then spinning, spooling, reeling, and hanking it. The job was so unbearable that Duniway later made it the prime punishment for "turbulent" Judith Reid of her first serialized novel (her only fiction dealing with early childhood experience).

> The little log loomhouse where my mother toiled throughout the long, hot summer to prepare the winter clothing, and where she shivered through the cold, bitter winter to manufacture our summer apparel—no wonder she slowly failed, poor thing—was to be my prison during the hottest months of the year. Wearily the work went on. Pick, pick, pick at the huge pile of burr-be-matted, abominable wool that lay heaped up behind the grim old loom.
>
> My fingers grew white—almost transparent—while my limbs seemed oppressed with an inward weight. I grew perfectly listless, and my mother would often chide me, saying it would do me no good to mope myself to death. But this state of apathetic indifference continued only during daylight. At night my whole nervous system was strung up to a state of intense wakefulness. . . . The most simple and ordinary sounds grew insup-

portable, and I frequently remained awake through the entire night, listening to the monotonous tick, tick, tick of the old hall clock.

The child suffers "a week of nervous prostration" before starting the work and another collapse before finishing, along with a personal crisis of identity which rings with the authenticity of probable autobiography:

> A sort of incomprehensible dread of my parents' authority took the place of the love I would gladly have given them. "*What* am I, and *why* am I, and what will become of me?" were queries that would not be answered. I was a sort of disagreeable incumbrance, an unnecessary evil, and·yet how could I help it, or how could I rid myself of myself? Queries of awful import for a child of seven years were these; but many such imaginative children have asked and many more, I fear, will ask just such unanswerable questions.[9]

Judith becomes convinced that nobody loves her, having heard her mother say, "She gives me more trouble than all the rest of the children put together!" and her father mourn that she is not a boy. Judith's mother assures her that Jesus "*will* love you if you'll forsake your wicked ways" and become "an obedient and good-tempered little girl" instead of "turbulent and obstinate." He even "pardoned the thief on the cross, you know." Judith, "stunned and stung" by the unjust comparison, "lay hushed and still in the deep bitterness of unutterable woe." "Jesus, the Saviour of sinners, loved the thief upon the cross; me he could not love. My parents wished me dead! . . . I loathed myself from a conviction of moral unworthiness, but no beam of peace could find its way into my heart." The fictional child flees from the house barefoot on a frosty night to her special place near the river, recovers her happiness as "Nature's child"—and is then taken so ill that she has to spend the rest of the winter in bed.[10]

This episode may well reveal a comparable trauma in Jenny Scott's own childhood; Mrs. Duniway incorporated autobiographical material into all her novels. However, though the sense of rejection became an integral part of Abigail Scott Duniway's personality, triggering defensive sensitivity and belligerence, her illness also provided a sense of destiny and vocation. Even among family members she was henceforth perceived as special, delicate, intellectual—more free than the others to pursue her own identity—within the limits of her environment. She was a "chosen one."

But she rebelled against Calvinist notions of salvation and damnation. The misdeed which precipitated Judith Reid's punishment was wandering away from a camp meeting, as Jenny Scott did too. Frontier preaching frequently led her to "the ragged edge of despair," Duniway later wrote, while the frenzy of camp meetings left her "religiously dead" and

made her eventually "if not skeptical, decidedly unorthodox." She was
terrified by revivalist preaching, remembering clearly the sermons of the
"kindly preacher" who

> seemed to find delight in holding the frightened penitent spellbound, . . .
> suspended, mentally, as by a hair, over a liquid lake of fire and brimstone,
> with the blue blazes shooting . . . beneath his writhing body; . . . his Heav-
> enly Father . . . waiting with scythe in hand to snip that hair.[11]

Uncle Neill Johnson claimed credit for "two considerable revivals of
Religion" during his years in Tazewell County, but his effect on Jenny
Scott did not last. She considered him "a striking example of a working
parson imbued with the practical idea of what constitutes a 'Church of
the Big Licks.' . . . [m]any are the beneficiaries of his industry and skill
who have long survived his ministry." She later compared fire and
brimstone preaching to mumps and measles—necessary but unfortunate
afflictions of childhood. Rebellion against piety, religiosity, church rules,
and dogma fueled the pragmatism of her own "circuit-riding" career as
well as her frequent battles with church authorities and religious women
in later years.[12]

One of the few bright moments in that terrible first decade of Jenny
Scott's life was the birth in February 1838 of Harvey Whitefield Scott. A
boy, at last, to carry on the family name and the family ambitions!
Named after the great eighteenth-century evangelist George Whitefield,
Harvey was greeted by his parents and all their relatives with rejoicing.
Brilliant, handsome, the "apple of his mother's eye"—and just enough
younger than Jenny to excite her sense of responsibility as well as her
jealousy.

Loyal to the death, Abigail Jane was stimulated by her brother's existence and occasional support, but stifled too by his superior opportunities, achievements, and self-centeredness. They worked together as
children, but they also fought together—and Harvey soon became
strong enough to beat up his sister regularly. As adults they both became
editors and writers, but Harvey's opposition and political power helped
prevent the success of his sister's woman suffrage campaign for forty
years—until after his death. Their verbal battles were notorious within
the family.

Harvey was Jenny's most admired sibling—and her most formidable
rival. The theme of jealousy runs throughout her work, both fictional
and autobiographical. Strong-minded but misunderstood heroines, usually the oldest among numerous sisters, are paired with brilliant, selfish
brothers who take male superiority for granted. Even the names are
similar—Herbert in *Captain Gray's Company*, Hal in *From the West to the
West*, Henry in *Amie and Henry Lee*, Hal in *Laban McShane*. The latter

novel, written when Duniway was almost fifty, opens with a twin sister bemoaning her father's decision to send Hal to college while she "must let others choose my road without regard to my preferences, and for no other reason than because I was born a girl." She continues:

> I used always to help you get the stovewood, hoe the garden, and drive the cows to pasture. Then, when your work was done outside, mine went on in the house. You went boating while I washed and mended your clothes; you went fishing while I washed dishes; and, for exercise, you played ball while I puzzled out your problems and mine in higher arithmetic and algebra. I've always done twice as much work as you have, Hal, and have led you mentally in everything in the bargain.[13]

There were such numerous and valid reasons for Jenny Scott's jealousy of her brother that it would have been abnormal *not* to feel it. The renowned Dr. Benjamin Spock explained to twentieth-century parents (who had the newfound leisure to worry about sibling rivalry) that "a phase of jealousy—if it is not too overwhelming and if it is gradually digested—may be a truly constructive experience..., inoculating and fortifying [the child] ... against future threats of the same sort."[14] Abigail Jane Scott digested a great deal of such jealousy, fortifying herself for a lifetime of competition and commitment, but the experience was so overwhelming that she never quite conquered the resentment she felt at threats of displacement, by either men or women. It was not easy to be the sister of Harvey Scott.

The three oldest Scott sisters, however, formed a loyal triumvirate. Fanny and Maggie were the foundation of Jenny's female "network," along with Kate (Catherine), Etty (Harriet), and Sarah as they came along. All of them, and their children, eventually became active suffragists. Among them, from childhood on, Jenny Scott was accepted and loved. Their support balanced Harvey's competition in her psychic makeup.

On the other hand, Jenny's relationship with her mother seems to have involved significant antagonism. It was her father who protected and encouraged her and with whom she most closely identified. She said of her parents, "My father was a generous-hearted, impulsive, talented, but uneducated man; my mother was a conscientious, self-sacrificing, intelligent, but uneducated woman. Both were devotedly religious, and both believed implicitly that self-abnegation was the crowning glory of womanhood."[15] Duniway admired generosity and impulsiveness; she spent her life trying to make women less self-sacrificing and more assertive. Mothers figure in her novels mainly as faultfinders or passive sufferers—usually dying in childbirth or punishing the heroine or warning daughters against marriage.[16] Her "poor invalid mother," as she always called her, served Abigail Jane as an example of what *not* to be herself.

The relationship of the fictional Judith Reid to her mother shows profound antagonism and even violence. The child attempts to invent a "cinder-catcher" for the tops of smokestacks on steamers such as she had seen on the Illinois River. After secretly stealing cotton thread from her mother and time from her own spinning, and after "a fit of violent, nervous head-ache" which made her "languid and miserable," Judith showed the contraption to her father. Though mildly interested, he warned her, "You are a poor man's daughter, little Judith, and your invention would not be noticed in Washington." The disappointed child went home to her mother "sweating over the red-hot stove," enduring the "acute suffering" of the "first months of gestation." "No wonder that mothers, under this double curse, often say and do unreasonable things, and . . . sometimes endow their offspring with ungovernable tempers and feeble constitutions," wrote Mrs. Duniway. Her story continued with Judith showing her "wonderful invention" just as something boiled over on the stove, making her mother's nausea even more unbearable.

> "You good for nothing hussy!" was the poor, dear woman's comment. "You've spent many an hour over this piece of tomfoolery when you might have been helping your mother!" . . . Then she discovered . . . the purloined spool of cotton. Rage got the better of discretion. . . . [S]he snatched a long switch from some nails on the kitchen wall, and proceeded to belabor my quivering flesh. I became frightened, then angry. . . . Then I snatched the switch, broke it into fragments, scratched like a wild-cat, and may God forgive me! in my frenzy I conquered my mother. . . . I am certain that I did not strike her; but I threw her to the floor and held her there, while my tongue . . . uttered unlawful abominations. It was the most wicked act of my life, but I had really passed beyond my own control.[17]

Abigail Scott Duniway's fiction obviously did not conform to Victorian stereotypes. She was equally candid about childbirth. Her third novel, published in her newspaper, the *New Northwest*, opens with a powerful scene which exemplifies the worst conditions of frontier childbirth and baby care. The frightened mother lay on a "low bed in the corner" while, "Old Aunt Betsey" with a lighted pipe watched. "Scream after scream pierced the smoke-laden air of the lonely cabin." Finally, "the patient clenched her hands, rolled back her great, shining eye and stared" in convulsions. Aunt Betsey "fell upon her knees" in "incoherent prayer," then "seized a half dozen large ears of Indian corn and plunged them into boiling water. . . . When they became hot and steaming she applied them to the sufferer's body, thereby relaxing the rigid muscles, and the patient awoke again to consciousness." When the baby was finally born, the mother exclaimed, "A girl. . . . It would be a Lord's blessing if it would never see daylight." And then, "Take it from me, or I'll *kill* it!" as she "writhed and raved" until she died.[18]

Ann Roelofson Scott's situation was not so bad as that of her daughter's novel; for one thing, she did not die. But she gave birth approximately every eighteen months for twenty years, and not joyously. The older girls all assumed responsibility for younger ones by the time they were six or seven. Abigail Scott Duniway still remembered at eighty, "when another little sister came to our crowded home, and my mother said, through her tears: 'Poor baby! She'll be a woman some day! Poor baby! A woman's lot is so hard!'"[19]

It was from John Tucker Scott that Duniway claimed to have inherited her fiery temperament—including her sense of justice. He encouraged her education and idealism as far as possible with limited means. A friend described him as

> tall, powerful and erect, with immense features, bold and strongly carved. He was ever a great thinker. . . . Morally he was a man of earnest purposes and positive opinions. He possessed deep religious convictions, and great courage, and was always ready for the furtherance of educational and religious enterprises. His feelings were invariably kindly and benevolent.

Another observer said, "there was in his face and eye a certain eagle-like quality . . . an element of humanitarian feeling, with a tendency to sympathy with movements . . . for the betterment of social and moral conditions." He even had "tendencies which might easily have made him an habitual agitator" and a "temperamental disposition toward utopianism." In his old age there were often "collisions of opinions" between the father and his conservative son, editor Harvey Scott; he was apparently closer to the "agitator" ideals of his daughter.[20]

Tucker Scott was in the audience when Abigail Scott Duniway toured Oregon with Susan B. Anthony in 1871. He took great delight in his daughter's writing and admired her courage. A few years before his death he wrote: "May God bless you, my daughter, and nerve your soul and body to endure the storms of ignorance and oppression, that from time to time assail you; for just beyond is the unclouded sunshine of His eternal justice. Affectionately, your old fogy father." In 1880, Duniway told her readers about

> the wise and thoughtful sire, who, even as in our childhood's days, views our future moves upon life's checker-board with concern, and hails every successful breaking of our enemies' "King Row" with quiet exultation, albeit he often gives warning lest we make moves rashly, and thus cancel past success and destroy the chances for future victory.[21]

Jenny Scott's first attempt to emulate her father was when she was six years old. During the election campaign of 1840,

William Henry Harrison was the presidential candidate, and, my father being an uncompromising Whig, I naturally partook of his ardor. I remember calling the village children together under the shade of a sycamore tree, where I climbed to a horizontal limb and harangued them about "Tippecanoe and Tyler too."[22]

It was the beginning of a lifetime of political oratory.

Abigail Jane Scott's education was gained almost entirely outside of any school. Her first lessons were at home, as part of her everyday communication with other adults, before she was even old enough to remember who taught her. Possibly it was not her "busy mother" as she later assumed, but rather grandmother Frankie Scott, who was dying of "pulmonary trouble" during Jenny's first three years. The death of Frances Tucker Scott was the earliest of her memories, followed by the "old Webster's Elementary Spelling book" which she later took with her to Oregon. (James Scott had bought a speller for his children in 1819.) In any case, quick-witted little Jenny "learned to spell, read and recite bits of rhyme" and became addicted to words and books for the rest of her life. She spent a few scattered months at the Pleasant Grove schoolhouse, where she may have witnessed her favorite cousin's daily whippings from schoolmaster Mr. Boggs. (Eight-year-old John Johnson began wearing a winter coat in summer for protection. His parents then discovered his black-and-blue stripes and dried blood, which no one had dared report for fear of Boggs. The Reverend Neill Johnson threatened Boggs with arrest and he disappeared that night.) Then Jenny attended lessons at "a little frame house in the edge of a village called Deacon Street, a mile or more to the North," but only "intermittently . . . unable, from some physical ailment, to be classed as a 'regular,' so received little benefit."[23]

Once having learned to read, however, Jenny Scott's primary texts became the many newspapers which entered her household. The journalism of politics and reform honed her intellectual commitments from an early age. Newspapers were as important to American pioneers as television in the twentieth century; they included local gossip, regional politics, and information about national and international topics. When there was not enough news, they reprinted poetry, fiction, and essays by the best contemporary authors. Every issue passed through many hands, while letters to the editors were frequently as informative or argumentative as the articles and editorials. Alexis de Tocqueville noted in 1830: "The American frontiersman penetrates into the wilds of the New World with the Bible, an axe, and some newspapers. It is difficult to imagine the incredible rapidity with which thought circulates in . . . these deserts. I do not think that so much intellectual activity exists in the most enlightened and populous districts of France."[24]

Grandfather James Scott subscribed to the militantly evangelical *Baptist Banner and Western Pioneer* as well as to the politically militant *Peoria Register* and *Pekin Illinois Palladium*, both supporters of Henry Clay and midwestern Whigs. The whole family read the influential *Sangamon* (later *Illinois*) *Journal*, edited by Lincoln's close friend and supporter Simeon Francis. Some relatives were also involved in printing. The Roelofson kin were regular readers of the *Missouri Cumberland Presbyterian* and various temperance journals. One which made a particular impression on the Scott girls was the weekly *Lily*, edited by a woman, Amelia Bloomer, and filled with eloquent arguments about women's rights by Elizabeth Cady Stanton.[25]

Circulation of thought on the frontier in the 1840s was expedited by one of the most important American newspapers—Horace Greeley's *New York Tribune*. Around 1848, when Jenny was fourteen, a young preacher who lived with her family subscribed to the *Tribune*. Jenny and her sisters read it avidly and regularly—and soon persuaded their father to do so too. Duniway later claimed that editor Greeley's hand had "done more to shape our destiny than that of any other living intelligence."[26]

Greeley was not only an enthusiast for the West as a land of opportunity and progress. He was also a publicist for all the reform movements of the day, from Fourierism to Graham's vegetarianism to female dress reform. In the *Tribune*'s pages appeared an extended debate between Greeley and popular Indiana socialist Robert Dale Owen, who advocated equitable divorce laws, emancipation of women within marriage, enhancement of the spiritual over the material aspects of love, and family limitation. Fourierist Albert Brisbane, in a regular column, stressed women's right to education and to equality within the cooperative "phalanx," which would be the nucleus of an ideal society. Writers called for "associationism"—with communal kitchens to relieve housewives' work—claiming that the isolated family was uneconomical, selfish, and unhealthy. There was discussion and criticism of Swedenborgian notions of "passional affinities." Although feminist Margaret Fuller was no longer literary editor, the unknown radical European Karl Marx was a contributor. In 1850 the *Tribune* was the only paper in the country reporting the annual Woman's Rights convention with honesty and respect.[27]

Abigail Jane Scott was anything but isolated from the currents of change and reform that were surging throughout the country in her youth. She was in her formative years and already acutely aware of the injustices she and her family had suffered. (Brother Harvey Scott, later to become a formidable intellectual opponent and conservative editor, was four years younger and less susceptible to notions of "True Reform." He was educated in Oregon by New Englanders—an entirely different experience.)[28] Jenny Scott responded enthusiastically to Greeley's conviction that "the Social evils which afflict mankind have their origin in the errors not of a part but of all, and . . . by the cooperation of all should they be overcome."[29]

Above all, Jenny Scott was impressed by Greeley's advice to aspiring writers: "when a mind crowded with discovered or elaborated truths *will* have utterance, begin to write sparingly and tersely for the nearest suitable periodical—no matter how humble and obscure—if the thought is in you, it will find its way to those who need it." She was to echo that advice herself in later years. She immediately began writing poems. One was soon published in the *Illinois Journal.* (No copies survive. Duniway later disparaged it for revealing "the new emotionalism of budding womanhood.")[30]

Jenny's sickly childhood gave her license to be intellectual, so her father chose her to be the first in the family to enter an academy. Fanny was older, but she was too useful and necessary at home. During the winter of 1850/51 Abigail Jane Scott spent five months in "an apology for an academy in Stout's Grove," about eighteen miles east of Groveland.

> The school met in a primitive Cumberland Presbyterian Church, and the studies ranged from primary grades to Higher Arithmetic, Grammer, Geography, Philosophy, etc., with recitations called before a grizzly-headed teacher. . . . My stay at this school was brief, as I was never a strong or healthy child.

Her main acquisition was an intensified suspicion of authority and external discipline. "I never did, could, or would study when at school," she later admitted. But she made friends among her fellow scholars, including Shelby M. Cullom, who was about to join Lincoln's law firm in Springfield, and Eva Parker, who was to become wife to Robert Ingersoll, the nineteenth century's most notorious and outspoken "infidel." (Twenty-five years later, Cullom invited Mrs. Duniway to lecture on suffrage to the Illinois legislature.) Cousin J. L. Johnson brought Fanny and Maggie to Jenny's "commencing exercises" just before the Johnsons left for Oregon. She wept "bitter tears" to see him go.[31]

ırons" and Yankees

"All of the family were thinkers and had deep convictions."

Abigail Jane Scott grew up in a clan-centered society. The transplanted
Kentuckians in Groveland and vicinity were almost all related, by blood
or by marriage. By rough estimate there were soon at least one hundred
close relatives within easy distance: the Johnsons—with twelve children—two Goudy families (married to Roelofson sisters), four Caffee
uncles (orphans brought up by James Scott—one married to another
Roelofson), the Norrises, Browns, Davises, Turleys and their offspring,
and uncle Peter Scott's family. Aunt Rhoda Scott was only six years older
than Abigail, while uncles Thomas and William Roelofson were thirteen
and ten years older. Besides grandparents James and Frances Tucker
Scott, grandparents Lawrence and Mary Smith Roelofson had moved
north to live nearby in 1835. The Montgomerys and Caldwells and other
neighbors had also been Scott friends in Kentucky.[1]

These kinfolk shared cultural and political loyalties too. They had left
Kentucky not only for land and opportunity, but also out of anti-Demo-
crat and antislavery conviction. They favored the Whigs, as did most of
Tazewell County, in contrast to the rest of Illinois. Kentucky's Henry
Clay was their political hero; they were united in their distrust of Easterners, bankers, financiers, and southern plantation owners. They were
frontier people, descendants of Appalachian pioneers who came mostly
from Scotland or northern Ireland or the German Rhineland, energetic,
hardworking, ambitious, passionate, and rustic. In addition, as Abigail
Scott Duniway once put it, "All of our family were thinkers and had
deep convictions."[2]

John Tucker Scott was the second of seven living children—five of
them girls. Ann Roelofson was the eighth of twelve—including nine
girls. Tucker Scott (so called to distinguish him from his cousin John
Caffee, brought up in the same household) was born on 18 February
1809, just six days after Abraham Lincoln and only eighteen miles away,
as all the Scotts later proudly emphasized. Ann Roelofson Scott was born
near Henderson, Kentucky, in 1811. Their parents, Abigail Jane's
grandparents, were extraordinary people whose lives helped shape the

character of all their kin. All her progenitors were path breakers, both literally and figuratively. Improvement, reform, progress, and change were the watchwords of her inheritance.[3]

The first James Scott in America died in 1757 in the French and Indian War. He had married Keziah Terry, daughter of Squire Benjamin Terry, a substantial landowner and slaveholder in newly settled Pittsylvania County in southwestern Virginia. Scott's brother-in-law Nathaniel Terry was in the House of Burgesses and later was an aide to General Washington during the Revolution. James Scott left his widow with five children and a significant accumulation of property for the time. Family tradition was that he had been "stolen" from London Bridge "with two of his brothers" and "carried off to sea" for "the service of the Crown" in the mid-eighteenth century, though another possibility was that he had escaped to America after fighting for Bonnie Prince Charlie at the disastrous battle of Culloden in Scotland in 1746.[4]

James Scott's widow married Richard Murphey and brought up her children in Surry County, North Carolina, just north of the Yadkin River in the mountains near the soon-to-be legendary Daniel Boone. Her youngest son, John Scott, married Chloe Riggs, whose parents were Dutch and Welsh Quakers from New Jersey. Quakers were already committed to antislavery, and Chloe apparently passed on her beliefs to her son James, Abigail's grandfather. Tall, resilient, and strong-minded, Chloe was the beloved Great-granny who lived with the Scotts in Illinois throughout Jenny Scott's childhood. She was one hundred when she died in 1852.[5]

Chloe Riggs Scott remembered "treking" across the mountains into Kentucky in 1797 with her eight children—"Jimmy" eighteen, "Polly unweaned in her arms, and Peter clinging to her skirts." Along with several Riggs families, the Murphey half brothers, and his married sisters, John Scott established his prosperous farm southwest of Lexington, not far from Nancy Hanks and Thomas Lincoln. Chloe Riggs, in fact, was acquainted with Nancy's mother. Chloe and John Scott's son James (Abigail's grandfather) became a fur trader, packing his merchandise over the mountains to Fredericksburg, Maryland, at a substantial profit. For reasons that are unclear his employer brought suit against him, but James was acquitted with the aid of one of Kentucky's leading lawyers, William Logan. That same year James was elected sheriff of Lincoln County and later constable of newly founded Lebanon, where he bought a center lot and managed other land for relatives.[6]

Frances Tucker became James Scott's wife in 1806. She was a warm-hearted, pious woman, orphaned in 1793 when she was seven by an Indian massacre which she vividly remembered. She was raised in the family of circuit-riding Methodist preacher John Tucker. (In 1799 there were only 10,000 church members in Kentucky's population of 220,955—and only 1,741 Methodists.) After years of illness, grandmother Scott died in 1838, much mourned by sensitive little Jenny.[7]

James Scott's legal and political activities caused him habitually to save every document or letter he received. His respect for the written word as a means to power and justice became an influential family tradition. In the flush times after the War of 1812, he bought more land and also books—including the speller so loved by granddaughter Abigail Jane. Both in Kentucky and later in Illinois he was a man who inspired respect among his peers.

Fellow Illinoisans remembered that "old Sheriff Jimmy Scott" was the kind of man who could chase and capture a horse thief and keep him chained to his own bedstead for two weeks while the county finished building a jail. (The man escaped during his first night there!) He could also "dry out" any alcoholic willing to reform. It was a two-week process, perhaps the same method his granddaughter Duniway later publicized to Oregon readers. Scott's management of family land claims and investments required toughness as well as intelligence, for at frontier land auctions,

> If a speculator should bid on a settlers farm, he was knocked down & dragged out of the office, & if the striker was prosecuted or fined. . . the case must come before a jury . . . selected from among the settlers. . . . [N]o jury would find a verdict of *guilty* against a settler, in such a case, because it was considered a case of *self defence*. . . . [T]he last resort would be to "burn powder in their faces."[8]

Furthermore, James Scott was as opposed to slavery as he was committed to squatters' rights. This was his primary reason for uprooting his family in 1824. He renounced his Kentucky status and security and impoverished himself to grant freedom to his slaves. His formidable spirit and intense convictions left lasting impressions on his children and grandchildren.

Long before the formation of the northern abolition movement, antislavery ideas were widespread among the small planters and Protestant revivalists of the back country South. As early as 1792 David Rice, a major figure in the Second Great Awakening, gave an eloquent speech on the subject to the Kentucky constitutional convention. Kentucky Baptists formed the Friends of Humanity for the purpose of freeing slaves in 1806. New converts at revival meetings were urged to forswear slavery along with alcohol and other sources of sin. Methodists also disapproved; in 1799 the Reverend John Tucker, Frankie Scott's stepfather, stipulated that his sixteen-year-old slave Stepney should be freed at thirty-one. The tightening of southern legal codes and manumission policies in the 1820s was aimed at the South's antislavery whites as much as at blacks, and it had the desired effect. It forced the strongest opponents, like James Scott, to seek free territory and leave the "peculiar institution" behind.[9]

Scott's action was the culmination of a clan dispute which had simmered for two generations, a microcosmic version of the one which would eventually rend the nation. In 1771 James Scott's great-grandfather Terry left twenty slaves in his will to be divided among his ten children. He specifically designated that two of the slaves represented the first James Scott's legacy to his five children. In 1809 Zadock Riggs, David Austin, and others who had married Scott sisters filed suit against stepfather Richard Murphey and brother-in-law John Scott to prevent the slaves from being taken out of Kentucky and to obtain their share of the slaves' value. James Scott became John Scott's executor when he died in 1811. The original two slaves had also died, leaving five grown slaves to be divided among four other Scotts, three Murpheys, and assorted grandchildren. Some heirs sold their shares to Scott for $15 each. But two Murpheys and Zadock Riggs refused.

In 1818 and 1819 Scott hired out two of the slaves, complicating things even further, since Riggs and the Murpheys each claimed one-eighth of their hire. Finally the circuit court ordered Absolem sold in order to pay them. James Scott bought him for $400. In 1823 Scott paid $1000 for another slave and in 1824 $700 for a young girl, both Absolem's children. He borrowed the money from the Bank of Kentucky. Meanwhile, cousin Thomas Dean had obtained the Murphey brothers' two-eighths interest and was suing Scott for payment—and also for assault and battery. Clearly Scott's hot temper was fully involved with his antislavery principles. Faced with possible bankruptcy, Scott would have to sell some of his slaves and perpetuate the system—or leave the South and allow his property to escape.

Family tradition said James Scott bought Absolem and his children in order to set them free. He declared insolvency on 7 August 1824. That October he headed north to Illinois with his ill wife, aged mother, seven children, four orphaned nephews, and the freed slaves on their way to Canada. Negroes could not stay in Illinois without being prime targets for slave hunters seeking to collect James Scott's Kentucky debts, not to speak of the discriminatory Illinois laws. But Tazewell County was as far north as one could settle in 1824, and very different from the proslavery southern counties. It was a move to freedom even for the Scotts.

Jenny Scott's Roelofson grandparents were as strong-willed as the Scotts. They had left Kentucky in 1821 to live in Carmi, Illinois, not far from Robert Dale Owen's New Harmony. But they came north to live next door to daughters Ann Scott and Esther Johnson in 1835. Red-haired Mary Smith Roelofson, daughter of Scotsman Thomas Smith, who had deserted the British army in the Revolution, was the kind of woman who at forty-five had ridden horseback with her twelfth baby through one hundred miles of wilderness to visit her parents. She maintained her stamina and courage during years of pain after moving north, where granddaughter Abigail Jane Scott was her observant neighbor.

For, instead of being able to help her daughters, Grandmother Roelofson became a tragic victim shortly after she arrived in Groveland. She was bitten on the leg by a wild sow and spent the next seven years in "great and constant pain." The wound was infected and would not heal. Her son bitterly remembered that gangrene had forced three separate amputations "at the hands of an unskilled doctor" with "crude instruments, no anesthetic." This was done in her log cabin on a table with a saw. The doctor died before her son grew old enough to fulfill his desire to kill him![10]

Eventually grandmother Roelofson resumed her housekeeping, resting her knee as she moved on "a common frame chair, . . . and when she stops she always has a chair to sit on." Her grandchildren remembered "the rude puncheon floor, scrubbed so white and clean with the marks of Grandmother's crutches all over it," and how she had been "so particular with her milk covers and crocks, . . . constantly telling how very bad the rats were in the *milk house.*" Her example of courageous endurance profoundly shaped young Jenny Scott's perception of womanhood. Even at eighty-one Mary Roelofson was "quite pert, and . . . manifested but little mental dotage."[11]

Grandfather Lawrence Roelofson was another formidable personality, a wilderness survivor. In his youth, alone or with other hunters, sometimes including Daniel Boone, "with his gun and a well-filled powder horn" he rode horseback over the mountains or between the scattered and besieged Kentucky settlements of the postrevolutionary era. A tall, blonde, fearless man with a piercing blue eye and an empty socket (injured with a penknife when he was thirteen) covered by a knitted patch, Roelofson spoke only German until he was nineteen. His father may have been a Hessian soldier. He vividly remembered the revolutionary war when his mother nursed wounded soldiers in their home, supposedly after the battle of Trenton. He taught himself arithmetic, reading, and writing and moved with his family to western Pennsylvania after the war. From there he moved with numerous kinfolk in flatboats down the Ohio to western Kentucky in the early 1780s.[12]

"The difficulties under which the first settlers of that part of Kentucky labored, were almost insupportable," his nephew later wrote. They had to live in stockaded forts in near-starvation during the first year, subject to Indian raids and frequent disaster. Nephew Isaac Knight was kidnapped in 1793, not to return for two and a half years. In 1829 he published an account of his captivity which circulated among relatives—another legend of pioneering courage for the family repertoire.[13]

Like thousands of other Kentuckians, the Roelofsons were victims of invalid land titles. Early Kentucky was a "Pandora's box of evils," caused by "extensive frauds, duplicating and overlapping boundaries, huge and multiple grants to the same persons, concentration of holdings, and a large amount of absentee ownership." In the 1780s and 1790s "sufficient land had been promised to cover the state four times over." Tax records show that even after twenty years of privation and hard work Lawrence Roelofson owned only one horse, eight cows, and two mules. Not until 1801 was he able to buy land—one hundred acres for $200 "at Thomas Smith's N.E. Corner," in Henderson, Kentucky.[14]

But grandfather Roelofson had intangible wealth which made up for all deprivation. In 1795, at the age of thirty, the same year he was married, Lawrence Roelofson experienced an "awakening" as one of the earliest and most dedicated converts of a fiery Presbyterian preacher named James McGready. McGready was well known in the Appalachian backcountry from Pennsylvania to North Carolina before he moved on to the Cumberland Presbytery of southwestern Kentucky. His zealous eloquence led in 1800 to the first great camp meeting of the Kentucky frontier. (Twenty-five thousand came to the Cane Ridge revival in 1801.) Many conservative Presbyterians objected to the emotional "arminianism" of McGready's style. But Lawrence Roelofson was one who broke their lock on the Red Banks church near Henderson in order to let him preach.[15]

The Awakening was "essentially a populist movement," says one eminent historian. Certainly it was seen as revolutionary in its implications, stressing emotion over doctrine and action over prayer. For robust frontier people "camp-meeting conversions were not decorous religious transactions." Sentimental excess and wild gyrations were common. Worst of all, uneducated pioneers themselves were allowed to preach.[16]

Grandfather Lawrence Roelofson was one of the first "licensed exhorters" in the Cumberland district. He immediately eschewed whiskey and tobacco forever, and his "active, zealous Christian course" became known throughout Kentucky, Indiana, and Illinois. But the Presbyterian Synod, with its "monumental dogmatic tradition," commitment to a scholarly ministry, and firmly established hierarchy, objected to "watered-down" doctrine, open Communion, denial of absolute predestination, and hunter-farmer clerics. The Cumberlands were cast out as heretics and became a small but extremely active sect. They retained respect for learning but admired most the self-taught variety. A contemporary said, "the first generation of Cumberland Presbyterians were the most intensely spiritual people that I have ever known."[17]

Lawrence Roelofson was one of the four organizers of the Illinois Presbytery and trained the next generation of preachers, including Jenny Scott's uncle Neill Johnson. Another organizer was James Scott's nephew, the Reverend D. W. McLin, a possible first link between the two families. McLin was outspokenly antislavery in 1829, long before other churchmen, when he felt "obliged to silence some . . . ministers" who refused to oppose slavery. In Groveland almost all thirty members of the Cumberland congregation were Jenny Scott's relatives, with Tucker Scott the main contributor. They were too poor to build a church until 1847 or even to support their own preacher, Neill Johnson. But their intense spirituality was unwavering.

Even in old age, grandfather Roelofson "could do more work than any of his sons." He especially loved to sing. He always "'raised' the tune and kept it going" and was the "first to offer his services in behalf of any who needed help." In the 1840s age reduced him to making axe handles, baskets, and brooms, but his charisma still impressed his many grandchildren.[18]

Southerners were not long the only ones in Tazewell County. By the time Abigail Jane Scott was born, Yankees too had begun to settle there. The completion of the Erie Canal in 1825 had opened the way west for New Yorkers and New Englanders, for speculators and businessmen and town builders of different training and heritage. Chicago, newly settled in 1830, became a thriving city within five years. Noting the changes caused by the Yankee influx, Harvey Scott later wrote: "They were mercantile traders or speculators mostly; . . . a class apart from the rough pioneers. They did not like the rough life of the woods or farms, but took up the professions or 'kept store.' They showed some study and refinement of dress, managed to afford better furniture . . . and held their religious meetings quietly, while the pioneers liked the Cumberland Presbyterian revivals or Methodist camp meetings." According to a local observer, "the Southerners regarded the Yankees as a skinning, tricky, penurious race of pedlars, filling the country with tinware, brass clocks, and wooden nutmegs. The Northerner thought of the Southerner as a lean, lank, lazy creature, burrowing in a hut, rioting in whiskey, dirt, and ignorance."[19] Cross-cultural rivalry, confrontation, and adaptation provided a turbulent but creative milieu for Abigail Jane Scott's development.

Poet William Cullen Bryant took the road north from Springfield in 1832, describing the rich prairie landscape which it still traverses today. He almost purchased a quarter-section of land in Pleasant Grove, as a speculative investment, because "the soil is fertile and well watered, . . .

and the region more than usually healthy. . . . [I]t is within convenient distance of a market [at Pekin]; . . . and saw-mills have been erected on some of the streams." His account shows that northerners were already in control of much of the new territory, however, for he was advised to seek information from Milton Shurtleff of Plymouth, Massachusetts, rather than the neighboring Scotts from "old Kaintuck."[20]

In 1834 a three-man committee from New England acquired a huge tract of land just south and east of Groveland, laid out the town of Tremont with Yankee efficiency, and moved in fifty families to establish "the culture, refinement and enterprise of the East" in the new country. A substantial donation of land and money convinced the county commissioners to make Tremont the county seat, to the horror of "the open-mouthed Kentuckians, Tennesseeans, and Buckeyes" in nearby Pekin. The town was built so fast that Abigail's uncle, preacher Neill Johnson, returning in 1835 from eighteen months in another pastorate, found his whole environment changed:

> The open prairie that lay east of me that I had thought would not be settled for fifty years was all bought up by a colony from the east, and a flourishing town had sprung up only one mile from my farm, called Tremont . . . my place that had been thought an out of the way place, had now one of the most public roads in the county, passing immediately by it. Everything people and all seemed to have made advances in worldly matters and left me far in the rear.[21]

Before the founding of Tremont, James Scott and his kin held the balance of political power in the vicinity. He could route the main highway past his farmstead gate and his son's sawmill, and could borrow or lend the school commission funds. Tucker Scott was postmaster. Political plums, however, along with the economic advantages, were lost when the Yankees came. The "southrons" could elect Neill Johnson justice of the peace only until 1847, when he lost by two votes and was forced to leave for lack of income. Uncle Hezekiah Davis "was compelled to abandon" his tannery business when the Tremont "colonists bought up all the timber land and he could get no more bark."[22]

Nevertheless, surrounding farmers prospered from the market created by the new town and expanding population. The 1830s were boom times in the west. Easy credit, extravagant plans for internal improvements, the opening of the Erie Canal, and increased migration all contributed to rising prices, speculative investments, and high expectations. Grandfather Scott built a large frame house to replace his log cabin in 1835. He also began investing in land and town lots. Tucker Scott's sawmill did a lucrative business among the treeless residents of the growing prairie community. Younger brother Lindsey Scott and cousin John

Caffee opened a general store. Land agent Thomas Jefferson Farnham sold the three of them land in the northwestern Illinois mining district.[23]

The boom did not last. Things began to go bad in 1837 throughout the country, following President Andrew Jackson's destruction of the National Bank and his Specie Circular requiring hard money for the purchase of land. Small farmers and land speculators were in great trouble. As a contemporary put it, "a sort of farmers' bank" created in 1834 "operated like setting out huge steel traps to catch their plantations" when money became scarce, and state "internal improvements" had caused a huge state debt and grandiose expectations. By early 1838, James Scott was having difficulty collecting from his debtors and Thomas Jefferson Farnham sued the firm of Caffee and Scott for payment of his loan, forcing its dissolution.[24]

Both John Tucker Scott and grandfather James Scott became seriously ill during the fall of 1838 after grandmother Frankie Scott's death. An epidemic of fever afflicted the whole area, along with a prolonged and ravaging drought. Almost everyone shook with the ague (malarial fever) each autumn, just when the harvest required attention and preserving food for winter was essential. Severe typhoid infections were often called "nervous fevers" or "brain fevers," while rheumatism from cold and exposure was normal. But in 1838 "the pestilence claimed its victims in almost every house," said Eliza Farnham, whose son and sister both died. (She had come west in 1835 to marry the land agent and visit her sister who lived about a mile east of the Scott homestead. She soon wrote a book about the experience.) Tucker Scott suffered a relapse the following winter. Little Jenny and her older sister Fanny had to take over the family maple sugar industry—building the fires, collecting and boiling the sap—a cold and exhausting job on winter nights and mornings, which made them both too sick to go to school.[25]

Another tragedy struck the Scott family during 1838. Tucker Scott's brilliant younger brother Lindsey Scott, who had suffered from some kind of debilitating disease ever since childhood, was arrested, charged with theft while drunk, and later murdered. Tucker Scott bailed him out of jail, but Lindsey jumped bail in order to haul some iron to Iowa and collect a $900 debt. Prairie pirates attacked and beat him with more than one hundred lashes, some as deep as the bone. A resulting "fit" caused his death a few days later. Tucker Scott, still recovering from his own illness, had the unhappy task of identifying the disinterred corpse and testifying at the murderers' trial. Meanwhile, newspaper accounts spoke of Lindsey's "insanity," others suspected he was a drunkard, and his brother was left to pay the forfeited bond and other debts of the defunct Scott and Caffee business. All the relatives were heartbroken and mortified. Ignoring the evidence of Lindsey's illness, they remembered only his alcoholism. Nor did the scandal improve their status among the refined easterners in Tremont.[26]

Lindsey's disaster tipped the financial balance for his brother's family. It was apparently anxiety over his debts which drove Lindsey Scott to jump his bail. Tucker Scott lost his farm in 1840 and finally succumbed to the epidemic of Illinois bankruptcy declarations in June 1842. The whole family had to spend the winter of 1840/41 "in a well-appointed, though tiny, steamboat cabin of several apartments." Jenny Scott never forgot the "dapper-looking business man" (probably T. J. Farnham) who foreclosed on their farm, "and we children . . . wondered, after he had departed from his bootless errand, if the man were cloven-footed, like a person of historical notoriety whom we called 'Old Splitfoot.'" "The failure of the Gallopolis bank, and the bankruptcy that followed, linger in my memory like the shades of a half vanished nightmare," she told her son in 1914.[27]

She also remembered the disdain and disapproval of neighboring Yankee settlers. The town of Tremont, for example, contained a significant number of the few Unitarians to be found outside of New England. That church's highly educated activist members "articulated the moral and religious dimensions" of upper-class Boston culture, stressing humanitarianism, rationality, and toleration rather than the emotional sentimentalism and hard Calvinism of other frontier churches. Unitarians in the west at that time were even more unique than Cumberland Presbyterians. There were also a few Episcopalians, some non-schismatic Presbyterians (now in union with the New England-based Congregationalists), and the zealously evangelical Baptists and Methodists. As Eliza Farnham dryly observed, since religion did not affect the value of land, the people of Tremont "were less restrained in the expression of these opinions [on religion]. . . . *Orthodox* and *heterodox* . . . were terms in frequent use . . . the sources of all sin, or the parents of all virtue. Unlike political opinions, these extended to the feminine population, and were . . . the single cause of whatever dissension or difficulty existed among us."[28]

Religious controversy touched the Scott family, too. In 1839, a year after the death of his first wife, James Scott married Jemima Brown. She was the daughter of a Baptist minister, and Scott at once became a deacon in Tremont's Baptist church with a "great chair" near the pulpit. The Cumberland Presbyterians had lost an important source of financial and moral support, just at the depths of the depression. His relatives considered him an apostate. Hard feeling between Scotts and Browns lasted a lifetime.[29]

Meanwhile, uncle Neill Johnson reaped frequent spiritual harvests at his camp meetings, and his pragmatism enabled him to handle emergency situations in ways his Yankee neighbors found appalling. One Christmas Eve, for example,

> several young couples who wished to be married gathered at a cross roads which he must pass. . . . The night was cold and stormy and Rev. Johnson was delayed so it was long after dark before he came by . . . and . . . he was in a hurry. He instructed them to join hands, and said a group ceremony. When it was over one young lady discovered she had not been holding the hand of the man she expected to marry. Consternation seized the group, but Rev. Johnson . . . calmly reassured them saying, "You are all married. Now sort yourselves."

Johnson noticed the Yankees' disdain for his style and understood their prejudices: "They generally called on one of their own preachers to Solemnize their marriages, . . . but . . . they called on me to officiate at their funerals. . . . I infered they thought me not refined enough for a Yankee weding but enough so for a funeral." He remained undaunted.[30]

The Scotts and Roelofsons were considered uncouth and rustic, but they were equally disdainful. In Abigail Scott Duniway's first novel, the Gray family planned a wedding, inviting "the rustic neighbors for miles around . . . while Yankees, as they called all people of refinement, were slighted with impunity, because . . . 'They think themselves a *heap* better nor their neighbors.'" The Johnson boys, her cousins, were able to attend school in Tremont because their father was a JP, but they too noticed the "enmity between the Town boys and the Country boys." The fact that Jenny Scott's uncles, William and Levi Caffee, were both notorious alcoholics made things worse. William Caffee was finally tried and executed for murder after a tavern brawl in Wisconsin.[31]

Jenny Scott remembered with both admiration and resentment the behavior of Yankee ladies. Cold, aloof, and educationally superior to their "southron" counterparts, these women kept their emotions under control and their manners restrained. They were arbiters of culture and respected by their men. In Yankee families, Duniway wrote, "the menfolks saw the necessity of taking the rougher part of the chores off of the shoulders of the women." Ladies like Eliza Farnham, wife of the land agent, rode by in carriages on excursions and paid only "an occasional out-of-door call" on such "primitive settlers" as the Scotts. Farnham too noticed the "indolence" of western men, while their wives "cannot be indolent if they would." In contrast, the Yankees' mother-dominant standards of child-rearing produced children who, in the words of a character in Duniway's novel *Captain Gray's Company*, "cared nothing for their father's commands, but a word or look from 'ma,' was all that was necessary to make them obedient." The father answered, "'No wonder they mind her,' . . . 'she'd chill a fire-coal to an icicle by looking at it!'"[32]

Tremont was a town of cold-water teetotalers. At a Fourth of July celebration in 1837, a visiting minister found it "a very cheering sight to witness the predominance of *tumblers* over *wine glasses* on the table, more than half the company toasting in pure *cold water*." This was an aspect of the town's "New England character," and it involved disapproval of rough pioneers as much as of the pioneers' whiskey. Genteel teetotalers wanted controls placed on those "unaccustomed to the yoke." Their prohibitionist aims became dominant in the temperance movement during the 1830s—the same era which included a shift in abolitionist leadership. Westerners resented the change and its implications, calling it "Protestant Jesuitism"—"a campaign . . . to destroy the liberties of the American people. . . . [C]oercion not reform."[33]

Grandfather Lawrence Roelofson had been a teetotaler since his religious conversion in 1795, but the Scotts were certainly moral suasionists rather than prohibitionists. The issue was openly political during the election campaign of 1840 when "Whig log-cabins in nearly every village dispensed hard cider with enthusiasm, while the Democrats referred to them as 'groggeries' and urged the enemies of the liquor traffic to beware." In 1842 Tucker Scott joined the Sons of Temperance (as did Abraham Lincoln). The organization included many reformed alcoholics, but it was frequently denounced by cold-water Yankees as a "secret order" opposed to legal prohibition and sometimes even to "true religion."[34] Abigail Scott Duniway remembered all her life the political overtones of the temperance and prohibition movements.

Even on antislavery the "southrons" and Yankees disagreed. The Scotts, as we have seen, were firmly opposed to slavery. Family tradition says they took part in the Underground Railroad, one route of which passed through Tazewell County and had several "depots" near Groveland. During James Scott's term as sheriff, from 1827 to 1835, one of the other two constables was Quaker William Wilson, whose farm was a stop on the escape route. Pleasant Grove was a recognized center of antislavery sentiment, and the *Peoria Register,* to which James Scott subscribed, was the only paper in Illinois which protested the killing of abolitionist Owen Lovejoy in 1837.[35]

But Tucker Scott had no use for "incendiary abolitionists." Yankee abolitionists in turn acted within their own networks and churches, ignoring the defunct Friends of Humanity and other southern groups. Tazewell County Kentuckians were cognizant of the economic implications of freeing slaves and favored gradualist, personalist solutions. Like Henry Clay and Abraham Lincoln and even most northerners before the 1850s, they considered slavery an unfortunate but legal evil because it was sanctioned by the Constitution. Voluntary emancipation and legal prevention of slavery's expansion into free territory were their pragmatic alternatives to imposed righteousness.[36]

Protecting their own political rights was the Scott priority. The question of who was qualified to vote and why was being discussed throughout Jenny Scott's childhood. A major issue in Illinois in 1840 was whether unnaturalized aliens, most of whom would be Democrats, should be allowed to vote. Whigs won a welcome victory in the legislature when aliens were disallowed. Perhaps Abigail Jane Scott also heard that Abraham Lincoln argued in his campaign of 1836 that he favored suffrage for *all* "who pay taxes or bear arms (by no means excluding females)."[37]

Lincoln was a popular man among Tazewell County Whigs. The presence of the county courthouse in Tremont brought him there frequently; he even served as Tucker Scott's lawyer at least once. In Tremont James Shields challenged Lincoln to a notorious duel in 1842.[38] There stump speakers harangued and issues of state were argued, along with the everyday battles of a turbulent, growing society.

Lincoln's closest friend, the charismatic politician Edward D. Baker, was responsible for a profound change in the Scott family fortunes. In 1846, through his brother in Pekin, he extended credit to Tucker Scott to buy the first circular sawmill west of Ohio. The Scott family was finally able to move out of a log cabin and into "the big elm tree homestead," and Ann Scott received her first cookstove—"a huge, awkward affair" which she considered more trouble than her fireplace. When Baker's brother died in 1849, Baker made Tucker Scott his exclusive agent for selling Page's Portable Saw Mills throughout Illinois and Indiana.[39]

James and Tucker Scott were at last able to pay the Caffee and Scott Company debts, while the young Roelofson brothers eventually became "substantial agriculturalists" on the profits from their own sawmill business. The Groveland Cumberland Presbyterians began to build a church, with Tucker Scott as the largest contributor. And Tucker Scott was elected, like his father twenty years earlier and his great-grandfather Terry one hundred years earlier, county road commissioner.[40] It was all a lesson in practical politics which Abigail Jane Scott would not forget.

The juxtaposition of "southron" and Yankee, of family pride and envious aspiration, of remembered hardship and precarious success, of female drudgery and ladylike refinement, provided both clan unity and personal challenge to the whole Scott relationship. Jenny Scott felt the added challenge of ill health, with concomitant family expectations about her intellectual potential, and the daily rivalry of her younger brother. Her environment and her reading exposed her to the most stimulating reform thinking of her day. Her father and grandfather Scott provided examples of the effects of practical politics, while grandfather Roelofson and uncle Neill Johnson were models of active commitment to a cause. Jenny's negative reactions to religious excess and to her mother's self-sacrificing drudgery reinforced her pragmatic individualism and her concern for justice and equality. Childhood in frontier Illinois prepared Abigail Scott Duniway both negatively and positively for a life of action, independence, and courageous commitment.

CHAPTER 3

Overland to Oregon

"And then we realized that we were bereaved indeed."

The "main highway" a few hundred feet from Abigail Jane Scott's childhood home was only a rough dirt track, but before many years it became the route along which "long lines of covered wagons were driven daily, in Spring and Summer, laden with the crude belongings of emigrants, bound for Missouri." In her autobiography Duniway remembered

> troops of bare-foot children coming to our home at sundown, carrying hickory and walnut sticks to bear away the fire coals my mother kept covered with ashes for her own use at cooking time, and that she always had brands, or coals, at hand to divide with the wayfarers in the lane.[1]

Oregon was as yet only an exotic name to most Americans, though covered wagon migration had been common for fifty years.[2] Romantic myths about ever-moving, free-spirited frontiersmen were also common. As neighbor Eliza Farnham wrote:

> The emigrant . . . has . . . the advantage over the first settlers. For as the numbers of the former increase, the latter retires before them as the Indian has retired before him. . . . When the *Yankee* homes thicken about him, and farms are opened within two, three, and four miles, he begins to feel straightened, oppressed; he wants more room, and resolves to sell to the first Yankee that offers to buy. He . . . commences his journey westward, shaking the dust of the Yankee settlements from his feet. He . . . journeys on, always toward the setting sun, for he knows that freedom such as he seeks has retreated thither.[3]

The Scott family saga shows that the reasons for "shaking the dust of the Yankee settlements" were much more complex, but freedom and space were certainly important factors. On 1 October 1838, in the midst of the Scott family troubles, John Tucker Scott and his uncle Peter Scott, along with Thomas Jefferson Farnham and many others, attended a speech in Peoria. Methodist preacher Jason Lee, one of the first American missionaries to Oregon, was crossing Illinois on a fund-raising trip to the East. He gave an impassioned description of the beauty of the country, the importance of bringing civilization and Christianity to the Indians,

26

and the necessity of settlers from "the States" to lay claim to the territory and take it away from Britain. The New England missionary society was publishing a monthly magazine called *The Oregonian, and Indian's Advocate* to "save" the Indians beyond the Rockies through publicity and fund-raising, and to obtain Oregon's rich agricultural, forest, fish, and commercial potential for America through encouragement of settlement. Tucker Scott and his slightly older uncle immediately became two of the three Illinois agents listed in the magazine.[4]

That summer's drought and disease made Jason Lee's description of Oregon's mild, humid, fertile Willamette Valley particularly enticing. Within a few months land-agent Farnham organized nineteen men, including several of Tucker Scott's friends, to go on a colonizing expedition. The "Peoria Party" left for Oregon in 1839. Only Amos Cook, Francis Fletcher, and Joseph Holman actually settled there, sending word back about the richness of the soil and mildness of the climate. Farnham returned in 1840 to write a book. He said, "no portion of the world beyond the tropics can be found that will yield so readily with moderate labour, to the wants of man."[5]

But for the Scott family difficulties at that time, John Tucker Scott might soon have followed his friends to Oregon. The "new country" was his favorite subject throughout Jenny Scott's childhood, while his log cabin and his sawmill became, as one historian put it, "a center of infection in the spread of that 'Oregon fever' which, by the spring of 1843, was raging all along the middle western frontier." Though the Oregon Provisional Emigration Society stopped publishing its magazine, Scott collected every book and report about Oregon he could find and became increasingly restless. He certainly was tempted to accompany the Peter Scott family when they migrated in 1845 to settle near Amos Cook in Lafayette.[6]

Nor was Oregon the only goal he considered. Around 1844, when his fortunes were lowest and the log cabin drafty and crowded, he apparently also thought of going to Texas. The family all remembered six-year-old Harvey Scott asking, "Is Texas a tight house?"[7]

Abigail Scott Duniway described her father as a man of "adventurous disposition." By 1850 he was at last reasonably prosperous, with enough assets to be able to consider a move.[8] Malaria still stalked the country every autumn, and Yankees now controlled local politics and much of the land. There was little prospect of great progress in Groveland. (It looks almost the same today as it did then.) Furthermore, Gold Rush enthusiasm had affected all Americans. Thousands were surging toward the West Coast, preparing to strike it rich in the gold fields or else as farmers and merchants supplying the miners. Sons left their families, husbands left their wives and children, quiet Spanish California suddenly became a state with over 100,000 Americans, and newspapers everywhere were filled with reports. California's statehood also brought to the nation increasing turbulence over slavery, fanned by the Compromise of 1850 and its strict Fugitive Slave Law. Free Soil men like Tucker Scott and his brother-in-law Neill Johnson saw Oregon as a sanctuary from the evil effects of the slave system, a place where one could be prosperous, healthy, and free. (Even Abraham Lincoln was tempted. He was appointed secretary of the Oregon Territory in August 1849, but he had his sights set on Washington, as did his ambitious wife, and turned down the position.)[9]

Meanwhile, agitation among Westerners for land and homestead legislation finally resulted in the Oregon Donation Land Act of 1850, which entitled a married man to 320 acres, and another 320 in his wife's name—the first "free" land in America's history. (Those who arrived after 1850 and before 1855 got half these amounts.) With additional purchases a farmer could obtain a substantial estate for himself and his children.[10]

Uncle Neill Johnson, who had moved his large family to Iowa in 1848, decided to copy the example of the Tremont Yankees who had changed his life in Tazewell County. He publicized among Cumberland Presbyterians a constitution for a proposed colony in Oregon where all would "join and buy a body of land, lay off a town in the centre. Sell out the choice lots . . . to the highest biders," and build a church and schoolhouse. Led by "divine direction" and a family "caucus" (though his family perceived his "roving disposition" and "Gold Fever"), preacher Johnson was commissioned to be one of the three founders of the Oregon Cumberland Presbyterian Church. He crossed on the Overland Trail with his twelve children in 1851. Enthusiastic letters back provided the final impetus for Tucker Scott's decision to go.[11]

That September Ann Scott lost her twelfth baby in another difficult childbirth. She remained a semi-invalid. Her husband became convinced that a better climate might cure her. Family letters frequently mentioned Ann's attacks of ague (malaria) and "lung fever" during the first stages of the journey. Levi Caffee, required to abstain from alcohol by his brother-in-law, suffered several bouts of pneumonia and pleurisy too. Farfetched though it seems today for families to undertake a two-thousand-mile journey by wagon train for the sake of health, it was a common reason in 1852. People were accustomed to migration, and guidebooks designed to encourage national development minimized the difficulties. As a character in Duniway's *Captain Gray's Company* exclaimed: "Pshaw! Everything that's worth having is worth working for and crossing the Plains will only be one summer's work."[12]

Besides Ann Scott, the young wife of cousin William Goudy was also sick. She had a six-month-old baby and "had daily drooped and faded," ever since its birth. The journey to Oregon was undertaken "in the hope of restoring her to health," wrote Catherine Scott Coburn many years later. Catherine, who was thirteen at the time, also said:

> the rank and file of the ox-wagon brigades . . . might be reckoned as possessing more than ordinary courage, but for the fact that they did not realize fully the vastness of their undertaking, or the tremendous stretch of country that they set out so boldly, with such primitive means of conveyance, to traverse.[13]

Ann Scott did not want to go to Oregon. Nor did Fanny, who was deeply in love with nineteen-year-old George Landes. (He was obliged to remain in Illinois to support his parents until he was twenty-one.) When John Tucker Scott made up his mind, however, his reluctant wife and daughters obeyed. In *From the West to the West* Duniway described the scene:

> "It's all settled, mother. I've made terms with Lije. He's to take my farm and pay me as he can. I've made a liberal discount for the keep of the old folks; and we'll sell off the stock, the farming implements, the household stuff, and the sawmill, and be off in less than a month for the Territory of Oregon."

The mother "shrank and shivered," saying, " 'You know we've always lived on the frontier, and civilization is just now beginning to catch up with us,—mightn't it be better to stay here and enjoy it?' " She and the children, she added, had never yet even seen a railroad. " 'Don't be foolish, Annie!' exclaimed her husband. 'We'll take civilization with us wherever we go.' "[14] The imposition of a father's will on his family was a major theme in all Duniway's fiction.

During the winter of 1852, one of the items most carefully sewn was a padded feather bed for the "Mother's Wagon." All excess possessions had been auctioned, but Fanny's young man bought her mother's prized "gaudy Dutch plates" and returned them to Fanny as a parting gift. Sewn inside the feather bed, which her father slept on all the way, they made the trip safely. One plate still exists in the Duniway home in Oregon.[15]

The route of the Scott journey was to be across Illinois to Quincy, then across Missouri to St. Joseph's, across Nebraska to Fort Kearney and up the Platte River to Fort Laramie, through South Pass and on southwest of the Grand Tetons to the Snake River. The last half of the trip was along the Snake River, across the Blue Mountains and the Grande Ronde Valley to the Columbia River near The Dalles, and then over the Cascade Mountains to the Willamette Valley. Beyond St. Joseph's the land was still unsettled Indian territory, while the magnitude of the Rocky Mountains was virtually unknown to average Americans. Filled with romantic concepts of the picturesque and the sublime, adults as well as adolescents set off across America looking for the "Eden of the West" like determined tourists on a working holiday.[16]

John Tucker Scott did not anticipate, however, that the Oregon Trail migration of 1852 would be the largest in America's history. In addition, the ravages of a nationwide cholera epidemic plagued all travelers. Even in the modern era the numbers on that trail would have constituted a health hazard. In one of his several reports back to the Tazewell County *Mirror*, Scott said that by 29 May officials at Fort Kearney, Nebraska, had counted 16,279 persons, 3,689 wagons, 4,777 horses, 2,905 mules, 37,883 cattle, 2,801 sheep, and 1 hog. By 14 July the figures were 28,625 persons, 7,516 wagons, 7,793 horses, 4,993 mules, 74,783 cattle, 23,980 sheep, and (still) one hog.[17] Except for the earliest and fastest travelers, the journey involved food and grass shortages, polluted water, extremely dusty roads, unscrupulous traders, disease, and frequently death. By the time their six-month passage ended on 1 October 1852, the Scotts had experienced a full gamut of excitement, hardship, and never-to-be-forgotten disaster.

All concerned knew that their departure was permanent; as letters frequently reiterated, they would never see the grandparents again until they all met in heaven. Catherine remembered "silently weeping women and sobbing children, . . . an aged grandfather standing at his gate as the wagons filed past, one trembling hand shading his eyes, the other grasping a red handkerchief, his thin gray hair blown back by the fresh breezes, and the soft spring snowflakes falling gently, around him." Harriet remembered "the long line of covered wagons, so clean and white, . . . so battered, torn and dirty afterwards! The loud callings and hilarity: many came to see us off." As they ferried across the Illinois River, "we looked back and saw our old watch dog . . . howling on the distant shore. Father had driven him back saying, 'Go back to Grandfather, Watch!' But he never ate afterwards, and soon died."[18] (The incident is in several Duniway novels.)

The journey of no return began on 2 April 1852. Five heavy green and yellow covered wagons stood outside the farm's gate with five yoke of oxen hitched to the provisions wagon and eleven yoke divided among the other four. Twenty-seven people were in the party: eleven Scotts, uncle Levi and aunt Martha Roelofson Caffee and their two sons, cousin William Goudy with his sick wife and baby, cousin John Goudy, and five other young men as drivers. Three travelers accompanied them, including a photographer. In Missouri they added twenty-two other wagons.

The Scotts carried $2,000 in cash hidden in the family wagon to use when they reached Oregon.[19]

Like many western emigrants, Tucker Scott planned to keep a record of his trip for future travelers. It was a major responsibility, intended for eventual publication. He assigned the task to Abigail Jane, who could not resist including personal details despite orders to the contrary. While her sisters did domestic chores, seventeen-year-old Jenny, "partly from innate ambition, but chiefly because she was under orders from which she knew there could be no appeal, kept, through all the tedious journey, a diary."[20] Seventy-three years later her younger sister wrote:

> I still can "see" her as she was, a slight young girl, evenings after the weary stretches of travel with that old book in her lap—sitting either by the tent—or perchance one of the waggon wheels—or sitting on the ground—while our father was giving her commands to lay the Diary correct!—she was too weary at times to write—But always did her best.[21]

Thus the role which became a major part of her life's work was first established for Abigail Scott Duniway by her father.

Sentimental innocence marked Jenny Scott's first journal entry:

> April 2d. . . . to me it was a great trial to leave the home of my childhood, the place where, when care to me, was a stranger, I was wont to roam oer hill and dale, and where, when I came to know more thoughtful days I have loved to silently muse over the varying vicissitudes of life and loved to wander alone to the sequestered grove, to hold communion unseen by mortal eye with the works of nature and of God.

Except for the sickness of Mrs. Scott, Miranda Goudy, and Levi Caffee, the first part of the journey was easy. It was Catherine rather than Abigail who described the accommodations for invalids, perhaps because Kate, being younger, often rode in the wagon. Miranda rode in a heavy springless wagon packed with boxes which were removed and replaced with a feather bed and pillows at night. She sat sideways on a small chair, "with barely room in front to place the feet, a space utilized by the babe, when tired, as a place to sit, the mother providing the handbreadth of floor . . . by lifting one foot to the side of the wagon."[22] Ann Scott, in similar conditions, kept her two youngest beside her as much as possible. Sarah was five and Willie three.

Jenny and her sisters, however, either walked or rode horseback all the way. The pace of the oxen was only around three miles an hour, twenty miles a day on the open prairie, so the girls were often "running over the hills and admiring the scenery around us." They learned very early "not to loiter behind the wagons unless we wanted to take a long walk" (7 April). But weeks later they got caught in a hailstorm trying to climb Independence Rock and discovered that "the wagons . . . had all crossed the river except the last wagon in the train which by hard runing we managed to overtake." The men "intended to let us wade it (it was waist deep) to learn us not to get so far behind the train: I would have liked the fun of wading well enough but did not like to get joked about being left" (29 June).

Jokes had not ended, even by 4 September, when Jenny and her sister decided to avoid the dust by walking ahead all afternoon. When they stopped they learned that the camp was two miles back.

> It was then sun-down and the road . . . was through heavy timber, which appears dark in daylight; we . . . met our little sister coming after us on horseback; We went back all the way in a hard run and just before we reached the camp met a man, who . . . told us it was three miles back . . . through the darkest road he ever saw, or heard of; . . . we almost concluded to wait till morning among the trees . . . , when we met Father who was more uneasy if possible than we, and who was quite out of patience at our ludicrous mistake. . . . In running I wore the soles off my moccasins against the sharp stones, and blistered my feet.

The Scott children were appalled by their first encounter with slavery in Missouri. Harriet remembered visiting "negro huts . . . to see some little Negro babies."[23] Jenny recorded the family's disgust:

> Noticed quite a contrast in the conditions of persons on the different sides of the river. Farmers in Illinois near Quincy were seen as we passed along, contentedly following the plough while on this side the negroes do the work and to me the contrast was so great that I could think of little else all day; Saw a man to-day who said he owned seven slaves of a good stock—he had raised them himself and two of them were worth one thousand dollars apiece; but he had not got enough of work out of them yet, and in a few years they would be worth more: May none of *us* ever be guilty of buying and selling the souls and bodies of our fellow creatures; slavery is a withering blight upon the prospects happiness and freedom of our Nation. [15 April].

Jenny's first letter back to grandfather Scott (25 April) detailed the family illnesses and then assured him they were not unhappy and that his "imagination of it would have been a great deal worse than the reality has been. We have in no case felt discouraged." After listing more difficulties, she continued: "You will probably want to know if we regret starting; I can only speak for myself. . . . I left home with a firm determination to be contented and I have succeeded so well that I cannot call myself anything else but happy. I never enjoyed myself so well before and never had as good health before in my life. . . . [N]o one knows what he can endure until he undertakes it." The words were a manifesto for the rest of her life.

Abigail Jane Scott reported the "much confusion" and work for everyone in camp, but "if I do find time to write there is so much talking and laughing, which you know I always have to join, that I can think and care about little else" (letter, 6 May). They were camped at St. Joseph, Missouri, having tried for four days to cross the river by ferry. Already she felt herself to be part of a great historic event: "It is estimated that the emigration across the plains this year will be greater by at least one third than has ever been known before," she said. A week later she enclosed with her letter of 13 May "a composition addressed to 'My Grandfather' for the Mirror." (The following March she asked him whether her poem had ever been published.)

Crossing rivers was always a memorable experience. As they waited at the Missouri, delayed by high water, "the mud on either bank looks sufficiently deep to completely mire every horse and ox in Missouri," wrote Abigail. Tucker Scott wrote his father about fording the Platte River eight miles above Fort Kearney, "where it was near 2 miles wide and about knee deep on an average with a *tumbling sand bottom.* The water is very muddy & roars & foams like a mill tail. It puts one in mind of a great braggadocio!" Harriet also remembered that episode:

> The melting snows had made the streams high; the roads nearly impassable. The Platte river, swift and swollen, didn't seem to have any banks. We had heard of the dangers of quicksands. My father had, with the help of his drivers, raised the beds of the wagons, so as not to dip water—oh! the excitement—I feel it yet! When everything was in readiness, all of us were tucked inside the wagons; my father put me, last of all, inside the back end of the last wagon, told me to keep still and not be afraid. The loud voices of the drivers as they yelled and whipped up the oxen, the jogging of the wagons through the surging waters and over the quicksands, the memory is with me yet! When they got over the river all were accounted for but they couldn't find me. Finally I was pulled out from under the bows nearly smothered.[24]

Abigail Scott's journal frequently noted the "splendid looking prairie" with "blue tinged timber in the distance, the wild flowers and shrubs beneath our feet and the numerous herds contentedly grazing near us." She called them "picturesque and sublime" (30 April). On 10 May she bubbled: "The soil is fertile and lacks nothing but improvement to make it one of the first places in the world in agriculture." She and her sister climbed a hill and "took a farewell view of St. Joe. and the United States." Jenny was fascinated by Indians and her first buffalo and Platte River thunderstorms—major events in almost all Overland Trail diaries.

Teenagers especially found humor in collapsed tents and sublimity in thunder and lightning.[25] On 3 June "the rain fell in torrents . . . while the thunder and lightning was to some the most terrific and to others the most sublime of any thunder-storm we had ever witnessed." On another occasion, "One of the tents got blown over and the many laughs and jests occasioned by the predicament the inmates of the tent were left in . . . made us all forget to regard the fury of the storm" (12 June).

As the caravan approached the mountains, Jenny Scott saw "the most romantic scenery . . . since we started; Columns above columns of sand and sand stone formed in massive bluffs shaped by the hard winds of this region into rude appearances of images which the traveler gazes at and is forcibly reminded of . . . the renowned ruins of magnificent structures of the Old World" (11 June). Her father also used such popular rhetoric, for he wrote the Tazewell *Mirror* on 13 June: "the scenery around is picturesque in the extreme. I am now in full view of the Solitary Tower—the far-famed chimney rock, and the renowned Scott's Bluffs. . . . To describe these curiosities would require a more graphic pen than mine, . . . they are of the most sublime works of Nature!"[26]

By mid-May the company began to notice numerous new-made graves, some deaths from measles and some from "colds and diarrehea brought on . . . by exposure and fatigue; but we think most generally from imprudence in eating and drinking." Not unduly alarmed, the Scotts felt they could avoid such mistakes. "Several of our company have been attacked with diarrehea attended with violent hemorrhoids but by taking a strong preventive at first and abstaining almost entirely from eating a day or two they get along without any dangerous consequences" (19 May). (In her fictional *Captain Gray's Company,* Duniway later emphasized disease and its proper treatment. The captain's bottle of "No. 6" is the standard cure-all,[27] while his insistence on the dangers of a bacon and biscuit diet may be Duniway's hindsight rather than fact.)

Traffic increased daily. On 5 June there were "upwards of sixty teams ahead of us besides two large droves of cattle; while behind us as far as we could see others were moving on." One hundred teams passed on 13 June as the Scott company rested for the Sabbath. (Emigrant registers at Fort Laramie indicate that 26,024 people with 5,790 wagons passed the fort that year during June alone, not to speak of their animals.)[28] Often the Scotts could find litle grass for oxen and no buffalo chips to make a fire for cooking. The soil and marshes were so impregnated with alkali that the only safe water for cattle or people was in the Platte River itself (16 June). But "the scenery is grand, high ranges of hills on each side adorned with cedars and pine, while numerous wild flowers and plants of evry discription adorn the valeys below. . . . if we only had plenty of 'Adams ale' we would have a delightful camping place" (18 June).

On 19 June Jenny described "several delightful springs" in which "the water was as clear as crystal" and "as wholesome as any in the '*States.*'" They were in eastern Wyoming, about twenty miles from "Laramie's peak," and thought they had reached "the long wished for hills at last." "The breeze," Jenny went on, "seems to inhale us with new life and vigor. Some of the hills are three hundred feet high and to me who had never seen a mountain they seemed to be one continued chain." The evening was "cloudless and pleasant" but for one discovery. A woman was dying in a wagon about one hundred yards away.

Nevertheless, "the part of our train who were sick are much better and improveing all the time. Those who were sick in the first part of the journey are getting healthy. It is most generaly the case if persons are sick and their health is restored they are much healthier than they had been for some time." Indeed, on that day Ann Scott had climbed in and out of the wagon, walked around the camp, and appeared to be almost well. Everyone went to sleep with a sense of accomplishment and hope.

Tragedy struck at two in the morning on 20 June, the Sabbath. Ann Roelofson Scott suddenly felt the violent cramps and diarrhea of "plains cholera." She told no one "until daylight when everything was done . . . to save her life; but her constitution long impaired by disease was unable to withstand the attack, and . . . between four and five o'clock her weari-ed spirit took its flight and then we realized that we were bereaved indeed." During the hours before her death, lying on the ground in the shelter of a tent, Ann Scott gave parting words of love and advice to each member of the family. Her last words were "all is well."[29]

The family was devastated. Harriet called her mother's death "a crushing blow to all our hopes." Abigail remembered that Harvey, "then a boy in his early teens, mourned her death with the intensity of feeling characteristic of his strenuous nature." More than fifty years later, Harvey told her "that sometimes he would awaken in the night, and recalling our mother's arduous lot, would rise and pace the floor, the victim of unavailing retrospection and regret."[30]

Abigail Jane Scott was the family spokesperson who finally sent the news back to Illinois, almost a month later: "As Father at present has no taste for writing," she said, "it becomes my duty to commence the (at this time painful task) of writing to you. Since we last addressed you, the mysterious, relentless hand of Death has visited us and we are now mourning the decease of our beloved Mother!" After describing everything in detail, Jenny added a crucial piece of information which was not in her journal.

I was sick that day and had been for some days; and during the whole of my sickness she had manifested the greatest concern for my recovery, and as I afterwards learned had frequently remarked that she did not believe I would get well; . . .

On Sabbath morning, (I slept that night with her) she arose early, before I was awake, and remarked to father that she was sick; he immediately went to prescribing medicine, and two physicians passed in a short time, both of whom were called to her assistance. The diarrhea was soon checked but her constitution so long impaired by disease was unable to withstand the attack and she began to sink. . . . [W]hen father tried to get her to talk, she said she had a great deal to say "but" said she "I shall die with weakness." . . . She had long felt willing to go at any time, and had felt for two months that she would not get through to Oregon.[31]

Did Abigail Jane Scott Duniway blame herself for her mother's death? Had she been too sleepy to help when her mother first awoke? In Duniway's 1905 autobiographical novel, the daughter, Jean Ranger, underestimating the first symptoms of her mother's illness, gives her some medicine but tells no one else until morning when it is too late to save the mother's life. "Jean could never forgive herself for not sounding an alarm." If impressionable young Abigail, already filled with ambiguous feelings toward her mother, actually carried such a sense of guilt into her adult life, it would have been a major component of her intense commitment to the rights and needs of women. As she herself said in the last sentence of *Path Breaking,* "The debt that each generation owes to the past it must pay to the future."[32]

They buried Ann Scott the next morning. The men chiseled a grave in the sandstone while Jenny recorded the location in hopes of finding it again. (They never did.) It was "on an eminence which overlooks a ravine intersected with groves of small pine and cedar trees. In about the centre of this ravine or rather basin, there wells forth from a kind of bank a spring of icy coldness, clear as crystal. In the outskirts of this basin clusters of wild roses and various other wild flowers grow in abundance." Above them "reposes the last earthly remains of *my mother*" (21 June). Jenny did not mention—but Harriet remembered—the stones. "We had to journey on and leave her, in a lonely grave—a feather bed as a coffin and the grave protected from the wolves by stones heaped on it. The rolling hills were ablaze with beautiful wild roses . . . and we heaped and covered mother's grave with the lovely roses, so the cruel stones were hid from view."[33]

John Tucker Scott wrote a poem about "The Golden Bowl Broken" which he inserted in the journal after reaching Oregon:

T'was midnight and he sat alone—
The husband of the dead,

That day the dark dust had been thrown
Upon her buried head;
Her orphan children round me sleep
But in their sleep do moan
Now bitter tears are falling fast
I feel that I'm *alone.* . . .

If gentle-hearted Tucker Scott had known what lay ahead, he might have preferred to stay beside his buried wife!

The company moved on for three more months, through sagebrush wastes, past foul-smelling alkali marshes where cattle could not graze, over rocky, dusty mountain trails which were as hard on the oxen's feet as on their own. By 3 July, "We see a great many abandoned, lame and worn out cattle and the air is literally filled with stench from dead oxen. We passed one as often as every half mile through the day." They were just one day behind a murder and hanging on the trail, learned from inscriptions on two new graves, side by side: "Charles Botsford murdered June 28th 1852," "Horace Dolley hung June 29th 1852." Details were obtained from the party ahead, which included the murdered man's wife and two children. On 15 July another murder in a nearby train required the Scott company men to act as jurors in a trial. They found the man innocent by reason of self-defense.

Reinforcing the family prejudices, a Mormon trading post sold the Scotts flour and food at outrageous prices (30 June). Then they passed a trading post "kept by french and half breeds with some specimens of humanity for their wives which plainily tells of the extent of their ambition. They are squaws of the most disgusting appearance" (3 July). Yet there in the wilderness, in the midst of their misery, they also met

a Mountaineer who had been in the mountains since '39—he is a native of Kentucky and the best specimen of a backwoods man I ever saw . . . his name is *Caldwell, his uncle Mr Wm Caldwell was one of our nearest & most intimate neighbours in the "Sucker State."* . . . [H]e appeared much rejoiced and quite glad to see us, particularly Father whose hand he grasped in honor of old Ky. His broadcloth coat and silk neck-kerchief contrasted strangely with his buck skin pants & moccasins; and his long, flowing hair and whiskers. He was mounted on an Indian pony and armed with two horse pistols, and was engaged in driving cattle. [21 July]

On 24 July a driver carelessly drove into a mudhole, upsetting the heavily laden wagon in which several of the girls were riding. As Harriet remembered it, Fanny, "as soon as she could extricate herself, poked her head out of the hooded wagon and cried, 'Oh Lord, come here quick!' The canvas bows were all broken and much of the contents spilled out. But Uncle Levi retained his sense of humor. He came running up and

exclaimed, 'hadn't you better call on some of the company?'" In this
accident Tucker Scott's carefully preserved cache of money disappeared. He was so angry that he told the teamster either to leave or be
horsewhipped. The man chose to leave.[34]

Tragedy soon struck again. Just above the Snake River's American
Falls on 30 July, the cattle, mad for water, stampeded across the rushing
river. In order to retrieve them two of the young men tried to swim
across. One of them made it, but "as the other one had never swam in
swift water he was carried down the river by the current and drowned! It
was impossible for any one to render him assistance as he floated down
so fast that a man could not run on the bank and keep even."

Catherine, who later identified the man as Jenny's "sweetheart," the
man she might have married if he had lived, said the swimmer panicked
and tried to return before being "hurled swiftly out of sight."[35] Jenny
wrote:

> His name was John McDonald. He was about twenty one years of age; was
> going through on his own resources with another young man . . . from Mt.
> Sterling Brown county Illinois and had traveled with us from Missouri. The
> deceased was a worthy young man; and being sociable affectionate and
> accommodating he won the esteem of all, and was beloved by every one who
> knew him. His untimely death has cast a gloom over every countenance. . . .

After detailing the rest of the day's events, she concluded:

> I am seated in the same place where I was when writing last evening but
> alas! how changed are our prospects, how greatly changed our meditations!
> The roaring of the river is no longer pleasant music to my ears, but is a
> jarring discordant sound, and I startle and half rise to my feet at rustling of
> the leaves about me; and these huge rocks which I then looked upon with
> admiration, now only terrify . . . but still I love this spot as It corresponds
> with my feelings.

The company's terrors were by no means over. The man who had
succeeded in crossing the river could neither drive the oxen nor return
himself. Tucker Scott and Levi Caffee decided to go eight miles up-
stream, where they had all fished for salmon the day before, and cross
with three horses. The horses were too weak for such swift waters. Before anyone knew what had happened to the men, the girls "saw the
white face of our old mare 'Sukey' bobbing up and down in the boiling
waters. She was such a loved old mare that we could not bear to leave her
at home in Illinois!"[36] How they worried until their father returned!
The stranded man meanwhile endured first the sun and then a ferocious hailstorm without cover. Tucker Scott paid thirty dollars to hire
two men to rescue him, though they could not budge the cattle. The man

was "so weak . . . he could hardly stand." Harriet claimed "his skin all peeled off and he nearly lost his mind from his awful experience," while Catherine mentioned the "ravenous mosquitoes" and the fear of Indians.

Next day they built a raft for crossing, but no one dared to go. Another precious sixty-four dollars paid two other travelers to cross, but still the cattle would not move. Finally, Scott "corked a wagon bed, placed an air tight water cask on each end and a large log at each side," and the desperate men forced the cattle to swim back by ten o'clock that night. In addition, the few animals that had stayed with the caravan ate something poisonous and died, including an indispensable cow that collapsed right after her milking. They named the place Camp Desolation as they "left its gloomy precincts, not caring to cast a glance backwards."[37]

Perhaps it was this experience of the river which made the Scott party fearful of crossing the Snake twice again at Glenn's Ferry and Fort Boise. Instead, they stayed on the south side for the next 140 miles, even though grass, wood, and water were known to be more plentiful on the other side. Soon Tucker Scott became ill, Jenny had a severe toothache, and the oxen began to weaken and die. Two men left after McDonald's death; now five more used the bed of a wagon, which Scott was forced to abandon because of lack of oxen, to float down the river to Boise. The weather was unbearably hot. Dust filled their nostrils and eyes. Almost everyone was ill, four more of them to die before the trip ended.

Among the dying was three-and-a-half-year-old Willie Scott. He had "cholera infantum, or dropsy of the brain" (25 August), and he lingered suffering for nine days before he died. For part of that time, Tucker Scott was also so sick with diarrhea that he could not stand. By the twenty-sixth, though, he was "some better" and managed to walk all day "though he totters as he walks. Our hope is in God." Harvey and John Henry Scott later claimed that only Fanny's special care had saved their lives. Jenny wrote:

> Aug. 29th Two months and seven days this morning since our beloved mother was called to bid this world adieu, and the ruthless monster death not yet content, has once more entered our fold & taken in his icy grasp the treasure of our hearts! Last night our darling Willie was called from earth, to vie with angels around the throne of God. He was buried to-day upon an elevated point, one hundred and fifty feet above the plain in a spot of sweet seclusion.

(Twenty years later, Harvey returned to Willie's grave and found the juniper tree in which Tucker Scott had carved Willie's name. He took a piece of bark to give to his father.)[38]

Close calls came to everyone on the Overland Trail. Eleven-year-old Harriet had "to keep up the loose stock" on the way. She rode an old one-eyed, swaybacked, sorrel mare named Shuttleback.

> She was a big powerful animal, and when she'd get a whiff of an Indian she would kick and plunge and many a time would throw me off. One day . . . both Shuttleback and I needed water. I was about a mile behind the train and off at the side of the road a grove of willows was growing, it looked like water might be there. . . . I gladly got off the saddle . . . and first let the mare drink. It was a steep place. The mare began to plunge and I soon saw she was in quicksand. I held on tightly to her rein, yelled with all my might, knowing there was a man behind me also driving stock. He heard me and rushed to my assistance, telling me to hold on and not be afraid; he would bring help. He rushed ahead and brought back my father and three other men, and with ropes and a long pole pried her out of the quicksand and floated her down the stream where she finally landed on her feet. I fully expected punishment but my father just picked me up, sat me down on the wet, muddy saddle, slapped the mare and said, "now, go on!"[39]

On another occasion, late at night, women and children were told to get out of the wagons in order to get them down an "all fired steep" hill to the camping place. Corpulent Martha Caffee hated to move.

> The angry protest of the tired woman ceased, however, with a suddenness that surprised her fellow travelers. Astonishment gave place to dismay, when something like two minutes of silence were followed by muffled shrieks, which seemed to come from the very bowels of the earth. They grew more distinct as the poor woman caught her breath fully, and an impromptu search with lanterns discovered her far down the mountain side, hanging to a scrub juniper tree, which was the only object intervening between her and further descent into the darkness of the nether world. The voice of her husband had not been gentle a few minutes before, but compared with this, when, after much tugging and straining, she was towed into camp, . . . it was as a summer zephyr to a howling nor-easter. She was only placated the next morning by the discovery that he, having left the conjugal couch in a huff, had made his bed in the darkness, close to the leeward of what in life had been a fine gray mare, but which, being now, some days defunct, he had mistaken in the darkness for a friendly rock. The shout of laughter that went up at his expense was turned upon his spouse, as he explained that the smell of sulphur had been so strong upon the night air, when he rolled up in his blankets, that he was not able to detect any other odor.[40]

For six weeks the girls were reduced to walking barefoot—their shoes had given out. They were covering eighteen to twenty miles a day over rocky, dusty terrain. Fanny carried five-year-old Sarah through the Grande Ronde Valley. The area was covered with prickly pear cactus.

When the spines "broke off in your feet they had to fester out." Jenny made ink out of berries in order to keep writing.[41]

By September the first emigrants to arrive in Oregon had spread the news about the horrors of the 1852 crossing. Oregonians began to raise supplies and men to help needy travelers. On 13 and 14 September, cousins John and Foster Johnson and Lawson Scott unexpectedly met the Scotts on the trail, two hundred miles from their destination. It was a joyful meeting and the diary recorded it characteristically: "They were just from the Garden of the *World* and we were all much rejoiced to meet each other, in this wild and romantic spot."

The Johnson boys brought a quarter of beef and some flour. Lawson Scott, said Abigail (no one else in the family would have told the story), brought

> a bottle of "oh, be joyful," thus horrifying our teetotaler crowd. It was little wonder that a relative [Levi Caffee], whom my father was bringing to Oregon to reform him, got gloriously tipsy, and engaged in a carnival of drunken songs; much to the diversion of the children, to whom it was all very funny.[42]

The cousins also contributed their labor to the heartbroken, exhausted family. The last hundred-mile journey over the Cascade Mountains included the worst ascents and descents in the whole trip. Neill Johnson had sent two yoke of fresh oxen to supplement Tucker Scott's worn-out animals, so the Scott party was able to take the rough, primitive Barlow Road instead of rafting down the Columbia River from The Dalles. Rafting, the only alternative for many emigrants, was a dangerous and difficult process, and it provided substantial profits to hosts of gougers and traders taking advantage of desperate people.

At The Dalles, with the little money he had left, Tucker Scott bought his barefoot girls new shoes. But he could do little to help other members of his company. Both Miranda Goudy and George Stevenson (who had joined them in Missouri) were now too sick to go further. Both died in October, leaving bereaved spouses and orphans stranded in the "promised land." Though Tucker Scott brought some of their belongings with him over the mountains, young Ruth Stevenson and her two small children had to find their own way down the river after George's death.

The Barlow Road was little better, only cheaper. It was on that route that the Scotts came close to starvation. The little food they had been able to buy at The Dalles' exorbitant prices turned out to be mildewed and rotten. Catherine remembered "boiling an antiquated ham bone and adding to the liquid . . . the few scrapings from the dough pan in which the biscuit from our last measure of flour—which . . . was both musty and sour—had been mixed." Even uncle Levi Caffee lost his sense of humor. The girls taunted him with "his own words . . . when romancing over the anticipation of a famine. . . . The poor fellow, who was really suffering from hunger, lost control of his temper." Abigail learned never again "to tantalize a hungry man, no matter what the temptation."[43]

On Saturday, the twenty-fifth of September, they descended the famous Laurel Hill on the west side of Mt. Hood, "an almost perpendicular descent of two miles, with three benches, where the teams could stop to rest." They chained the wagon wheels and fastened drags of heavy trees behind them to hold them back. It was here that "poor sister Margaret fell and rolled down and down. When she picked herself up Uncle Levi was there with his humor. "Maggie, aint this the damndest place you ever saw?' 'Yes, it is!' 'Well, you swore and I am going to tell your father.' "[44]

Six more days of travel brought the Scotts finally to French Prairie. They spent a day helping the ferryman repair his boat before they could cross the Willamette River. Then came a joyful welcome from Neill Johnson and his family. Penniless, exhausted, and grieving, they could rest at last.

Seventy years later, Harvey Scott's son Leslie concluded a compilation of the record of the Scott family journey by accusing Neill Johnson of a "grievous mistake" in advising John Tucker Scott to take his large family to Oregon. The printer of the book, an old pioneer, strongly disagreed, so Leslie Scott appended the printer's note to the text: "That journey made the character of John Tucker Scott's children," the man insisted, citing Harvey Scott's accomplishments. He continued: "Where else would daughters [like Abigail Scott Duniway] develop the determination to win a fight for a principle, lasting through two generations, than in that plodding, toilsome journey they record? . . . The Three Wise Men followed a star, and the world since has rejoiced. John Tucker Scott was a fourth, and, some day, state and Nation will honor him for the descendants he gave to both."[45]

CHAPTER 4

The Farmer's Wife

"I put my trust in the Lord till the breeching broke,
then I began to look out for myself."

Like so many other American immigrants, the Scotts found shelter in the new country among relatives. They recuperated for two weeks with the Johnsons, then moved to nearby Lafayette where uncle Peter Scott had settled in 1845. (Cousin Lemuel Scott was postmaster and George Goudy had recently organized the first Masonic lodge.) Lincoln's close friend Dr. Anson Henry and many other fellow Illinoisans had also just arrived. Amos Cook of the 1839 Peoria Party was now a prosperous farmer, merchant, and hotel owner in Lafayette, the county seat of Yamhill County, Oregon (later changed to McMinnville).

Historian Frances Fuller Victor called Yamhill County "one of the finest agricultural portions of the State, . . . celebrated for having domiciled, at one time or another, almost every person of prominence in the State, prior to 1868." The whole Oregon Territory, including what later became Washington, Idaho, and part of Montana, had only 13,043 settlers in 1850, plus about 5,000 new arrivals in 1851 and 8,000 in 1852. Portland was still a village. Lafayette ranked in size and importance with Salem and Oregon City and was nicknamed the Athens of Oregon because of its intellectual pretensions. Margaret Scott boasted to her grandfather that the town had eight stores in the spring of 1853.[1]

Catherine and Harriet ("Duck" to her grandfather) expressed their exhaustion and bereavement in letters home. Despite "continual rain" and "dull and gloomy" November weather, Harriet liked "Oregon what I have seen of it very well but not so well as old succordom [Illinois was called the Sucker State]. . . . I cannot be running about in the grasslot and pasture and rolling down the barn in the Crib. I cannot be a-running to Grandfather with the newspapers." Jenny and Fanny were contributing to the family welfare with all the sewing they could do, at "two dollars for pantaloons and five bits for flannel shirts."[2]

Jenny Scott quickly revealed her characteristic iconoclasm. At a Campbellite baptismal service a gentle rain began to fall. "This will spoil the diptising," she said. "I hope I don't fall" on the slippery sidewalk to the

43

river. "A Godly old lady walking near me said: 'If you put your trust in the Lord, sister, you will get down all right.'" Abigail Scott replied, "I am like the old lady who was in a runaway, who said: 'I put my trust in the Lord till the breeching broke, then I began to look out for myself.'" The "pious sister" was horrified and Editor Enoch Adams of Vancouver "printed my remark in his paper next week."[3]

John Tucker Scott quickly found a place in the small and highly self-conscious population of early Oregon. He wrote a perceptive description for the *Tazewell County Mirror:*

> As to the manners and customs of the Oregonians, I may say that they are of that kind that might be expected from a "conglomerated" mass of crude materials being thrown together and all shook up and then thrown out upon the great chess board of life. In the same neighborhood the "guessing" Yankee with his neat conveniences around him; the son of the Emerald Isle with his "paraties"; the plodding Dutchman "mit" his cabbage garden; the tight Frenchman with his native "vife" and surrounded with his half-breed "responsibilities" and Spanish cattle and "mustangs"; the enterprising man from the Western and middle States looking all around him for a speculation, or how to advance and develop the resources of the country, all classes full of money and good feeling; and you will have a faint picture of society here.

Scott was an "enterprising man" and proud of it. Having recovered from his harrowing journey, he was also proud of the new land he had found:

> Now, sir, fancy to yourself a tract of country stretching from north to south some four hundred miles, and from east to west some one hundred and fifty, with a navigable stream in the centre, and another cutting it in two and a spacious "sound" easy of access from the vast Pacific, and a sea coast on its western border, with two lofty ranges of mountains, with occasional peaks covered with eternal snow, lifting their grim vissages above the horizon, and all this grand outline "filled in" with hill and dale, timber and prairie, of the finest kind, and springs and brooks and rivulets, with numerous Kanyons and Cascades, and you have a *faint* picture of that portion of western Oregon—that lies between the summit of the Cascade Mountains and the Pacific coast, known as the Will-am-ette Valley and Puget Sound.[4]

For the next sixty years the same enthusiasm echoed through the writings of John Tucker Scott's children, including both Harvey Scott's measured editorials and Abigail Scott Duniway's pell-mell prose.

Scott had good reason to be enthusiastic, for he had himself "looked all around him for a speculation" and had found an answer. In early March he took over the management of Amos Cook's Temperance House, where important travelers often stayed and twelve to fifteen regular boarders paid $8.00 a week. His daughters made an ideal labor force—with the exception of Abigail Jane, who took a teaching job instead. The "large and commodious tavern house" provided a welcome roof over their heads and plenty to eat, though Maggie told her grandparents it involved "a great deal of work" as a "very profitable business." Twelve-year-old Harriet attended school that winter, but the other girls had to keep house. Among their important guests were Judge Matthew Deady, associate justice of the Territorial Supreme Court and a prominent Democratic politician, Republicans Reuben Patrick Boise, Oregon's chief justice in the 1860s, and attorney David Logan, son of Lincoln's law partner and mayor of Portland from 1864 to 1868.[5] Genial, generous, strong-minded, hardworking John Tucker Scott made an ideal innkeeper whom his guests respected and did not forget. The hotel gave the whole family status and wide acquaintanceship within Oregon's pioneer elite.

But Scott had no intention of remaining an innkeeper. He explained in a letter to his father that he did such a "strange" thing only because "I am *broke* and could not go onto a claim and make a farm with my family & at the same time make a living & in this business I can make a living & be able to improve a farm so as to be able to go on to it when the circumstances will justify." His "galls," he said, were "well pleased with the enterprise." He would obtain a claim in the vicinity, using the tavern only for six months or a year as a means of accumulating necessary capital.[6]

The Oregon Temperance House was similar to many others in America in the nineteenth century. Set up as alternatives to whiskey-selling taverns, such establishments usually did not eschew "soft" beverages like cider, beer, and wine. Hard cider, in fact, was a mainstay of the fruit-growing Oregonians, while moderation rather than total abstinence from alcohol was the ideal of many temperance advocates. It was the *public* use and sale of hard liquors, especially to the poor, to Indians, and to potential voters, which reformers particularly opposed—as even the new "Maine Law" indicated. That law forbade the sale of hard liquor in less than one-gallon containers and was the model for temperance agitation during the 1850s and 1860s.[7] Though prohibitionists came to favor much greater stringency, it was possible to be an ardent temperance advocate in mid-century America without being a total prohibitionist. This distinction Abigail Scott Duniway did not forget.

Now that he had a home and a living, Tucker Scott also could afford a wife. Ann Scott's death had left his children motherless and himself alone. Meanwhile, the attractive young Ruth Stevenson, whose husband had died at The Dalles, was destitute in the land of promise. She had two small children and, as a widow, no right to claim land. (Word had not yet reached Oregon of the law's amendment in 1853 allowing widows to "improve" a claim for four years if they did not marry.) Nor could Scott claim the extra 160 acres allotted by the Donation Land Act to a spouse, unless he remarried before the end of the year. The issue was on his mind, for he complained about the law's injustice to women in a letter of 30 March 1853 to the *Mirror*.

Six days after the Scotts moved into the Temperance House, Tucker Scott brought twenty-five-year-old Ruth Eckler Stevenson back from Portland to be his wife. They were married on 15 March by Methodist Reverend Pearne. The Scott daughters, still grieving from the loss of their mother, were not enthusiastic. (A father's second marriage and the resulting injustices for older daughters became an important theme in numerous Duniway novels.) But coolness toward their stepmother derived from an even more serious problem—so serious that it was kept secret for 125 years! Only because Tucker Scott's righteous brother-in-law Deacon Elijah Brown saved the explanatory letters for his descendants instead of returning them with other James Scott papers was the secret recently discovered.

On 3 July 1853 Scott wrote a cheerful letter to his father describing his young wife "of medium size . . . remarkably healthy and of lively disposition." He reported that "the children & their step mother are *verry* agreeable. . . . [W]e all get along together very harmoniously." He wrote no more letters until the following spring. By mid-July it was evident that Ruth Stevenson Scott was pregnant. The baby was due in October— only seven months after the wedding. It was not Tucker Scott's.

Margaret Scott wrote her grandfather on 17 August to report the unexpected marriages of both Abigail Jane and Fanny. "Pa's health is not very good and has not been for some time," she added, without more explanation, while she herself was "in a perfect whirl of bewilderment" after the "Grand 'Shiveree." She mentioned her father's illness again and then resorted to the family propensity for puns about Jenny's "old man" and Fanny's "'tother half." "So you see that Jenny has Dun a way . . . with the name of Scott, and Fran has gotten above her business and taken A. Cook."[8]

Faced with the possible effects of the unfolding scandal in their family, the Scott girls felt an urgent need to separate themselves from a situation which might damage their own reputations. Fanny's sudden marriage to her father's longtime friend and benefactor Amos Cook, when he was thirty-seven and she twenty—she had hardly forgotten her lover George Landes in Illinois—enabled her to provide a home for Catherine, Harriet, and Sarah. Margaret went to the academy in Forest Grove. Fanny still remembered bitterly when she was ninety that she had never received the education her father had promised her. Amos Cook, however, was a "good man," Margaret later told her grandfather, "and I think

Fanny will always have a good home and plenty to live on." Jenny described him as "very industrious and . . . in good circumstances . . . [with] one of the finest farm houses I know of anywhere; Fanny is in high spirits."[9]

John Henry (known as Jerry or "Little Toot") went to live with the Duniways. Harvey alone remained with his father. The next spring Margaret married George Fearnside, a storekeeper in Forest Grove. Catherine went to live with her and attend the academy. Tucker Scott gave up his hotel to Martha and Levi Caffee soon after the first weddings and spent the next few months straightening out his own shattered love life.

Tucker Scott explained his actions to his father in a letter the following spring (10 April 1854). He removed Ruth "from the family to a comfortable house," where he "employed a good nurse and skillful physician to attend her and provided her with all the necesary comforts in my power until her fathers *family* arrived—(her father died on the plains) which concists of three brothers and two sisters. They are all living together." He also "obtained a bill of divorce."

Though no records of Scott's divorce survive (the Yamhill County courthouse burned in 1857), gossip certainly continued and blighted Ruth's reputation for life. (In the 1853 legislature's "memorable session," other celebrated divorce cases included Margaret Jewett Bailey's complicated complaint.) Tucker Scott told his father he only "applied for the divorce . . . to avoid technicalities in law. [A]nd also to divest the matter of any thing like necessity or compultion on either her part or mine." But Abigail Scott Duniway later told her grandfather that at the time "he said he could not live with a woman who was having another man's children, and would not hear to keeping the matter dark, or we would never have made it public at all." She also said her father forbade his children to write about his "difficulty," so she had waited more than a year after her own marriage. "I felt that I could not write and say nothing about it and I did not want to be the first one to mention it." She now did so only in answer to her grandfather's questions.[10]

Tucker Scott launched an investigation. First he insisted that the abject Ruth write out her story for him and for his father, in order to provide a *"true and correct* account of the whole matter." The unconscious eloquence and repeated words of Ruth's letter (written on 5 September 1853) attest to the labor and grief with which she wrote it. After her first husband died, she said,

> I was taken sick and haveing no place to stop or any acquaintances with me I started down the river and in comeing down I lost all my clouthing and almost everything I had and not much left and in a strange place I was left to my own resources for food & raiment for myself and children one of them sick . . . but is now stout and healthy I acordingly took in washing

which was a good price and also a good many advised me to do so & and of course become aquainted with a great many men & of different characters finally there came along one and which I am very much mortified in saying that he seduced me he was with me twice and after he lefte me the second time I got to studying about what I had done and come to a full sense of my shame and disgrace and on his comeing again I drove him from my presence I have not seen him since and hope that I never will again in a few weeks now I will be confined and bring into this world a poor unfortunate little being the rewards of a mothers weakness O had I only one friend then near me I would have been saved but now I am lost had Mr. Scott only written to me before that time both him and I would have been saved a great deal of trouble and anguish but why did I not tell him all about it[?] it was because I did not think I was in that way if I had known it I never would have married him never never no never would I have done such a thing but I thought that that there was nothing the matter with me and that he never would find it out.

Like many another woman in her situation, Ruth felt the full burden of blame and disgrace of her sin. "No one knows or can conceive the anguish the anguish of my heart," she wrote, her repetitions reflecting her misery.

I know that I done wrong but . . . . if he can be content to let me remain with him I will I will never deceive him in anything again and I will be an obedient and faithful wife unto him so long as we both shall live but oh, if he cannot. . . . if we have to separate it will be almost beyond endureance altho I deserve it I know I do.

She praised the Scott family because "even now they all treat me the same as they ever did when they ought to have driven me from their presence."

Indeed, the conflict between nineteenth-century standards of morality and the dictates of the heart sorely tested the Scotts' consciences. Double standards, which Abigail Scott Duniway later so frequently protested, could not have been more poignantly exemplified for Tucker Scott's daughters. Women bore the unjust suffering caused by male lust and a moment's weakness. Men were not always protectors.

Ruth Scott's baby, born on 15 October 1853 (always listed as 1852 in family genealogies to hide the illegitimacy), was named Robert Stevenson. She was taken in by her relatives who came over the trail that fall, and they all moved to the newly organized Washington Territory. Deeply depressed, Tucker Scott followed six months later. After his "most serious thoughts," he wrote his father to "'ask your advice.' after you have looked it all over I want you to tell me what course you think would be best." "My concience," he said, "recognises her as my *wife*."

I know her to be worthy of a *good* husband and (with that one misstep) all that any reasonable man ought to ask, and besides this I will say that her deep marked sorrow for this wrong and the sincere repentance she has manifested and the earnest solicitude she has had toward my family in view of the whole matter renders the whole matter rather of a peculiar nature. . . . I have never entirely abandoned the idea of her being my wife.

Having waited for "circumstances . . . fully to develop themselves," he now believed Ruth "to be as *good a woman as lives*." He was taking up a claim in Washington in order to be near her while he awaited his father's answer.

Grandfather James Scott, the former sheriff, collected his evidence carefully before deciding. He wrote all the granddaughters for their opinions—nineteenth-century patriarchy with a decidedly egalitarian flavor. (Abigail Scott Duniway learned about freedom of expression from within her own family.) The daughters' disillusionment with their father is evident in their answers. Maggie Scott Fearnside, the most pious one, wrote:

And now it becomes my most unpleasant task to speak of his matrimonial affairs. We have none of us given him our *free* consent to marry her. I have told him he had better marry her if he can do nothing but grieve about her all the time but I cannot conscientiously have any thing to do with her. I consider she has given an insult to the family which no husband should forgive. She came into a large family of girls with a stain on her character which she knew in the unjust eyes of the world would for a time injure us. How often even now my cheek will glow with shame when persons of my acquaintance have no more feeling than to mention her. But from the fact that Pa will always be miserable unless he *does* marry her we have to give him our consent.

Abigail Scott Duniway responded with characteristic pragmatism:

had we ever had the least idea that he would want to live with her again we would all have done all in our power to put down suspicion in the first place and made no fuss about it; But pa seemed willing to divorce her and we thought he would think no more about her. . . . [N]ow that the noise of the divorce has died away we none of us feel willing for him to raise it again. She may be in earnest in her professions, but when she deceived us so far what reason have we to believe what she says? I hate to say anything to Pa about it for fear of hurting his feelings . . . , but I believe that he is blinded in her & that if he takes her he cannot be happy. [O]ne thing certain he is determined not to be happy without her and it is probly best for him to take her, but none of us girls can visit her or ask her to see us.

James Scott gave his approval. Tucker and Ruth Scott settled "about two miles from the head of Skookum bay" on Puget Sound. There were still only thirty voters in the whole county. They lived a primitive "shantee" life, but fish and game were plentiful, and Scott considered it the "*next best* place" to the Willamette Valley. Ruth had to contend with hungry, hostile Indians. The Yakima War broke out in 1855, forcing them to flee twenty miles by canoe across the sound to Olympia. Ruth's next baby was born an hour after they reached the fort. (A son of this child became the eminent Yale University historian of China and Christian missions, Kenneth Scott Latourette.) They returned to Oregon in 1857, to Clackamas County near the Duniways, and then to Forest Grove. Scott became a successful farmer and sawmill operator and a major benefactor of Pacific University, where Harvey Scott was the first graduate. Tucker Scott eventually named Robert Stevenson coexecutor with Ruth Scott of his estate, and he was an accepted member of the family.[11]

The Ruth Stevenson episode not only shattered the physical unity of the Scott family, it also left psychic wounds and divisions. And it added another dimension to the girls' incipient feminism. Though Harvey shared the loss of opportunity which his father felt, in 1856 he returned from Washington alone to live in a makeshift hut, attend school in Oregon City, and prepare for college.[12] He became an independent, tough-minded, politically conservative, self-made man, with a lifelong nostalgia for his lost and idealized mother. The girls, on the other hand, found educational and personal opportunities truncated by marital responsibilities, and a revered patriarch turned out to have clay feet. They developed capable, self-sufficient, strong-minded personalities, increasingly sensitive to issues of male injustice or female victimization.

Abigail Jane Scott had sought independence from her family even before the scandal. In the spring of 1853, a few days after her father's wedding, she went to the small but ambitious village of Cincinnati (now Eola) six miles southwest of Salem to teach. Hers was one of the first schools in Oregon, located not far from the one recently used by Chloe Boone, Daniel Boone's great-granddaughter. Jenny boarded with her great-grandmother's grandnephew, a member of the Riggs family who had followed the same migratory pattern as the Boones.[13]

Abigail Jane Scott passed "a creditable examination" and received a first-class certificate, though she "was not questioned severely, except in the proverbial 'three R's'." Her teaching, like that in most other frontier schools, was based primarily on Webster's speller (she used the copy she had "smuggled" onto the wagon and brought with her to Oregon) plus whatever other books the children might own. It was not an arduous job but one with respectable status as well as her own small income. She had a mixed class of ten to twenty students at about $4.00 each per quarter and became the recognized "intellectual" in the community.[14]

Jenny also found herself suddenly popular among all the unmarried men of the vicinity. The provisions of the Donation Land Act combined with the severe shortage of single women in early Oregon resulted in the most serious epidemic of marriage fever in American history. Men felt compelled to marry before December 1853 in order to claim a wife's portion of land. There were many thirteen-, fourteen-, and fifteen-year-old brides.[15] Jenny Scott, at eighteen-and-a-half, had more suitors than she wanted.

One of them still remembered Jenny twenty-two years later. The girl he had married when she was fourteen and he forty had fallen in love with another man. He kicked her out of his house, sued for divorce, denied her access to her children, and blamed the whole debacle on the "pernicious teachings" of Duniway's newspaper, the faults of "Uncle Sam's" Donation Land Act, and the refusal of Abigail Jane Scott to marry him. He had courted Mrs. Duniway, the man said in an anonymous letter to her paper, when she was one of "only . . . eight single marriageable women" he could find as he "rushed all over Polk and Yamhill counties."

> One morning in July a man looking very much like myself rode up to your school-house door, called for the mistress, put a letter of proposal in her hand, waited near by till noon for an answer, was then very courteously informed that "he was too late," and only two weeks after that, the more fortunate B. C. D. carried the schoolmistress off to the minister, and from there on to his double land-claim, while I only got a cold quarter-section.

"All Oregon," the man continued, "was married off in 1853, and I had to wait for a new crop, and could not wait long or somebody else would snap them up." Thus he had married "the first one that would have me," despite her young age. "Was not all Oregon demoralized by that law twenty-odd years ago?" he exclaimed. He himself had been only "a worshiper of woman's loveliness, if of anything under heaven." He could not understand his wife's behavior, comparing it "to the visit of a simoon, where I was not even looking for a storm."[16]

Duniway returned fire in an editorial in the same issue. She well remembered the man—mounted on a "tall bay mule" as he made his "pell-mell chase" around Oregon "proposing matrimony indiscriminately to tearful widows of a fortnight, and little girls dirty with mud pies; and now, at a mature age, he not only has the cheek" to describe it, but also the "effrontery to boast of it, and the hardiness to attempt to palliate it." She defended the man's wife (though she did not condone the adultery), and scoffed, "A worshiper of woman's loveliness indeed! A worshiper of a quarter section of land, we should think if we were to judge the merits of his case from the testimony of the only facts." Not surprisingly, the man became an implacable enemy of woman's rights and Mrs. Duniway.

Still sensitive about her father's marriage, Jenny Scott was not likely to be won by such a man as that. But a handsome young rancher, just back from a winter's prospecting for Rogue River gold in southern Oregon, was another story. Benjamin C. Duniway, tall, warmhearted, and good-natured, with thick black hair and classic features, a dashing horseman who was considered "the best catch around," had heard about the sparkling wit and untamed spirit of the new schoolteacher. Six months earlier, amid the miseries of the last stages of their overland journey, Jenny had seen Ben among the many rescuers from Oregon bringing sustenance to beleaguered pioneers. When he turned up at the door of her schoolhouse, Jenny Scott, as she always expressed it, "met her fate."

Born in 1830, the oldest son among thirteen children, Ben had come to Oregon in 1850 from Griggsville in Pike County, Illinois. His family, like the Scotts and like most families in that part of southwestern Illinois, was previously from Kentucky. His grandfather had been among the first settlers of Daniel Boone's Boonesboro in the 1770s. Ben's mother died shortly after his birth, and the last of his father's subsequent three wives died on the Overland Trail in 1851. With characterisic generosity, Ben Duniway was paying his father's expenses for that trip from the proceeds of his gold prospecting and of his ranch—320 acres near his sister and brother-in-law, the Gibsons, on the rolling hills northeast of Salem in Clackamas County.

There is no record of the whirlwind courtship, except perhaps a poem which Abigail wrote in 1899 when she was sixty-five and Ben had been dead three years. Describing young skaters and sleigh bells outside her window, she remembered "an echoing song of the long ago."

Tis a song of the days when the clattering feet
Of my lover's white horses struck sparks in the street,
And his rosy cheeked lassie with her brown, wind-blown curls
Snugly tucked in her hood, was the happiest of girls.
And she sang that same song, her heart swelling with pride,
As she nestled in trust, her fond lover beside,
    While the sleigh glided swiftly over the snow.
Oh the deep tender bass of my lover's refrain
As he joined the glad chorus, again and again!
How it touches my heart as yon sleigh-bells are jingling
And the gay lads and lassies, their voices commingling
    Are repeating my song of the sweet long ago!

Ben Duniway was always a singer, as his sons remembered, and his voice must have been one of his most pleasing characteristics. In a letter to

Clyde of 24 December 1899 Abigail Duniway spoke of her loneliness and memories, including "your father also, with his goodness and his feebleness, and [I] can hear his voice as though it had sounded [in] my ears but yesterday."

Jenny Scott in every way resembled the girls in all her stories who are swept away by romantic passion for handsome strangers, who marry young and without careful thought, and who are carried off to drudgery or tragedy from which there is no escape. Ben Duniway certainly admired, respected, and adored Jenny Scott. Her status as a schoolteacher, her intelligence and ready wit, even her independent spirit, appealed to the openhearted, horse-loving rancher. He believed in her talents and ambition. But the very generosity which made him lovable also caused the burdens which made their married life so difficult. In the bright, happy, horseback-riding summer of 1853, neither could see the runaway troubles which lay ahead.

Despite her infatuation, eighteen-year-old Jenny remembered the principles of exalted love she had absorbed from her reading. At her wedding on 2 August 1853 she omitted the word *obey* from her wedding vows and was "sustained in the refusal by a good Methodist minister," the Reverend J. W. Miller of Lafayette. Such a marriage was to be based on love, not lust; it meant that a wife would be free to refuse excessive pregnancies and that her husband recognized her right to do so.[17]

After the wedding Ben took his bride to the "wilds of Clackamas County," the hill country south of Oregon City, near the Mollala River. Tall, gray-green Douglas firs then covered the area, except for clearings here and there. The well-timbered banks of Rock Creek ran through the middle of the 320-acre Duniway claim. Off to the east one could see the white cone of Mt. Hood when the weather was clear, but the square mile of section 16 reserved for future schools, just east of their cabin, remained untouched wilderness. It was good land for hunting and stock raising, which was Ben Duniway's specialty, but the best land for farming lay nearby on the fertile prairies claimed by earlier pioneers.[18]

Because Ben Duniway had come to Oregon before 1 December 1850 he could claim 320 acres in his own name but nothing extra for his new wife because he had not married within a year after his arrival. Thus Abigail Duniway did not share the good fortune of some other pioneer women. She remained propertyless. Ben bought other claims also, and the work involved on all of them was extensive and tedious. Sparse population and huge donation land holdings intensified isolation and retarded both rural and urban development. Abigail Jane Duniway nicknamed their neighborhood Hardscrabble,[19] and soon came to resent the unaccustomed loneliness of her life. She had hired men to feed, and numerous other chores, as much or more drudgery than she had ever had before. She also became, immediately, pregnant. Clara Belle Duniway was born 26 May 1854, nine and three-quarters months after the wedding.

Proud of his new wife, Ben was delighted to invite his friends to admire her and relieve her loneliness. But they were not entirely welcome, as Duniway indicated in almost every account of her early married life. In one version she recalled:

> My husband . . . was the envied center of a group of about a dozen unmarried fellow ranchmen; and nothing delighted him more than to mobilize them at meal time at our cabin home in the wilderness, where it fell to my lot, whether the babies or I were well or ill, to feed the crowd to repletion, as is the habit of most wives and mothers of the frontier settlements unto this day.[20]

In another reminiscence she mentioned that these bachelors usually wanted their laundry washed as well, probably because they had no other access to soap. The huge soap-making kettle, along with the candle molds and the butter churn, kept every housewife busy when she wasn't making preserves and pickles and salted meat and bread, or milking the cow or tending the pigs, or making the clothes and sewing the quilts, not to speak of nursing her baby and washing her own family's laundry.

Something may be guessed about the quality of Mrs. Duniway's housewifery from her answers to correspondents' letters in the *New Northwest*. For example, on 30 June 1871 she wrote: "Though our soap was always excellent, we had no precise *rule* for making it, but like Mother Matthew with her potato pudding, we only wanted necessary 'ingregiencies.' Our ingenuity did the rest." The same column mentions her failures at tending ducks and her preference for chicken feathers in making pillows.

Jenny's troubles started almost immediately. "The first year . . . I ran short of preserves and delicacies of that nature long before the Winter came to an end, so our only dessert was, perforce, dried apple pies. But we served them with rich, thick cream." Though she acquiesced in serving Ben's friends, she rebelled at the frontier expectation that she should do it even when he was not there. One day, when Ben had gone off on horseback to tend his cattle,

> I was making a quilt, my husband's half brother, a young boy, was with me. . . . We had eaten lunch and I had washed the dishes and started work at the quilting frames, when four men came to the cabin. They sat around the fireplace and talked. I replenished the fire and then went ahead with my quilting. After an hour's stay I noticed they were becoming restless. Finally one of them said, "Well, I guess we might as well go; I don't see any indications of dinner." I was shortly to become a mother. I had been working hard; it was after the dinner hour when they arrived, so I said: "If you

had told me what you were waiting for you could have gone home an hour ago." I will never forget how troubled and shocked my husband was when I told him about my lack of hospitality.[21]

Benjamin Duniway was a "southron," accustomed to a man's world of camaraderie, horse trading, cattle raising, wild game hunting, unquestioning hospitality, and subordinate women. Gentle as he was by nature, he could see no injustice in expecting as much from his wife as from all the other women he had known. But Abigail Duniway had once glimpsed a world in which men did not sit and talk while women replenished the fire. Furthermore, quilt-making was a task so distasteful to her that it remained a bête noir for the rest of her life.[22]

Attacks of rheumatoid arthritis, which had begun when she was a child, now recurred under the strain of childbirth, farm labor, and psychological frustration. Twenty years later Mrs. Duniway told her readers.

We remember, when we used to follow the avocation of a supported and protected woman on the farm, that we were often so jaded and worn, and so tortured with pains and aches that we would involuntarily utter exclamations of pain, although we kept a-going about the usual occupations connected with our protected condition. . . . One morning after a restless night . . . one of the hired men expressed surprise at seeing us at table, saying he thought, from the complaints he had heard, that we would be too ill to get breakfast.

"Oh," said our gracious liege, as he patted the chubby hands of the baby in the high chair beside him, while we rocked the one in the cradle with our foot, as we stood in a half-bent posture and poured coffee for a half dozen "protectors," who were helping themselves to fried chicken and potatoes; "you needn't be uneasy about *her*! If she should once quit *complaining* and quit *working*, I'd feel sure she was going to *die*!"[23]

(Mrs. Duniway's compulsive work habits continued even after she became a professional woman. Her story continued: "We've been *sick* for the past ten days, and in that time have given four lectures, organized the suffrage society, visited a dozen families, done one day's sewing, written two chapters of the serial story and ever so much other MS, and yet we see no stopping place, although *compelled* to forego much that our voice and pen are longing to attempt. And now, finding that overtaxed nature will not longer obey the whip of ambition without a *rest*, we reluctantly lounge . . . , longing to write to you, good readers. . . ." She goes on to detail the events of the week!)

Ben was a hard worker too, clearing land and fencing in his stock, hunting the wild game which was a major source of their food, and growing and harvesting wheat. Of course, Ben worked outdoors and with other men as companions. His visitors, however, often supplied Abigail Duniway with the audience her temperament so desperately needed. In the midst of her complaints she was already writing up experiences "to read to my rustic neighbors. . . . [T]hey were sufficiently diverting to attract crowds to our cabin home, often to remain over night, and always till after dinner."[24]

Jenny Scott Duniway was proud of her ability to cope with hardship, and ambitious for the success of their enterprise. Much as she hated the work, especially in retrospect, she threw herself into it and did it well enough. Years later, in answer to an opponent who claimed that a woman could know nothing about "the roughening influences of physical toil," she claimed to have "milked milk enough with my two hands to float the Great Eastern (the largest streamer at the time afloat) and . . . made butter enough for market with the propelling power of my hands at an old-fashioned churn . . . to grease the axles of creation." The heroine of Duniway's *Captain Gray's Company* boasts of producing 2,000 pounds of butter for market in five years, as Duniway probably did herself—a substantial contribution to the family economy.[25]

She even helped her "old man" butcher hogs:

One time our liege had a large pen full of rapidly fattening porkers, and many of them were very ferocious, having been captured wild in the autumn by well-trained dogs. One day a merchant having ordered one of the fattest . . . , Mr. D. . . . undertook the job with the assistance of his protected and supported spouse. He first shot and killed the hog in the pen, causing all the others to become very furious. . . . Then he placed a heavy slab across the top of the pen and directed us to stand upon the slab and help him pull the carcass on it. To say we "hankered" after the job would require a stretch of imagination of which we prefer not to be guilty; but we climbed upon the pen, stood upon the slab, and waited the next move. Mr. D. . . . stooped down and caught the defunct porker by one hind foot. As soon as he raised the animal enough to allow us to reach the other foot, we did so, and both gave a tremendous pull. Mr. D's hands were wet, and the foot he was pulling slipped through them suddenly, leaving the whole weight upon our clenched fingers. . . . [W]e, too, . . . "let go," and with such a vengeance that we were pitched backwards into the oozy, abominable mud, eight or ten feet away. . . . Our mud-soaked cloathes were ruined, and we were somehow led to the conclusion that a woman's right to butcher hogs was one which we would ever after willingly delegate to the men, and insist upon their sole possession.[26]

Misfortunes seemed to stalk the Duniways. In June 1855 a tornado and hailstorm totally destroyed their cabin, barn, fencing, and newly sprouted crops. Abigail Scott Duniway was alone with her baby. She milked all the cows and gathered a good supply of wood before finally realizing that the strange noise and approaching ominous cloud was more dangerous than anything she had ever seen. Cowering in a corner with her child, she just missed death as the twister tore off the roof and smashed the furniture. Then hail pelted their defenseless bodies. When the storm subsided Abigail slogged for a mile and a half through mud and swollen streams with her baby, arriving at her in-laws' cabin so hysterical and distraught they could hardly believe her story. The Gibsons hailed Ben late that night as he headed home. Next morning, when they both returned to the farm, Ben was aghast. "You didn't tell it by halves!" he exclaimed. With the exception of a few fallen trees, no other damage had occurred in the whole vicinity. Neighbors gathered to rebuild the cabin and share supplies, but the loss was far more than could be replaced.[27]

Eight months after the tornado, Jenny Duniway gave birth to her second child. Willis Duniway, almost two years younger than his sister, was born on 2 February 1856. When sister-in-law Mary Gibson and neighbors Mrs. Ingalls and Mrs. Elliott were called from their homes nearby to act as midwives, they knew immediately that a doctor was needed. The baby was unusually large for such a slender mother. (Four months later he was "nearly as heavy as [two-year-old] Clara.")[28] After giving birth in the customary squatting position, Abigail was carried to the bed, where she hemorrhaged dangerously for hours. Fifty-eight years later she remembered her labor as "a season of indescribable suffering." Meanwhile, Ben Duniway had been dispatched on his horse. The night was dark and stormy and he was frantic. That excellent horseman and devoted husband, a man who had been roaming the Oregon countryside for five years hunting and trading and helping his neighbors, got lost. For hours he was gone. Finally, giving the horse the reins, the master arrived safely home—without a doctor. Willis was born unharmed.[29]

Fortunately, twenty-two-year-old Abigail Jane Duniway did not die. But she became an "invalid" all that spring. "Compelled to spend hours of each day in a reclining position, . . . occupied with our own intense thoughts," she began to "scribble" poems and stories.[30]

Catherine and Harriet came to help their sister, and the gaiety they brought to the troubled household was medicine, too. When they all wrote a letter to "Pa" that June, just before Kit was to start teaching school on Barlow's Prairie, Jenny crowed, "Clara & Willis are pretty *near some*. Willis looks so much like Willie used to that you really ought to see him." Harriet ("Dug") Scott, who was "almost froze to see" her father, also praised Willis as a *"bouncing boy,"* "a perfect *Scott*." But Ben was "almost laid up with the sore eyes." He was hoping for $200 from the cattle he gave Tucker Scott to sell in Washington. It was a late, wet spring. The roads "worse now than . . . in december" were delaying a longed-for trip to see "Mag" and George Fearnside in Forest Grove. Jenny's letter ended with a revealing slip of the tongue. She wrote "A J Scott" and then underneath, "Oh that wont do, it's Duniway." Married less than three years, the presence of her sisters and the misfortune of her illness must have made her long for Scott family girlhood again.[31]

The declining economy of 1855–56 made things worse. When the Scotts arrived in 1852, Oregon was still in the midst of a commercial boom caused by the California Gold Rush and the tremendous influx of immigrants. The miners of Jacksonville and the Rogue River in southern Oregon also needed Oregon wheat and apples. But prices had been falling ever since the bright summer of 1853; by the fall of 1855 times were "exceedingly stringent." Then the Duniway cabin burned down in the summer of 1856, making the debacle nearly complete. As Harriet told one of the children, "In those days at Hardscrabble life 'was more than pioneer'—it was strenuous and haphazard at best."[32]

Jenny Duniway began teaching again—a term at Butte Creek, another at Needy—the first of many times in which her labor served to rebuild the family finances.[33] The next year her father brought back her "Journal of a Trip to Oregon," renewing her desire to write and reinforcing her confidence that she had something to say. In September "Jenny Glen" published a poem called "The Burning Forest Tree," sent to the *Oregon City Argus* on a piece of brown wrapping paper, accompanied by a characteristic note: "I have to write with one foot upon the cradle rocker; I live upon a farm, cook for workmen, make a great deal of butter, and tend two babies."[34] Further inspired by "Viola," a Salem housewife who also published poetry in the *Argus*, Jenny Duniway produced another poem which hardly presaged her "revolutionary" future. She showed the "bourgeois" sentiments of most nineteenth-century women activists, who longed to overcome the privations of frontier living and live among the comforts of refined, urban civilization.

"Say, what do you live for, my bachelor friend?
  Tell me, why don't you get a good wife?
You have plenty of money a woman could spend
  In making you happy for life;
Then, instead of salt pork for your supper, you see,
  A wife could prepare you bread, butter, and tea,
You could build a good house, buy a sofa and table,
  Some chairs and some carpets, a cook-stove and cradle,
Begin life in good earnest, and then, when you die,
  If you've been a kind husband, somebody can cry."

Though Duniway always fancied herself a true poet, the editor of the

Argus, William L. Adams, wisely steered her toward a different course. He printed her next poem, he said, "to please the writer. We think 'Jenny Glen' could write a very fair prose article, and would suggest that she try her hand on that kind of composition hereafter."[35]

W. L. Adams, or Parson Billy as he was often called, who thus so decisively influenced young Mrs. Duniway, was, like most other frontier newspaper editors, the salty-tongued spokesman of a political faction and a way of life—a fighter for a cause. Trained as a Campbellite evangelist, Adams organized the Oregon Republican party in 1855–56, "stumped the state, writing his editorials on his knees, armed with two revolvers and a bowie knife," and had "the pugnacity of a bull-dog, never happier than when lampooning his opponents." Under the name Breakspeare he published a biting satire about the Democrats of the "Salem Clique," especially powerful editor Asahel Bush of the *Salem Statesman*.

Adams owned land next to Ben and Abigail Duniway. Their Hardscrabble area of Clackamas County and the whole Silverton country along with Lafayette and Oregon City were hotbeds of Whig and antislavery sentiment in Oregon during the explosive pre–Civil War years.[36] The most popular book in the local Butte Creek library was *Uncle Tom's Cabin*. In Woodburn uncle Neill Johnson and his sons were active in antislavery groups. William Rankin McCord, who married Harriet Scott at the Duniway home in 1856, was "doorkeeper at the loyal Legion." As war approached, Union meetings and rallies were often held in the vicinity. Finally a southern sympathizer among Cumberland Presbyterians called for a presbyterial trial of the "abolitionist" preachers Thomas Small of the nearby Abiqua church and Neill Johnson. Local Presbyterians heard the charges and exonerated Johnson and Small, suspending the *accuser* for slandering the gospel ministry.[37]

At this time many Oregonians were suspected of planning secession in order to set up a separate Pacific Republic under former governor Joseph Lane, vice-presidential candidate on the southern-Democrat Breckinridge ticket in 1860. The Union lasted only because Douglasites among both Democrats and Republicans united behind Lincoln at the beginning of the Civil War. In that uneasy alliance, people like the Scotts and Duniways and W. L. Adams never conquered their distaste for Missouri "border ruffians" in their midst—and the feeling was mutual. Southern Democrats and "Douglas Republicans" remained powerful in post–Civil War Oregon. They were significant factors in Duniway's later political activities; the same regions which voted for Breckinridge in 1860—southern and eastern Oregon—also strongly opposed her women's rights campaign.[38]

Women's rights were early associated with Republicans. From its first issue on, the *Argus* reflected the agitation throughout the country in women's magazines and progressive circles. It published articles on spiritual affinity in marriage, not marrying too young, giving women education and rest from excessive labor, even birth limitation. Editor Adams commented that *Godey's Ladies' Book* had a ubiquitous circulation among Oregon women.[39] He was hoping to appeal to some of the same women. Among the *Oregon City Argus's* first subscribers in April 1855 was Abigail Jane Duniway. Adams and his paper became models for Duniway's own *New Northwest.*

The 1857 Oregon constitutional convention also debated the justice of women's rights. Republican David Logan was the lone advocate of woman suffrage. In the midst of a discussion about naturalization and residency requirements for voters, with specific concern for who would be voting on the new constitution, Logan introduced a motion "to strike out *male* before *citizen*." It lost. Property rights, however, were taken more seriously. Discussion of that "woman problem" was heated. Several men wanted to strike out all provisions protecting a married woman's property and rights, those "she had at time of marriage or obtained afterwards, by means of which the husband was not the meritorious cause." George Williams, chief justice of the Oregon Territorial Supreme Court, exclaimed: "In this age of woman's rights and insane theories, our legislation should be such as to unite the family circle, and make husband and wife what they should be—bone of one bone, and flesh of one flesh. . . ." Divorces resulted from separate property. Such a provision would even require laws whereby husbands and wives could sue each other, he said. (Judge Williams later became the senator who introduced the Fourteenth Amendment, and then the United States attorney general who argued *Minor v. Happersett* in the Supreme Court in 1875, winning the ruling that the amendment did not confer the right to vote on women.)[40]

David Logan, supported by Republican Thomas Dryer, editor of the *Oregonian,* led the defense of woman's property as a "protection . . . against the improvidence or spendthrift habits of her husband." One Democrat, Delazon Smith, agreed that "it was not separate and distinct property which caused divorces; it was the want of affection—the want of marriage of the heart." The most stringent measure was defeated. But women also did not receive the right to all property held at marriage or obtained by their own efforts afterwards. The convention specified that "only the wife's property obtained by gift, devise and inheritance should be exempt from the debts and contracts of the husband" (a provision much more advantageous to creditors, bankers, and other businessmen). And the legislature would have to pass laws "for the registration of the wife's separate property." Without such registration (which could easily be overlooked by the uninformed), the exemption could not be enforced.

Meanwhile, with improved health and hopes, Abigail and Ben Duniway moved to a better location, near Lafayette in Yamhill County. The town gave Jenny the sociability of other "intellectuals" and of her sisters Fanny and Sarah. (Catherine had married John Coburn, a Willamette River steamship officer, on 23 June 1857. She lived at Canemah, just north of Oregon City.) The new Duniway home was a frame-constructed "mansion" which Jenny called Sunny Hillside.

Benjamin Duniway hoped to emulate the most successful farmers in Oregon by establishing orchards on his beautiful location, high on a hill overlooking the wide valley and town. Like Seth Lewelling in Milwaukie, who had brought a wagon-load of saplings across the Oregon Trail in 1847, David Newsom, founder of the Oregon State Agricultural Society, Neill Johnson, who had planted 400 saplings in 1852 and now had 30,000 trees, and many others, Ben expected to take advantage of the apparently bottomless market for Oregon fruit in California and the Sandwich (Hawaiian) Islands. Oregon apples were even being shipped to China and Europe in the 1850s. Respected men like Newsom advised throughout 1857 that the demand for Oregon fruit would undoubtedly last "for all time to come." "Fruit growing," he said, "is *the* business for the people of Oregon."[41]

Increased assets also meant increased labor, but Jenny Duniway was at last free from the "Farmer Gray sort of neighborhood" where "the women, generally speaking, care for nothing but making butter and cheese, and raising chickens for market, besides making patch-work quilts, and 'goin' to meetin'." She read Dicken's *Dombey and Son* and other books; his work became her standard of literary excellence. Other novelists also stirred her imagination. She named her third son Wilkie Collins Duniway after the author of *The Woman in White*, which appeared shortly before his birth in 1861.[42]

Mrs. Duniway probably also read the first novel ever printed in Oregon—*Ruth Rover* by Margaret Jewett Bailey. Mrs. Bailey was a pious woman who had come to Oregon in 1837 with idealistic dreams of religious sacrifice, but her novel, an autobiographical indictment of hypocrisy among Methodist missionaries, provoked vicious criticism of the author's virtue and of the book's plot, style, diary quotations, and "pornographic" realism. Jewett's mistreatment, unhappy marriage, and tragic divorce in 1853 stirred female compassion despite her rather saccharine piety. The reviews made her a martyr.[43]

Abigail Jane Duniway also had a story to tell. But she had a much more positive message for the world about the potential greatness of Oregon and the condition of women. Why not use her own diary to write an Oregon story? At the age of twenty-three she began to write a novel.

CHAPTER 5

Stepping Forth

*"But whether you prosper or not, I shall never
cease to love you while I live."*

Captain Gray's Company, or Crossing the Plains and Living in Oregon, was the
first commercially printed novel in Oregon. It appeared in April 1859, a
month after the birth of Abigail Scott Duniway's third child, Hubert. Its
epigraph was "Westward the Course of Empire Takes Its Way," from
the poem which had become the standard literary formulation of America's "manifest destiny." (The poem had also just been reprinted in the
Oregon City Argus.)[1] Duniway's publisher was S. J. McCormick of Portland, a well-known Catholic (within a predominantly Methodist pioneer
population), who was one of Oregon's earliest settlers and a frequent
supporter of liberal causes.

In her introduction, Duniway sounded the notes which would echo
through all her work. She described herself, apologizing for any defects
in her writing, as a woman who "has to be lady, nurse, laundress, seamstress, cook and dairy-woman by turns, and . . . attends to all these duties, unaided, save by the occasional assistance of an indulgent husband
who has cares enough of his own." (She was always defensively aware
that nineteenth-century women writers were not generally farmers'
wives; they were middle-class women of urban and intellectual background, even if they happened to live on the frontier.) She also asserted
that her "first literary effort of magnitude" was going to "assail time-
honored customs . . . because I earnestly believe in the principles advocated, and wish the reader to *think* and *investigate.*" She would not "scale
the giddy heights of romance" for the leisured classes, but would "write
a book which the world's workers, the stay and strength of our land, shall
read with benefit." She hoped it would "be instrumental in causing the
sterner, to look more to the welfare of the . . . weaker sex."[2]

Through her heroine, Duniway expressed the sense of literary vocation and exalted purpose with which she entered her new career. A
writer, "possessed by his thought and multiplied fancies," she said,

> sees far down through the dim past. . . . Others have not seen the light as
> he sees it; and with his pen, an instrument more powerful than the sword,

an invention more mighty than steam, he controls the minds of many thousands. . . . He exposes folly, subdues error, and exalts virtue as with a magic wand, and multitudes are blessed and enlivened by his visions.

She had not yet moved beyond the cautious feminism of *Godey's Ladies' Book* sentiment, agreeing that women are "properly prevented by the rules of society from public speaking, or filling public stations." But their words could be "blessings to the tried and suffering of earth; . . . companions to the happy, . . . messengers that speak of hope and mercy to the erring."[3]

Captain Gray's Company proves that the idea of publishing a newspaper was not a sudden inspiration to Duniway in 1871, but a dream that had gestated for years. The heroine plans "to start a Magazine that will be inferior to none in the Union," describing "Western life and incidents as they are" and "equal to any ladies' magazine in the East, and at their prices." Unlike other women, she will not be fearful of criticism or mortified by opposition, and "her writings will all be of a moral nature."[4]

The book focuses on two women, one gradually replacing the other in importance, each representing aspects of the author's own personality. Shy and sensitive Effie Goodwin and her precocious fifteen-year-old brother Herbert are counterbalanced by the assertive and successful young lady from Ohio, Ada Mansfield, who soon marries a paragon of intelligence, erudition, and medical information, Maurice Stanton. Though Herbert's diary entries are cited for the first portion of the overland journey, it is Ada's diary which provides the "quotations" for the rest of the trip. And though Effie overcomes all injustice to win an essay prize at the academy with her brother and the heart of her wealthy employer's son, it is the independent spirit and practical intelligence of Ada which makes her an acknowledged leader in Oregon society.

> Her's was no common nature. . . . She was impulsive, agreeable, witty, and energetic; and everybody agreed to that; but prudes shook their heads, and cautious, hypocritical mammas charged their daughters to beware when in her company. She was *wild!* That awful stigma. . . . Because she would ape nobody's manners, was blithe and frank in her conversation with those of the opposite as well as her own sex, fearless in maintaining her own opinions, and somewhat excitable in temperament, many, who would gladly have possessed her tact and intellect, turned away, prophecying evil in her future pathway.[5]

Ada is also an active campaigner for women's health. As a hardworking farmer's wife, she gives advice to all the women in the vicinity. She is "the same wild romp I used to be. . . . [W]hile everything animate rejoices, and all nature wears such smiling charms of loveliness, I shall laugh, and ride horses, and jump ropes, and climb hills, no matter what prudish matrons will say. . . . I would not be unfeminine, but I would be *healthy, active,* and *happy.* How sad I sometimes feel, when I reflect upon the way that most American women live!" Opposed to excessive child-bearing, she refuses to "have more than two children in a year" [*sic*]. She expounds hydropathic theories about health, comfortable loose-fitting clothing, "bathing, exercise and [proper] food, and *no* strong medicine"; she deplores the excess of bacon, lack of fruits and vegetables, and use of brandy, calomel, spirits of turpentine, and hot mustard poultices on the Oregon Trail. Her husband treats cholera with nothing but water, and some of his patients recover. Lecturing both mothers who work too hard and farmers who let them, Ada exclaims, "Does it cost as much to hire a cook as to pay a doctor? Or will all the hoarded gains of a lifetime atone for the suicide of a mother?"[6]

Abigail Duniway was undoubtedly influenced by two young hydro-pathic doctors who arrived in Salem in the spring of 1858. Ada and Gideon Weed came directly from training at Dr. Russell T. Trall's Hygeio-Therapeutic College in New York and were welcomed by the *Argus's* editor Adams (who eventually became a water-cure doctor him-self) and others of his political persuasion. The *Argus* had been publiciz-ing hydropathic theories for several years.[7] Ada Weed lectured and practiced medicine throughout the Willamette Valley and quickly gained notoriety for her treatment of female diseases and obstetrical problems. She also distributed copies of Dr. Trall's books on sex and marriage and of the *Water-Cure Journal,* which he edited. These de-scribed the evils of masturbation, the necessity of sexual restraint for the sake of good health, and the importance of obedience to the "natural laws" of rational love. Water, good food, and exercise were to replace the drugs and patent medicines—often laced with opium—so freely pre-scribed and used by regular doctors and their patients.[8]

Such opinions were perceived as aspects of political radicalism in 1858. Ada Weed was roundly insulted by Democratic editor Asahel Bush in the *Salem Statesman,* despite his "respect for the sex to which Mrs. W. claims to belong." She endured accusations of obscenity for her lectures to women—during the very months when Abigail Duniway was preg-nant with her third child and writing her novel. Bush snidely claimed that "gallantry" made him "correct the errors in orthography, syntax and punctuation, which abounded in the manuscript of our fair corre-spondent." Ada Weed attempted to defend herself in an eloquent, well-reasoned letter.[9] (When Bush reviewed Duniway's *Captain Gray's Company* he again complained of "bad grammar . . . liberally inter-spersed with slang phrases.")[10] It was no accident that Duniway named her lively, health-minded heroine "Ada" just when Ada Weed was under such attack.

In this book, as in all her later writings, Duniway made use of real events as well as personalities. Even such a minor incident as parents separating Ada Mansfield from her future husband Maurice Stanton is not just contrived nineteenth-century sentimentality. Abigail's favorite cousin J. L. Johnson complained that his parents did the same thing to him during their crossing in 1851. The real life lovers kept in touch by writing the romantic name "Laurie" on buffalo bones along the trail and eventually found each other again in Oregon.[11]

Duniway's sympathetic rendition of Farmer Gray's Kentucky dialect is one of the realistic aspects of the novel for which she was criticized, while the depiction of class distinctions is ubiquitous. "La bless us," exclaims Captain Gray when he "hearn tell" that the Goodwins wanted to join his caravan to Oregon. "Who'd a ever thought that as great a lady as Miss Good'in would a tried to go across the Plains?" Effie Goodwin and Ada Mansfield, however, both come from "Yankee" rather than "southron" backgrounds—a suggestion of Duniway's perceptions about the source of cultural superiority. They are not like the upper-class Mrs. Weldon in the first part of the book, however, who wears bloomers and "repelled all attempts at intimacy." Nor like the society lady Mrs. Munson, who hires Effie Goodwin as a servant, insisting that she keep her place and work long hours on poor food and low pay. Mrs. Munson leaves the care of her baby entirely to Effie, while she groans away her life as an invalid surrounded by medicines. She is "a bear, who wears the mask of a beautiful woman. To prevent herself from too close inspection, she keeps herself surrounded by disagreeable odors, sickening enough to turn the stomach of a skunk." Even the local academy, which Effie is finally able to attend when her brother returns with gold from the mines, involves the snobbery of society daughters until Effie's intellectual achievements win their grudging respect.[12]

Duniway's resentment of class restrictions and her identification with the rural rather than the urban middle class, as well as her attacks on hypocrisy and ostentation, began long before her commitment to the cause of suffrage. She was an agrarian reformer, like most of her relatives and friends. Fair treatment for women was a corollary of that reform. She was also an Oregon booster, convinced that the "new country" was the best country—and determined to be in the forefront of its advancement.

During the winter of 1858/59, the controversy over women's rights, which had begun in the *Salem Statesman* in regard to Ada Weed, moved to the *Oregon City Argus*. One suspects it was Duniway herself who wrote under the pseudonym Xenittie, calling for equality in the home and in property rights as woman's "utmost limit of . . . commendable ambition." While the nation moved toward Civil War, the Territory of

Oregon was occupied by a "memorable Divorce Session " in the legislature, and Xenittie argued against the Blackstonian concept of "femme covert." Women, she said, were also burdened with too much work, especially washing (a complaint Mrs. Duniway was to repeat for the next thirty years). Husbands refused to help with children and engaged in the "heathenish practice of being needlessly gone from home about one third of [their] time . . . gadding about from house to house" or grog shop, drinking and talking politics.[13]

Xenittie was silenced temporarily by a letter from Lear in January 1859 saying that "she, with that microscopic vision peculiar to monomaniacs, has made mountains out of molehills. . . . But if you are single, pretty, accomplished, and under thirty, . . . and if I can prevail on you to become my better half, I solemnly pledge myself, at all convenient times, to take care of the baby."[14] Others joined the fray, arguing for and against women's education and women's rights.

Finally, Abigail Jane Duniway, in her own name, "enraged" by Lear and others, "wielded her pen reclining on a sick bed" ten days after the birth of a new "'small man.'" A mistreated wife who left her husband would also lose her child, she pointed out. "It isn't society men who give up their places to women that are being complained of," she said. Nor did she approve of woman "seeking honors and rights out of her sphere." Society women were often treated with more respect than they deserved, but others were often "the victim of wrongs which our laws cannot punish or will not alter." *She* wanted "to see ladies content . . . to use *cradles* for ballot-boxes, in which they have a right to plant, not votes, but *voters*."[15]

Other women then took issue with Mrs. Duniway for not being courageous enough, though Lear said she was "the only one who has presented a case that can be seriously entertained." M. P. Owen of Salem said equality should include the right to vote, for her little girl did everything that boys do. "If they were not taught differently, they would grow to be men and women with the same habits and dispositions." Vivia of Ingle Dell described a "suffragist in the Mississippi Valley" who was also an efficient and gracious housekeeper, proving that voting rights were not out of her sphere. Consuello wrote eloquently about the importance of equal wages, coeducation, and job opportunities. Though laws could not solve particular marital problems like who tends the babies or does the chores, they could and should protect a woman's right to property. "If man and wife cannot live happily together," she concluded, "they should separate; but if circumstances are such as in their judgment to make it wisdom to remain together, they should do so mutually and upon equal footing."[16] Clearly, the issue of women's rights was already important to numerous other Oregon women.

For Abigail Duniway, however, dreaming of glory for her novel and suffering from a case of postnatal depression besides, that spring of 1859 was a nightmare. Her book did not receive rave reviews; in fact, it was not even enthusiastically received by her friends. The *Argus* and the *Oregon Farmer* merely noted its publication and its cost. Aunt Louvisa Turley in Missouri later expressed the opinion of most Scott relatives. She told her father, "I cant see any sense to it more than any other fool love story." Only Tucker Scott was enthusiastic. He talked of a New York or Illinois edition, where it "no doubt would be eagerly bought" because it had "caused a great sensation here." The *Statesman* panned her "bad taste" and "slang phrases." The Reverend Mr. Pearne, the Methodist minister who had married Tucker Scott and Ruth Stevenson, wrote in *The Pacific Christian Advocate* that he was "sickened with the love stories of the book" and the "artificial" plot.[17]

One letter-writer to the *Argus* said, among other things,

> From a certain insight Mrs. Duniway has allowed us in her domestic affairs, 'Etc.' cannot help but suspect that Mr. Duniway is what is vulgarly styled a 'hen-pecked husband.' She even goes so far as to boast of making a nurse of him. . . . [P]oor man! he dare not *say* anything, but very complacently sits in his corner nursing the baby, while she expatiates on poor (!) woman's 'wrongs,'—and he saying 'Certainly, my dear,' to anything and everything she may propose.

In the same issue was an open letter from Duniway herself to Brother Pearne. She accused Pearne of jealousy, of having wanted to publish the book himself. He was in complicity with "your colleague, Bush, whom I have always considered beneath *my* notice." "Such prudery as yours . . . makes *prostitutes* and *profligates*," she wrote. "To stem the torrent of your propensities, animal or critical, is a task too herculean for *my* pen—but I'll remember you in my next public effort in a character that you can't mistake. . . ." A month later she apologized for "having given way to resentment in such a manner. I have no excuse to offer except that a sense of attempted injury, with 'malice aforethought', prompted me to this reply to a man whom, in my usual health, temper, and spirits, I consider beneath my notice. . . . The letter . . . was written when I was excited by a fever on the brain, caused by overthought and overwork at a time when I should have been at rest in both mind and body."[18]

Abigail Scott Duniway was so devastated by the criticism that she kept apologizing for her book for the rest of her life. When it was reprinted in the *New Northwest* in 1875 she claimed she could not bear to look at it again.[19] Attacks on her own marital situation had apparently hit too close to home. The anxiety and anger which surfaced in Duniway's writing *did* have a personal basis. Ben Duniway, with characteristic confidence and generosity, had recently cosigned several loans for a friend "at two percent per month, to be compounded semi-annually until paid." Abigail was convinced "that it would ruin us financially if those notes were signed," but her husband said, "'Mama, you needn't worry; you'll always be protected and provided for!'"[20]

She had reason to be angry. Oregon's depression grew progressively worse after 1858. California was producing more locally, while Oregon's only trade connection was by ship. Abigail's butter and eggs were the main source of cash, and these were selling for only half the price of five years earlier. The same was true of cattle and apples. The winter of 1859 was "the worst . . . for forty years past," followed by drought and heat which destroyed spring crops. Agriculturalist David Newsom now reported that Oregon fruit raising was "at a *dead stand-still,* and our people are horror-stricken and ready to cave-in." "Golden visions" had been replaced by "sober reality," he said. Ben Duniway, however, spent $500 for an adjoining farm in 1860, ignoring his wife's desire for household help or comfortable furnishings.[21]

The poor crops of 1859 were followed by bumper crops in 1860, causing immense surpluses and forcing farmers to sell at a loss or go without cash. Hard-pressed by Ben's borrowing and the new land he had bought, the Duniways were under constant stress from worry and overwork. "As I look back over those weary years," wrote Abigail Duniway when she was eighty, "the most lingering of my many regrets is the fact that I was often compelled to neglect my little children, while spending my time in the kitchen, or at the churn or wash tub, doing heavy work for hale and hearty men."[22]

To relieve the pressure, both financial and psychological, Mrs. Duniway kept on writing. She became a regular contributor to the new *Oregon Farmer,* analyzing the economic crisis and offering solutions under the pseudonym A Farmer's Wife. Women, she wrote, must buy Oregon goods, not send money out of their own country "for costly fabrics that ill accord with other surroundings" like extravagant merchants' wives. Farmers should avoid debt and merchants should keep prices down. Californians should not blame Oregon women for butter adulterated by traders. "We Oregonians, who do the *work,* are going to form ourselves a UNION, to see if we can't have a *part* of the *profits,* and the merchant who will help us shall in due time have his reward." That letter brought a response from San Francisco businessman J. B. Knapp (who later moved to Oregon and became one of Mrs. Duniway's staunchest supporters); she was right, he said, about merchants' deceptions and their destruction of the market for Oregon butter. He offered to sell *her* butter without commission for six months to prove it good again.[23]

None of these ideas were uniquely Duniway's. Other Oregon farmers, like David Newsom (also a *Farmer* columnist), agreed. A meeting at Lone Butte schoolhouse in December 1858 organized "a general unity" of Oregon fruit growers. One of these solid American farmers wrote the *Argus* in favor of agricultural unions as a protection against profiteering by speculators and merchants. He explained, "Labor is the basis of wealth; capital cannot compete with it properly directed; and it should rise to be master of capital rather than continue a servant. Injustice to labor is one of the great errors, if not *the* error of all government."[24] (This was nine years before the publication of Karl Marx's *Das Capital.*)

The Farmer's Wife columns were controversial in only one area. Mrs. Duniway began to agitate for hired help for farmers' *wives*. She claimed that the high cost, due to Oregon's shortage of single girls, would be more than offset by the saving of lives and the improvement in management.

> With farmers' wives rests much of the power to bring about a different state of monetary affairs. Dried and preserved fruits, butter and eggs, soap and candles, pigs, pickles, vegetables and chickens, come under our legitimate supervision. . . . [W]e want time, strength and opportunity to attend to all this, so that we may preserve—or, if we had lost it—regain, excellent health and buoyant spirits, accompanied by that spirit of independence which makes everybody who possesses it happy.[25]

Shocking some of her more prudish readers, Mrs. Duniway compared the way farmers cared for expectant mares and expectant mothers:

> Now listen! ye husbands! while I tell you something which, notwithstanding your talk about horses' and cattle's pedigrees around your firesides and in the papers, you will think *me* very indelicate for talking about. . . . The working women of America are a race *going to seed.* And, as a too rapid rotation of crops will in time exhaust both crop and soil, so the over exertion of all our physical powers will cause us to multiply in *numbers* in the ratio that we decrease in *vitality or strength.* . . . Health, and the improvement of mankind are of more importance than politics or fine horses.[26]

Eight months after the date of this letter Abigail Jane Duniway gave birth to her fourth child, just two years after the previous one. Benjamin Duniway was known throughout the Willamette Valley as a breeder of fine horses. Abigail Duniway herself had no hired help.

A vitriolic reply from Amigo soon appeared in the *Oregon Farmer*. "We will not tacitly submit to her abuse any longer," he wrote; farmers cannot afford such help, and Duniway's sympathies are all for mothers—"how about the lords?"

> three-fourths of those weak, worn-out women are . . . just such women as

"Farmer's Wife." . . . Peevish, ill-natured, irritable, fault-finding scolds, always mouthing; they imagine their trials, troubles and tribulations, greater than anyone elses. . . . [H]er vulgar, abusive tirade, does not meet the approbation of farmers, or farmers' wives, in this section of the country, and furthermore, if she has any respect for herself or her sex, she will stop her malicious babblings at once.[27]

Abigail Duniway was less easily crushed than before. Not only did other letters come to her defense, but she claimed to know who Amigo was; a particular "disappointed, crusty *old bach,* with nothing but 'Cayuse horses, Spanish cattle and sheaf oats,' to recommend [his] fascinating person to the notice of the fair of 'Santiam Forks!'" Far from being quarrelsome, she said, she was "so remarkably docile and quiet . . . that she succumbs to the argument of a donkey the first time she hears him bray! *Of course* it is *cheaper* to let one wife wear out and marry another than to care for the one on hand."[28]

The *Oregon Farmer* at this time was printing numerous other letters and articles which advocated family planning and voluntary motherhood. "If you have such a mean, lazy *lummux* of a husband that he cannot stay in and take care of the children while you milk the cows or take a morning walk, do not present him with the second until the first is old enough to take care of it," wrote one strong-minded Oregonian. Mrs. Duniway urged young girls, "Be not in haste to marry anybody. . . .[Y]ou may find at twenty-two that your tastes are in every way different from what they were at sixteen." But she still believed that farmers' sons made the best husbands and that pining for city luxuries was a mistake. "The green fields, the garden and the dairy are your natural 'elements,' and you might not like fashion, folly, glare and glitter."[29]

As the emotional election of 1860 approached, Abigail Duniway's interest in politics also increased. She was elated that the Scotts' Illinois benefactor, Colonel Edward D. Baker, had become an Oregonian and was running for the Senate as a Republican. In 1860 he gave a campaign speech at Lafayette. Abigail overcame the objections of her "honored liege" that women never attended such events and "repaired to the village" with her "little ones" in tow. Starting with Mrs. McBride, wife of a judge who was the only Republican in the 1857 state constitutional convention, she persuaded six other women to brave the hisses of men and the reputed danger of being insulted by *Oregonian* editor Dryer's dirty jokes. "Many women were shocked," said Duniway later, "but among all those shocked ones not one could be found who was willing to stay away from the next political meeting."[30]

Baker was elected by a bare minimum of votes in deeply divided Oregon and helped carry the state for Lincoln. As the new president's closest friend and political ally, he introduced Lincoln at the inauguration and then, seven months later, became one of the first Union "martyrs" when he was killed by a random bullet at the battle of Ball's Bluff. Duniway's loyalty to the Union and to the Republicans could have had no more definitive seal of commitment.

But neither loyalty to the Union nor political audacity could solve the multiplying problems on the Duniway farm. Anonymous stories which began to appear in 1861 in the *Argus* and *Oregon Farmer* clearly bear Duniway's imprint, especially since some of the same incidents and characters turn up in her Farmer's Wife letters.[31] "John Smith" and his neighbor "Jobson," for example, debate the merits of staying on the farm or packing off to the mines of Idaho, where a mini-gold rush was then in progress. "Farming don't pay," says Jobson. Besides, "Who wants to be always making fences, and gates, and stables, and barns, and plowing, and hoeing, and setting out trees, and pruning trees, and looking after stock, and making up subscriptions for schools and the like?" John Smith appears again as an insensitive husband who has "worked for a half-score of years, and . . . got rich,—just as rich as I want to be, and my wife isn't comfortable yet," because he won't let her buy carpets or furniture or a sewing machine or any hired help. "When you got rich enough to leave off making rails and digging stumps, did your wife get rich enough to leave the wash tub? Was she able to give up the churn and mop?" asks Farmer's Wife.

> "I don't care anything about nice furniture," [Smith] replied; and if your wife hadn't been the meekest and most long suffering of women she would have replied that she didn't care anything about your grey fillies either, and . . . that it was time for you to be thinking something about a comfortable lodging place for your beast of all burdens.[32]

The bitter sarcasm of an unusual letter from Farmer's Wife was probably obvious to many readers when it appeared just a month after the birth of Abigail Duniway's fourth baby. The column, published on 16 March 1861, gave details about how to cure horses of colic and dogs of strychnine poisoning. (A dog poisoning by the villain also occurs in Duniway's *Ellen Dowd*, written in 1872.) "Being an invalid," said Farmer's Wife, "I think that malady cannot be relieved in a more useful manner than by making known anything I have learned that may benefit the noblest of animals, man's best friend, the horse."

Perhaps the article was triggered by a joke which Duniway still remembered with "overpowering humiliation" sixty years later. An anonymous Valentine arrived just after Wilkie's birth on 13 February, when she was already struggling over a churn making butter to pay "for taxes and that awful interest at two percent per month on another man's debt . . . 'compounded semi-annually until paid.'"

On opening the big envelope, I discovered a gaily-covered, poster-like Valentine. Seated on a chair was pictured a typical hen-pecked husband, trembling as if in terror. Clambering over him were a lot of squalling children, and above his cowering form stood an irate, illy-clad, toothless, straggling-haired woman, brandishing a broom. Under this delectable picture were the following lines:
"Fiend, devil's imp, or what you will,
You surely your poor man will kill,
With luckless days and sleepless nights,
Haranguing him with Woman's Rights!"

Obviously, Jenny Duniway thought her husband was responsible, for she burst into tears and said, "Did I ever give you, or anybody else, a reason for attacking me with a thing like this?" His "impatient" reply was, "it was sent to you by some fool as a joke. If I had known what it was, or that you would care a rap about it, I wouldn't have brought it home."[33]

In late November 1861, "the heaviest downpour that Western Oregon has ever known" melted unusually heavy snows in the mountains and produced disastrous floods on all the rivers of Oregon. Raging torrents destroyed everything in their paths, surging four feet deep on the main street of Oregon City that December 7, even depositing an Oregon City machine shop on the shore near Astoria at the mouth of the Columbia.[34]

Farmer's Wife described the devastation. The newly built warehouse at Lafayette, holding 80,000 bushels of wheat, had been swept away along with much of the commercial section of town. "One man," she said, "who owed a merchant a large sum of money, was compelled [during the fall] to sell his wheat at 50 cents per bushel to pay the debt." It was just recompense, she thought, that the merchant, who had expected to make a profit by such purchases, was now also a victim of disaster. Then she launched into a poetic description of the beauty of being alive in Oregon on her Sunny Hillside with her hardworking husband and four lovely children.[35]

The man was probably Ben Duniway, who had already decided, before the flood, to go to the mines. Farmer's Wife gave up her opposition in an earlier-dated column which appeared in the same issue with the one about the flood. Let the farmer go, she wrote, if "through misfortune and bad management" he has to pay off a $1000 debt at 2 percent a month. Such a debt amounted to $240 a year, she went on, and even with "untiring industry" and the help of his "small boy" he could clear only $500 a year, and out of that he needed to support his family. "Mr. A is a pleasant man and loves his wife and children, but . . . he says he'll 'break' sooner or later if he stays at home and he can but 'break' by going, though to leave his family is indeed a trial."[36]

As often happened when Mrs. Duniway was under particular emotional strain, her next column was a testy one. She took issue with the paper itself for making mistakes in her January letter. The printer had been drunk, she claimed, adding a postscript, "My husband says I ought not to grumble at the mistakes of your printer, for I write so carelessly that the—I suppose he means *printer's*—'devil' can be excused if he can't read my scribbling."[37]

Abigail Scott Duniway had been noted for her hot temper ever since girlhood. On the last page of her overland journal she inscribed a paragraph written either for self-improvement or perhaps as a lesson from her father:

> There is no human folly so foolish as Anger the sight of an angry person is very unpleasant they render themselves very unhappy and disagreeable and also their friends. There are some persons that fly into an angry passion and when they get a little recovered they think that they have acted very foolishly one angry word may do a great deal of harm yet the best of us are apt to let our angry passions rise we should remember that we were never made to let our anger rise against one another.

It was a lesson she never did quite learn. The combination of hot temper with frequent physical and emotional exhaustion was to make many enemies for the hardworking Mrs. Duniway in years to come.

One last letter in the Farmer's Wife series appeared in the spring of 1862. Considering Duniway's later opposition to prohibitionists, the column is worth noting. Impressed perhaps by her uncle Levi Caffee's increasing alcoholism, which finally killed him in 1867, she painted a picture of the despair which had affected thousands of Oregon pioneers in those hard times. A poor old drunkard came to her door on a "cold, wet, miserable day in November." The man, who had been a friend of Lincoln and Baker and Douglas, she said, had turned "aside into crooked ways," and her "soul went up in a fervent appeal that the young men and boys of Oregon might awake to the necessity of waging a war of extermination against old King Alcohol. who is, if possible, a worse enemy to progress than the dire hallucination of secession."[38]

After Ben Duniway left for Idaho at the end of March 1862, Jenny Duniway returned to teaching. For a salary of about $40 a month, the family's only income until Ben might "strike it rich," she taught at a private school in town while she continued to manage the farm. History was repeating itself, she knew, as she remembered her father's bankruptcy and her uncles' tragedies after the depression of 1837; but perhaps for the Duniways it would be different. An unsigned article on marriage that spring expresses the disillusionment she was feeling. There are no perfectly happy marriages, it said, and people should not marry in haste or too young or according to their passions. "It is better to suffer a broken heart single than a broken head and heart married."[39]

Soon after Ben's departure came the sad news of eighteen-year-old John Henry Scott's death. Jenny Scott Duniway's little brother could not withstand the rigorous regimen of work and study which he shared with Harvey Scott at their father's sawmill and at Pacific University. One day he collapsed from heart failure and was already dead by the time his Lafayette relatives arrived. Fanny Scott Cook brought the Cook and Duniway children in her wagon, while young Mrs. Duniway, still lithe and active despite her numerous illnesses, rode horseback at a gallop the whole twenty miles to Forest Grove. She wrote to Ben that her "heart was almost broken at the thought of giving [John] up, yet I felt that it would be selfish to wish him back in this world of parting and sorrow and sickness."[40]

Still the dutiful farm wife, Jenny went on to tell Ben about the hired man's crossness for lack of tobacco, which she couldn't afford to buy, and of sheep shearing with the help of Catherine Scott Coburn's husband. A "ciota" [coyote] had killed a lamb right after Ben left, so she had "milked about a gallon of milk from the old ewe, before her bag went down to its old shape." Farm responsibilities did not end just because a man was not there.

Abigail Duniway was passionate and loving as well as dutiful. She was also a sentimental mother. Her letter continued:

O, my dear husband! you have no idea how lonely and desolate I feel. It seems as if I hadn't a friend left in the world. But the children, bless them! are mother's own! and if papa is away, he'll come home some day, if he lives, and then we'll be happy again. Clara sleeps with me. Last night, as she lay in my arms, she prayed for her absent father with a simple faith that made my heart thrill. Pa, who could be poor and have such a daughter? The first thing I heard this Sabbath morning was Wilkie calling *Pa*, as loud as he could hollow. Whenever we mention you to him he calls for your *likeness* and when he gets it, he puts his finger on your face and says "pa" over and over again. Money could not buy that likeness. . . . If you were only here, I could tell you a thousand things that I cannot write. . . . O, I do hope and trust that our business may be so arranged this summer that we will never have to part again. If the prayers and good wishes of your wife can avail anything you will prosper this summer. But whether you prosper or not, I shall never cease to love you while I live; though I do not expect to live very long, unless I can have a change of climate; which, please God, I shall have this next winter if you are successful in the mines. Take good care of yourself. I am afraid you will try too hard to get along and lay yourself up. I would rather you would come back healthy than rich. . . . Your loving wife, A. J. Duniway.

Despite the sentiment, Ben Duniway must have also noticed the letter's conflicting messages. Jenny longed for his return, but she also wanted him to strike gold. She would love him forever, but she expected to die soon unless his prospecting saved her. His children missed him deeply, but Hubert could have no shoes until Pa came home with money. . . . The longer Ben carried that letter, the more desperate he must have become; there was little gold for him in "them thar hills."

Back in Lafayette by autumn, Ben was still unable to pay his debts, and time had run out. "One busy day," wrote Abigail Duniway fifty years later (having repeated the story many times before),

> . . . just as dusk was coming on—my husband having been away from home all day—the sheriff came to the house and served summons on me for those notes! Now, observe that, when that obligation was made, I was my husband's silent partner—a legal nonentity—with no voice or power for self-protection under the sun; but, when penalty accrued, I was his legal representative. . . .
>
> As the night came down my husband came home, and, after he had eaten his supper, and while he was playing with the children, the hired men having gone to their quarters, I confess I felt a little secret satisfaction when I served those papers on him. I had framed up a little "spiel," which I meant to practice on him . . . but he turned so pale and looked so care-worn I couldn't even say, "I told you so!"[41]

This was the turning point in the Duniway marriage. Ben made arrangements to settle out of court by selling his farm and keeping a small house in Lafayette where his wife ran her school. He was "deeply depressed" and "blamed himself" for the loss. Both Duniways had good reason to resent for the rest of their lives the unjustness of an economic system which always favored people of means over those who lacked both luck and capital. The purchaser was Millard Lownsdale, son of one of the founders of Portland, who recognized "one of the most sightly and perfect locations for a great commercial orchard" and had the financial resources to hold and develop it. Lownsdale's orchards became notable throughout Oregon in the 1880s. The 300-acre farm sold in 1910 for $300,000.[42] Few remembered that Benjamin Duniway had planted the first trees.

If Ben Duniway blamed himself, there is little doubt that his wife blamed him even more. The whole episode appears as fiction in her first *New Northwest* novel. John Smith, the husband of Judith Reid, signs a loan for a speculator friend and thereby loses his farm after floods destroy the warehouse where their grain is stored. Though Mrs. Duniway never publicly expressed anything but respect and concern for her "faithful, invalid husband," the man in the novel is clearly irresponsible and reprehensible. Like Ben, the fictional Smith is away hunting when the sheriff delivers his writ. Upon his return,

I was fimly resolved to give the deluded endorser a "piece of my mind" about the rights of an over-burdened wife, but the poor fellow was so docile, pitiful and humble that my wrath oozed out at my fingers' ends, and, woman-like, instead of heaping well-deserved wrath upon his devoted head, I saw the necessity of doing something to sustain him in his dread calamity.

Judith starts teaching school to pay expenses, just as Abigail did. Smith

was utterly prostrate under the misfortune, and seeing me thus resolute, willing and equal to the emergency, he began to rely upon me in a helpless kind of way that was as repulsive as his previously professed independence had been unjust.

Men often utterly *break down* under the wheel of misfortune, whereas women bend and writhe under the same trials, yet come out in the end master of the adverse situation.

Almost immediately other women, including her friends, start blaming Judith for John Smith's ruin.

"A pretty mess she's made of it! Such misfortunates are sure to come when women step out of their sphere! Look at them now! Sold out by the sheriff, root and branch! And the poor man looks like he'd lost his last friend! How I despise a business woman."[43]

Unlike the real Ben Duniway, the fictional John Smith is a drunkard and deceiver who soon leaves his wife, thus enabling her to rediscover the true love and rightful husband of her youthful dreams. However, Smith's helplessness does mirror Ben's physical condition for most of the rest of his life. Taking a job as a teamster, which was the only work he could do to earn money for a new farm, Ben suffered one more tragedy in the fall of 1862. A runaway team of horses knocked him down and dragged a heavy wagon over his back, causing an injury which was a source of pain and physical weakness for the rest of Ben's life. According to all accounts by his wife and children, he was an "invalid" from then on, though the nature and extent of his injuries is unclear.[44] Undoubtedly he was treated with the standard medicines of the time, especially opium and the newly discovered morphine, which eased the pain but probably contributed to the weakness.

For Abigail Duniway, however, the multiple tragedies became a blessing in disguise. She liked teaching and the intellectual world which it opened up to her. Freed from the butter churn and the milking pail, she "led an easier life than . . . on a pioneer farm. My work was rest for both mind and body. Health improved and hope revived." The work was still enormous by anyone's standards. She lined the ceiling of her small unfinished attic to make a dormitory for boarding students, rose at three or four A.M. to do the work of the household, taught school all day, and then enjoyed "recreative, musical, intellectual" evenings with her family. Her teaching methods were creative precisely because of her educational deficiencies; she had to analyze each problem right along with her students. She had never studied "grammar, higher arithmetic or algebra" and never had time to prepare for classes. So, when necessary, she used as examples "articles in the room, such as the stove, doors, windows, sashes or panes, desks, seams in the floor, etc. . . . [A]dapting such articles to the solution of the problem before us, we would all begin to see through it at once . . . and the lesson would be mastered in fine shape— no student imagining that I had been catching the inspiration of it myself as we went along."[45]

Nevertheless, there were complaints—not about the teaching but about the supposed lack of discipline and about politics. Those three years in Lafayette, from 1862 to 1865, were years of wartime and years of bitter division in Oregon society. People chose their children's teachers according to whether they were Secessionist or Union, and both sides were equally belligerent. There was no doubt about the political sympathies of Mrs. Duniway and her Lafayette Union School, nor about those of her associate schoolmaster, Reverend Burnett, pastor of the local Christian Church and cousin of the first governor of California. As Duniway later wrote, "Teaching school . . . commenced our real battle with public life. Strong men, who might have been better employed in making rails, opposed our work, but we struggled on and succeeded."[46]

When she sold her school in 1865 "at a profit," there were some who said she had been forced to do so, though she opened a new school that fall in Albany, Oregon. Political troubles plagued her there also. At the school's Christmas exhibition in December 1865, nine-and-a-half-year-old Willis Duniway declaimed upon the glories of the United States flag, and all the other children cheered. The whole community turned out for such "tribal" ceremonies in the nineteenth century—and there were still two "tribes" in Oregon. To secessionist Democrats (in contrast to Douglas Democrats), praising a Union flag, even in December 1865 when the Civil war was over, was flamboyant and "political." James O'Meara, editor of the *Albany States' Rights Democrat,* accused Mrs. Duniway of dealing with "sectional matters" and inserting politics into educational practice. She replied by labeling him, in effect, a *"rebel* and *traitor,"* "whose own political friends are ashamed of him. . . ."[47] James O'Meara's bitter editorials and news commentary followed Abigail Scott Duniway throughout her suffrage campaign.

The Duniways' move to Albany had been prompted by both business and personal motives. South of Salem in the Willamette Valley, Albany was a rapidly growing town at the junction of the Calapooia and

Willamette rivers, where the steamboat landed regularly from Portland in the north and Corvallis further south. It was then the third most important town in Oregon. New mills were being built to meet post–Civil War demands, and it was a good place to buy land as well as to open a school. The Duniways bought an extra lot that June of 1865 for $100 and sold it for $200 in October.[48]

Abigail's sister Harriet McCord and her family now lived in Albany too, and a Presbyterian college had been founded by former Lafayette resident, the Reverend E. R. Geary. The Duniways were able to buy a house next door to old friends, the Fosters, while a new Republican newspaper competing with the established *Albany States' Rights Democrat* made the political climate sufficiently congenial. Ben was well enough to resume his horse trading while Abigail taught school.

Within a year, the enterprising Mrs. Duniway had also started a business. Like many other ambitious women of her era, she opened a millinery shop—the only other "respectable" source of income for women besides teaching. When her "health failed" again in 1866 (the standard euphemism for pregnancy), she converted her school into a store with another woman as partner. She took the steamboat downriver to Portland to buy her first stock with only thirty dollars capital, hoping to get a hundred dollars worth of goods on credit. Jacob Mayer, one of the earliest and best-known storekeepers in the still small city, laughed and insisted on selling her $1,200 worth, receiving as interest Mrs. Duniway's lifelong gratitude and support. Mayer, who obviously knew the extent of post–Civil War demand, got his $1,200 three weeks later, together with another order for $3,000. Soon after Clyde's birth, Mrs. Duniway bought out her partner and continued in business alone.[49]

Meanwhile, Ben Duniway invented a washing machine. Using his knowledge of coopering, learned in his Illinois youth, Ben made the machines out of barrels with a suction top and pump and an added wringer and sold them to numerous Oregonians. He taught his boys carpentry in his workshop and took them on hunting trips to the mountains. He also had a good-sized vegetable garden in the Duniway backyard. His specialty was breeding matched pairs of white circus horses, and he became widely known as the "craziest" horse trader in Oregon. For a proud and ambitious man, previously an active rancher and horseman, Ben's illness was frustrating and painful. But his notable kindness and patience won loyal friends for himself and his family. The Duniways were not wealthy, but they were certainly not poor.[50]

Abigail Jane Duniway continued to write, spurred on partly by her brother Harvey Scott's good fortune. He had been librarian for the newly established 5,000-book Portland city library. As Pacific University's first graduate and a law student of Judge Erasmus Shattuck,

Harvey became known for his erudition and photographic memory and impressed many important people. When he produced a brilliant and moving editorial about the death of Lincoln in the spring of 1865, he was immediately appointed editor of the small but influential *Portland Oregonian*. This was already the most important Republican paper in the state; under Harvey Scott's aegis it was to become the most important news publication in the whole Pacific Northwest. Brilliant, enterprising, and tough, with a mastery of history, literature, and the classics and a capacity for independent judgment and hard bargains, Harvey Scott became a man to reckon with in Oregon.[51]

Being Harvey's sister had advantages, though it intensified the antagonism of political opponents. Harvey's appointment at the *Oregonian* also stirred the old sibling rivalry. At twenty-seven the little brother who had been so favored within the family was now respected, admired, and financially successful, while Abigail's husband was a failure and an invalid. Above all, Harvey was an editor—the very thing she had wanted to be for years. "Writing always *was* our forte," she wrote a few years later, "and if we had been a man, we'd have had an editor's position and handsome salary at twenty-one."[52]

Soon Abigail Duniway sent Harvey one of her compositions for publication. A man of meticulous writing style who, unlike his sister, was noted for his careful revisions and scholarly analyses (colleagues doubted if he "ever wrote a careless sentence in his life"),[53] editor Scott rejected his sister's work for lack of polish. She was not pleased.

One of her *New Northwest* serials is probably based on this episode. Editor Henry Lee refuses to publish a brilliant composition by his milliner sister about hereditary drunkenness because she is a suffragist and his political ambitions prevent him from helping her. Instead, he burns the manuscript and says: "You will never earn your salt as a writer. Making bonnets is your forte." Fortunately, the sister writes it again, sells it to the *Great Weekly World*, and obtains a permanent publishing contract for $5,000 a year.[54]

Abigail Duniway, like her brother, had absorbed the lessons in her schoolbooks and in Greeley's *New York Tribune* about the value of hard work, ambition, and making money. She firmly believed in the "room at the top" for any "literary man or woman" with the "divine afflatus" who, "like a celebrated inventor, financier, teacher, musician, painter, editor, orator or preacher, is born, not made," and who is willing to risk the "lions in the way."[55] But she began to realize clearly that there were a lot more "lions in the way" of women than of men.

Duniway wanted to be a writer, not a milliner. She loved words and activity. She hated sewing. Much as she always boasted of her capacity for work, she also longed for "protection" from the constant labor and wearing schedule she had set for herself. One later novel features a milliner complaining about her career, exclaiming that she would never do such work if she were not forced to it by her improvident husband. Another fictional episode shows a young schoolteacher breaking up all the desks of her schoolroom in a fit of anger at the frustrations of teaching. The heroine of *Ethel Graeme's Destiny* tells *New Northwest* readers:

> the greatest mistake a wife can make is the determination, too often indulged in by the young and ambitious conjugal beginner, of voluntarily taking upon herself the task of earning and providing the family's substance. . . . I wish I had begun my married life with a fixed determination to do my duty in my household, and let everything like outside business take care of itself. . . . I could have borne it, . . . with much better grace when I was young and my children were little than I bore it in the after years when . . . my own strength had failed because of my long struggle to fill a double position and bear a double curse.[56]

Nevertheless, the millinery shop was the cause of what Abigail Duniway later called her "third and latest birth." It brought her into contact with numerous other women, and she discovered that many of her customers endured as much subjection as the poor widows and other housewives to whom she gave out her sewing. For example, there was the sickly wife of a well-to-do farmer, whose butter money, intended for her daughters' Sunday school coats, was appropriated by her husband to buy a fine racehorse. She was afraid to buy the coats on credit and begged for a sewing job, which Mrs. Duniway could not give her at the time. When the woman died in childbirth the next summer, the pious clergymen of Albany offered condolences to the bereaved husband, while Abigail Duniway, "who had had a glimpse behind the scenes, pondered long and deeply over that 'butter money,' the defrauded children, the deceased wife, and that thoroughbred race horse."[57]

And there was the woman with five children whose husband sold all their furniture and ran away. Duniway persuaded a generous neighbor to loan $600 for the woman to furnish a boardinghouse and make a living. The husband returned, took possession of the furniture, repudiated the mortgage (illegal without his signature), and forced her to divorce him and lose her children too. It was all "amazing proof" to Abigail Duniway "that the vast majority of men have been so much better to wives" than required by "barbaric" laws, "that we hear only now and then of a husband and father who is heartless enough to act toward his family as the law permits."[58] Such exceptions stirred Mrs. Duniway's crusading spirit.

Women throughout the Willamette Valley began coming to Mrs. Duniway as a benefactor and woman's advocate, simply because of the nature of her work. She made trips to San Francisco for the latest fabrics and styles, and accumulated ideas too. Having herself begun on credit, she now helped other women to do the same. When another small-town milliner, a woman to whom Duniway had sold supplies, had all her stock attached for a debt incurred by her husband *before* their marriage, Duniway was touched in her pocketbook as well as her heart.[59]

Other personal reasons increased Abigail Duniway's interest in the public world. In September 1865, twenty-nine-year-old Maggie Scott Fearnside, the third of Tucker Scott's "Three Graces," two years younger than Jenny, met her early death from consumption in the pioneer village of Tillamook on the northwestern Oregon coast. Married only eleven years, she left five little girls who were now divided among the relatives. Eight-year-old Annie joined the Duniway family. Maggie, the pious, dutiful, and intelligent girl who was also the most beautiful of the Scott sisters, had spent most of the years of her marriage in the comfort of Forest Grove near her father's home. But in 1863 her storekeeper husband took his family to the wilderness of Tillamook, where even ten years later the whole county had only four hundred residents.[60] The death of women under such circumstances, and the plight of their motherless children, became a recurring theme in Duniway's later writing.

Soon another misfortune struck. Catherine's husband, "steamboat man" John Coburn, was killed in a steamboat explosion in July 1868. In order to support her four children, Mrs. Coburn began teaching in Canemah, though her salary was deliberately lower than a man's because she was a woman. For six years she suffered such discrimination, until she joined Duniway's *New Northwest* as associate editor. A kindhearted and extraordinarily gifted woman, Catherine was also a more disciplined writer than Abigail—as even *New Northwest* readers noticed. After 1880 she was an associate editor of the *Oregonian* for thirty years. She was as devoted to women's rights and suffrage as her sisters, but without Abigail's notoriety. Equal pay for equal work was always one of their primary concerns.[61]

The Duniway family added two more children to the first four during these years. Clyde Augustus Duniway, named thus illustriously by his older sister Clara Belle, who was also his chief nurse, was born in 1866. Ralph arrived as "an afterthought" in November 1869. This sixth and last childbirth was almost as difficult as Abigail's second with Willis. The process of delivery, she later told Clyde, had made her a "cripple" for the rest of her life, forced to wear "artificial aids" at all times, and always in pain when walking. She suffered from an obstructed bladder and a prolapsed uterus, a very common ailment among nineteenth-century women, and one which caused many of them to become semi-invalids for the rest of their lives. The malady was sufficient to make any woman fear painful sexual relations and further dangerous childbearing.[62]

Abigail Scott Duniway had reached another turning point in her life. During her four years of schoolteaching in Lafayette and Albany, Mrs. Duniway claimed to have taught over thirteen hundred young Oregonians.[63] Her millinery store made her known to many hundreds of women. Her writing had given her a name in the Oregon publishing world, while her distinguished brother and numerous other relatives scattered throughout Oregon gave her a widespread reputation in the still sparsely populated Pacific Northwest.

Abigail Jane Duniway became increasingly restless with the "unintellectual" husband who once had seemed so romantic. As she said to her son twenty years later, "I know what the light [of love] *is*, but *alas*, I never, never enjoyed it." And she complained of the Duniway relatives, "they don't interest me at all. I've been sated to death with the illiteracy of the family, which, with the exception of the strain that runs through the Scotts, shows little or no improvement in a century."[64]

Duniway always credited her "good husband" with the inspiration and advice which led to her great mission. But the way in which she did so, in *Path Breaking* and elsewhere, suggests more rhetoric than reality. Using one of the most common slogans of nineteenth-century feminism, she supposedly exclaimed to her bedridden husband, "One-half of the women are dolls, the rest of them are drudges, and we're all fools!" She had just come from a day in court providing testimony in defense of a widow's financial interests because the law prevented a woman from managing an estate without regular court approval.

> [Ben] placed his hand on my head, as I sat on the floor beside his couch, and said: "Don't you know it will never be any better for women until they have the right to vote?" . . . The light permeated my very marrow bones, filling me with such hope, courage and determination as no obstacle could conquer and nothing but death could overcome.[65]

An important part of Duniway's personality was the need to maintain her image as a dutiful wife who was forced only by necessity to enter the public arena. Much as she would champion the rights of other women to divorce, independence, and freedom from adverse circumstances, she also recognized the price such women paid in loss of material security and public esteem. Though she appeared to the world throughout her life as self-confident, outspoken, and even tempestuous, there was at the core of her personality, nourished by the hardships of her childhood and marriage, a profound insecurity. Much as she feared and resented the hell-fire, camp-meeting religious rhetoric, she had internalized the necessity for both a higher calling and community acceptance. Much as she was determined to stand for the truth and live in freedom, she also longed for the respectability and status which she thought such truth and freedom deserved. A "circuit rider" for women she might become. But the circuit riders she knew, especially her own uncle Neill Johnson, were also loyal family men and ambitious, enterprising farmers. It seemed indispensable to her crusade that she be perceived as a loyal wife and mother, acting with the approval and backing of her husband and other right-thinking men. Her invalid husband loved and needed her too much to withhold his approval.

During the winter of 1870/71, just after Abigail Jane Duniway had weaned her sixth and last child, the thirty-six-year-old farmer's wife, novelist, teacher, and businesswoman was ready to incorporate all her talents, experience, and passion into the service of a new career. The hardworking wife of Ben Duniway, who had not prospered, was determined to provide for herself and her children in accordance with the highest pioneer ambitions. She was also determined to build a better world for every woman.

CHAPTER 6

Circuit Rider in the
Cause of Women

"I ought to have been among the richest women of America."

In early November 1870 Abigail Duniway met with two close friends in Albany to suggest the establishment of a newspaper. Mrs. Martha Foster, her next-door neighbor, and Mrs. Martha Dalton, a music teacher from Portland, were glad to help found a State Equal Suffrage Association, but their two-thirds of the association was dubious about the financial feasibility of a paper.[1]

Mrs. Duniway was a reader of the *Revolution*, published by Susan B. Anthony and Elizabeth Cady Stanton since 1868 to promote woman suffrage. She also met California suffragists during buying expeditions for her store. On 10 December 1869 Wyoming extended the vote to women, as did Utah in February 1870. The ratification of the Fourteenth Amendment in 1868 defined "all persons born or naturalized in the United States" as citizens. The Fifteenth Amendment in 1870 established that no citizens could be denied the vote because of race, color, or previous slavery. Though the amendments were intended only to enfranchise black men, women logically concluded that recognition of their own rights should quickly follow. However, to suffragists' dismay, section 2 of amendment XIV used the word *male* to modify *citizens* for the first time anywhere in the Constitution. This made women like Stanton and Anthony campaign against its ratification, despite their previous support for Negro rights. Sensing a battle to be fought for what nevertheless seemed certain victory, Duniway had found a cause to suit her temperament as well as her pragmatic and idealistic goals. She was one of many other women throughout the country who made their commitment to woman suffrage around 1870.[2]

Some respectable women even became voters. Women had voted in New Jersey before 1807 and, as taxpayers, participated sporadically in the public life of colonial America. But nineteenth-century laws and constitutions and the increasing influence of Blackstone's *Commentaries* in the hands of undereducated frontier lawyers had eroded the position of women during the same period which enhanced the rights of corporations and spread political democratization among men. Now, women of diverse places throughout the country began to test the definition of citizenship provided by the Fourteenth Amendment, claiming that they too were "persons" and "subject to the jurisdiction . . . of the United States" and their own states.[3]

In November 1868, one hundred seventy-two women in a southern New Jersey Quaker town cast their ballots, though the male electors "courteously refused" them. By 1872, numerous other women tried to vote, including "Mrs. A. J. Duniway, a colored, and two white women" in Portland. Susan B. Anthony braved arrest and trial in Rochester, New York. Along with women in New Hampshire, Michigan, and elsewhere, two Washington Territory farmers' wives, Mary Olney Brown of Seattle and her sister Charlotte Olney French of Grand Mound, successfully voted in 1869. Two women in the eastern Oregon village of Auburn claimed to have voted even earlier for Lincoln in 1860.[4]

An Equal Suffrage Society already existed in Salem, founded by a number of prominent Republican politicians like Colonel Cyrus A. Reed, proprietor of Salem's hotel and opera house and known as "the first, the original 'booster' for Oregon." Duniway's organization replaced it, but they remained supporters of woman suffrage in politically divided Oregon. Having heard that a woman suffrage convention was to take place in California during the winter of 1871, Abigail Scott Duniway notified the Salem Equal Suffrage Society that she was going to San Francisco for her millinery business and would gladly be Oregon's delegate to the convention. They appointed her and also gave her both a free railroad pass on the newly completed line from Albany to Portland and a steamship pass for the necessary ocean voyage. Such traditionally male perquisites, the first of many in years to come, gave Duniway a delightful sense of official power and status as she set out on her first railroad journey and first ocean voyage. (Her brother Harvey had been a guest on the maiden voyage of the steamship *Oriflamme* from Portland to San Francisco the previous year.)[5]

The new transcontinental railroad (completed in 1869), plus the city's status as the leading seaport of the West made San Francisco one of the most cosmopolitan cities in the nation. Strong women and crusading spirits surrounded Mrs. Duniway in the city's radiance that December. She spent Christmas with the well-known abolitionist Republican Colonel John Collins and his wife. She visited Laura DeForce Gordon, California Suffrage Association president, and Emily Pitts Stevens, who was publishing a woman's rights newspaper, the *Pioneer*. Duniway had already met Gordon in Oregon. She later credited Stevens and her *Pioneer* as the inspiration for her own *New Northwest*. This was true only in an immediate sense, however; Stevens named Duniway Oregon editor for the *Pioneer* during the paper's short life.[6]

Gordon at this time told Duniway that "Eastern invaders" were attempting to undermine her leadership. The complaint established at the outset of Duniway's own suffrage career a comparable suspicion in regard to her work in Oregon. Gordon shared Duniway's freethinking antiprohibitionism; the "opposing factions" perceived in San Francisco were probably the same that continued to divide the New York–based National Woman Suffrage Association (NWSA) from the more conservative Boston-based American Woman Suffrage Association (AWSA). "Easterners" often implied women of New England religion and gentility who had been trying to impose their refined, cold-water life-style on the West throughout the nineteenth century. The conflict even touched the remembered resentments of Duniway's Tazewell County childhood. She readily understood Gordon's sense of the importance of controlling her own campaign. She also quoted Gordon as saying in 1874, "I am . . . an advocate of temperance in all things; but I am not in favor of the Church's style of preaching prohibition. . . . If I think I need a glass of wine, I do not intend that anyone but myself shall be allowed to say I shall or shall not take it."[7]

Perhaps it was on this occasion that Duniway also met the Illinois lawyer and suffragist Myra Bradwell. Editor of the "most important legal publication west of the Alleghenies," Bradwell had been refused admission in 1869 to the Illinois bar because of her sex, despite the respect her *Chicago Legal News* earned among lawyers. A founding member of the Illinois Woman Suffrage Association and the AWSA that same year, she apparently came West to inspire western suffragists too. Abigail Duniway later told a Woman's Club audience that it was Bradwell's advice which made her mission possible:

> I was . . . struggling to make myself believe that my constant ill health was a wise dispensation of Providence. . . . Mrs. Bradwell opened to my anxious mind an illimitable vista. . . . "You are young, yet," she said, cheerily. "When woman shall have discovered herself, all women will be ashamed of being invalids." She then went on to explain . . . that woman's greatest need was mental *VENT*.

Prescribing a remedy for the youngest Duniway's teething pains, Bradwell said, " 'I repeat, you are young yet. By and by, when these babies are men, you will still be a young woman.' . . . And so it came to pass that I had a vision."[8] Duniway was only thirty-six. Bradwell herself had no more children after the age of thirty-one in 1861. Her advice may have been personal as well as professional.

On New Year's Eve 1870, Abigail Jane Duniway gave her first public lecture. Praised by her audience and the newspapers, she was immediately offered a salary for a speaking tour of California. Understandably excited, Abigail wrote to Ben that she would be gone longer than expected. A whole new world of experience opened before the erstwhile frontier farmer's wife.

Then came Ben's telegram. "Come home immediately; business requires it." Thinking there must be some emergency or illness, since she had a housekeeper and a store manager, his wife caught the weekly steamer at once. Stopping in Portland just long enough to put a notice in the *Oregonian* that she had been appointed Oregon editor of Stevens's *Pioneer,* Duniway arrived home only one month after she had left. She had turned down the lecturing offer and missed the last three weeks of the convention, only to discover at home "no visible need of anything but the salary I had relinquished in blind obedience to what I considered an unreasonable mandate."[9]

There must have been quite a battle. Knowing Abigail Duniway's temper and the things she was capable of saying to her enemies, one can imagine that Ben Duniway was forever sorry he had sent that telegram. Only one week later, on 25 January 1871, the Portland *Oregonian* carried the following notice:

> Mrs. A. J. Duniway of Albany arrived in this city yesterday morning to ascertain what interests can be raised here in behalf of the removal of the *Pioneer* newspaper from San Francisco to this city. . . . In anticipation of success she will remove shortly to this city. We have little doubt that she will find encouragement enough unless she entrusts the canvassing business to some blockhead of a man. When women go for their own rights they generally get them.[10]

The wording sounds like Abigail Duniway's, and the idea like Duniway in anger. She would move *now*—and fulfill her dream at last.

During the next three months, Duniway moved her family to a small rented house at Third and Washington streets in Portland. She set up a printing machine in the two upstairs bedrooms, hired a printer, and paid her two oldest sons as typesetters. Willis had already learned that trade as an apprentice at the *Albany States' Rights Democrat.* For awhile she kept her shop in Albany and opened another in Portland, supporting the paper with a $3,000 loan and the enthusiasm of high hopes and strong convictions.[11]

"I ought to have been among the richest women of America," Duniway wrote thirty years later, inadvertently revealing the speculative motive which accompanied her literary ambitions, "but my husband, having once pauperized himself by becoming surety for an ambitious friend, went to the other extreme and refused to put his signature to my papers . . . [to] buy property in Portland while it was cheap."[12] The complaint was one she made often in later years, especially as she watched brother Harvey Scott's investments make him, indeed, an apparent millionaire. For her, money spent in the cause of equal rights was not "extra" out of a stable middle-class income, as it was for so many other late-nineteenth-century suffragists. Her newspaper and publishing company was the family's main support; her career was a financial necessity.

Benjamin Duniway still provided basic wages however. Devoted to his children and to his extraordinary wife, Ben left behind his garden and his workshop and his pinto horses and stayed with his family. He took a job as a clerk in the Portland customs house for the next fifteen years. Harvey Scott, newly appointed by President Grant to the lucrative post of customs inspector, gave him the job as a kindness to his sister. She was appalled a few years later when a political opponent accused her of being thereby "entangled in 'debauching influences.'" Ben's was a "humble position," she said. "I really pity the man whose ideas of integrity are so badly warped that he imagines that a woman could be bought for a paltry sum of a few hundreds a year, which her husband receives as a salary, and which she never handles or meddles with and is in no way responsible for."[13] Given Duniway's awareness of the need for money, it is hard to believe she considered her husband's "few hundreds" as lightly as she claimed. On the other hand, Duniway could not be "bought" by anyone. She always assumed that any gifts or loans were justly deserved indications of support for her cause. If strings *were* attached, she did not recognize them.

Mrs. Duniway hired a Chinese cook and housekeeper to care for her family. While the boys worked on the newspaper, Clara at first managed the store and then gave piano lessons. She often sang solos at suffrage meetings too. Ben was the one who nursed the children through sicknesses, told stories, and sang rollicking frontier songs. His children adored him for his warmth and "gentle" kindness; they respected and admired their energetic and peripatetic mother. Duniway paid her children for their work and introduced parliamentary techniques into family councils, hoping to make her household a paradigm of the equal rights world she advocated. "It is one thing to be a good housekeeper, quite another to be a successful home-maker," she wrote, warning that a mother's "zeal to discharge her duty" might make her "assume what should be [her children's] burdens. As a consequence, the entire family finally come to regard 'mother' as a sort of necessary household appendage, old-fashioned, dowdyish and illiterate." As for wifely obedience, she said in another editorial:

If . . . a mother by overweening indulgence helps her son to become a

thoughtless scapegrace, her daughter a helpless drone; if a wife, by cowardly subserviency, converts her husband into a selfish tyrant, she has
committed a sin in self-sacrifice that not all the halo which sentiment can
throw around it can construe into a virtue.[14]

In coming to Portland, however, Abigail Scott Duniway had stepped
across an unseen boundary. Despite its blackened stumps, dirt streets,
wooden sidewalks, and population of only 8,000, Portland was now the
leading city in the Pacific Northwest and one of the richest of its size in
the country. It was the port of arrival for all incoming trade and the
center of financial and speculative ventures which involved all its commercial and political leaders. In contrast to the rest of Oregon, the
majority of Portland's leading citizens were New Englanders. The city
was said to "out-Boston Boston" in the rigidity of its caste system. Victorian urban ladies prided themselves on wifely obedience and devoted,
dutiful motherhood, and Portland wives were often several generations
removed from farmyard toil and kitchen drudgery. Even the formidable
and wealthy Harvey Scott, editor of the most powerful paper in the
Pacific Northwest, was never quite accepted in the "best" Portland society. A "vulgar" newspaper*woman* was beyond the pale.[15]

Meanwhile, sailors, miners, immigrants, and others frequented a
seamy side of the city which was also uninterested in reform. In 1871
there were enough saloons to make one for every sixty inhabitants—one
of them said to have the longest bar in the world—and there was widespread prostitution and opium use, both in and out of the growing
Chinatown district. The situation did not change for more than a generation. In league with some of the leading business interests and politicians, who also controlled the industrial and transportation systems in
much of the Pacific Northwest, moral and legal injustice was not to be
easily unseated.[16]

On 5 May 1871 the first issue of the *New Northwest* appeared. Duniway
told her readers that she was "naturally acquisitive, calculating, and fond
of active business life," with a flair for writing. She explained that her
newspaper would become "one of the permanent institutions of the
country." She had "outgrown the sentimentality and 'moonshine' that
characterized some . . . early productions"; her new fiction, she said,
would be based on experience and the "obvious facts" of women's existence. In her "chosen bailiwick" the *New Northwest* would represent a
great and developing territory, the forward edge of an American empire
which would eventually encircle the world: "the onward march of improvement . . . starting from the western shores of the Eastern
World, . . . shall . . . extend its career of conquest until it bursts upon
the Old World."[17]

To such manifest destiny boosterism, Mrs. Duniway added radical utilitarianism. Her paper would be "not a Woman's Rights, but a Human Rights organ, devoted to whatever policy may be necessary to secure the greatest good to the greatest number. It knows no sex, no politics, no religion, no party, no color, no creed. Its foundation is fastened upon the rock of Eternal Liberty, Universal Emancipation and Untrammeled Progression." A few years later the *New Northwest's* masthead was even more specific:

> A Journal for the People
> Devoted to the Interests of Humanity
> Independent in Politics and Religion
> Alive to all Live Issues and Thoroughly
> Radical in Opposing and Exposing the
> Wrongs of the Masses.[18]

The *New Northwest* and Abigail Scott Duniway's indomitable energy were the primary factors in the Pacific Northwest woman's movement for the next sixteen years. Exposing frauds, defending mistreated women, describing local prisons, asylums, and reformatories, reporting on meetings, business, and cultural events, and keeping track of legislatures and law courts, the paper carried far more than the "gospel message" of women's rights throughout the territory and beyond. As Mrs. Duniway harnessed the passionate rhetoric of frontier camp-meeting oratory to the great new secular cause of political freedom, she traveled thousands of miles and lectured to thousands of men and women besides writing tens of thousands of words in her paper. She cried out against evil, identified the "sinners," and converted the "lost" to the cause, counting on the power of her wit and logic and passion and anger to bring them to their knees. As son Willis Duniway put it: "the individual wounds she makes in curing the fallacies of the age, being made in mercy, are never long in healing. . . . She will not leave any community where she begins her work till the backbone of opposition is broken."[19] With the head-strong temper of a frontier preacher, she also created enmities, which only increased her conviction of a sacred calling. With her "pen . . . more powerful than a sword" she was free at last to "expose folly, subdue error, and exalt virtue" like her first fictional heroine. As the molder of a great new constituency of women voters, she hoped to be, like her editor-heroes Horace Greeley, Simeon Francis, William L. Adams, and Harvey Scott, a positive force to be reckoned with among the rulers of the nation.

Secure in her sense of virtue as well as innocent ignorance of the forces arrayed against her, A. J. Duniway, as she signed herself until 1877, filled the next sixteen years of her life with energetic dedication. She became a mentor for hundreds of women throughout the Pacific Northwest—persuading them to develop their talents, obtain educations, enter professions, or write for her newspaper. Young people from outlying farms and towns often boarded with the Duniways in order to attend school in Portland or to learn the trade of typesetting on the *New Northwest*. Bethenia Owens's young son stayed for a year while his mother attended medical school in Philadelphia. Owens's articles on suffrage appeared in the *New Northwest*, as did the writing of others whom Duniway "discovered" on her travels. Dr. Bethenia Owens-Adair was one of many who later testified to receiving crucial aid and encouragement from Abigail Scott Duniway.[20]

Before examining the content of Duniway's preaching, one needs to know something of the sheer physical magnitude of her endeavor. The *New Northwest* appeared every Thursday, its four folio pages filled with six tightly printed columns of news, editorials, reprinted literature, serialized novels and stories, and long, descriptive "Editorial Correspondence" sent back by Mrs. Duniway about her travels. She had bought old, unusually small type, which was not replaced until 1880, so her columns contained much more than the average.[21] Among the authors she printed were John Ruskin, Bret Harte, Frances Fuller Victor (until 1874), Mark Twain, Fanny Fern, and many "unknowns," like Joaquin Miller's wife, whose talent she encouraged.

Some idea of the energy expended is revealed by Duniway's "Record of a Year's Work" for 1886, the last year of publication. After her daughter's death she gave 181 lectures (219 the previous year), traveled "3000 miles by stage, rail, steamer, buggy, buckboard and afoot," endured "more than the usual quota of persecution, hypocrisy, malice, gossip and hate" (especially from the Women's Christian Temperance Union, whose members prayed for her at their meetings), wrote 400 columns of material for the paper, and personally canvassed for subscriptions in every town she visited. By that year transportation facilities had improved somewhat, though the Pacific Northwest could still claim the worst conditions in the country. Primitive mud wagons often took the place of stagecoaches, and the few railroads were often just narrow-gauge lines run by mining companies. Regarding stage drivers Mrs. Duniway once wrote: "If there are degrees of exaltation in the great hereafter, where merit meets its just reward, faithful stage drivers will occupy some very high seats, despite their temptations and falls."[22]

That 1886 record included Abigail Duniway's attendance at the NWSA convention in Washington, D.C. She was one of the five vice-presidents—along with Susan B. Anthony, Matilda Joslyn Gage, Olympia Brown, and Phoebe W. Couzins—recognized by all as the foremost leader of women in the West. (Elizabeth Cady Stanton was then president.) Duniway had been attending NWSA conventions ever since 1872, making her way across the country by varied means each time. Often she received passes for free travel by rail and steamship, courtesy of transportation tycoon Ben Holladay or brother Harvey Scott.

She went by steamship to San Francisco and then by railroad to the convention of 1872, where she was immediately invited to a platform seat. In 1876 she came East again, this time for ten months. Starting with only a free pass up the Columbia and twenty-five dollars, Duniway lectured her way across the country to the Centennial Exposition. Along the way she visited relatives in Illinois and gave a speech to the Illinois legislature. She also composed *David and Anna Matson,* an epic poem on a theme borrowed from John Greenleaf Whittier (and recently used far more successfully by Alfred Lord Tennyson in "Enoch Arden"). Dr. Clemence Lozier and other women in New York found her a publisher and held author's receptions in her behalf. The attention and appreciation was thrilling.

(*David and Anna Matson,* however, was the worst thing Duniway ever wrote—in conception, use of language, versification, and moralistic fatuousness. It was also a flop. She claimed to readers that it had been well-received, and she continued to sell it wherever she went, but the kindest critical comment was from an Illinois paper which remembered her childhood and urged readers to buy it because of the beautiful cover. The *New York Graphic* made a more typical remark: "It is a sad, sad story, and we congratulate Mrs. Duniway upon having got rid of it." One creative critic said: "Some might be perplexed to decide whether they would choose to be Achilles, or Homer who sang of him. Possibly there would not be much hesitation in deciding between sharing David's trials [as a slave to the Barbary pirates] and writing such poetry.")[23]

Again in 1880, 1884, and 1886, Mrs. Duniway crossed America, describing early Pullman coach travel and blizzards and visits in Minneapolis, Chicago, New York, and Boston. Always she lectured in every city, town, or village, delighting Easterners with her salty frontier manner and being delighted in turn to meet so many of the most eminent women of her day. Though her primary affiliation was with the NWSA, she was equally at home with both national suffrage associations. For example, the *New Northwest* exchanged papers with Lucy Stone's and Henry Blackwell's AWSA *Woman's Journal* and frequently reprinted from its columns.

The first of Duniway's many lecture tours occurred in the fall of 1871. Hoping to capitalize on the fame of Elizabeth Cady Stanton and Susan B. Anthony, who were in California that summer, she invited them to accompany her and split the fees. To Duniway's disappointment, Stanton had no desire to tackle the wilds of Oregon and Washington Territory. Anthony, on the other hand, was desperately trying to pay off the $10,000 debt on her defunct *Revolution.* Recently hissed and vilified in San Francisco when she blamed male "protectors" for the notorious Laura Fair's murder of her false lover, she welcomed the invitation and the free steamship pass which Duniway sent. Assuring Anthony that there would be at least $1,000 to $1,500 profit from the trip, enthusiastic Mrs. Duniway planned a two-month, two-thousand-mile itinerary over the most rugged of frontier territory. For the fifty-year-old Miss Anthony, who was seasick all the way from California, the ten weeks she spent in the Pacific Northwest with Duniway were both miserable and memorable.[24]

The first lectures in Portland were reasonably successful. But the new editor of the Democratic *Oregon Herald*, Missourian Sylvester Pennoyer, published a poem aimed at both Duniway and Anthony:

Along the city's thoroughfare,
A grim old gal with manly air
Strode amidst the noisy crowd,
Tooting her horn both shrill and loud;
. . . .
A meek old man, in accents wild,
Cried, "Sal, turn back and nurse our child!"
She bent on him a withering look,
Her bony fist at him she shook,
And screeched, "Ye brute! ye think I'm flat
To mend your clo'es and nurse your brat?
Nurse it yourself; I'll change the plan,
When I am made a congressman—
    Women's Rights and Suffrage. . . .[25]

Later, in Seattle, the devoutly evangelical editor Beriah Brown, noted for his Civil War secessionist sympathies, which Duniway had exposed in the *New Northwest*, scathingly denounced Anthony as a "revolutionist, aiming at nothing less than the breaking up of the very foundations of society, and the overthrow of every social institution," an advocate of "licentious social theories" merely disguised by her argument for woman suffrage. An antisuffrage lecturer named Mrs. J. Blakesley Frost followed them to all major cities.[26]

One of many incidents foreshadowed Mrs. Duniway's future problems on both the regional and national level. At Umatilla on the upper Columbia, described by Duniway as a "dilapidated town [which] bewails its wind-worn raggedness and weeps o'er days departed" when it had been the base for gold prospectors in Idaho,[27] Anthony met the long-lost son of an old friend back East, a barkeeper who expressed his respect by offering her wine. Susan B. Anthony took a polite sip to avoid insulting the man and handed back the glass.

By the time the suffragists reached Walla Walla, word about Anthony's downfall had spread to the local preachers. No church was available for her lecture, nor was the local theater, since the Pixley Sisters were performing there that night. But resourceful Mrs. Duniway was not stymied. She scheduled talks anyway—including one in the Exchange Hall located behind a saloon, to the horror of the pious. Woman suffrage was denounced from all Walla Walla pulpits that Sunday—the first skirmish in a continuing battle by evangelical Christians against Duniway's "loose" principles. Anthony was pleased with her "fine audience" and felt that she had cleared up "*Free Love* and all to the satisfaction of Rev. Mr. Kimball." She also told Duniway, "If you want any cause to prosper, just persecute it," but slanderous publicity was certainly not what she preferred. Walla Walla remained a stronghold of opposition to suffrage and to Duniway.[28]

In Salem on 15 September the entire Oregon State Supreme Court visited Anthony and Duniway in the fine Chemeketa House hotel to discuss the suffrage issue. In many other Willamette Valley towns there were large audiences. Anthony enjoyed a three-day visit with John Tucker Scott and toured Forest Grove's Pacific University. At the Oregon State Fair in October, Anthony drew one thousand listeners to "a real Patrick Henry speech," while antisuffragist Mrs. J. B. Frost had only forty. But she had to give her lectures in the open, competing with the Pixley Sisters and a Fat Lady, a brass band and sideshow barkers; the crowds, though enthusiastic, were noisy. And she had to share a tent for a week with Abigail and Ben Duniway, Clara and three of the boys, and Sarah Scott Kelty and her husband. It was, according to Abigail Duniway, "a cozy little shanty, renovated each year by carpet and beds of freshest, cleanest straw, and affording a delightful nook wherein to rest and dress and sleep." But Anthony confided to her diary that they were "packed side by side like herrings—can't say I like it better than nice bedroom." Duniway, who had walked across the continent and lived more than half her life in a log cabin, reveled in the excitement—"Everybody hieth to the Donny brook of ye land of Webfoot, prepared to make money, spend money, . . . camp out, eat dirt, breathe smoke, sleep on the ground." Anthony made the best of it.[29]

The trip to Olympia, Washington, was so terrible that both women still talked of it years later. It involved primitive frontier hotels, indigestible food, canoe portages, and a ninety-mile wagon ride over the notorious corduroy Cowlitz road from the Columbia River to Olympia. According to Anthony, the "horses walked every step of the way." The rainy season made the muddy return even worse. In Olympia, the capital, a town of about 1,800 population, Anthony promised a third of one night's fees to victims of the great Chicago fire. She made only thirty dollars and then sent it all because ten dollars was so little. Victoria, British Columbia, a town so poor that someone was advertising for a family to occupy a house rent-free, provided largely male audiences, for whom "the idea of the ballot for women was even more unpopular than in the United

States, though all, by strange inconsistency, were intensely loyal to their queen."[30]

The frontier mill towns on Puget Sound insulted or ignored them. One kind woman in Port Gamble invited them to her home; her husband angrily ordered them back to the "wretched excuse for a hotel." With characteristically defensive belligerence, Duniway "wanted to stay it out and conquer the head of the family with [what she called] a little womanly tact," but Anthony insisted they both retreat at once. Ten rainy days on a Puget Sound steamer obscured any view of the spectacular scenery. Anthony wrote home that she was "tired, tired." Then, despite—or perhaps because of—her carefully reasoned arguments to the Washington territorial legislature that women as citizens already had the right to vote, the legislators passed a new law expressly forbidding Washington women to vote until the U.S. Congress should make it legal. Susan Anthony was serenaded in Olympia and received several marriage proposals. But she called her last lecture in Portland a "mortal agony" and finally headed home "as single-handed and penniless as usual."[31]

That first lecture tour did not dampen Mrs. Duniway's appetite for exploration. She had garnered many new subscribers and generated publicity. She had also discovered that she thoroughly enjoyed the give and take of a frontier lecture platform. Speaking extemporaneously, despite Susan Anthony's parting advice that she should "never attempt to speak in public without careful preparation and committing to memory everything I should want to say,"[32] Duniway both delighted and infuriated audiences wherever she went.

Her style revealed her rural origins and contrasted sharply with Eastern and urban rhetoric. A reporter for the *Oregonian* described her performance at the NWSA convention of 1886 in Washington, D.C.:

> There had immediately preceded her a Boston lady, a speaker whose words were carefully chosen, her modulation smooth, her a's and ew's given a scientifically correct sound, her gesticulations measured, her poise studied. Mrs. Duniway, being the next speaker, arose, stroked down the folds of her dress, walked to the middle of the platform as independently as a queen, and began her address in an off-hand manner that at once delighted her audience. . . . Force was substituted for excessive polish. As she proceeded, . . . the audience cheered lustily. They were especially struck with her unique comparisons, the incidents of Western life that she related. . . . I [was] proud of Mrs. Duniway and Oregon.[33]

Abigail Scott Duniway quickly built up a repertoire of metaphors and illustrative incidents which she could use with endless variations both on stage and in her writing. Even her enemies came from miles around to enjoy the entertainment of her presence in isolated frontier villages. Country ministers, anxious to preserve their parishioners' virtue, and perhaps also to avoid comparison with such a dramatist, often refused the use of their churches. Others, like the eminent geologist and evolutionist Reverend Thomas Condon of The Dalles,[34] welcomed her as an emissary of culture in a barren land.

Country women, farmers' wives, working women, and the laborers of America were Duniway's prime constituency throughout most of her life. She had no use for the sentimentality of "eastern poetesses," who knew nothing about the lives of "Women of the Border." When their history was written, she said, "and everywhere properly appreciated, many a hitherto unknown heroine, who stood guard in the front of the wilderness while humanity was filling up the vast expanse of acreage behind her, will form the theme for flowery pens." Such women were epitomized by a scene she saw from her steamer on the upper Columbia River in 1874. From "the great wild wastes of dreary upland, now used only for grazing, with here and there a forlorn hope of a farm-house . . . a solitary woman stands gazing at the steamer from the wind-worn stoop, looking as though the monotony of solitude had incrusted her in an impenetrable veil of reticence."[35]

The lecture tours provided news and subscribers for the *New Northwest* and also grist for Duniway's serialized novels—stories and characters and incidents which she could incorporate into her plots or embellish for her polemical purposes. The essence of her literary ambition "(aside from pecuniary reasons)" was to "lay facts before you; facts as parables; facts as lessons; facts as they are in the every-day life of more than one woman who pursues the allotted rounds of a life of heroic effort." But readers should not be "too inquisitive or critical about localities, identities, or even facts" because she had purposely disguised them with different names.[36]

Scribbling her novels as she traveled,[37] Duniway also enjoyed the hospitality of friends and relatives who had scattered throughout her territory. Her sisters and their children all became active suffragists. They led suffrage associations in their respective towns and acted as agents to sell the *New Northwest*. The first such association in Oregon was established in Forest Grove by Sarah Maria Scott Kelty in 1871. Sister Catherine Coburn was secretary of the state association formed in 1873, while Fanny Scott Cook was active in Lafayette. Numerous references indicate the continued activity of the whole family. Old friend Belle Cooke founded the Marion County Suffrage Association in Salem in 1874, while Clackamas and Yamhill associations were formed that spring.[38]

Other friends from Duniway's Clackamas County, Lafayette, and Albany days gave loyal support, either there or in the many other areas of

the Pacific Northwest where they resettled. When Duniway visited Pen-
ewawa, Idaho, in 1877, she stayed in a hotel run by former neighbors
whose son bore the name she had chosen for him twenty-three years
earlier—Charles Orestes Cram. The Crams named a street after her, so
she promptly bought a corner lot in the new town. In the town of Mt.
Hood, Oregon, she visited Dr. W. L. Adams, former editor of the *Argus*,
and Mrs. Adams. She often stayed with one or another of the nine
McBride sisters (two of whom were married to Adamses), daughters of
Lafayette's Judge McBride. Uncle Neill Johnson, who had moved to
eastern Oregon, and other members of his large active family were also
hospitable. Relatives in Illinois, Iowa, and Missouri subscribed to the
paper and entertained her on her cross-country travels, especially the
Turleys of Mt. Pulaski, Illinois. Duniway's young half-sister Rhoda Ellen
became a Latin teacher at the University of Washington before she was
married, while a niece arranged lecture dates in southern Oregon. She
often visited the Yeslers of Seattle, city founders who became millionaires as it grew, the Sylvesters of Olympia, proprietors there when
Tucker Scott staked his claim in 1854, and Madame Stahl of Walla
Walla, widow of a wealthy brewer and town benefactor. J. B. Knapp of
Knappton, who took Duniway on a tour of his sawmill and lumber
company in 1874, was the merchant who had marketed her butter in
1861. In Monmouth, Oregon, she "enjoyed the hospitality of the dear
friends of our youth, J. B. V. Butler and wife, in whose society we almost
grew young again."[39]

That Mrs. Duniway was an inveterate name-dropper is quite certain,
and that she delighted in the social distinction to be gained by having
"connections" is more than likely. Coercing people's support by listing
them as supporters was one of her most common ploys—one she was still
using even when she named them in *Path Breaking* and included her
brother Harvey Scott. But most people she mentioned were glad to be
favorably reported in her paper and flattered by the praise she freely
distributed.

On a tour of Idaho in autumn 1877 she visited the town of Colfax,
then only two years old:

> Charlie Hopkins, of the Palouse *Gazette*, and P. C. Sullivan, of Salem, were
> the first friends to greet us at the hotel. Then came Mrs. Wolfard, one of
> the stanchest friends of human rights in all the land, who invited us to her
> cosy and well-ordered home. . . .
>
> We found Ed. Beach and wife, formerly of Albany, Dr. W. W. Beach, of
> Buena Vista, the Davenports and Wolfards, of Silverton, and numerous
> other Willamette Valley friends in the place. . . .
>
> The town is growing like magic. Everything has an air of newness and
> hurry, but there are so: ? substantial improvements, including mills, dwell-
> ings, stores, and schoolhouses. . . . Ewart & Co. keep a large stock of gener-

al merchandise; Davenport & Wolfard furnish the flour for the multitude; Dr. Beach dispenses the drugs; and many other branches of business flourish, not the least being the *Gazette*, under the proprietorship of Messrs. Kellogg & Hopkins, who have suddenly struck a newspaper heaven.

Mrs. Duniway went on to explain that Charlie Hopkins was the grandson of her hero, Colonel Baker. He would certainly "make his mark some day, for 'blood will tell' in the second, if not in the first succeeding generation."[40] (This is a minor example of Duniway's propensity for impaling people with apparently harmless thrusts—in this case Charlie's parents.)

Charlie drove Mrs. Duniway to her next lecture in the even newer town of Palouse City. There she stayed in a hotel "with an obliging landlord and capable landlady, who partitioned us a bed-room with carpets, upstairs among the stars, and gave us food as nicely cooked as in the Palmer House, of Chicago, at the low price of twenty-five cents per meal." Such accommodations were better than what she often had in such towns, visiting in one-room "shanties," where she was "glad to get the corner bed, with two or more children as sleeping companions." Encomiums to far-flung and otherwise unknown hostesses made Duniway's visits cherished occasions for lonely frontier women. They also helped to sell the *New Northwest*.[41]

Here in Palouse occurred one of the many unique events in Mrs. Duniway's career.

> The dining-room of the hotel was chosen for the lecture, and the people had gathered in from every direction and filled it densely, and the speech was fairly begun when *crack* went the floor, and *smash* went the benches, and *down* went the people into the cellar below, leaving the undersigned well-braced against a tottering partition to prevent it knocking her on the head. Luckily nobody was hurt, but the confusion was indescribable. The fallen and frightened crowd after a while emerged from the cellar through the *debris*, somebody lifted the partition from the burdened shoulders of the speaker, and we all repaired to another room, where the lecture was resumed amid a general feeling of thankfulness that nobody had been injured. By morning the break was repaired and everybody was happy.

When Duniway wrote her autobiography thirty-five years later, she added that only her quick-thinking directions from the bottom of the hole preserved the crowd from panic as they climbed out.[42] As in many other instances, memory made Mrs. Duniway magnify her own importance.

Despite such "minor" difficulties on her lecture circuit, Duniway remained an unabashed booster of the whole Pacific Northwest. She intended her novels to provide "graphic descriptions of localities" but with "fictitious names and places" for "those who wish to supply their friends in the East with descriptions of Oregon scenery." (Susan B. Anthony wrote that she was reading *Martha Marblehead* to her eighty-four-year-old mother every week in 1877.)[43]

Sometimes the scenery was a little hard to believe. On J. S. Howard's farm in Paradise Valley, Idaho, Duniway claimed that

> carrots are not content with straight roots of even large dimensions, but they send out laterals in all directions, like monster lobsters, which they greatly resemble. . . . [O]ne hundred bushels of these persistent vegetables on a quarter of an acre this year. Parsnips grow six feet long, and onions seven inches across. Strawberries grow by tons to the acre. . . . There is room in this great, rolling, billowy, timberless, fernless, brushless, bunchgrass country for a million families.[44]

Duniway was in the habit of buying lots in many of the frontier towns she visited, so she was accustomed to investigating and reporting on land values. In 1875, she did so at Astoria, discovering that "its real prosperity is a myth, so far as the masses are concerned, and will so remain till those who wish to settle on the seaboard can buy Astoria property at San Francisco prices." She informed her readers that, having climbed the heights for the purpose of speculation, she found the price so exorbitant that "no sensible buyer will purchase" from the "primal squatters" who were unjustly monopolizing the land. She took her revenge by way of negative publicity:

> Astoria is very little for its age, and certainly the *dirtiest* town of its size we ever saw anywhere. There are many evidences, however, that its "second growth" has commenced. The streets, hotels and private houses are alike full of strangers, and were real estate held at its legitimate worth, many valuable buildings would soon take the place of the decaying vegetable matter and decomposing sturgeons upon the river banks, that, as they now are, would fill a less healthy atmosphere with a frightful pestilence in less than a fortnight.[45]

Eleven years later Astoria was still filled with "offensive smells," although produced by canneries, Chinatown, and "Swilltown . . . another unpleasant adjunct of the Venice of America," with its "barnacles of prostitution that protrude here and there through the sour swamp of the perverted appetites that feed the said barnacles." But it also had a new electric power plant, which Duniway visited with her usual enthusiastic curiosity:

> Mr. Gough, the young and gentlemanly electrician who has charge of the works, talks learnedly, but without ostentation, of "motors," "magnets," "insulated copper wires," "armatures," "commutators," "circuits," "arc," "incandescence," and so forth; and we wander in and out and around

among the intricate machinery, feeling like an elephant in a toy shop, and half afraid to turn lest we unchain the lightning somewhere. . . . We left the machinery and sallied forth in the brilliant glare of the mysterious illumination it had set free, devoutly prepared for the next great invention, which we are ready to believe will be the scientific and successful navigation of the air.[46]

Duniway occasionally noted with regret the devastation brought to the wilderness by some aspects of civilization. On a small stream near Seaside, Oregon, she saw that "great ruins of what once were spruce trees of vigorous growth and vernal loveliness, held aloft their skeleton arms to mock the ravages of girdling-ax and fire-fiend. . . . And the tangled growth looked up and sighed, and the feathery ferns looked down into the water and wept." Of the Rogue River hydraulic gold mines she wrote: "The bosom of Nature has been cut and scarified in a shameful manner in these parched areas, as though a cancer had left its horrible ravages everywhere—ravages that the wounded earth could never heal."[47] But, in general, she admired progress, development, and settlement, while she enjoyed the pleasures which an expanding society made possible.

From the mines and ranches and wheatfields of Nevada and Oregon and Idaho to the sawmills of Knappton or the fishing boats of coastal villages, Abigail Duniway visited, explored, questioned, listened to, and chronicled her society. Sometimes she joined in frontier wedding celebrations or attended an unexpected funeral. Once she witnessed the sudden recognition of a son long hidden from his divorced mother. One day in 1883 in the Lower Cascades, she joined two families whose children had just succumbed to an epidemic, as they took loads of flowers to the burial ground. On their return "the grown people rode a cowcatcher backwards over dizzy depths, the engineer of a passing locomotive kindly granting the privilege, himself taking care of the little folks in the tiny engine-room."[48]

The *New Northwest* carried accounts of Mrs. Duniway's visits to prisons and insane asylums, where she received grand tours by the administrators and interviewed the prisoners and patients. She frequently publicized such injustices as a woman's trial for murder without a jury of her peers or the refusal of Pacific University to admit an illegitimate child. She was on hand for detailed coverage of the trial of Nanny Thomas in a frontier courtroom in Colfax, Idaho, in 1881.[49] And she attended almost every session of the legislatures of both Oregon and Washington.

Duniway's descriptions of public figures could be devastating:

The sore-nosed member from Yamhill, who doesn't want women to legislate for themselves, and is equally determined that they shan't be legislated for, . . . is slightly below the medium height, and greatly above the average in adipose tissue. His head is powerfully developed at the base, where it is thickly set upon a pair of obese shoulders. The fishy eyes are surmounted by a forehead quite pointed in the region of the organ of obstinacy, bare at the summit, and embellished at the sides with scraggy fetlocks. Dear reader, don't laugh. We are aware that fetlocks don't usually grow upon the side of the head. We're describing an exceptional animal.[50]

The Washington legislature in 1881 provided one of many opportunities for verbal portraiture:

Yonder urbane member from Jefferson, with graceful gait and luxuriant hair, is the Roscoe Conkling of the lower House. He understands parliamentary tactics to a dot, and leads yonder grizzly-bearded gentlemen in high back heads through the bewildering mazes of amendments and reamendments, and rejoinders and sur-rejoinders, till he outwits them each and severally.

Yonder loud-voiced member is from Pierce. He is as active as the business end of a hornet; is, in fact, the Mahone of the combination, and he worries things terribly sometimes. There is a noticeable smooth spot on the top of his cranium worn there no doubt by the constant friction of his ideas against the acknowledged opinions of other people. . . .

Yonder gentleman in goggles excels chiefly as an artist. . . . That other member['s] *forte* is the persistent attempt at reconsideration of all measures passed through the brilliant maneuvering of the gentleman from Pierce.

. . .

Legislators can keep calm when discussing a hog bill; they do not lose their equilibrium when considering the merits of a game law; they can hold their tempers when discussing the woman question, and can smile urbanely when being bored by the hour by dissertations upon education, annexation, or river and harbor bills; but just let them get started on a money matter. . . .

It is simply impossible to sketch them now. A half dozen are on their feet at once, shouting "Mr. Speaker!" in stentorian voices. Some are buzzing about the hall, sucking so vigorously at the moist end of a meerschaum or cigar that you innocently wonder why they were sent to the Legislature to make laws for women before they were weaned.

The way they pelt each other with covert personalities is a caution to common courtesy. Eastern Washington is jealous of Western Washington. Clams bombard bunch-grass, and lumber interests menace gold mines. The members get so thoroughly excited that they remind the spectator of a swarm of bees whose queen is lost.[51]

While the starkness of some of Duniway's accounts make her a worthy predecessor of Hamlin Garland, the humor of others can be compared to that of her contemporary, Mark Twain. For example, she reported on a trip over the Sierras into Nevada in 1874:

Nine o'clock on Tuesday found us aboard the stage, with the usual crowd of passengers and baggage. We never saw a stage that wasn't capable of holding one or two additional passengers after it was already full. When about twenty feet from the hotel door, the horses plunged into a mud-hole, going down until, but for many similar observations, we should have expected to lose sight of their ears. But the horses came up, and down went the coach, throwing the travelers into a heap upon the forward wheels and righting them again with the next lurch. . . . Miles of tedious repetition of the first moment's experience sufficed to reconcile us to our fate; besides, when you get your spinal column snugly telescoped, you become in a measure stage-hardened; and you learn to endure everything.[52]

On other occasions she traveled by stage along the coast of Washington Territory:

[Beyond the neck] you see the same incessant chase, chase, chasing of sullen sea-foam, and the flinty beach, under the feet of your patient horses (if the tide is low) constantly disappears behind you, spreading new miles of the same unbroken surface as you proceed, while upon your right vast stretches of alluvial upland, with here and there a lonely farm-house and an occasional wheat-field, venture to show themselves from behind a tangled white-bleached heap of drift-wood, which you gaze upon (we mean the drift-wood), and your busy mind prances back to the days of your childhood (we speak from experience) and you almost wish you were a child again, commissioned as we were of old, to gather kitchen stovewood. Such is life.

After a while the tide flows and your horses wade and your wagon rocks in the rising waters. Once in a while a tidal-wave, mightier than the rest, strikes the vehicle unawares, and you watch the receding waves that almost engulf you, only to fancy that the stage is floating shoreward, and then— somebody gets sea-sick. Oh, it's fun—provided, always, that you are not sick yourself.[53]

Without knowing Emily Dickinson's "narrow fellow" in a New England garden, Duniway rendered a robust western railroad with less subtlety but comparable dexterity:

Our winding, snake-like train keeps adding freight car after freight car to its caudle extremity until, as the engine at last switches its tail of cars and goes thundering down the grade, we look behind us from the window and count *thirteen rattles*. Oh, *what* a snake! It follows us through the gloom and over the gorges; down the grades and up the grades; along the river and across the culverts; under frowning crags and over jarring trestle work, never ceasing its rattle and din, until at last we reach the Dalles, where the snake, rattles and all, curls itself away somewhere among the machine shops.[54]

She used a snake image again in describing her journey in Charlie Hopkins's horse-drawn open hack from Palouse City to Lewiston across the panhandle of Idaho. After a jogging trot for five hours in the rain, "wrapped like an Esquimaux" against the mid-November cold, they reached the top of the gorge above the Snake River with "the road below us winding in tortuous curves and zigzag angles for five miles on down."

> Far below us, to our left, the Clear Water came zigzagging down to meet the silvery Snake, as though unconscious of the fate awaiting it. The greedy Snake opened its mouth, and, swallowing it down, went writhing on, while on a flat just above this constant scene of reptile inebriety, and so far below us that she looked like a pretty toy, sat Lewiston, hemmed in alike by rivers and mountains, her regular streets bordered by Ritz poplars, and her neat, white cottages peeping from behind the trees like children playing at hide and seek.

On the drive "down the labyrinthine windings of that zigzag mountain," said the indomitable adventurer, "the grade was splendid. . . . How the blessed air of this upper country invigorates one's worn-out nerves."[55]

Duniway used metaphors from everyday female experience to produce uniquely appropriate descriptions. In 1881 she portrayed

> Olympia, the capital of Washington Territory, keeping guard like a queen over the grand inland sea. . . . Olympia's ample skirts are unevenly spread over the wide area of her undulating person, and terminate gracefully in a pretty bias flat, with scalloped edges that border her feet as they dip water in the edges of the bay.[56]

And on the "infinitesimal streamer" *Kataia*, going up the small Skipanon River from the Columbia, she described

> the labyrinthine marshes of a slough, so crooked that its banks remind you of the raveled loops of your friend's crochet work, with which the busy kitten has been playing until the whole combines a seemingly inextricable snarl. But the Kataia snorts, and pants, and labors, and you look out for the opposite banks and wait, never finding them where you think they ought to be, but fetching up at unnumberable kinks in the stitches, till at last, having "knitted ten, purled three, looped six, dropped eight and narrowed sixteen," as they say in fancy work, you "finished off" your last scallops and wind up at Skipanon landing.[57]

Frequently, episodes in Duniway's serialized novels can be correlated with events and places depicted in her "Editorial Correspondence" columns of a few weeks earlier. After one particularly hectic lecture tour where local newspapers had printed some scandal-mongering gossip, the heroine of her current novel exclaimed that women "are in the habit of continually suspecting some woman, and then, having socially killed her with calumny, they pounce upon and pick her to pieces like so many vultures upon the remains of a dead sturgeon. [But] . . . they are not morally responsible. The avenues of opportunity are closed to them, and their minds are dwarfed by jealousy and soured by envy until they cannot look upon a seemingly successful woman with the least degree of allowance."[58] In the same novel "Moll Seabank" of "Eagle Cove"

> was one of a class of protected and supported women which the traveler may often meet in wayside inns in pioneer towns. Her children were numerous, her trials many, and her duties legion. Ignorant and coarse she was, with her frowsy, red-brown hair, which all attempts to coax out of its desire to curl had only succeeded in bringing into a large wrinkled coil at the back of her head, while the stray locks that were not long enough to follow the coil rolled themselves into little rings around her perspiring, freckled and dirty face, as if trying to caress her in their mute sympathy with her life of unrequited toil. . . . As the years of marital drudgery had rolled on, and her condition of protected helplessness had become more and more hopeless, she had grown first irritable, unlovable, and slovenly, and afterwards morose, hard-hearted, loud, and exacting. And no wonder. . . . You may find [such women] from Maine to Oregon, and from Fuca to Florida, in squalid homes, in wayside inns, in dingy alleys, and oftentimes on well-tilled farms, where everybody's rest and interests and comforts are consulted except those of the woman whose additional burden of being mother to a race is consequently so badly borne that humanity is thwarted through the constant robbing of vital forces that are the God-given heritage of the unborn.[59]

Despite calumny and the heavy burden of her work, the controversial Mrs. Duniway was a happy woman during her *New Northwest* years. Much as she sometimes complained about her difficulties, her new career had enhanced both her physical and psychic freedom. One can almost feel the tapping of her foot when she describes the young people dancing at a "splendid" ball in Oregon City, even though, "our Presbyterian toes were never taught to trip fantastically. Sometimes we're glad, and again we regret it." Her "first experience in sea-bathing" came when she was almost forty-one. On a vacation trip to the Pacific, accompanied by Ben Duniway, who watched from the beach, she tried out the water with characteristic exultation:

> What a figure you cut, when, rigged in your neighbor's bathing suit, you take the hand of your host, equally charmingly attired, and literally *break* for the breakers. How you shrink and shiver at first. But, as the waves dash against you and you lose sight of the fact that you've always been a landlubber, you take a strange delight in watching the surf as it creeps murmuring toward you, shaking its white locks in your face as it approaches; and when,

with the strength of a mighty torrent, it dashes over you, as though determined to vanquish its daring intruder, you brace yourself and meet and conquer it, and watch it receding for a fresh onslaught, while you stand your ground victorious. You rise somewhat in your own estimation, empty your mouth of salt water, and go dripping to the bath-room, amid the cheers of the old bathers.[60]

At the age of forty-seven, as she admired the "bright young girls" at the Willamette and State universities, Mrs. Duniway added, "We . . . do not wish to be a child again. No, no. Theorists may prate as they may of the happiness of childhood and youth and the blessings of early womanhood. We would not exchange one year of middle life for it all; nor would we forego the promised fruitions of its approaching Autumn, even though its Winter of Death be close at hand, for all the blithesome laughter of the school-girl, or the rapturous re-awakening of 'love's young dream.' "[61]

Of Abigail Scott Duniway's many descriptions of herself, one concerned a trip from Lafayette to McMinnville in 1874:

we filled the wagon so full of Suffragists and their children, that a certain editor took a back seat on the hay, just over the wagon wheels, where "bump-ity-bump" she jolted along, swallowing dust in unknown quantities, and becoming so completely inhumed in the same, as to appear metamorphosed into a mummy from some ancient excavation.

When she was ready to return a few days later, after several lectures,

The proprietor of the Lafayette stage line [was] in a fever of disappointment. He had loaned his hack to some camp-meeting frolicers who had failed to come back. . . . This left us no alternative but to go to our appointment on horseback. . . . We hadn't ridden a horse for many a year; our "toggery" was anything but equestrian in style, and the basket, satchel, fan and parasol necessary to our comfort in traveling, made a formidable appearing load for a horse to carry in addition to our own avoirdupois. . . .
     When we reached Lafayette, the principal street was thronged with the beauty and chivalry of the place on their way to the lecture, and as we whipped poor, patient Rosinante with the parasol handle, and held on to the cumbrous basket, to keep it steady as we jogged along, we'll venture to assert that Don Quixote couldn't have outdone us in grotesque appearance had he tried.[62]

Abigail Scott Duniway was no longer like the lithe young girl of *Captain Gray's Company*, who rejoiced to ride horses and feel the wind in her hair. She weighed about one hundred fifty pounds and was "anything but feeble looking."[63] She was also unusually tall for her day. But the missionary zeal of her uncle preacher Neill Johnson still filled her heart.

And the indomitable spirit of old Sheriff Jimmy Scott, whose Kentucky long-rifle came to Oregon with Harvey Scott and whose ransomed slaves proved the idealism under his pragmatic pathfinding, lived on in his hardheaded feminist granddaughter, even with her parasol and basket on a jogging horse. A female Don Quixote she was indeed, but with a very practical goal. She reveled in the role.

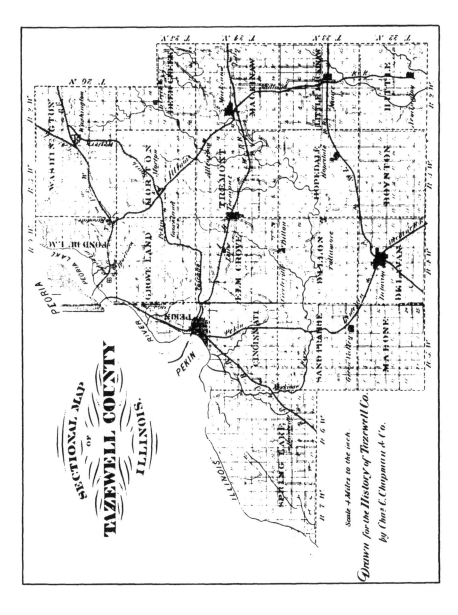

SECTIONAL MAP
OF
TAZEWELL COUNTY
ILLINOIS.

Scale 4 Miles to the inch.

Drawn for the History of Tazewell Co.
by Chas. C. Chapman & Co.

James Scott's farm: Elm Grove Township, section 2, northeast quarter of north half; Groveland Township, section 35, southeast quarter of east half; section 36, southwest quarter of west half; section 25, southwest quarter of east half (added in 1834)

Tucker Scott's farm: Groveland Township, section 25, southeast quarter of west half; section 35, southeast and northwest quarters of west half

Neill Johnson's farm: Elm Grove Township, section 2, northeast quarter of south half

Each section is one mile square. Tucker Scott's sawmill was in Groveland. Tremont was the county seat (previously Pekin). Railroads did not exist until 1850s, but were planned during 1830s. Eliza Farnham, author and wife of land agent T. J. Farnham, visited her sister Mary Roberts in southwestern Morton Township.

James Scott (1779–1860) of Pleasant Grove, Illinois

John Tucker Scott (1809–80), ca. 1870

Ann Roelofson Scott (1811–52)

Harvey Scott, 29 August 1857

Abigail Scott Duniway as teacher,
ca. 1862

Abigail Scott Duniway, editor of
New Northwest, 1871

Duniway home in Albany, Oregon

Ben and Abigail Duniway with children in Albany, Oregon, 1868. Standing: Hubert, Willis, Clara, Wilkie; in Ben's lap: Clyde; added: Ralph

Abigail Scott Duniway reading
from a copy of her book *David and
Anna Matson*, 1876

Ben C. Duniway, 1876

Duniway home at 5th and Clay streets, Portland.
Abigail Scott Duniway (at right) with her maid

Abigail Scott Duniway, with spirit of
Colonel E. D. Baker, ca. 1886

Abigail Scott Duniway, 4 October 1895

Abigail Scott Duniway at the polls, 1914

Abigail Scott Duniway voting, 1914

CHAPTER 7

To Loose the Bonds

"I am aware that I am treading now upon forbidden ground."

Like many other Americans, Abigail Scott Duniway believed that progress must begin with individuals, at the personal and domestic level. Without sexual and economic freedom, voting power would be meaningless. Without voting power, sexual and economic autonomy would be impossible to achieve. Women's political rights involved recognizing a woman's right to autonomy in every aspect of her life.

Mrs. Duniway was determined to publicize to the world the lives of "heroic" western women who combined "the toil of a bondwoman with the self-abnegation of a martyr, and the conscientiousness of a Christian with the lie-living existence of a hypocrite." She would preach the truth even to women who "fancied that politics meant something obscene, and that polling places were worse than gambling dens," women who were often "prostituted, soul and body, to the unholy behests of a besotted legal lord" and who "fancied that every other woman upon the face of the earth . . . was a social and moral reprobate." There were domestic implications to such a "revolutionary" doctrine. Duniway wrote in one novel,

> I am aware that I am treading now upon forbidden ground, good reader. . . . But all the outcry of all the Pharisees in all America will not cause me to swerve a single inch from my duty, which consists in declaring to you the whole power of the truth, God-made and humanity-violated. . . . There is, there can be, no other sin so heinous as that of unloved or unloving wedlock, for there is no other sin that so constantly breeds discord, crime and misery as this, and none other that brings them forth like this to curse the race.[1]

Although the birthrate had been dropping throughout the nineteenth century among the upper classes, America's farm population, especially in frontier areas, and particularly in Oregon, had one of the highest birthrates of any time or place in the world. Oregon in 1850 surpassed the national average fertility rate by more than 50 percent and led all other states and territories, while rural areas exceeded the urban areas of Oregon itself by almost 30 percent. A typical frontier housewife had

107

about eight children, while the ratio of infants to women was almost double that of India in 1961.[2]

Isolated and overworked, rural women had neither the freedom nor the knowledge nor the female support and companionship which became available to them even in the smallest towns. Cut off from their mothers and other women at an early age, they were often as ignorant about sex and related female problems as their husbands, who had never been expected to know about such things. Most of them did not even have the help of midwives, with their accumulated traditional knowledge, who were just at this time being squeezed out of the medical profession and who were also particularly scarce on the sparsely settled frontier. Knowledge of birth control, of abortion methods, of child care, and of female hygiene was in short supply on the same farms where, as Duniway so often pointed out, horse and cattle breeding was becoming a science.

Thus, when they could, women began to look to "scientific" medical books and literature for necessary information. Abigail Scott Duniway's advice about abstinence and spiritualized love was not unusual for her era. She repeated medical opinion which had been current since the 1850s and was common among reformers even earlier. It was also being publicized by other women writers in the *Revolution*, the *Women's Journal*, and *Woodhull and Claflin's Weekly*. For example, men as well as women were warned by doctors of the dangers to their health from "excessive" sexual indulgence—more than once or twice a month.[3]

Such advice was unwelcome to men and to most women too. Clergymen were concerned about gaining parishioners through family increase. Southerners considered a wife's nonobedience to her husband's demands a direct threat to family order and the social status quo. When the formidable Mrs. Duniway visited immigrant communities at the Carbonado, Washington, coal mines in 1883, ethnic pride also caused opposition. She seems to have forgotten the similarity to her own crowded childhood as she deplored the "many illiterate and thoughtless women" and their "swarms of dirty children." The immigrants considered her an imposing "lady," looking down upon anyone not "altogether as she is." The local *Tacoma Ledger* angrily accused her of "casting reflections" on "the generative capabilities of the women of Carbonado."[4]

Nor did it help that all the *New Northwest*'s first subscribers received bonus free subscriptions to *Woodhull and Claflin's Weekly* from New York. The controversial Victoria Woodhull had presented a suffrage memorial to Congress in January 1871, just before the NWSA convention, thereby scooping the association's publicity and gaining the backing of the whole organization. Even such prominent suffragists as Elizabeth Cady Stanton and Isabella Beecher Hooker praised and admired the fearless Woodhull, so it is not surprising that Abigail Duniway was glad to receive the *Weekly*, which Woodhull and her sister distributed free of charge.[5]

But the effect of Woodhull and her sister on public opinion during the early 1870s was out of all proportion to their actual importance in the woman's movement. "Protected," according to rumor, by Commodore Vanderbilt and a mysterious Colonel Blood, the beautiful and uninhibited sisters had risen from youthful degradation and misery to become successful stockbrokers and leading ladies in the seething society of post–Civil War New York. Captivating both feminists and spiritualists, they soon scandalized the nation—and thereby brought discredit on all suffragists.

The child of wildly schizophrenic parents in a huge frontier family, Woodhull's experience of revivalistic fervor and spiritualistic visions, her marriage to a drunkard at fourteen, and an agonizing childbirth in poverty which left her baby retarded, combined with her present beauty, wealth, and apparent power and virtue, made her particularly appealing to Duniway and perhaps also the inspiration for some of her fictional plots. The scandal was Woodhull's exposure of a love affair between the eminent Reverend Henry Ward Beecher and the wife of newspaper editor Theodore Tilton in September 1872. The case led to a lengthy, well-publicized trial which titillated the nation and destroyed Woodhull's reputation.

Apparently Duniway had not been reading the *Weekly* closely, for another item in the *New Northwest*'s first issue referred to "the hideous doctrine of 'Free Love,' [with] which so many frightened men seek to scare progressive women by casting at them as though they were in some way its aiders and abettors." Woodhull had specifically advocated free love a year earlier, defining it as "a single standard of morality." Not until November 1871, however, just as Duniway and Anthony were making their tour of Washington Territory, did nationwide headlines report Woodhull's defiant speech in New York's Steinway Hall. "I have an inalienable, constitutional and natural right to love whom I may, to love as long or as short a period as I can, to change that love every day if I please!" she said, adding, "Promiscuity in sexuality is simply the anarchical stage of development wherein the passions rule supreme. When spirituality comes in and rescues the real man or woman from the domain of the purely material, promiscuity is simply impossible."[6] Few were convinced.

Protests against *Woodhull and Claflin's Weekly* soon reached the *New Northwest*. Not only had Woodhull announced her candidacy for the presidency at a flamboyant New York convention one week after the first *New Northwest* appeared; she had also threatened "revolution" and "secession"—the most inflammatory of words so soon after the Civil War—if woman suffrage were not soon granted. "We will overthrow this bogus republic and plant a government of righteousness in its stead!" she declaimed as newspapers reported her words from coast to coast. Then, while most Americans still shuddered at the violence of the short-lived Paris Commune of 1870–71, Woodhull declared herself a Communist, committing a section of the International Workingman's Association, which she had organized, to woman suffrage and sexual freedom. This was too radical even for Karl Marx, who was among those who voted to expel her section from the organization.[7] Oregonians were no less horrified.

Duniway replied to complaints in her paper with "humble hope" that the free love charges were "mistaken, yet, should this sorrowful shame be true, as alas, it so often is where men high in political aspirations are concerned, we see no reason why all progressive and noble-minded women should be made to bear the opprobrium." Nevertheless, even Salem's Belle Cooke could not "conceive how any woman of delicate instincts or good moral perceptions can tolerate some of the doctrines" in the *Weekly*. One article on divorce seemed "unfit to be read by any pure-minded person. . . . [T]he advocacy of such principles will do more to injure the cause of woman than any other course." In this first of her many disagreements with more pious suffragists, Duniway did not back down. She defended Woodhull as "a sensational rather than a wicked journalist," an "unfortunate . . . intelligent, fearless, and remarkable woman" whose "able exposition of many of the glaring wrongs that curse society far more than compensate for the mischievous tendency of [her] *apparent* doctrine of free love."[8]

After meeting Woodhull in New York in 1872, Duniway modified her support. She referred to the "Woodhull farce" and to her "singularly obnoxious journal." But Duniway still agreed that "In the abstract, ten thousand of her theories are correct," and someday "humanity shall become sufficiently elevated to be a law unto itself." If Victoria could "awaken a demand for Woman Suffrage among the rabble whom none but herself and retinue can reach, I rejoice in her mission and bid her God speed in her labors." Ten years later, Duniway was referring to the "Woodhull-Claflin infamy" and its "filthy and obscene literature."[9]

Though Duniway stopped distributing the *Weekly*, her own *New Northwest* continued to publicize "wholesome lessons" about the importance of sexual control, family limitation, and wifely nonobedience. Such control was a major theme of all her novels and stories. For example, Judith Reid, the heroine of the first serialized novel, is "the lawful wife and legal mistress of a strong, passionate man" who insists on sexual relations during pregnancy. Judith loses her first "tiny bud of promise" (has a miscarriage) because "my over-taxed and much abused nature broke down. . . . [P]hysically I was unable to bear the burden of his inordinate desire." Duniway wrote the novel's next paragraph in her own voice:

> I deeply feel the dangerous and strong position that I here dare attack. I know that while the effects of these bestialities are plainly and palpably visible in every community and in almost every household, the discussion of this grave and awful subject is forbidden; but with a firm resolve to die, if need be, for the benefit of passion-cursed humanity, with fear and trembling, I plainly speak.[10]

In another chapter, Duniway urged that society "ostracize a man . . . who is so deeply encrusted in his own selfishness that he sacrifices the well being of the older members of his household to his ungoverned animal instincts" by having too many children. "Friends and brethren," she went on, "the next great lesson that man must learn is the control of his sensual appetites." He must "loose the bonds of personal *obedience,* with which he fetters woman, that thereby she, and not himself, may control the much abused functions of motherhood," just as female animals do. Duniway's "friends and kindred . . . sometimes begged me to desist" from such writing, she said. They claimed that "while things of which I speak are true, they should only be published in medical works and revealed to physicians and patients." But she cared for "the weak and lowly," for the "much abused, sadly outraged mothers of the race." "The *secrecy* of medical works, indeed! The very rocks and stones should all cry out against this damning shame!"[11]

Mrs. Duniway's ideal woman was self-controlled, not passionless. So was her ideal man. Woman's subordination stemmed from unjust laws and circumstances, not innate weakness. And women should be responsible for their choices. Therefore, it was necessary that they learn to assert themselves and to understand their own bodily functions, just as men needed to be taught consideration.

Like Elizabeth Cady Stanton, Duniway often gave lectures specifically directed to women's physiological needs, while other lectures were aimed at "Our Boys" and "Our Girls."[12] The "ecstasies" of sexual union in marriage were necessities for the full life of both men and women, she said. But "the unfailing source of . . . conjugal happiness" was to be found only in those "one out of twenty" marriages where

> the honored husband and equally honored wife had never ceased to keep ablaze the hallowed love-light that had glowed in their hearts in the roseate days of their wooing; that both had lived in understanding of and obedience to the laws of life, thus retaining health and vigor; and that each continually yielded to the other fullest recognition of individual liberty in everything pertaining to their mutual interests.

Though passion and sexual attraction were not abnormal, they were powerful forces which should be resisted for the sake of love. "Humanity . . . is ignorant of the moral and natural laws of constancy and self-control" which could be easily learned, she wrote, echoing the advice of hydropathic doctors and eminent scientists of the time. As the hero of *The Happy Home* explains, "God gave me great powers of loving for my own well-being, mother. He will not cast me off because I nurture, cultivate and control His highest, holiest gift." He would stifle his selfish passion with true devotion until Mattie was ready to marry, "believing that a husband's greatest triumph consists in conquering himself."[13]

Mrs. Duniway deplored "the time-honored system of 'courting' when the other inmates of the house are locked in slumber. Marriage should come of the *intellect,* rather than the passions; . . . There is a great deal too much bodily courting in this world of ours, and many are the fearful consequences." After marriage, restraint would preserve health and happiness. The "angular, pale-faced little creature, with a hollow backhead, large frontal brow, fiery black eyes, thin, electric, black hair and bony chest," of one novel, who had been having miscarriages "semi-annually" for ten years, was bitterly jealous of happy women, but "not naturally bad. Had she fully understood the laws of her own being and commanded their observance . . . she might have grown into a charming woman, . . . with those feminine graces . . . which she vividly remembered to have been her portion once."[14]

Marriage did not confer right of ownership. The plot of *Madge Morrison* revolves around the deception of Madge by the man she loves. He promised to let her return to her sick mother immediately after the wedding ceremony. Instead, to her horror, the marriage is consummated at once:

> "Certainly," interrupted the servant of the Lord who had tied the Gordian knot, as a shining piece of golden coin passed from the questioner's hand and disappeared in his capacious and often empty pocket. "We always have a bridal chamber, garnished and in order," he continued, rubbing his hands, and speaking in a deep, modulated bass voice, that Madge thought was somehow suggestive of molten brimstone.

As Madge "bit and scratched like a maniac," the preacher says, "But you surely wouldn't so wrong your holy office of wifehood, which implies obedience and submission, ma'am," and then tells the deceiving husband, "Carry her to your room. . . . She is yours, now, to have and hold till death do part you. What God hath joined together let no man put asunder."[15]

Madge's resistance, it should be noted, is based on concern for duty, not fear of sex, for in the next paragraph, where "George Hanson took possession of his property,"

The wild, ungovernable love that had induced her to become the wife of the man around whose form black shadows floated, still held sway over her senses. His caresses were inexpressibly dear, and his words of love so full and tender that, under the glamour of the spell they cast, it was little wonder that conscience for a time was quiet, and Madge's mother well-nigh forgotten.

In her last novel, written in 1914, Abigail Duniway was still advocating the same self-control and spiritualized sex she had always preached. *Margaret Rudson* insists on man's duty to "conquer himself," even though the future husband exclaims that he can't because "Our hot blooded natures are given us for a wise purpose." Margaret tells him she wants a business relationship, "a confidential counsellor, not a suitor or a lover." She sends him off to campaign for suffrage in order to keep him busy. On their wedding day, she insists that he leave to rescue a child in distress. At that point he deserts Margaret in fury, but she still considers herself right. "I rose for the moment . . . from wifehood, which is a selfish condition, into womanhood, which has no limitations of a selfish nature, because it includes the creative, protective and fostering function of altruistic motherhood." All ends happily when the husband finally returns and reciprocates Margaret Rudson's exalted love.[16]

Duniway referred to contraceptives only once, when one of her heroines expressed horror at "the numerous latter-day hypocrisies that have been invented and indulged to hide hymeneal villainies" in a "new-fashioned community."[17] In 1871 she encouraged *New Northwest* readers to purchase John Humphrey Noyes's book about the Oneida community, which contained his theories about nonpropagative, "amative" sex. But she did so mainly to help Minnie Myrtle Miller, the recently deserted wife of poet Joaquin Miller, who was selling the book in order to support her children.[18] In 1892 Duniway, with her oldest son, Willis, attended a lecture by the controversial theosophist Annie Besant; by then Besant's trial for obscenity (printing birth control pamphlets) in England in 1876 was almost forgotten.[19] She also listened to Cyrus Teed describing the Karezza method in 1893, but found it a "disgusting" doctrine.[20] Whatever she knew about contraception, she apparently still associated with prostitution, as did most other "respectable" women of her era. Rationalization and spiritualization of love was the goal she always recommended.

Like most of her contemporaries, Mrs. Duniway was well aware of the prevalence of prostitution. One of her earliest editorials contrasted the strict enforcement of laws against wandering cows in Portland with the notorious laxity towards bawdy houses: "Mothers of growing sons," she wrote, "we cannot banish the 'steps which take hold on hell' from our city limits unless we vote." Women must prevent "our sons and daughters" from "being snared by the sirens of sin whom we now meet on every pavement clad in the garb of luxury, which tells too well the melancholy story that their horrid business 'pays.' "[21]

But Abigail Duniway also sympathized with prostitutes, perceiving them as victims of the double standard which judged women much more harshly than men. She carried on an unsuccessful fight to have a prostitute's child admitted to Pacific University during 1872 (and another in 1880) and apparently knew the woman personally. One of her fictional heroines explained, "The sins of women are generally connected . . . with the sins of men, Mr. Lofty. Then how can women be more culpable than men for the same offense?" Another novel features a wronged wife in disguise as a Madame who maintains her purity of character as she listens to the troubles of men. She finally confronts her own fallen husband with the news that

> "I have tracked you the wide world over. I have found you in many a brothel, where assuming various disguises, I have captivated you. *Yes, sir,* under the blushing light of the twinkling night stars in almost every state in this Union, I have fascinated and entrapped you, winning from you in every case the most extravagant declarations of ever enduring love."[22]

The significance of the double standard argument in relation to women's rights can be seen in an exchange which took place between a clergyman and Mrs. Duniway at the Temperance Alliance meeting in 1872. When she called for an equal suffrage resolution, the man exclaimed, "Mr. President, I charge the sins of the world upon the mothers of men. There are twenty thousand fallen women in New York—two millions of them in America—we cannot afford to let this element vote!" Duniway replied, "How dare you make such charges against the mothers of men! . . . what say you, sir, to the twenty millions of fallen men—and all voters—whose patronage alone enables fallen women to live? Would you disfranchise them, sir?"[23]

Oddly enough, she ran into similar trouble, for an opposite reason, from another clergyman that same year. According to her version of what happened, as Duniway presided over a meeting in Lafayette, where she had been known for years, a "poor old preacher" recently arrived in Oregon from the East had "wrongs to redress" in regard to the renowned New England abolitionist Abby Kelly Foster. He accused both Foster and Duniway of favoring "spiritual marriages." When Mrs. Duniway could stand his "lascivious" talk no longer, she rapped her gavel and shouted, "Hush!" It did not work, and Duniway ended up calling the preacher an "infernal LIAR! an old beast! reprobate! a villain!" Half the audience shouted, "Go on, go on!" while the other half rose to leave, until finally another man managed to quell the disturbance and get the audience to resume their seats. In her newspaper account, Duniway mentioned that her nerves were fatigued from numerous previous lectures, but she asked no pardon for her own conduct. "God Almighty gave us combativeness with which to defend womanhood, and though we never will be the aggressor, we stand ready to rend an antagonist when he deserves it—if the encounter does make us sick." As on numerous other occasions, she spent four days in bed recovering from the "nervous prostration occasioned by the melee."[24]

As women alone were blamed either for becoming prostitutes or for not being sexually obedient to their husbands, so they were also blamed for abortion and infanticide. When an Ohio minister called for a ministerial conference "to look the evil squarely in the face" and do something about it, Duniway told her readers that it was actually none of his business. "The vast majority of mothers cannot for many coming generations be made to see and understand" that abortion is wrong, she said, because it is not mothers but fathers who are responsible. "The principal cause of all this crime is *enforced maternity*, and the crime will never be abolished till the cause ceases." She frequently deplored the prevalence of abortion and infanticide, publicizing incidents like the abortion death of an unwed mother at a Portland Medical Dispensary and fraudulent ads purporting to cure "ladies' disease." But the cause, "bodily subjugation of mothers," could only be removed by giving women political and economic freedom, she said. Moral freedom alone was not enough.[25]

Mrs. Duniway even went so far as to suggest that infanticide was sometimes right. Influenced by the growing eugenics movement of the time, she described in one of her novels a brain-damaged baby whose enlightened aunt advocated "a sleeping potion that would still these convulsions forever." "Good reader," Mrs. Duniway continued, "some day . . . the world will not raise physical or mental monstrosities, as now. Some day they will cease to be generated; but that day will come long after the world has learned to re-generate them [into spiritual life] through the merciful agency of anesthetics as soon as they are born." A later chapter specifically advocated "stirpiculture"—the scientific breeding of human beings.[26]

Fear of hereditary damage was as significant as "revolutionary" zeal in causing Duniway to warn that "social sins . . . are by no means confined to illegal associations between men and women," and that "the effects of adultery in wedlock will be visited upon the children unto the third and fourth generations." Birth defects, mental or physical, were perceived as divine punishment for parental misbehavior by many nineteenth-century authorities. (They were in fact often the result of inherited syphilis.) Thus the unfortunate mother of the brain-damaged baby in *Dux: A Maiden Who Dared* wailed: "'Happy children, or children gestated under right conditions, would never be as fretful as these last young ones, and nothing but a flagrant violation of the best and holiest of nature's laws would ever have created Charley.' "[27]

About divorce Abigail Duniway was somewhat more ambivalent. Contrary to contemporary custom, however, she refused to shun divorced women. Needing a companion to accompany her to the Oregon state legislature in 1872, she created a stir by choosing Salem's Dr. Mary Sawtelle, whose "sad domestic experiences appealed to me, from the first, as the principal reason why I should defend her openly." Another divorcée, Bethenia Owens, who had first met Duniway when they were both milliners, sent her son to live with the Duniways in 1871 while she attended medical school in Philadelphia. Married at fourteen to an irresponsible man, Owens had divorced him at eighteen and been self-supporting ever since. Duniway was glad to help her.[28]

But Abigail Scott Duniway still believed that "True marriage is indissoluble, eternal; a oneness as indefinable, as inimitable, and as necessary to the happiness of humanity as are the inexorable laws of attraction and repulsion which together operate to sustain the wonders of infinitude." Because "humanity so often errs," she admitted, "false marriages" might need to be dissolved, "yet we reiterate we cannot advocate free divorces."

> The immediate consequences are too fearful, too glaring; the opportunities given to men and women to marry without reflection, or with no intention of holding to their vows for life; the fearful wrong that would thus accrue to children; the many deserted wives; the many desolate firesides, all combine to cry out against the flagrant injustice of removing the marital responsibility.

Instead, women should be allowed to help make laws against child marriages or drunken, licentious, poverty-stricken wedlock. Those already caught in the web of marital misfortune must simply endure by asserting their "newly awakened womanhood" to "command the respect of the spoiler." They should concentrate on training their children "into a knowledge of the fundamental laws of common humanity, that thereby they, at least, may escape the maelstrom of conjugal misery and discord and shame."[29]

Duniway was preaching what she herself practiced. As she put it in *Edna and John*, if a woman has made a wrong choice in the past, it is nevertheless her duty, for the sake of her children, "to make the best of a bad bargain."[30] She noted ironically the "trepidation" of husbands who

> imagine that the *New Northwest* is going to take their wives away from them! Who ever heard of anything so ridiculous? Why, brethren, we have been the faithful wife of one man for almost a score of years, and intend not only to

remain his wife until death doth part us, but we shall do all in our power to persuade your wives to stay with you. We have no doubt but many of you feel that your wives ought, in justice to themselves, to leave you and earn for themselves and children a respectable living; but instead of our counselling them to do so, we shall content ourself with doing all in our power to enlarge their opportunities to benefit their families, not even excluding their frightened lords. We really were not before aware that so many men imagine that they hold their wives by *power* rather than by love and high and holy principle.[31]

Such disclaimers did not prevent accusations from "wronged" husbands against the *New Northwest*. A crusty old rancher who had tried to marry Jenny Scott the schoolteacher twenty-two years earlier remained convinced that his marital problems were her fault. The interrelationship of political and sexual opinion is strikingly illustrated by the non sequitur conclusion of the man's angry letter:

Let me give you another law that some of our Democratic friends, *distinguished at that*, have had the kindness to suggest to me as being violated. They lay the whole blame of my wife's defection to the pernicious teachings of the *New Northwest*, unsettling in the minds of women the sacredness of the marriage relation, constantly urging them out of their happy homes and household ways into the ways of men, where their modesty must become unsexed, and their virtue be constantly assailed, unless they are indeed both 'strong-minded' and hard-featured. . . ; that nothing but the good old Democratic doctrines of Jefferson and Jackson, and the equally sound dogma of Paul . . . can save the country. Some of them urge me to vote for Lane because you advocate Warren.

Duniway had printed the banished wife's sad letter of farewell to her family, whom she was never to be allowed to see again, in the previous issue of the paper. She now told the husband that she was unable to "increase the mental capacities or moral stamina either of 'Democratic friends' or weak-minded women," though she thought the unfortunate wife's adultery was "more deserving of pity than censure."[32]

Certainly it was possible for mistreated wives to find justifications for leaving home in Duniway's writing. The novel which was appearing when the above episode occurred included a romantic exhortation to her readers:

the day is coming, in the history of inevitable progression, when any other reason for the consummation of conjugal relations than the heaven-ordained one of an exalted affection will be everywhere held as a crime. . . . [M]en and women are often wrecked for life upon the altar of matrimony, made legal by statutes which are founded in ignorance and perpetuated under a system of superstition that lays the responsibilities of the comsummation of an unnatural alliance upon the Immutable, as though God, the Infinite, would desecrate the holy ordinance of an honorable union by libelous counterfeits upon marriage *as it ought to be,* and as it surely *would be,* were human laws and human knowledge in accord with the perfect laws of nature and of God.[33]

Mrs. Duniway's intention was to provide warning to the unmarried and encourage reformation of the married. She was willing to stand up for divorced women as the victims of unendurable conditions which justified their cases; "Women are getting too far advanced to longer endure drunkenness and brutality," she wrote. But "when men in general so regard it, and proper marriage laws are enacted, wives will have no cause to appeal to the divorce courts. . . . [S]hallow writers who prate of 'the early training of girls for the great stage of wifehood' would do vastly better by endeavoring to impress upon young men the responsibilities of husbands."[34] Only when the marital problems of Mrs. Duniway's own children became insoluble did she finally allow a fictional heroine to say:

> "Would it not have been far better for me and my children, when I learned . . . that I had made a grievous matrimonial mistake, if I had fled, like Hagar, to the wilderness? I thought to save my son from the fate of Ishmael, but I have failed. I have learned, alas! too late, that children brought up in discord, however securely the hatred and discord may be hidden from the world, are the innocent victims of a mighty wrong."[35]

Abigail Scott Duniway had always been as devoted to her children as to her career. She had invested a great deal of her ego satisfaction in the belief that her methods of child-rearing would produce better results and that her daughter and sons were near paragons of good behavior and intelligence. In *Captain Gray's Company,* Ada Mansfield Stanton had expounded her theories on the care of babies:

> Don't nurse him only just when he needs attention. Don't humor him to a lighted candle whenever he wants it. Make him know that his couch is his proper place until he gets over baby sleepiness. . . . Don't allow him anything but his natural nourishment until he gets some teeth. Teach him to love the bath-tub.

Duniway prided herself on the discipline and independence she expected of her children. She made a virtue out of her own hatred of domesticity and felt that giving them jobs and wages was as good for their character as it was for the family finances. She was sure she could "put her boys upon honor before the public" as few other mothers could.[36]

Nevertheless, Mrs. Duniway's favorite son remembered that it was his father, Ben Duniway, who "had special gifts in home doctoring and nursing." His mother "lacked the calmness and patience to deal with personal needs of ailing children. She was nervous, apprehensive, worried, when they were ill," preoccupied with "her literary and public work."[37] All her children were ambivalent about her work and her authority.

Duniway took little Clyde (whom she still called "darling C-o-y-d-i-e" or "Bumpsey" when he was thirty) on many of her lecture tours, but he retained "no clear memory of her personal influence . . . or of her public work."[38] She even took Ralph when he was only five, to "take care of mamma." One rainy morning they had boarded a Willamette River steamboat before daybreak:

> Somebody took Ralph by the hand and led him forward on the boat, causing us to lose sight of him in the darkness. We feared that he'd fallen overboard, and for a time were almost frantic. Then, after looking everywhere else, and calling ourself hoarse in a vain attempt to make him hear, we rushed into the cabin and found the Young American calmly superintending the porter, who was building a fire. If we hadn't been a Christian we might have spanked *one* embryo "protector." As it was we admonished him *very gently*, and received for answer, "Why, mamma, don't you suppose I'm able to take care of myself? I could travel alone to Boston if you'd only give me enough cash."
>
> We sighed for that child's prospects. He's bound to go to Congress or to be Governor or do some other damaging deed yet, if his precocity isn't nipped in the bud.[39]

When Abigail Duniway made her first lecture tour with Susan B. Anthony, she took Clara along on the first half of the journey to play the piano and sing for suffrage meetings. While they were gone, Willis Duniway was arrested in Portland for stealing pumpkins, possibly in an attempt to embarrass his mother. A letter in the *Albany States' Rights Democrat* claimed such motherly neglect was the perfect rebuttal for "all the foolish nonsense about 'woman's rights'" by the "noted female advocate of that dogma . . . perambulating this State with Susan B. Anthony." Duniway exclaimed defensively:

> When all mothers find employment for their young and growing sons *as we have* there will be no gangs of idle ruffians running loose in the streets to entrap children into mischief. Under man-made laws the city of Portland is so dirty and vile that children who have honorable employment cannot go into the street for a little needed exercise without being trapped into temptation by the children of mothers who "have all the rights they want."[40]

Gossip and slander were the most potent weapons employed against

Mrs. Duniway throughout her life, so she was very sensitive about her family's reputation. But her ideals often conflicted with reality, filling her with an ever-increasing sense of martyrdom for her cause. On one occasion she repudiated a claim that her "poor 'head of the family' was compelled to 'do without his victuals unless he cooked them himself.'" She replied that "a woman who is capable of carrying forward any great public enterprise is also able to hire capable housekeepers and manage her kitchen by proxy." Her home, she said, was "clean and commodious and healthful and plentiful."[41]

Rumors continued to circulate, however, frequently as jokes told by men who knew perfectly well that they were not true. A lady on a steamboat confided to Duniway, not knowing who she was, that the purser said Oregon's leading suffragist "drinks, and smokes and swears like a man." The man who had warned against votes for prostitutes at the Temperance Alliance meeting of 1872 accused Duniway herself ten years later, when he thought she was not present, "of indulging in Bacchanalian revelries with men" in her hotel rooms. She marched to the platform and demanded a retraction. She also got her revenge: "Suppose that I, . . . imagining that Mr. Driver was absent, had dragged his name before the assembly, and repeated the often circulated scandal, falsely accusing him of killing four of his deceased wives!" The gathering soon broke up "in profound silence."[42]

On a visit to Independence, Oregon, a southern-dominated town, Duniway encountered gossip linking her with Senator Nesmith, an anti-Mitchell Republican. "Relics of obscene stories," she wrote,

> which he is charged with having related as parts of conversation between him and ourself, are still sniffed as a choice relish by some of his filthy admirers, and we would not allude to them at all save for the purpose of informing the wives of some of these foul-minded beings that kind Providence has always furnished us with better company than J. W. Nesmith; that we never conversed with him on any topic in our life, and never rode in a stage-coach where he was; that we never spoke to him but once, and that was about a year ago, and by the merest accident; that he never introduced us to an audience in The Dalles or anywhere else; and we doubt that he ever claimed that he did.

Nesmith was not such a fool as to risk a libel case, she went on, so the gossipers had better "find out whether or not he is really guilty of saying he did [address us in improper language] before they condemn us everlastingly because of his sin."[43]

The gossip did not die. Nine months later it was published in the *Portland Sunday Welcome.* Before their mother even saw the paper, Willis and Hubert publicly avenged her honor by caning the editor and getting themselves arrested for assault and battery. When Mrs. Duniway went weeping down the street past groups of whispering men, Republican Attorney Dolph proffered his arm to protect her. The elderly Presbyterian minister Reverend Lindsley told her that Galileo, St. Stephen, and Christ had been martyred too, while Republican Prosecuting Attorney John F. Caples privately assured her sons that they "did exactly right." Harvey Scott's *Oregonian* carried "a blistering editorial . . . hotly excoriating any paper that tried to slur or slander the good name of a faithful mother." The Republican-appointed grand jury found no case against the Duniway boys, while the editor soon admitted the story was a mistake. But the caning as well as the gossip was picked up by other papers like the *Walla Walla Union* and continued to undermine Duniway's reputation among the pious.[44]

Under such circumstances, Abigail Scott Duniway's frequent attestations of loyalty to her "invalid" husband and repeated insistence that her campaign for women's rights was his idea are quite understandable. She had little choice. But reading between the lines of her novels and editorials and assessing the evidence of her family's behavior, one may judge that Abigail Duniway's marriage was seldom as harmonious as she claimed. Nor were her children unusually enlightened.

Benjamin Duniway's health declined precipitously during the *New Northwest* years, but at first he accompanied his wife on easier lecture tours. They went to concerts, plays, and lectures together, including a two-week Chautauqua one summer. Occasionally, after she rushed to catch a predawn train or late-night boat, she recorded Ben's presence carrying her bags and begging her to remain home a little longer. He advised her against using confrontation tactics, but she seldom listened.

When Abigail Duniway wrote up her *New Northwest* account of the hog killing on their farm, she added "P.S.—Mr. D. says that 'hog scrape' happened so long ago he guesses we'd better not tell it. (He spoke too late, though.)" Ben probably perceived that the incident would not help his wife's reputation with the Portland elite. Ben also had little confidence in Abigail's financial judgment, and this contributed to the family tradition that she was spendthrift and impulsive and could not manage money. An exchange between the two of them at the Oregon State Woman Suffrage convention of 1880 suggests a tension which was not entirely humorous. The meeting was debating the question of whether women could leave home to engage in public life and whether they would lose the high regard of men if they did. Mr. Duniway said "that he had no difficulty in running the home by proxy during his wife's absence. . . . There were always plenty of good looking women to hire— cheap." Mrs. Duniway remarked "that the best men of the country have a higher regard for the women who want to vote than for any others.

She said she was neither young nor handsome, but was sure she could marry again in a month if she were a widow."[45]

As the years passed, Abigail Duniway became increasingly resentful of Ben's failures. Though she loved him, she also felt that she had made a bad marriage, one that better laws and more knowledge would have saved her from. Again and again she claimed that a girl of eighteen was too young to marry, though she had done it, and some of her sisters had been even younger. By the time they were adults the boys all knew that "mother and father are not congenial." She herself wrote Clyde, "There's an end to everything under the sun but an unhappy marriage." His father had "sapped all my younger life."[46] Judith Reid's disgust with her husband in Duniway's *New Northwest* serial of 1871 contrasts sharply with the Mansfields' ideal marital harmony in her *Captain Gray's Company*, written in 1859.

Like her other novels, *Ethel Graeme's Destiny* shows Duniway's awareness of the need for secrecy about marital misery. The heroine, married too young, soon learns to fear and hate her drunken husband. But she also fears to disobey him because of public opinion, which will blame his drunkenness on *her* failures as a wife. Furthermore, "there is nothing that so humiliates a woman, or from which she will so intuitively shrink, as the acknowledgment that she has made a mistake in her matrimonial ventures." Ethel Graeme is "not a new-fashioned woman. . . . I deprecate, detest, and utterly repudiate the 'affinity' doctrines of certain latter-day reformers, who attempt to palliate and excuse their own derelictions by accusations, no matter how truthful, against their erring lords. Two *wrongs* never did make one *right*." Ethel is afraid that any "accusation against him would doubly react upon myself and his children."[47]

Why, then, does the heroine tell her story? She continues:

> The adventurous mariner who has guided his vessel through a long-continued storm, past rocks and shoals and breakers, striving vigilantly the while to keep his traveling companions in blissful ignorance of the common danger, does not forget, when the peril is past, to place beacons in the great highway of the ocean, as a warning to those who may come after him.

Ethel is so bitter that she cries, "rather than see my child compelled, even through a match of her own choosing, to walk such a road as I had traveled, I would willingly hang her with my own hands to a friendly tree."[48]

Mrs. Duniway was usually too busy for wedding anniversaries or other celebrations. Lecturing in Lafayette on the subject of marriage, she had to be reminded of her twenty-first anniversary by the minister who had performed the ceremony. The next year she made plans for Ben to join her at Astoria, but apparently *he* forgot. When she met the steamer he was not on it. Worried, she took the steamer herself back to Portland for the day and then made sure that Ben would join her a week later at Astoria. Her anniversary column was no paean to marital bliss:

> How memory darts back over the dreary distance that spans the intervening years! And now a vision comes of a hopeful bridegroom and pale young bride; a household in tears; . . . . with one vacant chair . . . for we were the first to leave the paternal home. . . . Gray hairs have slightly silvered the head of one of us, and deep furrows long ago traced themselves in the brow of the other; but twenty-two years of toil and pleasure; of trial, disappointment, and success; of mistakes, experiences, and hopes, have builded themselves a witness in a large family without one vacant chair. . . . Blessed be thou, O veil of Futurity, for thou hidest from the children of men the troubles in store for them. . . . Thou weavest sweet promises for the time to come, and leavest naught in the wake but Education, the handmaiden of Experience.[49]

No one can miss the emphasis on "dreary" years, toil, and disappointment, nor the repeated "vacant chair," which conveyed Duniway's sense of her youthful mistake—and the one she hoped daughter Clara would not make. In these early *New Northwest* years, Clara Belle Duniway was becoming an increasingly attractive young woman. Her mother was determined that Clara was to be a lady, albeit an enlightened, hardworking, woman's-right-and-suffrage lady. No man was good enough for Abigail Duniway's musical and gifted daughter—certainly not the man Clara currently favored!

Don Stearns, Clara's future husband, had arrived in Portland by 1875 and immediately usurped one of Abigail Duniway's own cherished projects. He started the first evening newspaper in Portland, something she had wanted to do herself two years earlier. Worse yet, Stearns was from Missouri—rough and uncultured by Duniway's standards, a man without money or class who was given to drinking, smoking, and "rakish" living.[50] The advice about "exalted love" which appeared in Duniway's novels during these years was primarily intended for her own daughter. In 1875, Clara was twenty-one.

Duniway's *Madge Morrison, Mollala Maid and Matron,* in which Madge had been enticed away from her mother to a runaway marriage, was filled with such literary gems as, "When a wholly practical man, with no more conception of ideality than an ox, gets his mind on matrimony, there isn't much poetry about it." The widower courting the widow in order to obtain her land "leaned heavily against her for an instant and whispered the old, old story, which ever is and ever will be sweet to woman, . . . even if her better judgment tells her that its fruit will be Sodom apples in her hands, its taste, at last, the taste of ashes to her soul."[51]

In 1877, two years later, Duniway called the infatuation of young lovers an "affliction" like smallpox, which "oftener destroys than restores those who are the blind victims of its ravages." "Sometimes love is like leprosy," she continued, "fastening its virus in the veins of its victim and fettering the subject for life to the chains of a slow consumption of all that was sparkling and hopeful. . . .[N]ot one married couple in twenty is mated; . . . the appearance of harmony in nineteen out of twenty homes is a delusion painfully apparent to one or more of the parties most deeply interested, if not to all the nearest friends of the victims."[52]

Such vehemence reflected the anguish of a profound disappointment. The passage was written immediately after Abigail Duniway learned that Clara Belle Duniway had eloped with Don Stearns. It happened while Mrs. Duniway was on her trip East to the Centennial Exposition. She left in June 1876 and did not return for ten months, partly because she had fallen ill for six weeks at a relative's home in Illinois—possibly as a reaction to the vicious reviews of her book. When she finally reached Portland, exhausted and depressed, at the end of March 1877, she discovered that beloved Clara was married. Don Stearns, who knew that Mrs. Duniway opposed the match, had persuaded Clara to a secret ceremony two months earlier, across the river in Washington Territory. Clyde Duniway remembered that when his mother was told,

> she broke out into one of her uncontrollable fits of temper, and during the course of things Clara fainted. It was then that Mother Duniway wished that her daughter would never come out of her coma. Later, though, everything was all smoothed over for the public eyes, and Mrs. Duniway had the wedding quietly announced, and held a party for her daughter. It was a secret that was kept within the family.[53]

The irony of Clara's situation was that it was foretold by her mother in several novels about elopements of innocent, foolish young girls misled by rash and dissolute men who brought them nothing but suffering and early death. For example, in 1872 Duniway wrote of Ellen Dowd, whose infatuation led her to marry "just over the border, within two miles of home." "The law failed to save my Ellen from herself! It failed to save her from the lust and poverty and wretchedness entailed upon her by a worthless nobody," mourned the mother. "The fond mother of a beautiful young girl may enjoin and enforce strict obedience from her as a minor until some hot-brained animal chooses to make her his legal mistress, and then a short ceremony of a few awful words of the law . . . makes of her an accursed nonentity, renders the further attempts of parents to protect their darling futile, null and void!"[54] Clara was not impressed.

In the spring of 1877, *Edna and John, A Romance of Idaho Flat* described

Edna's mother's reactions to "the fearful shock she had felt when the news of Edna's marriage had burst upon her like a thunderbolt." She would now live only for the day "when Edna, repentant and sorrowing, would yearn for the mother love that in her blindness she had cast from her" to become "the creature of a stranger's will." Mother love was the only kind that lasted, unselfishly; all else would fail. "Your mother . . . will permit herself to be unjustified forever in your eyes, rather than you shall feel the wounds recoil upon yourself that you inflict upon her. If you are a daughter who has been unfilial, your atonement will come when your own children trample upon your heartstrings." When a man "lures your child to a ruin that he can legalize by marriage laws, you can only welter in your own agony."[55]

The Duniways always disapproved of Don Stearns. Mrs. Duniway feared that Stearns was marrying Clara for her money, and she apparently also knew something about his personal life and character for which she never forgave him. Clara, however, with true Scott initiative, aspired to be independent of her mother. Shortly after her marriage she ran an ad in the *New Northwest* offering to act as purchasing agent, at 5 percent commission, for people in the country who wished to buy in Portland stores. She also helped her husband with his newspaper and continued giving piano lessons. A "very attractive and brilliant young woman," Clara was more like her mother than her mother wished her to be.[56]

The Stearnses floundered in financial troubles for several years. Forced to compete with the new *Oregonian*-sponsored *Evening Telegram,* Stearns's muckraking *Portland Evening Bee* survived only until 1880, when it succumbed to a merger with the *Telegram.* Though Don Stearns was "a wide-awake young man from Omaha," his "capital consisted almost wholly of super-abounding energy, hopefulness and desperate courage." Sale of the *Bee* enabled him to become a land speculator, planting prune orchards in Oregon and Clarke County, Washington, and then selling divided tracts at a large profit. His "visionary" schemes were backed by the *Oregonian's* H. L. Pittock until he tried to establish a paper company and resort at the shallow Lake Camus on the Washougal during the recession of 1884. Like one of Duniway's fictional villains, Stearns "brought his wife and small child up there to live in . . . swampy desolation," where Clara "was taken ill by something mysterious" which he treated for months with hot lemonade. In the summer of 1885 she came home, with her young son, suffering from consumption. Ben Duniway cared for her with the help of her brothers, while Abigail continued her lecture tours and writing. In January 1886, at the age of thirty-one, Clara died.[57]

During the preceding months, Mrs. Duniway had written an involved

novel about the "DeLauncy Curse," a curse that infected three generations with runaway marriages—a destiny inescapable which also led to
madness in its victims. The mother says to her daughter in the first
chapter,

> "I knew, when you ran away and married Andrew, that what you thought,
> in your youth and inexperience, was a love match was in reality a passion-
> blinded escapade, from which you would awaken too late, too late. Oh, my
> poor child! You sowed the wind. I knew there was nothing compatible
> between you two, but I prayed God that he would keep you blinded
> always."[58]

The theme of death pervades the novel, death as "one of earth's greatest
blessings" in age or infirmity and the beginning of heavenly happiness
and forgiveness for all sins, especially the sin of marrying without parental permission. Clara was reading the *New Northwest* until just before she
died, so that to a modern reader the words of her mother seem cruelly
lugubrious. But Abigail Scott Duniway came out of a Calvinist tradition
which freely spoke of death and sin in the presence of the dying. She
may even have intended to comfort Clara in her own tactless fashion.

Whatever the case, Clara's death deeply stirred Duniway's sense of loss
and mission. Five days afterward she reported Clara's last words,

> "I wish I could go with you darling," we said, with choking utterance, . . . as
> the dear one, struggling for breath, looked with an unspoken appeal into
> our tear-dimmed eyes. And as she fought feebly against her impending
> fate, she painfully gasped in answer, "You must finish your work, Ma!"

Then, in the same account, Mrs. Duniway listed all the signs of progress
in the condition of women which might indicate that her work could be
completed "within the next decade of years." She chose, under the circumstances, an odd analogy. Having referred in her first paragraph to
Clara as "the precious earth-life that has throbbed in unison with ours
since the days of our earliest womanhood," she now spoke of

> "our work," not because we have in any sense a monopoly of it, but because
> we have long been so completely submerged in it that we have come to be
> recognized as part and parcel thereof. The work years ago adopted us; and
> to the extent that the parent is the property of the child, the work is "ours".

A year later, after the *New Northwest* was sold, she said she felt as if she
had lost another child.[59]

Clara's marriage and death were not the only family troubles that
Abigail Duniway had to deal with during the *New Northwest* years.
Though Willis and Wilkie both followed their mother's advice about
waiting to get married (until they were thirty-eight and thirty-two, re-

spectively), Willis was known in the family to be passionate and fickle, and Wilkie, tempted by gambling, sometimes kept "bad companions." Wilkie later remarked that "Willis is all right at heart, but is troubled with weakness of the flesh. A pretty woman seems to turn his head." And his mother worried that "There is no forecasting the future of a man who goes wrong in *sex*."[60]

Hubert's problems were even worse. Young girls from the country frequently boarded with the Duniways while they obtained an education in Portland. In 1877 one of the boarders got pregnant. Ida Leslie and Hubert, both just eighteen, had been as foolish as many another adolescent in every era. There was another tempestuous episode, but Mrs. Duniway managed the situation in accordance with her principles. Hubert, she said, *must* marry the girl. She packed them both off to San Francisco to live temporarily. Then, after the baby was born in April 1878, Duniway took charge, bringing the three-month-old child home to Portland while Ida and Hubert waited in San Francisco. Duniway's *New Northwest* "Editorial Correspondence" of 1 August 1878 described her trip to California and "spontaneous" adoption of a "precious little orphaned waif." The "change of food and the hardships of the journey" on a cold and crowded ship caused him to die within a week, she said. Ida stayed on with the Duniways, but Hubert "behaved like a bachelor." He was already engaged to Cora Parsons before the "domestic and simple" Ida, stricken with tuberculosis, died at twenty-three. As brother Clyde put it, "If she had lived, Hubert might have felt tied down."[61]

Once again, Duniway's *New Northwest* novels reflected family events. In *Fact, Fate and Fancy; or, More Ways of Living than One*, published between September 1878 and May 1879, her theme was marriage and mismarriage. She included a young girl who went insane after having a baby because the man refused to marry her, and another whose husband had married her without love and caused her unending misery. Finally the latter takes poison in order to free herself and her husband. "Five years of unloved wifehood is a long time to live and suffer," she tells him. "I have called the great physician, Death, to release you from your bonds. You may be happy yet." A year later she was writing about the sin of unloving wedlock as the source of "discord, crime and misery" whose progeny can only be a "curse" upon the race.[62]

Believing as she did that children inherited bad characteristics from parental lustfulness, she saw her own children's behavior (and later that of Clara's son Earl) as evidence of such sin. Not only was the plot of *The DeLauncey Curse* based upon this idea; she also spoke of it to her children themselves. Referring to her hopes that Willis would soon be "happily and honestly married," she told Clyde that marriage would help Willis immensely, "provided he was pleased with his choice; otherwise he would be of all men most miserable. His unrest in this regard, as well as your own, is the heritage of ante-natal environment; and oh, I do *hope* it will not be transmitted to your children."[63]

Apparently Duniway had reason for concern. Another letter mentioned that the affianced Miss Baker (whom Willis did not marry after all), "seems to be just the mate Wis needs to correct his shortcomings. She knows *all* about him, but is so deeply in love that she has entirely forgiven his past mistakes, and says that just as she forgives the past, she by that measure will demand steadfastness in the future." (When Willis finally did marry, he became a devoted, sentimental husband for the rest of his life. He and Alice MacCormac had no children, but she suffered from some serious physical ailment almost every two years. One suspects frequent miscarriages.)[64]

Between the Scylla and Carybdis of exalted nineteenth-century public respectability and private morality, Abigail Scott Duniway was only one of many who struggled to keep afloat. She conveyed, through her writing and lecturing, despite family scandals and "necessary" hypocrisies, the values and norms of a revolutionary cultural change. To twentieth-century descendants of such reformers, Duniway's gospel of personal autonomy and sexual control may seem as repressive as it was liberating. But women who see the issue of rape as one of the prime symbols of male oppression throughout history[65] can certainly appreciate an unpublished poem found among Abigail Duniway's papers.

Entitled "Dream," the poem uses a monster to symbolize male lust, a red cloak to symbolize sexuality, a white veil for renunciation and freedom, and rape as the essential condition of unprotected and unfree women. Only an escape from forced sex and its consequences can make women free and equal, she implies. Walking "through crowded streets" with a "sister, fair and dear, / . . . / While ever in the distance—half concealed— / A hideous shadow seemed to hold us back," the poem's narrator "entered a great Council Hall" with "men of all degrees of culture":

And now the monster shade drew near and glared
With eyes blood red, like wild infuriate beast.
Fixing his gaze on me, his head bent low,
With one fierce plunge he laid me at his feet, . . .

A "brother" held the beast at bay while she prayed for deliverance. "Men gazed at us but seemed inert to help." She knew that only

by faith
I kept the monster down behind the man,
Who ever pressed more close; his arms, like fetters

Holding me, as in a tightening vise;
Until I knew not which I dreaded most,
The man or beast.

Two "Gen d'arms" arrived, but only replied to her cry for help,

"Be still, submit, or peradventure he may strike you dead."
Then in my wrath I cried "'Tis passing strange,
That no one dare attack this beast.
Are all men cowards?"

She then loosed the clasp of her red mantle, which she had heard "infuriates the beast." Making her escape, she found "a drapery of purest white" which, like a sail, sped her up "widening paths" and "a mountain grand." Suddenly remembering her friend, she thought,

Should I go back? Nay, nay, had I remained,
Could I have saved myself? By prayer and faith
I kept the monster down as in a spell;
But in some nerveless hour I might have slept;
And woe to those who sleep when danger threats.
Now was I free—to work for her, my sister,
And my sisters one and all.

The poem concludes with Duniway's own "Interpretation":

What was it that we feared?
Not man the peer of Christ,
In semblance, like unto the "perfect One,"
Who unto woman is a brother true.
But we did fear the beast in human guise,
Who erst controlled as slaves the weaker sex
By masterly brute force and power of might;
Coercing oft "with stick no bigger than his thumb."
For thus in English tongue proclaimed the law;
Impotent, hence, the law, to curb the beast.
Woman alone, through innate strength divine,
Must take him by the horns and free herself,
Thus freeing womankind; and best of all,
Re-forming in the man his better self;
That he may stand erect before our God
Whose image he doth bear.

The threatening sexual implications of the nineteenth-century woman's rights movement were very real. Arguments against double-standard hypocrisy and for the essential purity and spirituality of true love, along with a woman's right to give or withhold sexual activity as she herself judged best, were opinions which also profoundly affected the personal lives of men. When the price men were asked to pay for women's equality was abstinence and purity, the political issue of the ballot took on an emasculating social significance.

CHAPTER 8

Of Prayer and Prohibition

"A race of free, enlightened mothers will naturally produce
a race of free, enlightened sons."

To the pious women and ministers of the proliferating and competing evangelical churches, Mrs. Duniway's concern for sexual reform was often disturbing. But the freethinking radicalism of her religious beliefs was anathema. The Calvinism of Duniway's childhood had left its mark on her character, and biblical imagery came naturally to her rhetoric. Nevertheless, rebellion against hell-fire preaching led Duniway to an iconoclastic skepticism in maturity. She clashed openly and frequently with representatives of orthodox piety.

Religious and cultural loyalties in the post–Civil War Northwest, as in the rest of the country, were interrelated with attitudes toward woman suffrage. The uneasy peace which had followed so much devastation included an upsurge in sentimental piety together with an ever-increasing emphasis on propriety and conformity. At the same time, new developments in biblical scholarship and scientific research—most notably Darwin's evolutionary theory—made free thought, agnosticism, and the "scientific" investigation of spiritual phenomena both more appealing and more feared. Many Americans in the 1870s and 1880s shared emotional religiosity, even in sectarian diversity. Many ministers, threatened by the secularizing tendencies of urbanization and eclecticism, resented all reform and reformers that were not church-centered and piously orthodox.[1]

One of the most notable movements to grow out of this religious conservatism was a new and militant form of temperance agitation aimed at legal prohibition of all alcoholic beverages. Starting as a passionate crusade of middle- and upper-class women singing and praying in saloons until they were arrested and jailed, it swept the country in the winter of 1874 and became institutionalized in the Women's Christian Temperance Union (WCTU). The movement at first opposed female suffrage as contrary to true womanhood. Gradually its members joined and then transformed the suffrage battle. Prohibitionists in the Pacific Northwest became a major factor in the development of Abigail Scott

131

Duniway's political campaign.[2] Her troubles with the WCTU were almost inevitable.

At the beginning of the 1874 "Women's War on Whiskey" in Portland, Abigail Duniway welcomed the crusade in the *New Northwest* because it would "bring women to the knowledge that they can deviate from long-established customs without bringing down the heavens upon their heads." "We have much faith in the potency of singing and prayer," she added, only to contradict herself the next week: "We have no faith in prayer alone to accomplish anything." "Prayer," she went on, "is simply a form of expression of humanity's desires, . . . yet without works it is dead. 'Trust in God and keep your powder dry.' This is the watchword. . . ." Such frontier-style pragmatism did not appeal to the well-bred ladies of the Portland Temperance Crusade. Duniway also assured her readers that the ballot alone was worth more "than all the temperance societies, conventions, resolutions and crusades that can be formed . . . in half a century."[3]

"Called" to California to lecture that spring, Mrs. Duniway again antagonized the pious. A minister in a Stockton audience said suffragists were women who "consort with infidels." She shot back with a "bomb" in her usual extemporaneous fashion. Christ too had associated with publicans and sinners, she exclaimed, while she herself "believed in prayer and in Christianity, but not in the puffed up churchanity of the nineteenth century. Some hissed, some applauded, and some left the church." As after all such episodes, Duniway was exhausted from "a succession of bilious attacks, aggravated by constant travel and public speaking."[4]

When the Duniways moved to Portland, the first and only minister to call at their house was the Reverend Thomas Lamb Eliot of the newly established Portland Unitarian Church.[5] While many clergymen were dubious about suffrage, Eliot encouraged and supported it. Duniway attended his church regularly when she was in town, though she never actually joined it. Privately she was still skeptical, remarking to Clyde twenty years later that she had just heard Mr. Eliot "preach the only really powerful sermon I ever heard from his pen" on the Easter Sunday that her son Ralph joined the church. "I thought some of joining, but couldn't quite get down to it; it seemed so silly. Yet I was glad for Ralph to try it." The Unitarian emphasis on freedom of thought, moral responsibility, and intellectual investigation suited the temperaments of many mid-nineteenth-century reformers like Duniway. But antitrinitarians seemed so heretical to evangelical Christians that more than ten years after Eliot came on his chosen "mission" to Oregon he was still denied membership in the Portland YMCA and shunned by the orthodox. (As late as 1916, there were only four Unitarian churches in Oregon, with a total membership of 532.)[6]

Duniway's friendship with and support from Jews in Portland also contributed to her controversialism. She remained loyal to Jacob Mayer, the businessman who had given her a start in the millinery trade. Portland's Solomon Hirsch, financier, legislator, and Republican ambassador to Turkey, was one of her prime political supporters. In the 1882 Oregon legislature, he himself faced vicious anti-Semitic criticism. Rabbi Stephen Wise, later renowned among Reform Jews and in the liberal community of New York, began his rabbinical work in Portland, where he and Mrs. Duniway became good friends.[7]

Duniway was interested in spiritualism, too, as it related to her religious rationalism. She did not, as some biographers have claimed, escape into it after the death of her daughter, but rather had been intrigued for years by spiritualist teaching as a mode of scientific inquiry into religious truth. Duniway's sister Harriet became a practicing medium. Many notable Oregonians shared her curiosity and even joined in seances. But in the 1870s Oregonians also remembered that the notorious Victoria Woodhull had been national president of the Spiritualist Association and that contemporary scientists were apparently trying to discredit everything from creation to the Bible.[8]

Duniway claimed as early as 1873 that if angels had been able to talk to Abraham, Jacob, and Moses, it was "equally possible for them . . . to do the same today." She compared some spiritualists who "do wicked deeds" to some equally damnable clergymen who do not therefore "prove that there is no truth or good in Christianity." "We have seen," she continued,

sufficient evidences of the super-mundane power of disembodied spirits to satisfy us . . . and . . . we know . . . that any honest seeker after scientific facts can receive the same knowledge, if he is willing and will try. We look upon Spiritualism, not as a religion, but as a science. . . . We belong to no society or order of Spiritualists, and neither shall we. But we are . . . willing to investigate the phenomena . . . just as we investigate astronomy, the law of gravitation, the diurnal and yearly revolutions of the earth or the circulation of the blood.[9]

After Clara Duniway Stearns died in January 1886, Mrs. Duniway did indeed find her spiritualist convictions comforting. "I heard from her, through private psychic sources," she said later. That winter she also saw the guardian ghost of Colonel E. B. Baker in her photograph.[10] She was still defending spiritualist ideas in her later writings, though son Clyde scoffed at the dreams and telepathic communications she frequently reported to him.

The captain in *From the West to the West* tells his daughter, "All religions have their origins in human selfishness." " 'Better say they originate in

human needs,' replied Jean; 'but selfishness is universal, all the same.'"
Duniway did not wish to deny the need for religion, only to minimize the
importance of differences. In the same novel she had the brilliant doctor
say, "We can't know much about the mystery we call God. It makes little
difference to the humanity of the various nations of the earth, all of
whom must worship the Divine Idea, whether it be called Vishnu,
Chrishna, Isis, Allah, Jehovah."[11] This skeptical, open-minded ap-
proach to religion was an outrage to the orthodox. *New Northwest* readers
accused Duniway of blasphemy when she told them in an editorial in
1880:

> The fatherhood of God and the brotherhood of man is the creed of en-
> lightened religionists the world over; a creed that embraces the Golden
> Rule, whether it is expressed after the Christian, the Brahman, the Confu-
> cian or the Mohammedan form. Religion did not originate with Chris-
> tianity, nor do Christians alone embody the idea of conscientiousness.
> Everybody's God must necessarily differ from every other person's God. He
> is a creation of the individual's mind which conceives Him, and is the
> product of his own understanding. . . . It matters not to us whether God be
> styled Ormuzd, Isis, Bramin, Thor, Prometheus, Josh, Theos, Pan or
> Jehovah.[12]

A reader in 1881 accused the *New Northwest* of "taking a stand of open
hostility to the church." She answered that churches were indeed necessary to keep society from a "relapse into barbarism."

> This paper is strongly in favor of good and faithful progressive preachers.
> Its publishers are proud to claim as personal friends many of the foremost
> clergymen of the day. With humanitarian Christianity it has ever been in
> perfect accord. But the senior editor has often encountered a narrow,
> puritanical, blue-law *churchanity*, which bars its doors against her work, and,
> with an over-pious and super-holy air, turns its priestly back upon her
> mission. This bubble of pharisaical unrighteousness is always punctured in
> these columns when it attempts to blockade the pathway of human rights
> with the Bible. We are sorry our correspondent has failed to discriminate
> between the religion of the New Testament and the bigoted cant of the
> scribes, pharisees and hypocrites who sometimes attempt to thwart her
> work, and whom she never fails to denounce.[13]

Duniway attended a "holiness" camp meeting in Oregon one day in
1886. The fervent preaching and the mourner's bench reminded her of
her childhood, and her reaction was not enthusiastic. Nor was her perceptive analysis received enthusiastically:

> We believe their experiences are spiritual manifestations; . . . that the man-
> ifestations are caused by mental concentration and the physical contact of

the "altar," where they meet and kneel and mingle promiscuously, singing and shouting together, till they form a magnetic current, which communicates its force through invisible agencies to their entire circuit. We believe that all religious revivals are the result of the excited conditions that accompany physical contact, mind force, singing, preaching and prayer. We were converted in childhood through the same experience, and we never enter such a circle without a recurrence of the old-time thrill. Therefore, we never laugh at it, though we have analyzed and thus learned to comprehend it through years of critical investigation.[14]

In 1875, at the height of a nationwide fundamentalist revival featuring Dwight L. Moody's clarion calls to "Accept Christ and be saved" and then join some church immediately, Duniway gave her brother Harvey space in the *New Northwest* for a series of erudite articles about religion and evolution. When readers complained vociferously, accusing both Scott and Duniway of heresy, Harvey Scott wrote a spirited defense. "Religious excitation" is "no longer as prevalent as in the past," he said, but "with clearer views of the constitution of the universe and of the relation of man to the Supreme Power have come dignity, constancy, and self-possession, with also a wholesome leaven of disbelief in ecclesiastical dogmatism." A similar series of essays—this one on atheism and social justice, written by an Englishwoman in Idaho—appeared in the *New Northwest* in 1882.[15] Combined with Mrs. Duniway's disdain for hypocritical "churchanity," such theological independence made her politics appear threatening to clerical as well as sexual order.

Two eastern clergymen discovered as much when they met Duniway on a train in Illinois in 1876. They were returning from a Moody revival, and she let them know her opinion: "Certainly, if we could believe the plan of eternal salvation to be as stupendous a failure as most persons seem to imagine who are looking to Brother Moody to be saved, we should feel that Omnipotence was badly outdistanced by the spirit of evil. People in a revival are just as unreasonable as they are in a war." Shocked by her arguments, the ministers compared her to the "notorious unbeliever named Ingersoll," who was known throughout the country as "the Dwight L. Moody of Free Religion," "the nation's most outspoken infidel and a scourge of the churches." As a matter of fact, Mrs. Duniway had been a schoolmate of Mrs. Ingersoll and was proud to announce the relationship. She claimed to be both more radical and more Christian than the orthodox:

"Go to the root of evils," we answered promptly. "Quit insulting high Heaven by your senseless sanctimony, and demand that the precepts and example of Jesus be followed by all who name His name. Jesus said, 'Sell all that thou hast and give to the poor and follow me.' . . . Would you espouse any cause, even for Jesus' sake, if it cost you your fancied respectability to do so?"

When the ministers sneeringly suggested that Mrs. Duniway thought women's rights would solve all problems, she replied that it would take time, but

> if women had their legal, political, and financial rights—equality before the law in all things—they would wage a successful war against prostitution, the ally of the devil, who is making more sinners in a day than Moody can save in a twelvemonth. . . . Then, if wives and mothers had the rights against which you sneer, but which Jesus gave us in the Golden Rule, they could wage such a war against intemperance as would fail to glorify itself because a saloon changed hands and saved one man by destroying another.[16]

This friendly exchange took place just three months after another confrontation. While visiting relatives in Illinois during her trip East in 1876, Duniway reported with righteous wrath an inhospitable rejection by the Reverend J. R. Lowrance, the minister who had lived with her family before they moved to Oregon. He refused to meet her or to let her speak in his church. Duniway chose to forget that she had made known her own feelings about him in one of the first issues of her newspaper:

> A milk-and-water specimen of humanity, for whom we never entertained the smallest iota of personal respect, a thin-haired, thin-visaged and flabby-looking clergyman who made his home at our house, and whom we grumblingly worked for, performed the one good deed of his long sojourn by subscribing to the New York *Tribune*, and we would purloin it from his table and peruse it regularly.[17]

Now that she was planning a visit to Lincoln, Illinois, she told her readers,

> Chief among those whom we had most delighted (in our verdancy) to remember, was Rev. J. R. Lowrance, the pastor who received us into the church in our childhood, who knew us well in early womanhood, and whom we looked to greet after a quarter century's absence with the same gladsome cheer with which we have everywhere else been met since these tedious journeyings began.

She wrote to tell him of her coming, asking him to obtain a church for her lectures,

> inasmuch as he had, in the beginning of his ministerial career, made his home at our father's house for years whenever he had been so disposed,

which was not seldom, and had always enjoyed yellow-legged chickens and other creature comforts with as much freedom as they had been bestowed.

She herself had often "washed and ironed his dirty linen."[18]

An abrupt note, signed by E. J. and J. R. Lowrance,[19] informed Mrs. Duniway that the minister's house was full and that he had "no controll" over the local church. She went to another minister instead, sending Lowrance (and publishing in the *New Northwest* "Editorial Correspondence" column) one of her inimitable letters.

> Dear Brother:—I am very glad to get your note, seeing it was in your heart to write it. My house will always be large enough to hold you, even as my mother's ever was. And when you come to Portland, Oregon, though I have no pastoral "controll" of any church in the city, I have sufficient moral influence, which I shall gladly use, to get you a hearing in any of them. I . . . shall keep your card to show to my father that he may see the effect of casting bread upon the waters. In Christian love. A. J. Duniway.

Duniway next learned that a "low-minded, untruthful specimen of mental nastiness . . . another preacher's wife" had spread stories that Duniway advocated free love. Duniway secured a witness who could prove that she "had never visited the evil-minded crone at all . . . and . . . [that] the whole thing was a black and infamous *lie*."

> We charged the lie upon her, and if the church were governed by purity and dignity, instead of self-righteousness and vain-glory, it would rid itself speedily of Poindexter and her and Lowrance. The good people rallied to our support by hundreds, in spite of the slander, and if we didn't warm the wax in the enemy's ears, it wasn't the fault of the undersigned.[20]

Clearly, Abigail Duniway's combativeness sometimes carried her too far. The slander and cruelty which followed her everywhere aroused her frontier conviction that "self-preservation" was the "primary law" of existence.[21] When she was wounded, her militancy, quick temper, and natural tactlessness unconsciously invited attack. Her sense of being on the front line of the suffrage battle was to her both exhilarating and disturbing, but she succumbed to the temptation facing almost every reformer; she sometimes became egocentric and excessively paranoid. She certainly was incapable of practicing the meekness and piety so extolled by nineteenth-century "true womanhood."

Nor did she wish to be meek and pious. One reason she clashed with the women of the Portland Temperance Crusade in 1874 was that she so thoroughly disdained their upper-class status, religious hypocrisy, and open snobbery. Speaking the truth as she saw it, she described the crusaders as follows:

A pitiful picture has been drawn by some one . . . unacquainted with the *kind* of women engaged in this war—of the neglected household, the hen-pecked husband tending the baby, the ungoverned, hungry, crying children, of a generally disorganized, demoralized family. This is a mistake. . . . The women actively engaged in the movement are not those whose shoulders bear the burden of household drudgery, nor of daily toil . . . but the women of wealth, of position, who have many spare hours in life, the young ladies who sit in the parlor entertaining idle callers, or dawdling over novels. . . . Women who have turned with timid horror from the possible publicity and vulgarities involved in woman's voting have not deemed it too public to kneel in the open street, amid a half-jeering rabble, and tell Jesus the story of their sorrows, or too vulgar to enter the vilest liquor den and bandy words with degraded sots. . . . Welcome any excitement, any fanaticism, that will arouse in woman the desire to have an *actual existence:* the desire to be a concrete number in the sum-total of humanity![22]

Duniway confronted these women in person, too, along with their ministers. She did not like the two young antisuffrage ministers from the East who were organizers of the Temperance Crusade. Mr. Izer and Mr. Medbury, of the Methodist and Baptist churches respectively, had just joined their newly formed congregations in Portland and "had no notion that the women should do anything except as they should dictate." These conceited "ministerial boys" insisted on such "fulsome adoration" as to "nauseate . . . the great Omnipotent." (She respected Congregationalist "Dr. Atkinson, being a much older man, and consequently not over-conceited about his personal holiness." He was a pioneer of 1848.)[23] Izer and Medbury organized WCTU meetings during the summer of 1874 at which Duniway insisted on speaking in extemporaneous camp-meeting fashion about the importance of the vote and the uselessness of prayer without power. (Eastern churches were accustomed to having exclusive control of their membership and meetings, while Duniway's Cumberland Presbyterian background took for granted the sharing of churches and the freedom of all individuals to speak their minds within them.)

A little choir of hostile women was organized to sing me down whenever I arose to speak; and, at a signal from Rev. Mr. Izer, pastor of the flock, the women would obey his uplifted hand and begin to sing. As it would have been as impossible to out-speak a choir as to out-shriek a brass band, I would demurely take my seat; but only to rise again when the singing ended, and resume my plea for equal rights for the mother-sex, speaking for half a minute before the choir would again be ready to drown my voice.

Finally, the pastor desperately announced that Mrs. Duniway was to be prohibited from ever speaking in his church again.[24]

Not surprisingly, peaceable Ben Duniway wanted Abigail "to stay away from the meetings after that," but he "reluctantly accompanied" her the next evening. She went to her usual front seat, while Ben waited near the door. All went well for some time until Mrs. Duniway was "seized" with a "sudden inspiration." "I arose, raised my hand, closed my eyes and said, reverently, 'Let us pray.'" For twenty minutes she addressed her Creator, eyes closed, taking "no note of the time."

> When I was able to cease praying and open my eyes I beheld a silent, astonished multitude, in front of which, facing myself and choir, sat the pastor, his elbows on his knees, his open hands clasping his jaws, his eyes staring at vacancy. . . .
> The meetings, thereafter, soon ceased to draw crowds and raveled out for lack of patronage. But votes for women began to permeate the air.[25]

Abigail Scott Duniway had won a battle, perhaps, but not the war. Gradually the prohibitionists of Oregon, Washington Territory, and elsewhere became suffragists, mainly in recognition of the argument that ballots could help them make laws. But, from within the women's movement, their influence soon changed the significance and course of the suffrage campaign.

When Abigail Scott Duniway started her newspaper the temperance movement was still dominated by men. Having been a longtime supporter of temperance in Oregon—ever since her family's management of the Lafayette Temperance House—and convinced that temperance support would contribute to the achievement of suffrage, Duniway chose that group for her first public appeal. Democrats and clergymen were prominent in Oregon's Temperance Alliance, which mirrored the southern–northern split within the population of Oregon as a whole. They did not invite Abigail Scott Duniway to the temperance convention in Salem in the spring of 1871, but she announced in the fourth issue of the *New Northwest* that she intended to *go* anyway.

> We hope to lay before the honorable and well meaning committee a few potent and unanswerable facts in regard to the only possible means of allaying the horrors of intemperance. Let woman arm herself with the ballot, and we shall see if she cannot drive the liquor traffic to the abode of owls and bats. It's the only show.[26]

In 1872 she attended the temperance convention again, and this time the presiding officers tried to ignore women altogether. When someone nominated Mrs. Duniway as chairman of an important committee, the moderator feigned deafness until she "felt obliged to arise and speak for my sex." She was then nominated, "doubtless in ridicule," as vice-president at large, "which was carried with uproarious laughter."[27]

At the temperance convention of 1873, the Democratically controlled credentials committee, with well-known politician J. Quinn Thornton as chairman, "declared all delegations to be satisfactory (including those from the Penitentiary) except women, whom he styled 'setting hens,' 'belligerent females,' etc., after which he subsided with pompous gravity." Duniway then moved to admit the suffrage delegation, and "pandemonium" ensued. Thornton told the sergeant-at-arms to arrest her, saying "Take that crazy woman out of the house and take care of her," while several other men started taking off their coats to defend her. "The officer," said Duniway, "quailed before my uplifted pencil." George Williams, no friend of suffrage, but the Republican United States attorney general at the time and a close friend of Harvey Scott, called for order, insisted on a vote, and thus won women the right to sit in the convention. The "disappointed prohibitionists then seceded from the Alliance, and set up a 'Union' for themselves; but their confederacy did not live long."[28]

Duniway's use of the word "confederacy" reveals her estimate of those who opposed her in the alliance. They were Democrats who had been secessionists during the Civil War. Sexual antagonism, as is often the case, served as a mask for political antagonism—and J. Quinn Thornton had long been known for fighting tough with his opponents. Even the moderate Democratic *Salem Statesman* defended Duniway's accreditation to the convention, saying, "The delegates in question were treated rudely, and with such personal indignities as were unworthy of gentlemen engaged in a great reformatory movement." The newspaper cited Duniway's support of Republicans during the 1872 elections as the cause of the rudeness.[29]

Abigail Duniway's *New Northwest* in the 1870s constantly associated liquor and prostitution with Democratic politics. In running battles with editors Beriah Brown of Seattle's *Puget Sound Dispatch* and Sylvester Pennoyer of the *Oregon Herald* (who remained her ardent antagonist as Oregon's governor in the 1880s), both of whom were known for their secessionist sympathies,[30] Duniway often took her cue from their claims that "Our estimate of womanhood is too high to warrant us in aiding in an effort to drag her down to the filthy pool of party politics." "It is the presence of that filth which so outrages us," wrote Duniway.

> We have waited long for our brothers, who have made the filth, to arise in their boasted might and cleanse and purify their politics. . . . The reeking political slime in which they daily writhe calls aloud to us for purification. Women have hearkened to the call, and . . . woman, with her scrubbing brushes, her dustpan, her soap suds and her ready-waiting raiment of cleanliness, is baring her arms and fortifying her "constitution," to come to the rescue.

Directly following that editorial was one on prostitution in Portland as "one of the growing vices engendered and fostered by the 'filthy pool of party politics.' "[31]

She was quite right. The Portland city government in the 1870s derived most of its revenue from high licensing of the city's 149 saloons (one for every sixty inhabitants). Six out of nine members of the Democratically controlled city council were saloon keepers. One was chief of police, and the mayor was a frequent patron. Nor did Portland's financiers and businessmen wish to rock the boat to purify politics. The threat of women voters doing so appealed only to those without power.[32]

Mrs. Duniway thus early established her suffrage campaign on arguments from expediency as well as justice.[33] But the cleansing which she envisioned as the outcome of woman suffrage was based on political equality, not female moral superiority. Nor was it limited to any one issue, especially prohibition of alcoholic beverages. She believed, according to the eugenic theories of the time, that women with access to legal and economic freedom could refuse submission to drunken husbands and avoid conceiving drunken sons. Strong-willed mothers would produce strong-willed offspring who would not need prohibition laws to make them behave. Women with the ballot would war upon social and economic inequities of all sorts, thus creating the kind of society which precludes prostitution and intemperance.

Like the mid-century utilitarian philosopher John Stuart Mill, Duniway at first accepted the possibility of limited prohibitory legislation.[34] But her attitude was always the exact opposite of that of moralistic prohibitionists. They saw suffrage as an expedient measure for the purpose of prohibition—the "tail of the prohibition kite," Duniway called it. Instead she claimed, "It is wrong to accord woman the ballot just because she would vote against liquor. It is equivalent to saying that those only who oppose the traffic should be enfranchised, while certainly no fair mind would deny a woman her right to vote for the traffic, however much it would be deplored." Women would probably "have the good sense to favor prohibition," she said in this 1880 statement, but they should have the right to vote even if they opposed it.[35]

In one of her earliest editorials (and again many times later) Duniway stressed that alcoholism was a physical problem, not just a moral evil. "Intemperance," she wrote, "is a disease and should be treated as such. The victim should be cared for by the State as are the unfortunate inmates of an asylum for the insane."[36] Neither prayer nor prohibitory laws could be sufficient remedies, but rather only aids to personal rehabilitation. At a temperance prayer meeting in California in the spring of 1874, she tried to reconcile the two conflicting viewpoints. "Brother Anthony" was defending local option laws in opposition to a pastor who argued for regeneration, not prohibition. Her explanation was that "the views of both brethren were correct." No prohibition would be necessary in "the future state of man, yet many years away, when, having overcome his lower nature, he shall be a law unto himself. . . . But Mr. Anthony . . . was viewing life as it is now, with drunkenness as the bane of the people, for which a sudden and specific antidote must be supplied."[37]

Almost ten years later, when Frances Willard of the WCTU came to Oregon, Duniway said, "While we do not agree with Miss Willard as to the common sense of the crusade movement, we recognize it as the one absurd thing needed to shock the women of the nation into the proper recognition of their political status under a yoke of disfranchisement." She praised the work of temperance women in forming Bands of Hope in Portland (led by Harvey Scott's wife) to educate children about the evils of alcohol. Most of all, she welcomed Willard's insistence on the importance of suffrage—mainly because most temperance women had previously been antisuffragists. Citing the "hosts of blear-eyed, thick-tongued, babbling sovereigns, many of whom have no visible means of support," whose votes helped "foster the sum of all villainies, which is cheap whiskey and its accompanying train of murder, rapine, woe and want," she castigated the injustice of women having no comparable legal rights. Nevertheless, she insisted, "While we do not believe that prohibition will in our day become the accomplished fact that the ardent women of the WCTU are working for, we do believe that with woman's added power, as expressed through the ballot, will come her opportunity to demand that no son or husband shall be drunken or unchaste."[38] The distinction was clear to Abigail Scott Duniway. But it was too subtle, and too liberal, for most temperance reformers.

During the final year of the *New Northwest*'s publication, when opponents insisted that Duniway had once advocated closing saloons by means of the ballot, she tried to clarify her position once more:

> You may go to the files of the *Daily Oregonian,* the *New Northwest,* or any other paper that has faithfully chronicled our words on the subject of temperance from the beginning of our public career. . . , and you will find that we invariably have said that there was but one cure for intemperance, and that was not the ballot *per se,* but the independence, liberty, and financial and political standing that the ballot represents, which will eventually enable free women to hold men, though without any arbitrary show or exercise of authority, to as strict a line of moral rectitude as men to-day hold women.[39]

Actually, the ambiguity of some of Duniway's early pronouncements, as we have shown, was greater than she intended. Possibly her sister Catherine or her son Willis, during their terms as associate editors of the

New Northwest, had written some of the misleading editorials. For example, even as recently as 4 February 1886 her newspaper said:

> The *New Northwest* believes in temperance, is in favor of submission of the question to the people, and hopes that prohibition will prevail. It has its private views about the probable success of attempting to enforce prohibition, and also has a theory for the treatment of the liquor traffic. But neither private views nor individual theories will affect the matter, which must be faced as it exists in politics to-day. Therefore this journal is on the side of prohibition. As a question of principle, there is no doubt that the State has a right to prohibit anything that is injurious to the people; and even the most ardent supporters of the liquor traffic do not deny its baleful effects. The sole argument against it is based on the ground of expediency; and, since anything that is right should be made expedient, prohibition must ultimately win. It may not be now, it may not be in our day, but win it will when public sentiment shall have been brought to view all great progressive movements from the stand-point of right, leaving expediency to take care of itself.

The editorial went on to oppose any "third party demonstration in favor of prohibition" because it could not succeed and because it would antagonize the "large number of voters who cling to the old parties." Most people then, and since, were unable to understand the fine distinction Mrs. Duniway was making between prohibition as the long-term moral goal of an enlightened (and equal rights) society and prohibition as a political movement with legalistic, "tyrannical" potential.

But there can be no confusing the point of Abigail Scott Duniway's series of seven articles entitled "The Temperance Problem," which appeared during the summer of 1886. The first essay explored the political background and implications of the prohibitionist cause.

> Women who had always opposed the ballot; who had preferred sitting supinely in the prayer-meeting, singing "Where Is My Wandering Boy Tonight?" while the little hoodlum was out raising a rumpus at a Woman Suffrage meeting; and clergymen who had always commanded them to work for temperance on an "evangelical" basis only . . . , are the ringleaders in this new departure, in company with broken-down politicians, who have suddenly hoped to further their own interests through the women's votes, all heedless of the consequences to woman's liberty as a basic principle of right.

Mrs. Duniway recognized the source of such zeal:

> Many of the women who are frantically fighting the liquor traffic have been personal victims of the liquor curse. The husbands of some and the sons of others are diseased with drink. And to all of these the cry of "prohibition" comes like signal notes of hope, waiting tardily upon despair. . . .

We could not join them in this movement because . . . it began at the wrong end of the temperance reform. It pictured the drunkard as a martyr to the man who sold him intoxicating liquors, rather than a victim of his own bestiality and moral and physical disease. It sought to distract women from the basic principle upon which alone they might build a platform of liberty and justice.[40]

Knowing the fanaticism of prohibitionists, Duniway said, she had not made her position completely clear in early days by outright opposition. She had hoped to win them over instead. "But the knowledge of the storm that we would evoke did not justify our procrastination or cowardice during by-gone years, and for this alone we ask the public's pardon."[41] Now she wanted to make it clear that the "innate depravity" of all human beings made it virtually impossible to ban whiskey altogether. Even the Patagonians and native Alaskans, "the types of all humanity's early condition," were brewers of intoxicating beverages. Education was a better defense than innocence.

Give the children *knowledge*, dear mothers in Israel. The *truth* will make them free. Instead of praying continually to God to help you stop the liquor traffic, take your boy to the corner saloon, and in his presence select from any number of barrels on tap. . . . Pay for it and have it carted home. . . . [A]nd when you have it securely in your own possession, pull out the spigot and let the liquid waste. Then . . . let your boy see the sediment that is left behind after the barrel head is knocked in. From that day forward . . . he'll shun the vile concoction. . . . The experiment, including the purchase of the whiskey, will cost you less than your cheapest possible attendance upon the cheapest possible temperance convention.

Druggists would continue to dispense liquor as a medicine, while drinkers would inevitably circumvent prohibition laws, she said, giving specific examples of such practices. "Alcohol," she continued, is both "the result of decomposition, and . . . the basis of preservation. . . . Like everything else in nature, . . . it may be made an agency for both good and evil." Like fire, "it is not its sale or use, but its mastery over human appetites, that must be controlled by the laws and regulations of civilization." Using the analogy of an abscess in the body which, with an airtight and impregnable bandage, would send the virus "circulating with increased malignity through and through your diseased body until it would *rot you to your death*," she claimed that a "prohibition plaster" would rot "our national patient, the body politic, to its death."[42]

Duniway's last three essays were about her own proposed remedies to the problem. "Any legislation looking to the proper restraining of an evil," she wrote, "must first have the moral force of public sentiment behind it of sufficient power to sustain the law. Sumptuary legislation . . . is a direct violation of the fundamental law of the land, whenever and wherever attempted, all the supreme judges of all the courts of America to the contrary notwithstanding. . . . It is this fundamental law, ingrounded into the very heart of the nation's existence, which the people recognize as inalienable, that causes them to violate prohibition ordinances, even to their own undoing."[43]

A kind of inoculation was the best cure for alcoholism, she said. "We have known for years that drunkenness may be cured by simply overdosing the patient and confining him to a diet of 'whiskey straight' till he gets sick enough of the stinking fluid to imagine he is throwing up the soles of his feet. . . ."

> If a boy under our control should show evidence of becoming dissipated, we should as patiently as possible bide our time, and when we caught him in a drunken stupor we'd wrap and strap him securely in the sheets and blankets and proceed at once to inoculate his system through and through with alcoholic drinks. We'd set a bowl of whisky over a cane-seated chair with a lighted spirit lamp beneath to keep the liquor fumes in circulation through the closed room; we'd boil his potatoes in brandy and doctor his beefsteak with rum; we'd sprinkle the bedding with gin and wash his face in beer. He'd rave and fret and swear and beg and blaspheme by turns, but he'd be compelled to submit, for we'd have had him so securely bound in the beginning that he couldn't get away. If our patient were a beginner, twenty-four hours of such treatment would sufficiently inoculate him to effect a life-long cure. But if he were an old soaker, we'd keep him under treatment nine days, and when we were ready to let him go free, he would be free indeed, for he would at once and forever of necessity discard intoxicants, since he could no longer endure even the smell of them.[44]

Mrs. Duniway had advocated the same kind of treatment in 1878 and 1884 novels. It was a homeopathic "cure," the principle being, as she put it, that "the hair of the dog is good for the bite." This was also a contemporary notion about how to treat drug addiction.[45] But it was hardly the kind of cure that pious prohibitionists could be expected to understand or use!

Stringent laws against "spurious or adulterated liquors," she went on, as well as other common adulterations like "sand in the sugar, beet juice in the vinegar, lard in the butter, chicory in the coffee, meal in the pepper," would heal "the nation of its disease of drunkenness, since it is well known that drugged liquors destroy the human body much more rapidly than pure ones." High taxes, which should not be called licenses, would "dyke" the flow of liquor to "prevent its overflow; better than concealing it beneath the surface . . . by prohibitory laws." Church basements should be opened for "family" use, with constant "unbounded hospitality," games, reading, and refreshments, as a "counter-attraction to the saloon," and also as a means of increasing church revenue. She suggested regulating the size of saloons, forbidding tables, lunches, cards, or screened doors and painted windows for privacy.[46]

In the sixth essay Duniway insisted again, as she did throughout her career, on the dangers of third-party prohibition. Citing the elections of a Democratic Portland city councilman and Democrat President Grover Cleveland, she wrote:

> The great mass of people will soon tire of seeing Rummies placed in office by the reflex action of the Prohibition fiasco. They are not indifferent to the great game of coalition by which the party of the first part could easily be beaten at the ballot-boxes but for the stop-thief cry of Prohibitionists, who manage to decoy enough of the blinded but honest voting element from the [Republican] candidate who eschews fanaticism to elect the Rummy every time.

"The mean between the extremes is the only correct one, and the only one which promises the ultimate triumph of liberty, peace and soberness," argued Duniway, for "Iron-clad ordinances are not available in a land where absolute monarchies are not tolerated."[47]

In the same issue, 12 August 1886, she wrote in her "Editorial Correspondence" column,

> Liberty will open woman's eyes, and knowledge will enlighten her understanding. The ballot in her hands will ultimately assist the temperance reform; but it will never bring prohibition, for that is not temperance, but intolerance and quackery. The ballot in her hands will prove in time the magic key to the power which will enable women to rear a race of men who will be voluntarily free from drunkenness, because a race of free, enlightened mothers will naturally produce a race of free, enlightened sons.

Nevertheless, accusations that Abigail Scott Duniway had "sold out to liquor," published by the WCTU, now spread throughout the country. The August meeting of the Massachusetts Woman's Christian Prohibitory League held in a Baptist church in Boston decided that "Mrs. Abigail Scott Duniway of Washington Territory has brought disgrace on the Woman Suffrage cause." In words which epitomize the profound difference in philosophy, the ladies voted

> to censure most severely her action in attempting to conciliate the liquor power lest that power should be turned against Woman Suffrage; and we feel that we voice the sentiment of every true woman in America when we say: God grant that the ballot may never be given to women if, in order to obtain it, we must conciliate men.[48]

A whole new generation of eastern suffragists first learned about Mrs. Duniway in this way.

By the end of 1886, "old friends" Mary Thompson and Bethenia Owens-Adair, who were prohibitionists, suggested that Mrs. Duniway "step down" from her work. Hattie Loughary, president of the state suffrage association for a number of years, felt it "not best to call a State Convention of the Association until the prohibition fiasco . . . shall have a little more time to play itself out."[49] On 6 January 1887, Abigail Scott Duniway sold the *New Northwest;* it was "like parting with a loved and trusted child," she wrote. She bowed, temporarily, out of the front line of the battle.

CHAPTER 9

Dethroning the Idol Gold

"Every thinking and reasoning person clearly sees that there can be no real enmity between capital and labor, any more than between man and woman."

Abigail Scott Duniway wrote Clyde in 1893, "To be of real use in the world one must have power; to have power one must have money; to have money one must have opportunity; and this last will eventually put you in touch with the other two necessities." Abigail Duniway wanted to make a world where all citizens, including women, would have access to the opportunities which lead to money and power. She continued in the same letter, "[T]he doctrine of the 'survival of the fittest' is correct in theory, but the truth is that most of the fittest of a present generation have little natural chance for survival." Philanthropies are only "palliatives" because "the wrong is founded upon wrong conditions, fostered upon the masses by the fortunate few."[1]

In contrast to her wealthy brother Harvey Scott, who developed firm and unbending Hamiltonian convictions,[2] Duniway was a committed Jeffersonian, concerned for independent farmers and ordinary citizens—plus ordinary women. In general she reiterated the values of mid-century, midwestern Whigs like her father. She opposed the gold standard, favored antimonopoly legislation, and stood up for the rights of laborers and farmers as well as women during the volatile era of industrial and commercial expansion known as the Gilded Age. By the 1890s she was seriously interested in the Populist movement. Her ideas gained her many friends—and many enemies among the powerful.

Equality for women, Duniway believed, was as important to the welfare of men as to that of women. "A one-sexed government," she wrote, "is like a one-sexed home. It is like an unmarried man or an unmated woman. It is like one-half of a pair of shears. It is like the atmosphere with the oxygen left out. It is like love without reciprocity, light without heat, a world without an atmosphere, or magnetism without electricity."[3] Women should not seek to rule *over* men, only *with* men. Personal financial autonomy was the foundation of such political freedom, she insisted, as Jefferson too would have argued. Laws should guarantee that autonomy to all women, even to those married women who felt no need of it. "Men must learn that woman is an individual, complete and sovereign in herself," she said, "and not a machine to be guided 'as the law of man directs,' without volition of her own."[4] Autonomous individuals, in free cooperative association within marriage, community, and nation, working for the good of the whole, were Duniway's ideal.

At the Oregon State Woman Suffrage convention of 1880 Duniway introduced a resolution declaring that "the great labor reform of the age lies in giving woman, the great unpaid laborer of the whole earth, the fruits of her toil." (Elizabeth Cady Stanton had sponsored a similar wages-for-housework resolution at the NWSA convention in 1878.) But the resolution was opposed by Dr. Mary Thompson, a charter member of the organization who had been sparring with Mrs. Duniway ever since it began. (She was also one who urged Duniway to step down in 1886, and intrigued against her in 1906.) Thompson said it was "a blow at the unity of the marriage relation" and a matter which husbands and wives should settle between themselves.[5]

Duniway's conflicts with women like Thompson (who was also a prohibitionist) were based on the fundamental conviction that women are not "purer and better than men," as Thompson claimed they were at the convention in 1881. Duniway insisted that women deserved the ballot and recognition of their economic value "because it is their right" as citizens and persons under the Constitution.

> Without [that right] they are vassals and not sovereigns . . . , servants without wages when married and in the condition of perpetual minors. . . .
>
> A government of one-half of the people by the other half is only half free. It is not a republic, nor a democracy, but an aristocracy—an aristocracy of sex. . . . "Governments derive their just powers from the consent of the governed," and women are not governed justly because they are taxed to maintain a government in which they are denied the right to give or withhold their consent.

Mrs. Duniway told the legislators of Oregon in 1880 that "the generic term *men*" always includes women when it comes to tax-paying or law-breaking, but "the man has never yet lived who has said of a woman convicted of crime, 'May it please the Court and the jury. *I* represent this woman. Punish me!' "[6]

Such arguments were also woven into all Duniway's novels. In one case the heroine disguises herself as a young lawyer and proceeds to instruct her judge-employer (who is also her father) with a line by line analysis of the Declaration of Independence, the U.S. Constitution, and then the Oregon Constitution.[7] Mrs. Duniway told the NWSA convention in 1889, "The Declaration of Independence and Preamble to the Constitution of the United States formed the basis of my many sermons through all those weary years. . . . [W]e can only secure our right to vote by and through the consent of voters. . . . Whenever our demand for our right to vote is based upon an alleged purpose to take away from men any degree of what they deem their liberties . . . we simply throw boomerangs that recoil upon our own heads." For Abigail Scott Duniway, woman suffrage was a principle of justice, not just a step toward reform, though it would indeed have many expedient consequences.[8]

Unlike pious nineteenth-century proponents of "woman's sphere," Duniway insisted that all women are not naturally endowed with culinary or housekeeping skills or higher moral perception. But they all have particular talents which should be developed. She never ceased pointing out the flaws in arguments like "women do not fight in armies" or "women are not educated enough to vote intelligently." Many men don't fight either, she said, either because of illness, infirmity, weakness, small size, or even cowardice. They are not therefore denied the vote. Many men, especially among immigrants and laborers or freed slaves, were certainly less educated than many women.

Answering the common claim that women were incapable of equality because they had never produced the same great works as men, Duniway said, "man himself—and woman also—is the result of woman's untiring energy and painstaking toil. . . . That the permanent work of woman is noticeable in its effect, rather than in the labor itself, is no proof that the labor has not been performed, but exactly the reverse." She debunked the then current scientific theory that brain size proved male superiority by pointing out that "the elephant has a larger brain than a man, but his brain quality is of an inferior order." Stressing the importance of environment and opportunity, Duniway continued:

> Circumscribe the liberty and independence of man as woman is thus circumscribed, and he, too, is "unreasoning, positive and emotional." Woman changes her opinion more easily than man; and the radical difference between the human and the brute is that one can change his opinion and the other cannot. The donkey, for ought we know to the contrary, is the same yesterday, today, and for all coming time.

(Duniway used the donkey metaphor frequently as a rhetorical weapon against those opposed to change.)[9]

Like most other westerners, Duniway believed in coeducation rather than segregation of boys and girls, on the grounds that familiarity was the best preventive of excessive romanticism or passionate ignorance. Since nature made everyone part of a family, she said, men and women as well as brothers and sisters should live and work together—at home, in school, and in government. Opposing "female academies" of every sort, she also disapproved of segregated colleges. When Smith College was founded in 1875, she said that to be consistent it should at least have a woman rather than a man as president. She said the same of Bryn Mawr and Vassar, reiterating that "neither men nor women do their best in any life, shut exclusively away from each other. The competition that springs up between the sexes when associated together in educational pursuits, is a healthful one, and carries with it a stimulus that brings out all the latent powers of the minds of both."[10]

The principle involved was the same that made her disapprove of racial segregation and the decisions of the Supreme Court which ruled discriminatory voting laws in the South constitutional: "Any school-girl might see the fallacy of Judge Waite's ruling, and all the world does see it, so far as negro men are concerned; but only the wisest men can see it, so far as it concerns women, whether black or white."[11] Though she retained and sometimes expressed many common prejudices against black Americans and other racial groups, she was always ready to deal with individuals as fellow human beings, deserving of the same civil rights which she was so anxious to achieve for women. One of her most frequent metaphors was that there was "no Canada for runaway wives," and she constantly compared the injustice of woman's status to that of slaves. Duniway danced enthusiastically at a "Proclamation Festival" with "our colored brethren" in 1875, and she included "colored" people in her suffrage organizations.[12]

About the Chinese, it must be said, Duniway was somewhat more ambiguous. Along with most other westerners, she shared a low opinion of their potential. Shiploads of Chinese coolies were being brought to the West Coast, mostly to work on the railroads, but also as cheap labor in mines, homes, and factories. Hired in gangs and paid through their boss, who was usually part of a Chinese syndicate in various western cities, many laborers were indeed slaves in their working conditions and pathetically low pay. Thus they constituted a threat to free labor that became more and more serious as European immigration increased, western cities expanded, and various depressions occurred. Further-more, Chinese poverty led to crowded, unsanitary Chinatowns, where opium dens and prostitution flourished.

The Workingman's Protective Alliance was organized on the West Coast to agitate for immigration restriction and against the hiring of Chinese workers. Mrs. Duniway opposed the alliance and also the condi-tions which caused Chinese squalor. Let us have "consideration of the means to liberate from slavery all Chinese bondmen and bondwomen who are here," she wrote. Chinese laundries helped make American women free, she said, while capitalistic practices were a greater threat to labor than the poor coolies:

Yet we wish it distinctly understood that we believe Chinamen to be the means, ordained by Providence, to relieve the over-burden of washing and ironing and other work of menials and scullions from the shoulders of American women. We long to see free, independent Chinamen, whose highest aspiration is kitchen work, so plenty in America that every weary mother who is enduring the curse of "bringing forth children in sorrow" can afford to hire one. . . .

Let the Protective Alliance, while considering the pernicious effects of Coolie labor, exert itself to get a five or ten acre homestead for every homeless husband or wife, where surplus men or women can be employed at low rates in beautifying the grounds, doing the housework, and raising fruits, poultry, vegetables, etc., etc. Then there would be work for every man, woman, and child of every Nationality that could come to the Pacific coast or be born therein during the next two centuries.

Where our people suffer one disability from Chinese labor, they suffer ten thousand from land monopoly and exorbitant rates of interest.[13]

Duniway was more concerned about the exploitation of female labor, pointing out that the slight advantage over coolies was hardly worth praising. After a tour of the Oregon City Woolen Mills in 1882 she wrote:

The girls and women employed in the mills get ten per cent more *per diem* than the Chinamen, and about fifty per cent less on an average than the boys and men for doing the same grades of work. It is claimed that the increase of women's *per diem* over Chinamen's is due solely to the outcry made by voters against the employment of the "little brown men," while it is known that voters owe their fifty per cent advantage over women to the fact that women are disfranchised, and consequently have no influence of which the factory owners stand in awe.[14]

In 1886, when rioters swept Portland and other western cities, burning Chinese laundries, shops, and homes in organized terror campaigns, the *New Northwest* joined the *Oregonian* and the business community in condemning such lawlessness and cruelty. Duniway blamed her old Democratic enemy, Governor Sylvester Pennoyer, for encouraging the riots as a means of placating other immigrant groups suffering from the current hard times.[15] Such defense of Chinese rights did not endear Mrs. Duniway to the urban laboring populace.

The obvious first step in any woman's emancipation, said Duniway, was freedom from excessive physical labor. Hired help for overburdened farmers' wives and for women who desired to fulfill other talents was a major theme of the *New Northwest,* as it had been of her *Argus* letters. Duniway herself hired Chinese cooks and housekeepers, though she complained about their work as vehemently as eastern ladies did about their Irish maids.[16] In the 1880s she pointed out that no laboring men were planning to replace boycotted Chinese laundries themselves. It was women whose health and welfare would be most affected. One fictional character was moved to paraphrase the Bible: "Of what shall it profit a man if he gain entire surcease of Chinese labor and lose his own wife?" In a small Idaho village Mrs. Duniway found that Chinese were being banished, just as they had been in Tacoma and elsewhere, at the instigation of labor agitators and "reformers" of the "dirty clothes brigade."

> There is one "agitator" here, a pompous and condescending negro, who gave us polite occasion to inform him that if he were not a *voter*, the average "agitator" would make it as hot for him as he was trying to make it for the dozen Asiatics in the place whom he hates so heartily. He wanted to know "where the women were who did the washing thirty years ago." "In the graveyard," was our prompt reply; and the citizen of African descent subsided into silence.[17]

Primary symbols of woman's unpaid subjection, for Duniway, were patchwork quilts. Every year she attended the Oregon State Fair and described it in the *New Northwest*. New machinery, the increasing emphasis on horse-breeding and racing, the displays of baked and canned goods and prize fruits and vegetables, all received her attention and qualified praise. But hand-sewn needlework was anathema.

> Then, there were . . . tatting, darned netting, silk embroidery, and a thousand other trifles that impecunious women kill themselves over, causing the beholder to sigh for the wasted ingenuity that is so confined to futile nothings in its endeavor for expression that men falsely imagine that the women of the land are content to do nothing else.

Duniway feared "lest many members of yet other generations of the sons and daughters of women are to be robbed of vitality through the overwork of their mothers before they are born." Before she left the 1880 fair she suggested that premiums for women's handiwork be "more on a par with those offered for horse-racing." They should be "for babies, butter, starch, soap, candles, cookery, etc.," but not for "the ever obtruding and always ugly patchwork quilt." Duniway considered the other items valuable additions to the economy, but

> Any fool can make a quilt; and, after we had made a couple of dozen over twenty years ago, we quit the business with a conviction that nobody but a fool would spend so much time in cutting bits of dry goods into yet smaller bits and sewing them together again, just for the sake of making believe that they were busy at practical work.[18]

Similar comments about quilts appear throughout Duniway's writing. In fact, she had first made an issue of such "unnecessary" and unhealthful labor in her novel of 1859, *Captain Gray's Company.*

There is thus a particular irony—possibly evidence of Duniway's fund-raising intentions—in her plan to donate one of her own handmade quilts to the New York World's Fair in 1899 as an example of Oregon women's accomplishments. Immediately the other members of the Port-land Woman's Club raised a special fund to purchase the quilt for the Oregon Historical Society, claiming it was too precious to send out of the state. Duniway used the money to aid the suffrage campaign of 1900. The quilt is still at the historical society, carefully rolled and hidden from public view. It provides mute evidence that Abigail Duniway was both an abominable seamstress and possibly color-blind! No wonder she could not perceive the artistic value of quilts![19]

Just as quilt-making symbolized the economic subjugation of women in a society divided into men's and women's "spheres," so the lack of land for individual families appeared to Duniway as a form of subjugation inappropriate to American society. Despite her admiration for progress and the manifest destiny of American expansion, Duniway abhorred monopoly capitalism and its class arrogance, so often destructive to the autonomy of laborers, small farmers, and the poor—including women. Though she assumed that the solution to the plight of laborers and immigrants in an increasingly industrial society was to encourage them to farm or to be more frugal, their situation aroused her sympathy. She conversed with immigrant families on trains and welcomed them to Oregon, and for a beggar boy in New York in 1876 she almost bought out a bakery shop.[20]

Abigail Scott Duniway had grown up in a milieu where small farmers felt themselves to be the backbone of the community and the moral arbiters of American civilization. Her grandfathers, James Scott and Lawrence Roelofson, as well as her father, John Tucker Scott, with their strong personalities and their family histories of idealistic individualism combined with group loyalty, had provided examples of will power, industry, and accomplishment which no Scott offspring could ever forget. Justice for such frontier farmers was a matter of common sense, of rational, natural law, a matter of protecting the interests of individuals and families, not of corporations, trusts, and monopolies. Nineteenth-century society and nineteenth-century law increasingly eroded the rights of the former in favor of the latter, while the merging of common law and equity law "emasculated" the independent standards which had once provided some protection to women's financial rights.[21]

One basic tenet of the agrarian milieu was a pervasive suspicion of the rich. The large plantation owners of the southern states, who owed both their wealth and their political power to their control of unfree labor, were hated both because of their haughtiness and political injustice toward poor whites, especially those on the frontier, and because the slave system demeaned the dignity and value of free labor. Slaveholders were also perceived as corrupt and effete because they had been spoiled by leisure and temptations to immorality. Northern capitalists were equally hated for similar reasons.

Abigail Duniway's *Captain Gray's Company* opened with the foreclosure of a widow's farm and "humble log cabin" by a villainous Virginian "brought up among slaves" on his wealthy father's plantation. "He of course had a hatred for poor white folks, which his own poverty and debauchery had in no way diminished." The man claimed to have bought the "deed of trust" on the widow Goodwin's land and warned her that going to court to defend her title would be expensive. She agreed: "The lawyer's fee is equal to the oppressor's demand."[22] Many *New Northwest* serials involve legal injustices toward women and the cruel snobbery of inherited wealth toward the virtuous poor.

Duniway and her fellow pioneers were particularly suspicious of rich and "refined" Easterners. A frontier farmer or tradesman who had achieved wealth by his own labor was an admirable example of initiative, frugality, and virtue. It was normal and good to aspire to that kind of wealth. For example, describing the Seattle land boom in 1883 which took place in anticipation of the coming railroad, Duniway mentioned that "Among these leading land owners are our public-spirited friends, Hon. S. B. Yesler and wife, who, after years of patient waiting, awoke one morning and found themselves millionaires."[23] She never made any secret of her own desire for the just rewards of her labor and the kind of amenities which only money can buy. Only those who had not experienced equal hardships and whose definitions of propriety were shaped by the expectations of money and leisure since childhood were perceived as interlopers and arrogant tyrants.

The first issue of the *New Northwest* established Duniway's working-class credentials. Responding to what she called the "Phelps, Dahlgren and Corbett Manifesto," an antisuffrage "remonstrance" presented to Congress in the winter of 1871 (after Victoria Woodhull's prosuffrage petition), Duniway launched a vigorous attack on the female "establishment." "The wife of our worthy Senator [Corbett]," said Duniway, "the beautiful and 'shrinking' Mrs. Henry W., . . . imagines that she is capable of dictating to the toiling women of America concerning what they shall and what they shall not do." The remonstrants, she continued, were "fashionable butterflies, who nightly flaunt their finery—paid for by the people—through the gay throngs at the capital."

We toiling and tax-paying, but reading and reasoning women, who stay at home while these parasites upon the public bounty are flirting at the Capital, do not care a single straw if they do not vote. Let them bear the "heavy burden" of fashionable life if they like it. We even doubt their ability to vote. . . . [W]e most emphatically deny their right to interfere with our prerogatives. We have borne, and are today bearing, "other and heavier burdens" than the casting of a ballot or the voting ourselves of a salary.[24]

Mrs. Corbett was a leading member of Portland's social elite—the New England–born wife of Oregon's Senator Henry Winslow Corbett. Mrs. Dahlgren was the wife of an admiral and Almira Phelps was a prominent eastern educator of women and the sister of educator Emma Willard. (Corbett himself, who was one of the most wealthy men in the Pacific Northwest, traced his ancestry to "a military chieftain who won fame and name by service under William The Conqueror." His daughters were married to two other Portland financiers, Henry Failing and Thomas Robertson.) The antisuffrage remonstrants argued "against the oppression of having suffrage forced upon them" and feared the disruption of marriage and the social order by "discontented Amazons." They also explicitly called the "socialistic doctrines" of the suffrage movement un-American. Duniway, however, compared the antisuffragists to "certain mistaken but overzealous colored men" who had petitioned Congress during the Civil War in favor of slavery. She claimed they were all "worthy companions of Dame Partington, who tried to sweep back the waves of the Atlantic with a mop."[25]

Such rhetoric was a delight to the rural constituency which made up a large part of the *New Northwest*'s readership. Duniway certainly considered herself the equal of all such ladies and obviously enjoyed associating with the "best society" wherever she went, "dropping names" with alacrity and training her children in respectable manners and expectations. The ambiguity of her feeling is particularly evident in her novels, such as *Amie and Henry Lee,* where high society is vicious and selfish, but the heroine always aspires, on her own terms, to be accepted and respected within that society. Mrs. Duniway was a reformer but not a revolutionary. Her goal was to transform society in order to eliminate the distinctions of class and economic conflict, to provide for the greatest good for the greatest number by means of profit sharing, mutual investment, and cooperative communities and businesses. In such a society, all women would be ladies and all ladies would be working women.

Like most pioneering American farmers in the nineteenth century, Duniway shared the convictions about land which editor Horace Greeley had publicized in the middle of the century. He preached that the "principle of land limitation" was "the very key of the arch which is destined to upbear the unportioned millions from their measureless degradation and abounding misery." He spoke of state guarantees of land ownership to small farmers and of communal organization as the ideal replacement for the isolated individual family system. And he called for other reforms like regulated work hours, child labor laws, and distribution of capital profits among workmen.[26]

In an early issue of the *New Northwest,* Duniway deplored "the wanton distribution of public lands among rapacious and greedy politicians, the granting of large tracts of the public domain to railroad companies and steamboat corporations, and the consequent centralization of capital and power in the hands of a few individuals." She called for the people to "use their patent power as citizens" to "prevent a land-holding aristocracy from getting us under their merciless thumb, or 'we, the people' will soon be a nation of bankrupts."[27]

This issue was a major element of Mrs. Duniway's speech to the 1874 Oregon legislature, entitled "The Destiny of Our Republic," as the country recovered from the Panic of 1873. In opposition to pious moralists who considered evil social conditions the result rather than the cause of moral degradation, Duniway argued that poverty and suffering led to criminal behavior, while a happy environment nurtured virtue. It was time to consider claims of *humanity* superior to claims of *money.* "This country is or ought to be a government of homes," she said, "yet, such is our system of finance, such have been the manipulations of our money kings . . . that we are in reality not a government of the people and by the people, but a government of money, by money—a government of landed monopolies and corporations and cash."

At the rate things were going, she went on, within twenty years "fifty thousand men will own the entire landed domain of the nation." She deplored the "great corporations . . . buying up of vast landed tracts— the driving back of the settlers from the great, governmental domain, . . . so many thousand acres . . . given over to horses and sheep and cattle and swine." Nevertheless, "fifty years hence individual ownership in these large tracts of land will be just as obsolete as individual ownership in man is today." Although she declared she did not advocate the "torch and flame" of communism (already a word of violent connotations because of the Paris Commune three years earlier), there was danger that "the vast homeless, landless masses shall rise up in a great rebellion, compared with which the slaveholders' Rebellion was as child's play." The government should buy back all unused land at "fair valuation" in order to avoid such disaster. "We want the government of these United States to be so emphatically of the people and by the people that it can own its governmental right, our vast landed domain and hold it in trust for the *possessors.*"

Once the government established ownership, Duniway continued, each individual would pay an annual stipend and "be protected in his

inalienable rights upon the soil forever." Security for families and beau-
tification of the country would result, while millionaires could use their
riches to assist their neighbors. She foresaw a nation in which women
would finally share in lawmaking and mothers would show "no longer
the hollow eye, the bowed shoulders, the despairing look, the furrowed
cheek." They would be free to endow their offspring "with that grand
and perfect physical constitution which naturally and rightfully belongs
to every child of this Republic."

Duniway predicted that in one hundred years the country would be
"dotted all over" with "beautiful cottages . . . set round about with vines
and gardens, adorned with all that is pleasant to the eye, with all that is
elevating to the mind and the body." There would be many churches
"devoted to the service of a free religion," and many "grand, stately,
massive edifices" preparing every child no matter how poor with a free
education. There would be an end to "every penitentiary, every alms-
house, every gibbet, every asylum for the insane." These were "the
dreamings, . . . the aspirations" of her soul, of which woman's rights
were an indispensable part.[28]

The vision was similar to that of Henry George, who had published a
little-known pamphlet called "Our Land and Land Policy" in 1871. Duniway's idea about paying perpetual rent for the use of the land reminds
one of George's "single tax" on land values, an economic theory which
created a stir among westerners when he promulgated it in his book
Progress and Poverty, published in 1878. But the idea was also related to
eighteenth-century physiocratic theories which had been floating
around in Jeffersonian thought for a hundred years. However, Duniway
wanted the government to purchase back the domain from its "feudal"
owners, while George wanted the government to tax such ownership.
Duniway's reference to 30,000 landowners of Great Britain suggests the
influence of Irish Fenianism, publicized by George Francis Train in the
Revolution and also in speeches he gave in Portland and Salem, Oregon,
in the summer of 1871.[29]

Small farmers and businessmen might welcome such a theory, but it
was not appealing to those Oregonians who were already involved with
"landed monopolies and corporations and cash." Senator John Mitchell,
Duniway's prime political ally, and his friends among the bankers and
railroad men were engrossing new land faster than anyone else. Brother
Harvey Scott was accumulating land in and around Portland and was
involved in numerous other investments, from which he eventually became extremely wealthy. He made it clear to all *Oregonian* readers
throughout his career that "The dream of social justice never will do
anything for him who depends on it. He should quit that dream, take the
first job he can get and stick to it till he can make it the stepping stone to

another and better. Then he will find no theory of 'social justice' of any interest to him."[30]

Abigail Duniway herself, of course, was investing in land whenever she could, but generally she bought only small lots. The *New Northwest* had effectively tied up most of her capital, but even so she was unable, by law, to make any purchases on her own until after the Married Woman's Property Act of 1878. She later claimed that she had "earned and expended over forty-two thousand dollars in my long-drawn struggle for Equal Rights for Women, which if I had used in trade, or invested in real estate, would have made me several times a millionaire." She lamented being "handicapped" and prevented from gaining a "footing" in early Portland, Spokane, and Ellensburg. She wanted wealth as a source of power, a means of reforming society and obtaining social justice— though she admitted to Clyde that "maybe, if I had been allowed to grow wealthy I might have failed in *philanthropy* and *heart*."[31]

In one of Duniway's earliest *New Northwest* editorials, she asserted that women had been wrongly "cramped in the exercise of their executive qualities" by nineteenth-century custom and education. Extolling financial ability as "the basis on which the superstructure of society rests . . . the magic wand which makes the earth yield her treasures for the use of man; which brings all tribes and people of the world into . . . interdependence; which so distributes labor that the sciences, arts, and tastes which minister to man's higher needs may be cultivated," she said; "it is to the body politic what the circulation of the blood is to the human organization." A woman

> must recognize her duties to herself and to the world. Custom and society must unite in enforcing the performance of those duties upon her. The world must demand of her that she do her part of the world's work. If, by circumstances, temperament and organization, that work lies in the family circle alone, let her do her part there; but if, as often happens, a woman has tastes and capacities which lead her outside that circle, let her not hesitate to obey their dictates. The possession of powers is not only a warrant from God, but an obligation imposed by Him for their use.[32]

To carry out such obligations, women would have to develop some means of streamlining household work and of being remunerated according to its economic value. On Duniway's trip East in 1872 she probably heard Elizabeth Cady Stanton's opinions on the subject, if she had not already read her articles in the *Revolution,* or Harriet Beecher Stowe's, or Mary Livermore's in the *Woman's Journal.* In 1869, Melusina Fay Peirce, wife of the eminent Harvard philosopher Charles Peirce (who did not take her ideas seriously), had defined cooperative housekeeping in the *Atlantic Monthly.* Women would join as shareholders in a corporation organized to produce specific services, such as laundry, baking, or delivered meals. They would buy or rent a building and necessary equipment, share or purchase the labor involved, and charge their husbands for the service. The innovative Mrs. Peirce had even managed such a project successfully during 1870 in Cambridge, Massachusetts. Mrs. Duniway was certainly aware of these ideas, as well as of the mid-century utopian experiments in various parts of the country. The 1870s also spawned many farm and consumer cooperatives among men.[33]

By 1875 Abigail Duniway was delivering regularly a lecture with the title "Cooperative Housekeeping." In 1881 Yours Truly of Beaver Dam Farm described to *New Northwest* readers her plan for a local laundry; half a dozen families could together "hire a Chinaman" to live near the center of their village and do all their washing and ironing for eight dollars a week. Duniway's fictional Edith McShane, whom "Nature never cut . . . out for a cook," aspires to be "a practical philanthropist." She wants

> to inaugurate great cooperative schemes among women, schemes to classify and regulate their work as men classify and regulate theirs. I'd like women to learn cooperation in all the industrial pursuits that are peculiar to their own sphere. I'd like to enlarge their sphere of action, too, and make it comprehend and include the complex as well as the simple problem of right living.

The rhetoric is very similar to Peirce's, who published her book on the subject the next year. But, as Dolores Hayden says in regard to Peirce, "Capitalists could not accept her ideal of nonprofit cooperation. . . . Conservative advocates of 'women's sphere' found her emphasis on women's economic power distasteful."[34] Without financial or political autonomy, nineteenth-century women were unable to participate on their own terms in the great commercial and industrial expansion of the post–Civil War era. Even Abigail Duniway could only preach.

At the Oregon State Fair in 1883 Duniway told audiences of women about

> the good time coming, when a few master minds among them should be able to formulate a system of household work in which they could so cooperate in their manifold labors that the present complex system of drudgery that wears them out would give way to a double-complex system of combined labor and machinery as simple within itself as the cooperative plans of men who run threshing machines, steam plows, saw mills, grist mills, woolen factories, coopers' shops, carpenters' shops, merchandise of a hundred or a thousand kinds, railway corporations and steamer combinations.

One "weary listener" remarked that "Women ain't smart enough to do

such things." Duniway answered, "Give women equal rights with men
before the law; let their work, which is even more necessary than men's,
since no man or woman could be born or reared without it, become as
remunerative as men's, and we'll soon show you a Villard of our own."
She compared the recent completion of the Northern Pacific Railroad
under Henry Villard—whose seizure of railroad control to divert it to a
Portland terminus by means of a "blind pool" of investment capital had
been one of the great business coups of the century—with her own
hopes that

> A Villard among native-born women shall arise who will demonstrate . . .
> that the hundred thousand individual kitchens, in which women now wear
> out their lives in discontented efforts over a hundred thousand cooking
> stoves, can be so controlled by . . . cooperative discipline that woman's work
> may be made as simple, as effective, and as remunerative as man's.

A woman said, "I'm afraid you're only dreaming," adding sadly, "I wish
I had a thousand dollars to invest in a scheme like that." "Dear woman!"
wrote Duniway. "She had honestly and faithfully earned ten thousand
dollars of her husband's twenty, but she didn't know it, nor did he."[35]

Abigail Duniway was not just dreaming. She was already thinking of
becoming such an altruistic entrepreneur herself, if only she could find
the funds. She considered cooperative ventures the solution to industrial
monopolies and labor–management strife. And there was still room to
do it in the West. As she wrote in one novel, " 'The philanthropists of the
country are running wild over the proposed prohibition of the liquor
traffic '. . . . 'But I can see greater evils, worse monopolies, than even the
curse of the still.' "[36]

Abigail Duniway spoke of "land fever" regularly as she traversed the
vast plateaux and valleys of the still-virgin hinterlands of Oregon, Washington, and Idaho. On 22 December 1881, she printed a two-page,
eight-column description of the "scenery, soil, climate, productions,
prospects and possibilities" of the Pacific Northwest, for the benefit of
capitalists and immigrants who might wish to make investments there.
There was room for thousands of farms, she exclaimed wherever she
went. "We will be back," she remarked, as she described hours of lonely
staging through the fertile open wilderness from southeastern Oregon
to Baker City.[37]

Land fever also infected Duniway's son-in-law Don Stearns, who tried
a new venture just before the serious Oregon recession of 1884. Harvey
Scott and H. L. Pittock, who had recently bought out Stearns's newspaper, backed the project financially, while Mrs. Duniway publicized it
in her paper for the sake of her daughter. "What a Summer resort this
place is destined to become, and what a boulevard may be made for

driving or other pastime around its sylvan borders!" Duniway described the "wild, romantic beauty" of the "crystal waters of Lake La Camas" on the Washougal River twelve miles up the Columbia from Portland. There was "abundance of water power for every desirable enterprise," with an "immense paper mill" nearly completed. "Hundreds of laborers," as well as farmers and businessmen would do well to invest in La Camas Colony, Duniway wrote.[38] But those who may have followed her advice found the site swampy and malarial; the water power was inadequate for the paper mill. In January 1886 Clara Duniway Stearns died from consumption developed in the log cabin on the "sylvan borders" of the "wild romantic" lake.

That spring Willis Duniway accompanied his mother on a lecture tour through southern Idaho, investigating land values and irrigation schemes for the "great inland empire." She was depressed by Clara's death and political opposition, and ready for a new beginning. Plans for "making the desert bloom" (which were finally publicized and carried out a generation later) were already in progress during the 1880s. Willis and Mrs. Duniway caught "water-wheel fever" while visiting Boise. Encouraged by a tip from Harvey Scott about a proposed new railroad route, they filed claims for two large tracts of land in the Lost River Valley of south central Idaho near the villages of Hailey and Antelope Station.[39]

Abigail Duniway apparently hoped to put her cooperative ideals at last into practice. Proceeds from the sale of the *New Northwest* would provide development funds. But shortly after the purchase she discovered that her family did not approve. In September she wrote bitterly,

> If, when Henry Villard conceived the idea of completing the Northern Pacific Railroad, he had been obliged to ask his wife for the use of a little money, and she, not having given the subject a thought, or perhaps being unable to comprehend it, had refused not only to give him the cash, but had obstinately forbidden him to go on with the enterprise; if he, not content with such repression, had gone out among women to create that famous "blind pool," and had found that his bond was of no account because he was a married man, does any reader believe he could have carried out his pet ambition? . . . We know a woman whose plans for projecting and carrying forward a scheme for cooperative housekeeping are . . . quite as important as were the plans of Henry Villard. . . . Yet that woman has a husband who holds her fortune in his grasp, who is her legal representative and head, and he does not sympathize with her plans, so he withholds from her the means to make even a respectable beginning. She cannot go out among other women to create a "blind pool," for they are, like herself, financial paupers in the midst of plenty; so her magnificent brain power is lost to the world.[40]

Abigail Scott Duniway's plan was probably similar to what she de-

scribed in her unpublished novel *Margaret Rudson,* a cooperative indus-
trial-agrarian enterprise on a huge tract of land in Idaho. Together with
a handsome young man whom she converts to the cause of woman's
equality, Margaret plans to develop the land by means of a joint-stock
corporation, employing "the methods of great trusts and corporations"
in the most modern financial, as well as material, technology.

The proposed town of Utilitaria is established with her fortune as a
bond, while "humble" eastern factory workers and other immigrants can
either buy shares or receive half their wages in the form of stock. Along
with a dam and irrigation system, there is a huge hotel for one hundred
women, two hundred men, and four hundred children, shaped like a
letter H, with a public kitchen and dining hall where all are required to
eat. Margaret and her husband participate in governing as equal members in a workers' directorate. They are honored with a special apart-
ment, but individual homes are not allowed. Margaret's preference for
the privacy of family tables "as in first class hotels in cities" is voted down
by the directorate. Absolute marital equality includes hyphenated names
for husbands and wives; they become Mr. and Mrs. Rudson-Horner.[41]

Duniway apparently prepared an earlier version of the same story,
hoping that son Clyde could persuade the editors of the *Arena* or *Cosmopolitan* to publish it. It was about an "Altrurian Ranche," upon which

> my "altruist" forms a "stock company" with all the waters of his creek as a
> basis, puts his land on the market under bonds, and by a contract with each
> new resident, or little purchaser, turns over the lands when the last pay-
> ment is made, with sufficient acreage under alfalfa to afford the purchaser
> a chance to live from the proceeds of his corns [crops?], a creamery, etc.

Her scheme, she said, was not "radical or Utopian or didactic," just
"altruistic."[42] (The word *altrurian* was apparently borrowed from
William Dean Howells's *A Traveler from Altruria,* which had just been
serialized in *Cosmopolitan.* Duniway was providing a western locale for
the principle of cooperative community, which Howells too had borrowed. The most famous utopian novel of the era was Edward Bellamy's
Looking Backward [1888], about Boston in the year 2000. Actual experiments with cooperative boarding clubs already existed in several cities,
while the Rumford Kitchen at the Chicago Columbian Exposition in
1893, which Duniway attended, was a prototype for public neighborhood kitchens. Charlotte Perkins Gilman's famous *Women and Economics*
actually synthesized earlier ideas when it appeared in 1898.)[43]

Abigail Scott Duniway was an enthusiastic supporter of the Knights of
Labor, who shared her agrarian philosophy and concern for justice within the system. She objected vociferously, however, to the mass labor
movement led by "foreign-born demagogues" under the control of par-

ty politicians, and often manipulated to their own disadvantage. Her comments about the "foreign scum" and "ignorant rabble" in cities like Portland echoed the sentiments of her Know-Nothing relatives and friends in the 1850s—and for the same reasons. Rootless laborers were a basis of corrupt political power, bought by the promise of whiskey or bread and usually paid for their votes on election day. They also opposed woman suffrage.

Dennis Kearney, for example, the flamboyant and anti-Chinese labor agitator from San Francisco, who cast the lone vote against woman suffrage at the Greenback Convention of 1880, was often the subject of Duniway's blistering contempt. He was "California's greatest curse and deepest shame, the blatant blatherskite who leads the sandlot rabble," a "criminal, who was too shiftless to earn a living in his native land," a "worthless alien cur," a "truckling coward, who deserted his post when mate of a gale-tossed vessel," a "mountebank on the beer money of the Golden City's rough and tough elements," and a "brazen braggart," with a "following of corner loafers, midnight ruffians, sand-bag garroters, flannel-mouthed bog-trotters and adulterous political preachers."[44]

But again and again Duniway defended the virtue and industry of the poor. In a two-part short story called "Judd and John Mundane," published in February 1886 at the height of the western labor crisis, Duniway fictionalized her philosophy.[45] The poor sister-in-law of wealthy judge Judd Mundane bemoans the hard luck which had impoverished her husband John and led her to overwork and jealousy:

> "Why," she asked [her sister-in-law] fiercely, "should I, who have always been frugal, industrious, and, as far as I could have my way, enterprising, be compelled to live in poverty and drudgery, while you, who are certainly no better than I, may live in affluence and comparative ease? . . . Ah, sister, . . . I cease to wonder at the discontent among the laboring classes—the
>
>> "'Ninety and nine who live and die
>>   In poverty, hunger and cold,
>> That one may revel in luxury
>>   And be wrapped in its silken fold.'"

The woman says on another occasion:

> "The truth is that the whole financial system of the world is wrong. The few who get the inside tract become monopolists and crowd the many to the wall. Judd Mundane thinks he's a very superior man and manager because he holds a life lease on a lucrative position, which never ceases to yield its revenue in hard times or flush ones. He forgets that such positions are scarcer than hens' teeth, and only the fortunate few can get or hold them at all. Sister, I believe I have discovered the root of a poor man's discontent. It

lies in his utter inability to carve for himself a higher niche, because the places for higher niches are all monopolized."

Mentioning that he got his start "with a paltry five thousand or so as an inheritance," the judge claims, "If other people would accumulate property, they must do as I have done. They must work early and late and economize in every direction till they have saved enough to make them capitalists." His wife remarks, "There are few persons, even among the laboring classes, who couldn't get on in life with a start of five thousand dollars." Poverty-stricken John Mundane becomes a labor organizer, to the horror of his affluent brother, while his wife accepts the job of doing laundry for the judge's family because the Chinese laundry has been hounded out of business by the labor movement.

Knowing Harvey Scott's opinions and his frequent arguments with Abigail Scott Duniway, one strongly suspects an autobiographical background to the "Judd and John Mundane" story. Strikes and riots were occurring that February throughout the Pacific Northwest. Elsewhere in the nation conservatives were so fearful that they rapidly condemned to death three accused participants in the Chicago Haymarket labor demonstration of 1886. Meanwhile, Abigail Scott Duniway's newspaper proposed solutions which were both more radical and more old-fashioned than those of most of her contemporaries.

John Mundane, her fictional spokesman, tells a union meeting: "'The capitalist tells us that we are hungry because there is an over-production of bread. The minions of the law tell us that riots abound among us because we will not work. Wealth accuses us of improvidence, and power berates us for having speculated—and lost.'" Because he insists that the cause of labor's trouble is not the Chinese, Mundane's speech is met by "a storm of cat-calls, hisses, and cries of 'Put him out!'" But his brother the judge, hearing the speech and remembering his wife's advice about brotherly help, devises the perfect solution. A week later Mundane presents the plan to his fellow workers:

> "a couple of hundred of us, each with a capital of fifty dollars, might form a joint stock company and go to work, not to sell somebody something that nobody has any money to buy, but to manufacture something the world wants. . . . Gentlemen, there is an excellent body of timber land on the Sound shore. . . . There is timber enough on the land, if worked into lumber, staves, barrels and boxes by a joint stock company of two hundred, to make each of us moderately independent. There is land enough, when cleared of its timber, to make each of us a comfortable little home."

The judge agrees to surrender a mortgage without interest in return for the two thousand dollars raised by such a company. "The 'Anti-Coolie

League' changes its name to the 'Workingmen's Cooperative Union,'"
and "labor and capital gave up quarreling and joined hands in fostering
mutual interests."

Few immigrant laborers could put their hands on fifty dollars (the
equivalent of several hundred today) in 1886. Despite her good intentions, Abigail Scott Duniway was too far removed from them to understand their conditions. For example, she visited mining towns in the
company of managers, not miners. She remained fundamentally loyal to
capitalism, complaining only of its misapplication. She respected the
increasing wealth of her brother and other friends. She counted on the
support of the "better sort," who owned the railroads and mines and
banks and businesses of the Pacific Northwest—without realizing the
two-edged nature of that support. She wanted similar economic opportunities for everyone through regulation not destruction of the system.

Abigail Duniway disagreed with her brother about another controversial issue. She opposed the gold standard while Harvey made "hard
money" one of his most cherished principles. "Falsehood has no rights,"
he insisted, telling his readers that the intrinsic value of gold was a
matter of "fixed and unchangeable principles. . . . [T]he purchasing
power of money is exactly equal to the commercial value of the material
of which it is made." He knew that the "fundamental principles of monetary science are absolute, because human experience for 2500 years so
teaches. . . . Only ignorance, presumptuous folly or selfish interest ignore or defy them." Abigail Scott Duniway's monetary theories became
such a "disgrace" to the Scott family honor in the 1890s that Harvey's
wife, once a member of the Oregon Woman Suffrage Association
(OWSA), became an active antisuffragist. Duniway's own sons campaigned in 1896 for the Republicans and the gold standard.[46]

The ideas of the Greenbackers and later the Populists appealed to
Abigail Duniway, however, even though her suspicion of third-party
movements kept her from joining them. In 1880, as the Greenbackers
began to achieve prominence, she reported from a town in southern
Oregon that "the mercantile interests are almost at a stand-still, owing to
the absence of money to move the business. It is little wonder that the
greenback theory is meeting with favor among the people." Tying her
opinions to the antislaveholder metaphor, she said she was "ready to
predict that Gold, like Cotton, will some day prove to be not a king, but a
commodity."[47]

Mrs. Duniway told *New Northwest* readers: "there is no more inherent
value in gold or silver than in lead or copper . . . . The world would
suffer no loss . . . if gold and silver were to disappear from the face of
the earth. Their value is not based upon their real worth in usefulness,
but on their fictitious worth, which depends, first, upon their scarcity,

and second, upon the fiat of Nations." Any form of currency, including paper, "must depend alone upon the credit of the Nation which issues it, while the credit of the Nation itself must depend upon its resources in arts, manufactures, commerce, and all other useful industries."[48]

Duniway went on reiterating this idea all her life. In 1893 she told Clyde Duniway that she had believed it for twenty years—thus connecting her conviction to the currency controversies of the 1870s and the "Crime of '73," which had cut back the money supply by discontinuing the minting of silver coins. In 1896 she put it even more explicitly; she favored " 'commercial credit,' or a national and international paper standard, of which I have been an adherent since 63."[49] (It was Lincoln's Congress which had passed the National Banking Act in 1864, creating the paper notes which were the first uniform U.S. currency.)

Mrs. Duniway argued against both the "silver elephant" of the West and the "gold bug" of the East:

There is no such thing as real money. The thing is a fiction, a phantom, a pretense as any one can see in a panic. The only tangibly stable thing is government, either of monarchies or by the people. Credit based upon government is not "panic," if the government is stable. No government of any magnitude can ever pay its demands in gold. . . . But the world will never get over periodical panics, caused by the cowardice of gold (which would bravely face the racket if it were a *real* power and thus *prove* its alleged tangibility) until the scales fall from the eyes of enough of the world's under millions to cause them to repudiate the unlimited power of any sort or all sorts of alleged real "money."[50]

Revealing her agrarian origins and populist leanings, Duniway told Clyde she favored government regulation of the money supply:

Now, as to finance: . . . I would have the government of the United States, under it's constitutional power to coin money, re-declare its independence [of British financiers]. . . . Do away with the National banking system entirely. Stop all tampering with any sort of currency; that is, all brokerage and all trickery to bull and bear money markets, by taking control of all the gold and silver bullion that comes to its mints. . . . The Government has the gold and silver in inexhaustible quantities in its own mines. It has the power to take charge of its own property. If you say "paternalism will not do in government," I say "aye, aye." Paternalism is just what is the matter now. The bankers enjoy it to the uttermost under present conditions. As favored sons of the government they have the power to wreck every thing whenever they choose to combine and close their doors. "A fair field and no favors" should be the nation's watchword.

If the rest of the world refused to trade with America under such circumstances, Duniway said, "let us be patriotic enough to reenact that Boston tea party on a grand, grand scale."[51]

In 1886, while Clara was dying, Abigail Duniway wrote an extended analysis of her economic theory in the *New Northwest,* advocating "such changes in the administration of human affairs that they shall no longer operate to make the idle rich continually richer and the industrious poor continually poorer." She called "the hackneyed objections to the silver standard" a "re-hash of the old threadbare arguments against greenbacks, and . . . the result of the same cause, namely: the desire on the part of the money kings of the earth to retain the power." Though the Pacific Northwest had no "really poor, *i.e.,* none who cannot get a comfortable living and good honest wages by working for themselves on lands of their own," she thought, "and this last is always best for the industrious poor," she wanted to warn the powerful:

> While the writer does not recognize or accept the theory that there is a natural antagonism between capital and labor, and therefore takes no stock in sand-lot politics, we do see, in the legislation that for threequarters of a century has bowed before gold as its supreme lawgiver and king, a daily menace to the people's liberties that may well arouse to action the most exalted patriotism.

As labor riots swept the country and "robber barons" furiously manipulated for control, Duniway's "revolutionary" rhetoric continued with the metaphor so hated by Democrats: "Time was when cotton was called king. But the mutations of war dethroned King Cotton and exposed to view the power behind it—the slave power—that enabled the Southern planter to grow rich, with cotton as his medium of exchange, and slave labor as the fulcrum upon which it turned." She hoped the "idol gold" could be dethroned without the ravages which dethroned cotton, although "In holding our own [as a nation off the gold standard] a good many millionaires will go to the wall, just as, in dethroning King Cotton, the Southern planters who fought to keep the ascendancy failed to sustain themselves."

Duniway's ultimate heresy was comparing unions to other financial associations. In answer "to those who will complain of the sentiments of this article" she wrote,

> The example for trades unions and the organization of Knights of Labor was set long ago by money kings, who jumped the lands and held them, . . . and have ever since held the advantage through associations that have protected their assumed interests. It was an example set by bankers, capitalists and mercantile unions, all afterward combined into a great syndicate known as the Board of Trade; . . . [whose] emissaries now seek to throttle labor and the professions everywhere, . . . even as they have wound their

sinews of law and gold around the mines, the lands and the forests, holding them by a title as fictitious as the once supposed-to-be divine rights or title to individual ownership in man.[52]

Historian Lawrence Goodwyn has said the questions of financial theory and "fiat money" were "central to the ongoing problem of economic inequity and corporate concentration in America" during the post–Civil War era. "The possibility of a mass democratic politics free of decisive hierarchical business influence was a remote one."[53] This applied to Mrs. Duniway's cause even when she championed business as well as labor interests. For example, she greatly admired the Northern Pacific's Henry Villard, son-in-law of abolitionist William Lloyd Garrison, and was delighted to be included among the invited guests on the speakers' platform when Portland held its great celebration in December 1883 in honor of the railroad's completion.[54] But Villard's financial wizardry was a colossal disappointment to citizens of Washington Territory, who had expected the railroad to end at Tacoma. With the Washington legislature about to vote on woman suffrage that fall of 1883, Duniway's enthusiasm for Villard strengthened her ardent enemies in Tacoma. When Villard lost his control in early 1884, there was a political shift in both Washington and Oregon and a heightened resentment of railroad interests. Agitation became widespread for railroad forfeiture of excess land grants in Washington. Willis Duniway, now associate editor of the *New Northwest*, wrote editorials saying that forfeiture of railroad lands was undesirable—thus exposing his mother to the charge that she had sold out to the railroads.[55] Mrs. Duniway also mentioned that her friends in Seattle, the Yeslers, were now "burdened with heavy grievances" because of Villard's overthrow, which "changed the tactics of the Northern Pacific as well as its officers, leaving them out in the cold." She was concerned, she said, for all of Washington Territory and its need for transportation; therefore, "the present hostility to the grant . . . would result disastrously to the best financial interests of the people of Puget Sound outside of Tacoma." Government, she insisted, must "deal in good faith with the interests of corporations according to contract."[56]

Duniway certainly appeared to be condoning the speculations and profits of her friends while opposing those of her enemies. She also now frequently mentioned a relative among the managers of the railroad. But she herself knew she had not "sold out" because she still opposed monopolies and advocated the very regulations which the railroads hated: "the real issue in railroad questions is in the future, when men and women shall have grown wise enough and free enough to demand a railway system that will enable the government to control the carrying trade and transport freight and people at a rate in conformity with our

present postal system."[57] The idea of nationalization did not please railroad magnates or make them more favorable toward woman suffrage.
Duniway was on everyone's wrong side.

Abigail Scott Duniway's ambiguous commitment to economic opportunity for all can be compared to Thomas Jefferson's belief that "all men
are created equal," never considering women and slaves. The new conditions of an industrializing, capitalistic society created both opportunities
and inequities which could not always be reconciled. Duniway recognized the problem even as she hoped for the ideal solution. In an editorial which appeared on 15 September 1881 she wrote:

> Debt is the farmer's bane, the merchant's curse, the consumer's ruin, the
> editor's annoyance, the debtor's chagrin, the poor man's enemy, the rich
> man's friend, and the usurer's glory. . . . Without it the rich would have no
> chance to grow richer, the poor could not grow poorer, and everybody
> would have enough. Without it the world would learn the beauties of coop-
> eration and the delights of untrammeled action. . . . But, bad as he is, he
> does many necessary and wonderful works. He starts great enterprises and
> carries forward mighty improvements; he backs the steam engine that
> moves the world's commerce. The earth is not yet ready to do without him;
> nor will she be till "swords are beaten into plowshares and spears into
> pruning hooks."

Abigail Scott Duniway's philosophy exalted the values of the American
classless society as it supposedly had always been, in which almost every
laborer was also a small capitalist cooperating with business in expanding
and settling the country. As she said in 1886 in a speech called "Labor
Strikes and Political Upheavals," "Every thinking and reasoning person
clearly sees that there can be no real enmity between capital and labor,
any more than between man and woman."[58] She became more and more
"soured," however, "toward people who have no more sense than to be
'hewers of wood and drawers of water.'"

> The multitudes who toil unceasingly in the noise and danger and drudgery
> that accompany alledged "labor saving machinery" might be sifted seventy
> times seven, and you would hardly find one in a thousand who could
> comprehend your altruism sufficiently to help himself after you had pro-
> vided the means and shown him the way. Meanwhile you'd get only your
> sacrifice for your pains, and the money you'd spent in the effort would be
> worse than wasted. You can't make a silk purse from a sow's ear, nor a
> whistle from the tail of a pig!
>   And yet, I do not agree . . . that the case is hopeless. . . . It is not *indi-
> viduals*, but *averages*, that count in the great cycles of philanthropic endeav-
> or. The glacier moves slowly—*but it moves*—and from the *debris* of its mor-
> aines arise continents.[59]

CHAPTER 10

The Cesspool of Politics

"We have earned, and should of right hold,
a lucrative position in the Republican party."

From the time she stood on the limb of a sycamore tree, at the age of six, and imitated her father by shouting for "Tippecanoe and Tyler too," Abigail Scott Duniway had been fascinated by politics. Republican Senator E. B. Baker, her childhood hero, was one of her frequent lecture topics. She had been attacked by Democrats during the 1860s for running a Union school. She took the stand for woman's rights with a long-established reputation for Republicanism.

Her brother's *Oregonian,* the "overshadowing journalistic power" in the whole Pacific Northwest for forty years,[1] was also Republican. Though Harvey Scott and Abigail Scott Duniway disagreed on specific issues—especially on the gold standard, the importance of public high schools, and finally on suffrage itself—their family relationship was never forgotten by opponents. Resentments toward Harvey Scott were often extended to his sister, while she continued to assume that his fame and importance were advantages to her cause. She trusted her brother—perhaps more than she should have.

The *New Northwest*'s masthead reference to "Eternal Liberty, Universal Emancipation and Untrammeled Progression" was a red flag before the many Oregonians who were Democrats, Secessionists, or southern sympathizers. An influx of Missourians and other defeated southerners after the Civil War made Oregon even more deeply divided. In fact, in the 1868 election, Oregon was one of only three northern states which voted for a Democratic president. When it came to woman suffrage, southern Democrats did not easily forget that Susan B. Anthony's brother was a friend of John Brown in Osawatomie, Kansas, that Elizabeth Cady Stanton's husband was in Lincoln's cabinet, or that Abigail Scott Duniway was a radical Republican.[2]

In 1871 the city of Portland, despite its large New England and Republican population, was controlled by a Democratic machine, as were its newspapers. Even the *Oregonian,* which had been and would be so staunchly Republican under editor Harvey Scott, was temporarily in the hands of Democrat W. Lair Hill from 1872 to 1877.[3] Furthermore, most of the revenue which supported the city government was obtained by the high licensing of local saloons. Democratic politicians had good reason for favoring such a license system rather than outright prohibition of the whiskey business. Republicans opposed licensing, though later on they wanted to take advantage of the same revenue source. To prohibit would require money for enforcement, while high licensing would instead produce money for hard-pressed city governments.[4]

Scandals within the Republican Congress and the administration of President Grant were just beginning to be uncovered in 1871. The party split in 1872, while exposés continued after the 1872 election, affecting the reputations of most of Grant's supporters. After the collusion in gold pricing which led to Black Friday in 1869, and the exposure of Boss Tweed-Tammany Hall corruption in New York, there were also revelations of bribery among customs agents and the notorious Credit Mobilier kickback scheme for the Union Pacific Railroad in 1872. By September 1873 the nation plunged into a major depression as Jay Cooke and the Northern Pacific Railroad went bankrupt, and the Whiskey Ring—hundreds of distillers who had been bribing Treasury officials in order to avoid taxes—was revealed to the nation. Farmers in the West were deeply distressed by hard times and lack of money, while suspicion of government, of the corruption of officials, and of whiskey dealers was understandably rampant. Post–Civil War retrenchment had begun.

Abigail Scott Duniway, nevertheless, plunged directly into both national and local politics, fully convinced that women wielding the power of the pen would soon be granted the power of the vote as well. Oregon was her political "bailiwick," within which she claimed to be a chosen "representative . . . through the voice of the press and by long years of earnest work . . . of my large and otherwise unrepresented constituency." Outspokenly aware of the personal sacrifices she was making for her cause, Duniway applied to herself the same philosophy she advocated for others; she asserted her leadership and demanded respect for her methods. She expected those who had come later or at smaller cost or from other parts of the country to acknowledge and appreciate her significance. As she told her sons, "the world belongs to those who take it."[5]

Having arrived in 1852, Abigail Duniway could consider herself one of the early settlers of Oregon, in contrast to those who poured in after the Civil War. She had been nourished on the outspoken rhetoric of "Oregon style" journalism and the unfettered give and take of frontier politics; the *New Northwest* was intended to be a political instrument as well as a literary venture. Fellow pioneers, both male and female, were among Mrs. Duniway's first and strongest supporters in the territories of

Washington and Idaho and the new state of Oregon. That many of them were now also leading citizens of their communities was an initial advantage, too.

Abigail Scott Duniway's commitment to the Republican party of Lincoln and Baker, of antislavery and moral reform, was as pragmatic as it was idealistic. She began praising Horace Greeley, the potential Republican candidate for president, in the first issues of the *New Northwest*. She remembered his *New York Tribune* and longed to "shake the hand that has . . . done more to shape our destiny than that of any other living intelligence."[6] Her chance to do so came when she went East in the spring of 1872 to the NWSA convention in New York City.

Duniway gave a speech in Greeley's favor at the convention. She assumed he still favored women's rights as in the past. But Susan B. Anthony, who knew otherwise, appointed Duniway to go with her to interview Greeley. By this time Republicans had split, and Greeley chose moderation in order to gain wider support. When he revealed his "chilliness" toward woman suffrage, the quick temper of Duniway's platform rhetoric was immediately turned on him: "And now, Mr. Greeley, mark my words," she exclaimed. "You'll never be President! You will find that women can tear down, if they are not permitted to build up." Duniway later claimed she would have been "more diplomatic" if she had not been such a "novice," but the evidence of her life suggests otherwise.[7]

There was only one alternative to Liberal Republican Greeley—who was soon also endorsed by the Democrats. The Republicans already in power were running President Grant again. Despite his flaws, the party platform included a plank favoring woman suffrage. Encouraged also by most eastern suffragists, Duniway explained to *New Northwest* readers the necessity of supporting Grant Republicans. In Oregon, however, this involved also supporting controversial John Mitchell for the Senate against incumbent Liberal Republican Henry Corbett. Duniway did so, ardently, and thus became embroiled in one of the most vitriolic political wrangles in Oregon history.[8]

Accusations against Mitchell's personal morality as well as Grant's corrupt administration had solid foundations that Mrs. Duniway did not know about. When the truth finally surfaced, after the election, that Mitchell was a bigamist and an adulterer, Duniway insisted that she must "consider everybody innocent until proven guilty" in a court of law. Claiming that her influence used against him might have ensured his defeat, she called upon him to make "restitution" for any wrongs he had done to women "by becoming the special champion of the rights of all women. . . . [L]et his Senatorial career be one continued grand atonement to all womanhood for the errors of his youth." (Possibly Duniway was motivated by loyalty to the second Mrs. Mitchell, an uneducated frontierswoman noted for her malapropisms and inadequacies in Portland society.) No less unscrupulous as a politician than he was as a man, Mitchell retained Duniway's support, and he never did "atone."[9]

Abigail Scott Duniway was a firm believer in the spoils system as an aspect of representative government. She made no secret of her own ambitions, remembering Senator Edward Baker's help for her father's sawmill and governmental rewards to editors W. L. Adams, Simeon Francis, and Harvey Scott.[10] In March 1873 she told her public:

> We have earned, and should of right hold, a lucrative position in the Republican party. . . . Men who have never aided the party in any way will bear the light are appointed to positions that belong to us, while women, wielding an influence that will, if turned against the party, ruin it in a future election, are left to struggle in pecuniary embarrassments in publishing an influential Republican paper.

The *New Northwest* suspended publication until June, ostensibly because of an epidemic of measles among the Duniway children. But among Republican politicians the threat bore fruit. A few months later, Mitchell's law partner and a Portland banker gave the *New Northwest* interest-free loans to continue business.[11]

The Temperance Alliance meeting of 1873, at which Duniway was so rudely treated, occurred just after Mitchell's election. Then, in the winter of 1874, just before the women's prayer war on whiskey, temperance advocates, including many opponents of the Mitchell faction, formed the Prohibitionist party. Duniway opposed a third party, claiming that it would "cripple" the suffrage movement because it did "not consider the enfranchisement of woman the first need of this Nation. Enfranchise woman and the temperance question will soon settle itself." Splitting the vote, she said, would only help elect Democrats.[12]

At this point the enmity which her opinions aroused became so strong that Duniway resorted to a pseudonym. Yours Truly columns, which appeared in the *New Northwest* for the next ten years, purported to be by "a young girl of the period," and from internal content might have been daughter Clara's, but the style seems unmistakably Duniway's. With the hurt pride and defensiveness so integral to Abigail Scott Duniway's personality, Yours Truly compared her opponents to Revolutionary War Tories or Civil War Rebels, motivated by the "fell spirit of oppression," trying to destroy the cause of woman's equality by destroying her. Though they insisted, "'We wish the cause all manner of success! Our clamor is against the Duniway!'" she wrote,

> These fellows know full well that the Woman Movement without Mrs. Duniway would be like a locomotive without steam, an army without a

leader, a France without a Napoleon. . . . [B]ut for Mrs. Duniway the Woman Movement in Oregon and Washington Territory would be just where it was three years ago.

Yours Truly went on melodramatically about Mrs. Duniway's "long and self-denying" fight; "Then persevere, brave, struggling heart. Be not intimidated by the rage of your enemies. Your friends will stand around you as a wall of impenetrable fire," warding off "the poisoned arrows of malignity."[13]

A week after this outburst, Catherine Scott Coburn joined the *New Northwest* as associate editor, a position which she filled with diligence and talent for the next five years. Duniway informed her readers that her sister would "soften all the asperities which some of you complain of in us, and thereby please you far better than we alone can do."[14] Despite Duniway's requests, the OSWSA's second annual convention that February (and in future years) refused sponsoring funds for the *New Northwest*. Instead, it provided an able new lecturer who became almost as peripatetic as Duniway. Hattie A. Loughary, wife of a prominent Yamhill County farmer, campaigned for suffrage and wrote up her travels for the *New Northwest* for the next twelve years.[15]

Abigail Duniway spent that spring lecturing in California. When she returned she began her unwelcome "lectures" at the WCTU meetings. She also launched an attack on Addie Ballou, a San Francisco "poetess" featured at a Spiritualist camp meeting near Salem, who apparently snubbed Mrs. Duniway. Ballou's friendship with editor McDonald of the *Salem Statesman*, whose frequent criticism of Duniway was freely reciprocated, led the *New Northwest*'s Yours Truly to imply an affair between Ballou and McDonald. The column brought a rebuke from longtime suffragist Colonel C. A. Reed of Salem. Addie Ballou, according to Reed, declined to defend herself, saying only, with refined disdain,

"I have no time to lend from humanity, to idle in picking up the gauntlet of warfare [Mrs. Duniway] seeks to force upon me, even though it were not crimsoned with the heart's blood of my innocent children, or of a lone life, dedicated to misfortune's victims. The most abandoned of my sex and your own have need of sympathy more than rebuke. Shall she have less?"[16]

Duniway was not repentant. Instead, Yours Truly wrote another barbed "letter" suggesting that Colonel Reed was "a little smitten with the lady, too." Only an "acute sense of injustice, as well as of the ludicrous and ridiculous, . . . [had] prompted her to write the captured *Statesman* up as she did." Obviously

the couple were "smitten" and "spooney," . . . but Yours Truly's remembrance of her own first love affair . . . prevented the suspicion from ever crossing her mind of any other than honorable relations between the parties. . . . Mrs. B is a smart woman, who understands angling for men's praises to perfection. But that she is an angel in dimity, or indeed an average woman in philanthropy and nobleness, Yours Truly does not believe; because . . . she never would have countenanced a newspaper or its editor, when that paper, through its editor, was seeking to destroy the leader of the Woman Movement.[17]

Addie Ballou ignored the discomforting debate—except to write a brief note to the *New Northwest* asking for extra copies of the paper so she could show her friends "what one woman could say about another" in the great Northwest.

Throughout this same summer and fall, Mrs. Duniway was serializing *Amie and Henry Lee* in the *New Northwest*. The novel was one of her most virulent attacks on social snobbery, set in the fictitious town of "Portsmouth" with a virtuous dance hall hostess as heroine. Many readers probably recognized themselves or their friends among the maligned society characters, while Democrats must have been infuriated by the political implications of its plot. For example, there is a Democratic victory banquet where the destitute heroine's editor brother, who had refused to help her because of his own social ambition, gives an anti–woman suffrage speech. After making the standard arguments about wifely purity and female virtue being above politics, he also argues that political corruption would no longer be possible if women were to become free and equal:

> Go, for instance, to the 'Walk in and Welcome.' There are always to be found in that saloon, from half a score to half a hundred women, who rule to-day the political affairs of this city. Or, rather, I should say—*ahem!*—that we who are leaders in politics, through them, and the influence they wield with arts and embraces and whisky are enabled to carry elections just about as we choose.[18]

In January 1877 Duniway joined with Republican judge John F. Caples to establish an Open Temperance Society as an alternative to the prohibitionist Temperance Alliance. Holding meetings in the new YMCA hall, the group soon aroused the ire of the orthodox in a dispute over rent payments. In her typical "blasphemous" rhetoric, Duniway told her readers:

> These hide-bound believers in a seven-by-nine heaven, who would vastly prefer to send all people to a Miltonic hell rather than have them gain everlasting paradise by a route not pointed out by themselves, are jealous of the audiences these meetings draw, the enthusiasm they excite and the good that they do, untrammeled by creed and cant.[19]

Duniway also continued to attend meetings of the Temperance Alliance. In 1880 she engineered its acceptance of a woman suffrage resolution. Opponents claimed she did it through trickery in a "still hunt" during the stormy convention session.[20] Mrs. Duniway insisted for the rest of her life that the still hunt—political maneuvering and personal persuasion rather than "hurrah" campaigns—was the only way to win the vote. What she did not realize was that the method could be used just as effectively against her.

Abigail Scott Duniway boasted about being sponsored by many of the leading businessmen and financiers of Portland—all very wealthy and all Republicans. Names included Harvey Scott, Ainsworth, Reed, Denny, Mayer, Hirsch, Mitchell, Sprague, and Pittock when she listed them in 1879. Her business had just been reorganized as the Duniway Publishing Company with Willis and Hubert Duniway co-owners. The backers, she said, "wouldn't grant permission for us to thank them openly if we asked it, so we will not ask."[21] It obviously never occurred to her that such backing might be a two-edged sword.

That summer Mrs. Duniway visited Jacksonville, a Democratic stronghold in southern Oregon. After being rudely treated by several leading men of the town, Mrs. Duniway included in her weekly *New Northwest* "Editorial Correspondence" the "true" story about Democrat Judge Prim and his wife. "His protected and supported wife, whom he once banished from her home and children for two years because he was weak enough to permit somebody to slander" her, had finally been welcomed back "for her children's sake and his own convenience." Duniway's column then coyly continued:

We bear letters of introduction from various lower valley dignitaries to various masculine nabobs in this beautiful region; and, after we've had time to see what we can do on our own responsibility, just as we used to be compelled to do everywhere, we'll present the letters, and then, dear, confidential reader, we'll tell you all about the fun. There are a number of would-be prominent men in this place who have tried their best, because of their ignorance of our position, to snub and ignore and ridicule us, who, did they but know what their impudence will cost them, would bow like monkeys and chatter like magpies. It's too jolly for anything.[22]

The result of Duniway's story was "a mighty tempest in the social and political teapot," she reported the next week. "Squads of men are holding indignation meetings on the street . . . , and it really looks as though they'd be calling out the militia pretty soon for the express purpose of fighting a lone woman whose offense against them has consisted in simply telling the truth." That night, as Duniway finished writing her column, she added:

The plot thickens.
"On, ye brave!
Who seek for glory or the grave!"
The "militia's" been out and egged us! And they've burnt us in effigy, the image being a fair likeness of George Washington, so we're told, though we didn't see it; and it wore a white apron with the words "Libeller of families" on it in big letters—a fitting name for the cowardly *canaille* who seek, under cover of darkness, to exhibit their true inwardness. . . . Only one egg hit us, and that was fresh and sweet, and it took us square on the scalp and saved a shampooing bill.[23]

Duniway's Republican loyalties certainly contributed to her enjoyment of Judge Prim's discomfiture. When he lost the 1880 election, she was quick to take credit for his defeat. But ever afterward the case of the egg-throwing—"Jacksonville arguments"—was cited as proof of the "hoodlum element" opposition to woman's rights, as if politics were irrelevant and Duniway were entirely innocent of provocation.[24]

Throughout the 1870s, Abigail Scott Duniway had been advocating direct action by the legislature, as in Wyoming and Utah, rather than a state constitutional amendment, to grant woman suffrage. Like her friend Samuel Corwin, who had introduced House Bill No. 42 in 1872 calling for "the elective franchise to citizens without regard to sex," Duniway believed that the "better class" of elected representatives were far more likely to act justly than the mass of voters who would have to ratify an amendment.[25] Her methods were designed on the basis of this assumption. Republican Senator Charles Fulton from frontier Clatsop County invited Mrs. Duniway to speak to the 1872 legislature—the first woman so honored in Oregon. He introduced the suffrage bill in the Senate and remained her supporter always. The 1872 vote was very close—twenty-one in favor of suffrage, twenty-two opposed.

At the same time, Duniway's other women's rights efforts bore fruit. The legislature passed a Sole Trader Bill, which allowed a woman to carry on business legally even in the absence of her husband and to keep her property without liability for her husband's debts. Mrs. Duniway submitted petitions for a suffrage law to every Oregon legislature thereafter. In 1878 she rejoiced that a Married Woman's Property Act finally gave wives the right to own property, keep wages, and manage, sell, or will their property—the same kind of law which had been reluctantly passed in New York and Massachusetts during the 1850s. Women taxpayers also received the right to vote on schools—a significant form of power in local politics.[26]

But in 1880 prohibitionist legislators introduced both a prohibition and a woman suffrage amendment to the Oregon constitution. This provoked months of squabbling, while Duniway opposed "undignified" lobbying for "personal hobbies" by temperance women. She refused to involve the OSWSA in any cooperation "with the fanatical nonsense that demands only a one-sided 'temperance ballot.'" Nevertheless, when the suffrage amendment finally passed, Duniway was quick to organize a ratification jubilee and claim credit for the victory.[27]

The constitutional amendment would have to be passed again by the 1882 legislature and then by a general referendum in 1884. But Oregon suffragists were jubilant. Hattie Loughary immediately suggested a well-organized county-precinct-neighborhood campaign to ensure final victory. Duniway, fearing the "ignorant rabble" and assured by politicians of their support, preferred her own methods. Having been included, along with brother Harvey Scott, among the Oregon dignitaries who accompanied President Hayes during his tour of the state that fall, she felt her newspaper and political position could insure victory.[28]

In 1882 Nebraska's voters defeated a suffrage amendment similar to Oregon's. Duniway's New Northwest analysis of what happened reveals her own complacency about a potential Oregon victory. "First. . . . Had the matter been discussed throughout the State for more than ten years, as in Oregon, they might and doubtless would have regarded it differently. Second.—One-third of Nebraska's voters are foreigners . . . [who are] almost solidly against the amendment. Oregon has but a small percentage of this class. . . . Third . . . burdensome regulations in regard to the wording of ballots. Oregon will not be similarly hampered." She discussed how blank or wrongly worded ballots afforded great chances for "rascality," remarking that Oregon's suffragists would have "no absurd regulations about the form or style of ballot to militate against the ratification of the amendment."[29]

Unfortunately, the differences were not so great, as we shall see. Oregon was changing rapidly in the 1880s. Construction of the Northern Pacific Railway brought workers and immigrants; Portland's expansion exacerbated the political corruption; even the New Northwest's publicity and the 1884 balloting was muted by dirty tricks. Mrs. Duniway's trust in her eminent brother and his friends made her much more vulnerable to deception than she realized.

As one man later told Wilkie Duniway, it was "almost inconceivable to what lengths the brutal and coarse of that day would go" in order to disrupt Abigail Scott Duniway's work.[30] Her habit of standing her ground and fighting merely publicized such injustices, which she considered a good thing. But the results could be otherwise. For example, when an irate husband tried to refuse his wife's subscription to the New Northwest, Duniway told him to learn "that if his wife wants a dinner she is not compelled to do without it if he doesn't desire to eat too." The postmaster then delivered a whole bundle of New Northwests to the woman, claiming they were so addressed. The husband sent the bundle COD back to Portland. The Duniway Publishing Company brought suit against the postmaster, charging willful malfeasance against the postal inspector who investigated the case and endangering both men's jobs. The *New Northwest* got no satisfaction, but the son of the inspector was the editor of the *Sunday Welcome*, which published the slander about Mrs. Duniway and Senator Nesmith (see chap. 7).[31]

The founding of the *Northwest News* in January 1883 seems to have been another deliberate attempt to undermine the suffrage amendment and to put Duniway's paper out of business. The suffrage amendment had passed the Oregon legislature for the mandatory second time that fall so the public referendum was scheduled for the biennial election in June 1884. The *Northwest News* was outspokenly prowhiskey, and it consistently deluded and enticed *New Northwest* subscribers. Though no one seemed to know much about its various owners, Harvey Scott gave a surprisingly detailed description when he wrote Portland's history. The paper lost as least $200,000 during its short existence, he said, and was finally sold to a "stock company, composed of a number of the leading republican politicians of the city" with Duniway's implacable enemy James O'Meara as editor.[32]

The Duniway Publishing Company brought suit immediately against the use of its name. The Duniways testified to receiving barrels of molasses by mistake and numerous bills for paper and printer's ink which they were forced to pay. But the judge took seven months to rule no conflict, forcing a Duniway appeal to the Oregon Supreme Court. The Multnomah County Court judge was Democrat Raleigh Stott; the bailiff of his court was a man whom Duniway had publicly exposed for his immoral behavior at houses of ill fame. The man's father, influential doorkeeper of the legislature, had warned Duniway in October 1882 that he and his son "*could* and *would* defeat the amendment," by "methods we didn't dream of" which he wouldn't scruple to use, even though he had always favored suffrage in the past. The case stayed in the Oregon Supreme Court for nine months—until two weeks after the June 1884 suffrage referendum. Then the ruling favored the *Northwest News*, requiring the Duniways to pay substantial court costs. Having won its case, the *Northwest News* was immediately sold—and changed its name.[33]

Meanwhile, bogus stories about Mrs. Duniway's supposed connections with liquor interests appeared in many other newspapers. Thousands of defective ballots were printed by a Seattle wholesale liquor dealer with the suffrage amendment crossed out or marked "NO," even though Duniway had arranged for OSWSA to furnish ballots printed by the Duniway Publishing Company. Both Republican and Democratic central and county committees had supposedly guaranteed to "handle 'yes' tickets in such a way that fair play could be secured."[34]

Economic conditions were bad in 1884. The completion of the Northern Pacific Railroad had released thousands of laborers and brought hordes of needy immigrants, many of whom worked in the hop fields. They were warned that women voters would probably close their saloons. They were also paid up to $2.50 per antisuffrage vote.[35] The woman suffrage amendment was soundly defeated, 28,176 to 11,223, even though Oregon Republicans were victorious. All rural counties voted for it, but Portland's Multnomah County negative votes outweighed them.

Duniway claimed railroad workers from Washington had been rounded up and herded to the polls like sheep. But she blamed their stirring up on prohibitionist women. They said *she* was responsible for the defeat. WCTU influence had been burgeoning since charismatic Frances Willard visited Portland in 1883. Abigail Duniway liked Willard better than most prohibitionists, calling her "a Christian without cant, a temperance advocate without bitterness, a Woman Suffragist without acrimony." But Duniway still insisted on her own preeminence in Oregon. She continued to rely on Republican promises and rural support as Democrats multiplied and farmers stagnated. (Her report on the 24th annual Oregon State Fair in the *New Northwest* on 25 September 1884, is much changed from those of the 1870s, now describing the "waning power" of the agricultural association, the "worn-out field" mortgaged to Asahel Bush, the decayed wooden camps and "tents all gone," the hard times and low prices.) Duniway was sure that avoiding the liquor issue would have made the politicians keep their promises.[36]

Abigail Scott Duniway was so certain of victory that she went East to the annual NWSA convention during the spring of 1884. She used contributed campaign funds to print ballots, pay poll workers, and send the *New Northwest* to "all known enemies of suffrage." She had decided against "local and imported speakers" in favor of organizing "as men often do to win in cases where nothing is to be overcome but ignorance, hatred, vice and prejudice." She was horrified that the WCTU undermined her plans by hiring Massachusetts prohibitionist Mrs. Mary Clement Leavitt to campaign all spring about suffrage as a means to liquor control. She was also angry that numerous antisuffrage editorials appeared in the *Oregonian* for three months before the election, while Harvey Scott was out of town. She felt he had betrayed her, but she blamed the women more.[37]

Loyal Mrs. Loughary, president of OSWSA, wrote the *New Northwest* that she had not really dared hope for a victory. "Tears fill my eyes till I cannot see the lines," she wrote, but they were tears for the excess cruelty and injustice of the defeat. "Scarcely any Democrats voted 'Yes' . . . and every ignorant whisky man of the Republicans voted 'No,'" she claimed, because of rumors that it was a Republican and a prohibitionist measure. Nothing stopped obscenities like the men of Rainier waving a cross decorated with women's underwear on election day.[38]

Abigail Scott Duniway, without embarrassment, admitted right after the election that she used a significant part of the campaign money to commission an engraving "containing the honored faces of the host of friends of equal rights who have aided in the work in the past." It was to be "a work of art and beauty," showing the "Goddess of Liberty in the act of crowning kneeling womanhood" among her "loyal subjects." Because of the defeat she was now considering an additional, cheaper engraving "portraying . . . the polls wherein the rag-tag and rough-scuff elements of the slums unite with gamblers, pietists, foreigners, libertines and all coarse and silly women to beat back the tide of progress."[39]

When Abigail Duniway invited NWSA to hold its annual convention in Oregon that year, tactful Susan B. Anthony courteously declined. She told Duniway she was "doing splendidly" and should ignore the "envious and jealous." "All you have to do is to work right along—as the moon did when it was barked at. You shouldn't even stop to brush off the flies that light on the ox's horn." (The metaphor took root among Duniway's enemies.)[40]

During these years Duniway also spoke regularly to the Washington territorial legislature. There in 1873 a suffrage bill lost 18 to 12; in 1875 it was 15 to 11. A constitutional convention in 1878 defeated suffrage by only 8 to 7, while in 1881 it passed the house 13 to 11 and lost in the council (that is, the senate) 7 to 5. Washington women, however, did receive their property rights in 1881.[41]

The political proclivities of Abigail Duniway were major issues of the Washington Territory suffrage battle too. The 1883 legislature was considering an act to remove the word *male* from voting requirements, thus repealing the law enacted in 1871 after Susan B. Anthony's visit. When Mrs. Duniway arrived in Olympia on 12 October 1883, she found the Washington women in a "panic." They had been warned by several Democratic prosuffrage legislators that they must keep out of sight, and especially that they must keep Mrs. Duniway away. "It makes the members mad to see you on the streets! . . . Your very presence will kill the bill!" one of them told her.

Reluctantly, Duniway took the advice at first and left Olympia, promising not to return until the bill had passed. But she doubted "the wisdom of the present 'still-hunt' policy." She wanted to go frankly and honestly among the Members on suitable occasions, form their acquaintance as in former years, abstain from personalities or heated discussions, and let them know that we rely upon their patriotism, chivalry and sense of justice, because we have a better opinion of them than some of them seem to have of each other.[42]

How easily she had forgotten her pungent *New Northwest* legislative caricatures!

But it was the prohibitionist evangelical Democratic wing of the suffrage movement which feared her presence. Editor Clarence Bagley of the *Puget Sound Courier*, a Democrat, accused Duniway of "childish ignorance of politics." He and others favored an amendment to the law, rather than repeal. She was sure theirs was a "subterfuge" to ensure defeat. While Bagley railed against her in his paper, a young lady legislative clerk from New Tacoma (where hostility to Portland financiers and railroad interests ran particularly high because of the diversion of the Northern Pacific Railroad to Portland instead of Tacoma) wrote the Tacoma *Ledger* that "the suffrage bill would probably pass through the Legislature if Mrs. Duniway could be kept away." The latter considered that "an unprovoked slap in the face" as she was "struggling to establish justice for all." No women would have ever been employed as clerks, she said, if it were not for her years of hard work on their behalf.[43]

Urged by her friends, Duniway quickly returned to Washington. Longtime suffragists and freethinking pioneer Republicans like herself, the Olney sisters—one of whom was now president of the Washington Suffrage Association—Mrs. Sylvester of Olympia, and Mary Shelton, an Olympia storekeeper, accompanied Duniway to the legislature. She detailed the whole legislative battle to *New Northwest* readers, foretelling the exact vote and designating the two council members who were "pledged to whiskey." Her bill passed while the other was remanded to committee.[44]

Opposition to woman suffrage and to Mrs. Duniway was fundamentally political. Some even feared that Abigail Scott Duniway wanted to be governor of Washington Territory, which she vehemently denied in the *New Northwest*. However, some New York suffragists, including Lillie Devereux Blake and Dr. Clemence S. Lozier, did petition the president to give her the office, and the *Washington Post* took it seriously enough to write an editorial opposing her candidacy. "I am seeking liberty for womanhood and not office for myself," said Duniway, but she saved the *Post* clipping, which appeared on 24 January 1884, in her scrapbook. Her astute editor friend John Miller Murphy of the *Olympia Standard* (who had once been with the *Oregon City Argus*) compared Duniway to abolitionist William Lloyd Garrison and called Bagley of the *Courier* one of a "presumptuous band of professional politicians which seeks to profit from her life-long labors" by reading her out of the suffrage party. "If it was not feared that she would be an important factor in politics, an independent power that cannot be swayed by factions, the effort would not be made thus early to destroy her influence," he said.[45]

Nevertheless, times and politics had changed a great deal since Abigail Scott Duniway began to publish her newspaper. As soon as Washington women obtained the right to vote they launched a massive Local Option campaign, which Duniway perceived as one cause of Oregon's 1884 defeat. She campaigned energetically against the Local Option bill, which was narrowly defeated in June 1886. The WCTU was furious, but Duniway was convinced that liquor interests, both local and national, were actually promoting prohibition as a means of discrediting women and preventing them from getting or keeping the vote. More research needs to be done to corroborate or discredit that belief, if possible, though Norman H. Clark's study of the Washington prohibition movement, *The Dry Years*, shows how complex and devious the political maneuvering and the social situation actually were. In any case, Duniway's insistence that the proposed law was designed to be circumvented by the sale of alcoholic "medicines" seems justified. She insisted that

> Women . . . must first secure the perpetuity of their own liberties . . . [and not] be driven blindfold over their weak little equal suffrage bridge and made to break it down, carrying with it not only their own enfranchisement, but the fond hopes of the millions of women in other States and Territories. . . . [I]t is not the ballot, per se, but the power that the ballot represents, that is destined to do their work for temperance in coming years; and [wise women] know better . . . than to make their fire too hot, lest they cook their own as well as other women's ballot yeast.[46]

As we have seen, Abigail Scott Duniway retained her philosophy of agrarian independence and individual rights even as many of the farmers she knew (not to speak of urban leaders like her brother) were changing with the times. The political power of the "old pioneer" Republicans, whom she so admired, gradually came to be based on financial clout rather than on population. For example, Portland financiers like C. H. Lewis loaned funds to farmers like Ralph Geer. They also served on the board of directors of the powerful Oregon Railroad and Navigation Company (which had absorbed the Oregon Steamship Company), were involved in Henry Villard's scheme to divert the railroad terminus to Portland in 1883, and intrigued for other benefits with congressmen, senators, and legislators. The most important developing industry in both Oregon and Washington, even by 1875, aside from railroads and transportation, was hop-growing and its related breweries. Republicans Ralph Geer in the Silverton area of the Willamette Valley and Ezra Meeker in Washington's Puyallup Valley were two of the most successful of those pioneer farmer-entrepreneurs. When European hop crops failed in the mid-1880s, Meeker alone did a $100,000 business each year and employed around 1,200 harvesters. Oregon was the largest hops-producing state in the country. Entire families joined in the harvests each season, often earning "enough to supply . . . the necessities of life for half a year."[47]

The situation in Walla Walla, Washington, provides a microcosmic example of the whole Pacific Northwest. Tension over the issues of woman suffrage and prohibition had been high in that town even when Abigail Duniway and Susan B. Anthony first visited in 1871. The town's closed churches and the suffrage speeches the two women gave behind saloons helped establish Duniway's reputation in the vicinity. The source of the tension, however, lay in the town's foundation as a teetotaling Presbyterian mission, while its economy became dependent upon beer. In 1886, Duniway repeated to her *New Northwest* readers the sad story of "Mrs. Stahl, owner of the Opera House, and widow of the great Walla Walla brewer." (She told the story all spring in her speeches, too.)

> My husband and I worked eight years in Canyon City, he at butchering and I at the wash-tub. . . . When we came to Walla Walla, we brought *twenty-five thousand dollars*. . . . My husband started a brewery . . . and made a market for the people's barley. He gave fifty dollars or more to every church, and he helped build the bridges. There was no hall, and he built one. And after while we moved out here and he built these brick houses. They cost *forty thousand dollars*. By and by he die, and there was a debt of *twenty-two thousand dollars* left on the property. I go to work, I make a slave of myself, I keep the business together to raise my children. Now, they say I shan't sell beer any more. . . . (italics mine)[48]

Economic depression in the 1880s caused decreasing sympathy for the rich. Nevertheless, Mrs. Duniway chose wealthy Mrs. Stahl's example to explain her scheme for practical politics. She noted that Walla Walla's proposed prohibitory law was "good—as far as it goes." The problem was that it provided no compensation to persons deprived of their businesses. Arguing that no "town, county or precinct" has the right to deprive individuals of their means of livelihood without "paying damages," she castigated impractical Christian agitators who despised

> money that has helped in its way to build every church, school-house, bridge, road and other public work in the land, as well as the jail, the penitentiary, the insane asylum, the gibbet and the alms-house. It is the money power behind the liquor traffic that makes it strong; and the fact

that prohibition agitators, like most women, have comparatively little taxable property themselves, and therefore have nothing to lose, has contributed largely to the present excitement.[49]

Mrs. Duniway told the women:

> If, instead of joining men in this conflict for prohibition, which . . . cannot be enforced, except by bullets, you will utilize your newly acquired power by forming a corporation to buy or lease that great building [Mrs. Stahl's brewery]—if you will convert it into a cannery, or creamery, or both, and give employment to that woman and her children, and to the wives and children of all the men in your midst, . . . the fame of your philanthropy . . . and the success of your business methods will inspire the voters.[50]

The effect of Abigail Scott Duniway's suggestion was the opposite of what she intended. Prohibitionists immediately accused her of having "sold out to whiskey." The libel spread across the country, causing such things as the Massachusetts Woman's Christian Prohibitory League censure resolution. When Duniway repeated the story in her speech to the NWSA convention in 1889, Susan B. Anthony coldly shifted her allegiance to Anna Howard Shaw.[51]

In a society which expected women to be purer and better than men, Duniway appeared to be defending the indefensible and "playing politics like a man." She herself expected to benefit from the process, as she knew others did. When Democrats accused her of being an unscrupulous political schemer for whom the end justifies the means, she retorted that

> Women who are not ready to go down into the very cess-pool of politics, and so trouble the waters there that the angel of Freedom may have opportunity to enter and purify it, do not deserve the blessing of individual liberty.

Women, she said, "must submit, for the time being, to an order of things with which they cannot assimilate," but which they must take advantage of, working "from a practical, rather than an ideal stand-point" to gain their victory.[52] To temperance women, in the Pacific Northwest or Boston, such behavior was simply selling out.

Washington women did lose their voting rights in 1887 in a rigged court case, brought by a saloon-keeper's wife. They were not reenfranchised for twenty-one years.[53] Only in Idaho and Colorado did women get the vote any sooner, and neither state had significant temperance agitation. But Abigail Scott Duniway, who remained a Republican despite her flirtation with populism, and whose sons became pillars of the Republican party in Oregon, never regained the power she once thought she had in Pacific Northwest politics. Nor did she ever hold "a lucrative position in the Republican party." There was no spoils system for women without votes.

Nor for women without a public voice. The events of 1886 had taken their toll both publicly and privately. Clara Belle Duniway Stearns's death in January left her mother particularly susceptible to discouragement, just as political opposition had become most virulent. Mrs. Duniway's carefully reasoned arguments against anti-Chinese agitation, capitalist oppression, and prohibition legislation, made all politicians anxious to be rid of her. By mid-1886 she was persuaded to sell her newspaper "at a handsome profit."

Willis Duniway was now associate editor of the *New Northwest*, and the devious Hubert Duniway business manager. Willis was already showing symptoms of the heart trouble which would eventually cause his death. Benjamin Duniway's health had also deteriorated, and he longed for the ranching life he had left behind twenty-five years earlier. The family persuaded Abigail Duniway that the paper was no longer prospering financially, though its record books seem to indicate an income twice as high in 1886 as in 1880.[54] The subscription list had been only around 3,000 throughout most of its publication, though readership and influence were much higher. Duniway herself did much of the selling and collecting of bills throughout her travels, making her lecture tours even more exhausting. She too was tired.

Harvey Scott apparently helped in the persuasion. Soon after the publication of Duniway's story "Judd and John Mundane" in February, he told the Duniways about a potential railroad route in Idaho and may have offered to "forgive" a mortgage just like the fictional judge.[55] Meanwhile, Dr. Mary Thompson—a charter member of OSWSA, Dr. Bethenia Owens-Adair, and other "old friends" insisted that it was time for Duniway to step down. Thompson, a prohibitionist who firmly believed that "every woman, in the average, is more moral than man," had been clashing with Duniway for many years about the goals of the woman's right movement.[56]

Portland businessman Oliver P. Mason, a close friend of Harvey Scott, bought the *New Northwest*, promising to continue Mrs. Duniway's columns. Unfortunately, he went out of business after two months.[57] Harvey Scott promised space in the *Oregonian* for his sister's contributions, when he did not find them objectionable. The sale of the Duniway Publishing Company provided funds for co-owners Willis and Wilkie to obtain ranchland in Idaho. The boys moved there with Ben Duniway in July 1886, while Duniway stayed in Portland to complete the paper's last year of publication.

Within a year Harvey Scott gave Wilkie Duniway a job as typographer on the *Portland Evening Telegram;* then, from 1894 to 1905, Wilkie was editor of the *Weekly Oregonian.* By 1888, Hubert Duniway had established the H. R. Duniway Lumber Company with expectations of a "big future." Next he became manager and agent for the Brower & Thompson Lumber Company. Willis Duniway helped Ben manage the ranch for a few years, until in 1894 Harvey Scott obtained for him the lucrative post of secretary to newly elected Republican Governor Lord.[58] Without cash, printing press, or newspaper, Abigail Scott Duniway was—almost—silenced.

CHAPTER 11

I've Been Robbed

*"I will die as I have lived, misunderstood by those
I love best and serve most."*

Abigail Scott Duniway had great hopes for the Duniway ranch. There
were two large tracts of land in the Lost River Valley of south central
Idaho, obtained through the Pre-emption Act, the Homestead Act, and
the Desert Reclamation Act.[1] Like some others who participated in the
western land boom of the 1880s, she imagined irrigation schemes and
development potentials which were not to be achieved in her generation.
Hoping to carry out the joint-stock plan she described in her fiction,
Duniway was ready for the new beginning which the purchase represented. But her family had other ideas; they wanted no part in utopian
dreams or social reform projects. Ben wanted to raise horses and cattle.

Mrs. Duniway went to Idaho for two weeks in January 1887—then
retreated to the warmth of her home in Portland. She went back again
only in the summers. She was the Fourth of July orator at nearby
Houston, and she encouraged Clyde to fulfill his ambition to go East to
Cornell. In 1888 she even helped plan a classic frontier "shoot-out" in
defense of the ranch. Clyde remembered that episode vividly:

> Just then two ruffians "jumped" one of the family "hay claims" on Antelope
> Creek. Ralph brought the news to the Alder Creek cabin, some eighteen
> miles, where Mother and I were. That same evening Willis arrived by
> buckboard from Challis. There was a solemn family conclave on the crisis.
> Helped by the pioneer experiences and spirit of Mother it was decided that
> lawless force must be met by force—there being no peace officers within
> sixty miles, and the sentiment of the frontier requiring all but cowards to
> defend and vindicate their rights. Never shall I forget the Spartan courage
> and advice of Mother as she stood beside me while I was loading the maga-
> zine of my Winchester rifle. "Be awful careful, son. Don't shoot unless you
> have to. But if you must shoot, be sure you kill the wretch the first shot." We
> three boys left about midnight on our mission.

After her sons returned safely, Mother Duniway gave a "tongue lashing"
to the constable who tried to arrest them and insisted that Clyde should
leave as planned, immediately, for college.[2]

Except for her summertime visits to Idaho and some lecture trips, Abigail Scott Duniway remained in Portland from then on, attending cultural events, keeping boarders to cover living costs, and trying to concentrate on her writing. She soon realized that her sons had given up any interest in her "life-work" and now seemed to "regard the part they have enacted in it as a misfortune." She talked more and more of her regret that the ranch was so far away and by spring of 1892 she placed an ad in a New York paper to sell it. She wanted her share of the family business, which had all been invested, and she hoped to get at least $25,000. (This was before the Panic of 1893. After years of expensive litigation over water rights, plus drought and depression during the 1890s, the Alder ranch finally sold in 1900 for $2,150. The other ranch was sold to the ranch foreman in 1896.) Her sons no longer wanted to stay there, and "father" had grown "too old and feeble." "If I were able to do my part as in former years," she told Clyde, "I would go there and stay five years by myself—but it is a physical impossibility." She was then almost sixty herself, gaining weight and frequently ill with headaches, rheumatism, and stomach troubles.[3]

The loss of the *New Northwest* and the frustration of her "original design" for the Idaho property left Abigail Duniway stranded and depressed. After spending the summer of 1892 at the ranch, she became convinced "that father can not while he lives, make any more provision for me than he did when you were all babies; and now, he has my spare means entirely in his control." The "germ of future competence" within her boys would enable them to make arrangements for her, she said. "All I want is a moderate independence, and I am sure you feel that I have earned it," as a "just reward for my life of effort." She wanted to be free of financial worries in order to concentrate on her writing. With "exaggerated faith in the value of the Fifth and Clay home property [in Portland] and a small acreage . . . in Washington County," Clyde later claimed, and in return for her equity in Idaho, she decided to ask her sons to support her as she had in the past supported them. The result was not nearly as equitable as hoped, partly because of the disastrous nationwide depression which began in July 1893.[4]

Hubert and the others wrote Clyde to explain the deal they arranged. A trust agreement would put all of Abigail Scott Duniway's property into the ownership of her five sons and guarantee her $100 a month for the rest of her life. Since the present value of her Clay Street house, aside from all her other investments, was "probably $15000 or $16000," Hubert was sure it would be a good business proposition, "aside from our filial duty and our desire to render mother's life easy and as happy as possible." Hubert then explained in another letter, "Owing to mother's way of looking at business, we must *buy* this property from her on installments just as though we were buying from a stranger. If she is left to feel that she still owns it, . . . she will probably insist on managing it." Duniway soon mentioned that Hubert had shown a sudden "filial awakening," apologizing for his previous "neglect," and that Ralph was at last "very courteous to *me*." She had been haggling about the boys' proposed financial agreement, refusing to accept their original terms, but she now supposed "Willis will do his part, and I must try not to mind his pessimistic nagging. He is loyal at heart, and, after he has had his 'say' will generally be reasonable. But he has kept me weeping till my eyes are very weak and much swollen."[5]

Willis explained, that Christmas of 1892, that he felt "it was unwise for mere wage-earners to go to putting up regularly for mother while she has so much property," but by taking title it might be made to "pay." Though Clyde expressed a few doubts, the other four overruled him, and they all gave their mother an Astrakhan fur cloak for Christmas.[6] Within two years Ralph and the others began to have doubts. Ralph remarked on 7 April 1895, "The way times have tightened, we are paying entirely too much money to mother." (Clyde tore off the next few lines of the letter, as he did to numerous other letters when the subject of his mother's happiness was being discussed.)[7] Ralph continued: "Father is no trouble because his wants are simple and economical. What shall we do with mother? . . . The serious question before us is, by what course can mother and father be provided for, and at the least expense?" Hubert and Ralph soon stopped paying, and Ralph reported in September: "The 'trust' arrangement and the money spent under it has not made [Mother] any more contented than before." Clyde tore off another sentence. She "misstates the facts to all the relatives and some of her friends in telling her tale of woe. What to do to provide for her is a great problem. Father is easy to care for. He wants but little, i.e. kindness and his physical wants supplied." Ralph was distraught. "There is absolutely no money to be made on the arrangement mother had us make with her. The only hope is that a sale can be made that will get something over the mortgages, to be used in support of mother."[8]

Modifications in the "trust" were made at that time, and again in 1899. By then Ralph was still unable to pay his share, and Hubert was four years behind. In 1904 Hubert and Ralph dropped out altogether. Duniway scribbled on the back of an 1899 letter from Hubert to Clyde which reported that she was "satisfied" with their inability to pay, "I did not tell the boys I was 'satisfied' with their proposition. I said I would *try* to get along. But, to do it I must devote all my time to keeping boarders." Abigail Duniway received $100 a month from the trust from 1893 until the spring of 1895, when it was reduced because of hard times to $75 a month. After Ben's death her income was reduced to $40 a month plus the right of occupancy and income from boarders in her house. By 1904 a new agreement stipulated that she receive $50 a month, and in 1914 she began to receive $90. Hubert was manager of the trust until Wilkie took over in 1904. Clyde always referred to it as a "pious fraud."9

Abigail Duniway had discovered, as she examined the account books for the ranch in 1892, that there was no profit to be had in Idaho, and that bank loans of at least $4,000 still had to be paid. Most of the approximately $8,000 put into the project during its first year by Ben, Willis, and Wilkie was money from their shares of the Duniway Publishing Company—the end of the *New Northwest*. How Ben Duniway had gained control of all his wife's "spare means" is not clear, but apparently he had registered his claims only in his own name, and the ranch costs were much higher than expected. By 1893 Ralph told Clyde that "she thinks she has been robbed—(!) and what to do with her I don't know." That fall, Duniway wrote, she "overhauled the Idaho matter" with Willis, Wilkie, and Ralph and "*settled* it. I am obliged to be satisfied. The thing is buried and I will die as I have lived, misunderstood by those I love best and serve most."10

She remained bitter, however. Complaints about lack of money and her lack of freedom and independence filled her letters during the 1890s. She told Clyde, seven months before Ben's death,

> Of course I *ought* to care for him, and am quite willing to do it; but when all my means was *confiscated* and nothing left me but the *confiscator*, with not half enough of income to maintain him, I'd have to be an idiot to enjoy it! It is a comfort, though, when I see how feeble he is, to realize that he has no knowledge of his own failures!

The Duniway sons, identifying with their "good" and "gentle" father, were deeply troubled by their mother's lack of sympathy and patience, and agreed among themselves that *she* was the one who lacked financial sense.11

Deprived of the means to avoid household work, Abigail Duniway told Clyde in 1893 "this is one reason that I am *shelved*. You are the *only one* of the family that thinks enough of my capacity for public duty to ever urge me to keep on the harness. Perhaps I ought not to mind the *wet blankets* others throw over me when I try to make starts." She felt that

> the rest of the boys seem to have stopped, . . . determined to let all progress go on without them. How much their attitude on these questions has influenced me in later years it is hard to estimate; yet I know it has done much to paralyze my whilom ambition. Then, too, the financial embarrassment, resulting from giving all my savings away to another (who had previously sapped all my younger life), has been an active factor in effecting my asphyxiation.

She wanted to break "these octopus-like arms. . . . If I only *could* get rid of the grind of household drudgery! But that takes capital—something I am never to possess."[12]

During the summer of 1894 she told Clyde:

> I want oh, so much, to raise a fund to carry out my corporate—not exactly cooperative idea on the lands at Alder Creek. But there is no use in wanting. My hands are tied by the inexorable fate against which it is useless to struggle. I can't think of it for a second without my poor worn-out eyes get red with tears. So, let it go! I'll take a new start in the next world—by the holy Gods!

A month later she confided,

> Oh, how I did *hope* in the bygone years, that when my sons were men I might be free to *travel* and develop somewhat of my long repressed desire to *be* and *do!* But the dream is over. To live to eat and eke, and patch the blunders of another and—others—is my fate. Someday—and, but for the thought of that I would do something awful! Someday I'll get out o' this old body. It has been my only prospect for nearly half a century. But life is so long and dreary, when hope is dead—and you are only living to end it![13]

Forbidden to carry out her cooperative development scheme at the ranch (which indeed might have failed in the hard times of the 1890s), Abigail Scott Duniway tried to keep "scribbling." But this, too, without her own newspaper, turned out to be frustrating and discouraging. "I could do a great deal of literary work in these comparatively idle days if I knew where to turn for a publisher," she told Clyde. She sent him stories and novelettes which she hoped he would place in eastern magazines like *Scribner's* or *Youth's Companion.* (She had received personal rejection notes from the editors of *Arena* and *North American Review.*) She told him, "I wrote so many years under impulse of publication that I can get up no inspiration to write at all under other conditions."[14]

Many stories had Idaho settings. "Altrurian Romance" was about a cooperative joint-stock venture. "Eliphalet's Girl: A Story as a Man Would Tell It" concerned a husband who was glad to get away from being "overshadowed"; he felt like the "honorary but unnecessary adjunct" and "worthless appendage" of his worldly and active wife. In *Margaret Rudson*, Margaret's father Abijah was a fictional rendition of "poor old man Williams who went insane from living alone at Antelope station." "His fate," Duniway said, "has made me think much of *father*."[15] Eastern magazines were not interested.

The Idaho expenses and the loss of her *New Northwest* left Duniway with no spare funds to use for promoting suffrage or financing another newspaper or other forms of publication. It also made her more sensitive to issues of money—payment for lectures, expenditures to outsiders in suffrage campaigns, or costs of her own participation. She lacked the financial security of the new upper-middle-class reformers, who in turn could not understand her seeming crass materialism or her preference for inexpensive campaigns. Abigail Duniway felt so straitened, for example, that she could not sleep for days after losing a purse containing $21.00. (By 1909 the trust was worth only $5,000 to each of the two remaining Duniway owners.)[16]

Duniway still gave lectures on suffrage whenever she was asked—to the Idaho constitutional convention and the NWSA in 1889, to the Columbian Exposition in Chicago in 1893 (where she advocated homesteading for women looking for independence and achievement), to legislators and Fourth of July celebrants always. In 1892 she introduced the controversial Kansas "hell-raiser," populist Mary E. Lease, to a Portland audience. A Duniway speech on the topic "Removing the cause of strikes," given before 2,800 striking laborers in 1894, earned her the title of "Patrick Henry of the Northwest." (Harvey Scott's *Oregonian* refused to print it.)[17]

But Abigail Scott Duniway, once vice-president-at-large of the NWSA and the acknowledged representative of frontier American women, was now "de trop" among national leaders. When she went to Chicago in 1893 she found the Woman's Council "a most extraordinary body of the world's notables, among whom your mother, not being a member of anything 'federated,' . . . is not a leader. But . . . at future conclaves of the kind I will be in position to receive the recognition which long ago would have been mine if I had not been asphyxiated by circumstances." Nevertheless, at the National American Woman Suffrage Association (NAWSA) convention in Atlanta, Georgia, in January 1895, she was disappointed to find an "intrigue" among other women against her, apparently dating from the 1889 convention, where she spoke against prohibition just before the two suffrage organizations merged. She told Clyde she had agreed to a paid lecture tour of Idaho, but when the campaign began there in 1896, she learned that her lectures were not needed. Perhaps this was because the new organizing chairperson for NAWSA was Carrie Chapman Catt, who considered Duniway, and also Anthony, not a "safe campaigner." In fact, she responded to Duniway's objection to outside interference in the coming Idaho campaign with the charge that "we want a State Association there . . . made up of the best people, with the right kind of persons as leaders. They write me that the right kind of people are not the leaders there in Boise City. . . . [I]t was not the upper tendom that attended your lecture but the middle class people."[18] (One of the "wrong" sort of people in Idaho was Duniway's close friend and disciple May Arkwright Hutton, a goldminer with a questionable past and a flamboyant nature who was anathema to many other suffragists. Hutton had traveled with Duniway in Idaho, campaigning for suffrage in 1895, though she did not strike gold and become a millionaire until 1900. Despite her differences with other suffragists, she was an invited guest on the platform for Duniway's seventy-eighth birthday celebration in 1912.)[19]

Invited instead to California, after Ben's death, Duniway discovered that the eastern committee in charge of the campaign was "determined to send me to out-of-way and almost inaccessible stage stations," as she put it. They "would not permit me to accept invitations to go to large centers to continue my very popular and acceptable work," so she "got *sick* and came home instead and they are not happy." She told Clyde that California women agreed they might have won the ballot "if left to themselves" instead of being "dominated" by the easterners, who took $11,000 of the $15,000 raised. She also gave the easterners themselves "a plain but courteous talk about *combing the West of its cash in its hours of trial*. I think they won't invade my bailiwick any more except by invitation." It is not surprising that Duniway decided not to go to the next national convention, claiming, "There is nothing in it but to sneeze while Aunt Susan's body guard takes snuff, or pay the fiddler while the ring does the piping."[20]

Idaho, with a noncontroversial campaign managed mostly by local workers, approved woman suffrage in 1896. California did not. Carrie Chapman Catt, with local support, personally obtained the endorsement of all political parties. Idaho's sparsely inhabited Custer County was the only one against suffrage, perhaps partly because of antagonism toward the Duniway ranch, the litigation over water rights, and Republican Justice of the Peace Willis Duniway. But the many years when Abigail Duniway was the only suffrage worker in Idaho had prepared the way. Duniway rightly claimed more credit than she received.[21]

Meanwhile, in Oregon, the suffrage issue languished. After the legislature refused to pass suffrage bills in 1886 and 1888, nothing further was done until the OSWSA began pushing for another amendment in 1895. It passed the legislature at that time, but in 1897 the politicians were embroiled in such serious rivalry over the issue of free silver that the legislature of 1897 never organized.[22] The amendment's second passage was delayed until 1899, followed by the unsuccessful referendum of 1900.

Other reform-minded women were engaging in many activities in the 1890s. In Portland they now had a flourishing Ladies' Aid Society, an orphanage, and a Woman's Exchange. Abigail Duniway participated in the foundation of the exchange, but told Clyde she had been unable to continue because of lack of money. She joined enthusiastically, however, in the new Woman's Club movement, which had begun in Washington under the aegis of her friend Abby Stuart. The Oregon Equal Suffrage Association (OESA), which Duniway reorganized in 1894, cooperated with the State Federation of Women's Clubs, though many federation members were opposed to suffrage. Duniway considered the clubs "consciously or not, great recruiting grounds for the Woman Suffrage cause." Duniway was the OSWSA president, and often held parlor meetings at her home, but numerous younger women were now major activists. For example, Duniway gave credit to Dr. Annice F. Jeffreys, vice-president-at-large, for the entire process of steering the suffrage amendment through the 1895 legislature while she herself was absent.[23]

For a brief period Abigail Duniway edited a new journal, *The Coming Century*, but lack of money prevented its continuation. Later, with the backing of Frances E. Gotshall and her father, leaders in the temperance movement, Duniway edited the *Pacific Empire* for a couple of years. But she was not comfortable under someone else's authority (mild and cooperative as it was). She had taken on the project with high hopes in the fall of 1895, but the Gotshalls were unwilling or unable to provide the extra $3,000 investment she thought necessary to make it successful. Frances Gotshall's father was a second cousin of Clyde Duniway's employer, Henry Clay Frick, "but *not* a financier." His daughter, said Duniway to Clyde, "shows the Frick spirit, tho . . . she has a good many religious cranky ideas, the result of a narrow Methodist environment, out of which she is already beginning to grow." Duniway "admire[d] the girl," but she soon felt overworked and underpaid at a particularly difficult period in her life. (Duniway was also accused of being "coarse and shocking" for publishing stories like "Shock Locks." When Clyde read the story he agreed with the critics. Apparently no copy has survived.)[24]

As the Woman's Club movement grew, Abigail Duniway finally became acquainted with the elite "400" of other Portland women, who had previously ignored or snubbed her. She was very pleased to tell Clyde how Mrs. H. L. Pittock, wife of the *Oregonian's* publisher, upon joining the Portland Woman's Club in 1896, "advanced and took my hand and thanked me for being her 'inspiration for a quarter of a century!' "[25] But even though Duniway was soon elected president of the state federation, she managed to antagonize many members by her assertions of superiority; she herself felt no shame in saying, "for a long time our chief public diversion [was] to call club women to order whenever they would, inadvertently, break the [parliamentary] rules by offering some motion, tending in our direction, from the floor." On the other hand, she too "was frequently called to order by some good suffragist, and was sometimes deeply humiliated as a result of throwing hot shot, myself, among women" who claimed to oppose suffrage.[26]

After the sale of her newspaper, Abigail Duniway met regularly with her friends the Lewellings of Milwaukie and other prominent Oregon intellectuals, to discuss the problems of government and society. From this study group emerged many progressive twentieth-century reforms—including the "Australian" secret ballot, initiative and referendum, and direct election of senators—which came to be known as the "Oregon system."[27] Duniway contributed as much as she learned from this group, and many of her early letters are explanations to her son of ideas gleaned from books they were reading together. She told Clyde in 1892 that the Republican party was "dead," because it had lost its "moral purpose" and was ruled by the "almighty dollar. I do believe the Populists will eliminate enough of their crudities to make of this new party a moral force, so divested of cant and trickery that the rank and file of the Republican masses can become allied to it," she continued, mentioning her interest in the newly formed Industrial Legion of the United States. By 1893, she had "concluded to let everything go in Idaho and begin at the bottom in my old age." She would try to get the Oregon legislature to pass an amendment striking out the words "white male" in order to open the way to woman suffrage by the back door. "This . . . will put me squarely in the fight again in a year or two. I feel that it is wrong for me to be silent when there is so much for me to do, and that is one great reason for my long despondency."[28]

Family problems contributed to her despondency. Aside from grief over the death of Clara, Mrs. Duniway now carried on a running battle with Don Stearns over the custody of Earl Stearns, Clara's young son. She was convinced that Don Stearns would be a bad influence on the boy. She was also concerned that Stearns would not provide enough funds for his care. The ranch provided little Earl with a home for a few years, but after Ben Duniway returned to Portland in 1894, Earl lived with his grandmother. It was not a very successful relationship. She badgered him about health, morals, and money (or the lack of it); he complained about the food—and even left home after Ben's death for several weeks to eat in restaurants, until he ran out of funds. When he suddenly enlisted as a private in the Army during the Spanish-American War, she sent frantic letters to his commanding officer in the Philippines trying to get him released because of his "ill health." (At the same time, Harvey Scott was trying unsuccessfully to get Earl a commission!) Afterward, Earl became a cowboy in Arizona. When he wrote his grandmother a letter describing his job, she scribbled, "To think that Clara's son has come to this!" on the back of it and sent it on to Clyde. He later became a trapper in Wyoming and died of pneumonia in 1918.[29]

Duniway was intensely worried about her sons' amorous concerns. She thought Willis was fickle. (So did his brothers. Ralph said he was "peculiar and streaky as ever," while Wilkie referred to his "weakness of the flesh.")[30] With the help of her avid matchmaking, Willis became engaged to one of her boarders, and then broke the engagement. (He preferred to marry "wealth, position and style.") Often he sulked or refused to talk to his mother or went out on unexplained business. In his mid-thirties, his journalistic career uncertain (though he had worked briefly in Idaho and in Washington, D.C.), still living at home with his mother and brothers, Willis was apparently as despondent as she was. His appointment as the new Republican governor's secretary in December 1894 was a great relief to all concerned. Abigail Duniway told Clyde, "The position is better for him than to be *governor*. The salary is much better and the responsibilities nominal."[31] Willis moved out and married Alice MacCormac on Christmas Day.

In 1906 Willis was elected Oregon State Printer, under the aegis of the Republican party, a lucrative political position and one which enabled him to amass a small fortune. This position had once been held by Duniway's Democratic enemy Asahel Bush, so Willis's achievement was a particular pleasure to his mother. When he and the party fought a great battle against Progressive reformers to retain the profits from state printing jobs instead of receiving a fixed salary, she rejoiced in his victory as evidence of the legislator's respect for Willis's integrity. This was still an issue in the 1912 election. He died from heart trouble in 1913 with an estate of $100,000. His wife gave away almost all of it to worthy causes before she died.[32]

In May 1894, Wilkie Collins Duniway married Wilhelmina Barck, described by his mother as "firm as a rock." They boarded with Abigail Duniway for several months. When Harvey Scott made him editor of the *Sunday Oregonian* he too moved to his own quarters. (Wilkie became Oregon's billiards champion in 1907, and third in the nation in 1913. After 1905 he was foreman of the *Telegram's* typographers—a good location for a relative of the owner. The new owners who had replaced Harvey Scott fired him in 1915, shortly before his mother's death. His eyes then began to ulcerate. Within two years he was blind. Abigail Duniway was very fond of Wilkie and Minnie's children.)[33]

The situation in the Duniway household while the boys were still at home was not idyllic. Hubert wrote Clyde that his mother's "not having much to occupy her time and mind had a good deal to do with her working herself up into one of her impatient fevers (you will understand what I mean, I suppose)." He added:

> While mother and Willis and Ralph don't have many, or any, open ruptures, there is very little in common between them. Mother thinks they don't show her proper consideration, which is partially true; and they get

impatient and out of humor over some of her little peculiarities. . . . [I]t keeps mother feeling "injured" about half the time. . . . Wilkie and mother have seemed to be more companionable for a long time than she and the other 2 boys; but now that he is married, his time out of the office is mostly given up to his "birdie," (they seem quite happy) so that mother misses him, I think, more than she understands, altho' they *are* in the same house.[34]

In September 1894, Ralph also got married. The youngest Duniway was a serious, hardworking, determined young man who had joined his brother Clyde at Cornell for two years to earn a law degree. He made his career in Portland both in private practice and later as Republican city attorney. He often worried about the nation's money policy and about "the moral cowardice and hypocrisy that I see in 'good' men and women." At twenty-three he fell in love with Kate Schermerhorn, a one-hundred-sixty-five-pound schoolteacher from a wealthy German family, who was "energetic and inconventional in her actions for a woman." Because of lack of money they postponed having children, and Kate taught kindergarten, despite Ralph's concern that a married woman should not have to work. But by 1898 Ralph was able to tell his brother that "marrying a good, unselfish woman, and having a child by her, is a great educating and broadening experience, and it makes one a better man." Troubles existed for years between Kate and Mother Duniway, so that even Hubert remarked that he wished Ralph's wife "was more friendly and congenial to the family, especially mother, whom she never has treated with common courtesy, and sometimes not decently. None of us know the reason, but I suppose Ralph does." Kate also had a serious "difference of opinion" with Clyde at the time of Ben Duniway's death. A few years later Ralph was afraid she might "break down" altogether.[35]

The trouble with Kate was serious enough to cause Abigail Duniway to turn down a significant opportunity in the spring of 1896. She refused to run for county school superintendent in order to avoid jeopardizing Ralph's nomination for city attorney. The job would have been just what Duniway had always advocated for women, a position with power and remuneration and meaningful work. Perhaps she secretly lacked confidence enough to face such a political test. Anyway, she told Clyde:

I sent a letter to the nominating committee of the Taxpayers League, . . . saying that I thought it inadvisable for a woman to risk antagonizing *voters* by pursuit of any position where labor is light and compensation heavy. . . . Of course my real reason for declining was the fear of handicapping Ralph. . . . I did not want to give Kate a shadow of excuse for laying the blame of his defeat upon me, as she would naturally have done had a Duniway name been already up for office. Yet I should like to be a county school superintendent, aside from the pay in it; and I believe I would have been elected if I had made the canvass.

Willis, Hubert, and Ralph, on the other hand, enthusiastically campaigned throughout Oregon in 1896 for the gold standard and the Republicans, despite their mother's populist proclivities.[36]

Hubert's life during these years was filled with disasters and uncertainties. His lumber business was so badly affected by the depression and the floods of 1894 that he went bankrupt. But by the end of the decade, he was shipping lumber all over the world. He became more and more unhappy with his fashionable wife and his mother-in-law's complaints. Cora Parsons had married Hubert in 1884 (soon after the death of the unfortunate Ida), and her mother now lived with them. They had no children except for adopting the small daughter of a dying friend. Though Cora was active in Mrs. Duniway's parlor meetings for suffrage, often singing solos or helping with preparations, the family remained dubious about her "painted face," and Duniway always sided with Hubert in their arguments.

The most characteristic comment in Hubert's repertoire—one which appeared in almost every letter he wrote and was recognized as typical by his brothers—was that he was terribly sorry he couldn't meet his financial obligations, but he "firmly believed" his business would improve soon and he would then immediately even up the score. In one letter he claimed that Clyde owed him money—and the letter is covered with Clyde's penciled notations about Hubert's errors! As Wilkie later remarked, Hubert "is always willing to settle *in the future.*"[37]

Indeed, Hubert did "settle in the future," but not much in accord with his mother's theories about women's rights. His dealings with Cora and daughter Ruth were as ambiguous as his dealings with money. When Hubert left for China in 1901 (after years of being gone from home on various extended business trips), he wrote Clyde that he planned to stay for "several years" but had not told anyone at home and did not plan to until Cora changed the "tone" of her letters. Meanwhile, he wanted Clyde "to write me . . . when you learn of something which I ought to know. . . . I hope nothing disquieting will arise, but if it does, I want to know it. The truth—and a full knowledge of it, even if painful—is better than ignorance." At the same time, Hubert told his mother that Cora had been carrying on with traveling salesmen. He also informed Cora that if she left Portland she was to "put Ruth with Minnie and Wilkie." When Cora offered to go to Asia with him, he did not accept her, and he later complained that she had insisted on the expense of coming to see him in New York in 1903. By 1906 he explained that he was "not going to let things drift this way much longer," and again remarked on Cora and her mother "talking and criticizing and scolding as they always do when they don't get their way in everything." Fortunately, everything was finally settled. "Relative to the divorce can say that it does not distress me at all. On the contrary, it is a great relief. I have been slowly developing matters with Cora to induce her to do just what she has done."[38]

Hubert remarried in 1910, deeply offended that daughter Ruth "has never written me a line of congratulation." He refused to let Ruth live with him in New York, especially when he learned that "she had planned for me to send her to a dramatic school." He applied very different standards to Ruth than to himself.

> I have not offered to pay her debts, and I think it is best that she should economize and pay them herself, because such a lesson is necessary, or she will do the same thing again. . . . I can't afford [to have her come live with us], and I am sure it would not be best for her . . . because of her wrong ideas about the stage. Having to work and support herself is the best thing.[39]

(Abigail Scott Duniway was especially fond of Hubert's lonely daughter; Ruth Kerby became the only grandchild who was not afraid of her grandmother. She eventually married a foreign correspondent who became an editor of the Peking *Far Eastern Times*. She died in Europe in 1969.)[40]

Clyde Duniway's career was a source of great joy to his mother. He had won an $800 scholarship to Cornell, where he was an outstanding student under Moses Coit Tyler. He supported equal rights for female Cornell students and gave a commencement oration on "Universal Suffrage." When he graduated in 1892, the president of Cornell recommended him as a tutor for the son of Henry Clay Frick, general manager of Andrew Carnegie's steel mill empire. Clyde took the job, acting also as Frick's home secretary at $2,000 a year, just before the famous Homestead strike and its bloody suppression at Frick's mills in July 1892, "the most spectacular conflict in all this period of industrial war." Clyde accompanied the Fricks on five tours of Europe. From 1893 to 1896, Frick paid Duniway's expenses at Harvard in return for having Frick's son live with him there.[41]

Clyde Duniway wrote a Harvard Toppan Prize Ph.D. dissertation later published with the title "The Development of Freedom of the Press in Massachusetts," a subject obviously related to his mother's work. He was the concluding speaker for a victorious Harvard debating team against Yale in 1894, and in 1896 he spoke in favor of woman suffrage before a Massachusetts legislative committee. Mrs. Duniway's lengthy discourses on finance were written in answer to Clyde's letters during these years. When he took issue with her populism, she told him tolerantly, "I do not expect you, my son, to harbor convictions differing from your present environment. For your own conscience's sake it is better so—for you.

But, my dear, the world is moving! The agitation, under which the country is being stirred as never before, began with the public schools and will never be settled till it is settled right, and in the interest of all the people."[42] Clyde became a professor of history at Stanford University for the next ten years, and then successively president of the University of Montana, the University of Wyoming, and Colorado College in Colorado Springs. Later he taught at Carleton College in Minnesota.

With Willis, Wilkie, Hubert, and Ralph all married by the end of 1894, Mother Duniway was delighted that her distant "C-o-y-d-i-e" was also confiding to her his matrimonial hopes. But apparently he was refused when he "popped the question" at Christmastime 1895; Ralph wrote him in January with sympathy for his "great disappointment and bereavement": "Why or how a woman could cause you a disappointment is beyond my comprehension," he said.[43] (Clyde made a happy marriage to Caroline Cushing in 1901.)

Benjamin Duniway's condition was a continuing problem during the 1890s. Even while he was at the Idaho ranch his judgment was a worry to the family and a constraint on his wife. But in the fall of 1894, Ben Duniway told an Idaho friend that he was going home to die. At sixty-four his arteriosclerosis and sciatic pain from the ancient back injury made him almost helpless. Besides the pain, he suffered from sudden "attacks" of some sort, frequent bad coughs, and morning nausea. Cold all the time, he loved to sit by a hot stove, even in July. A doctor said, "that fistula, *contracted years ago on the beach*, . . . is insidiously poisoning his whole system" and would "close the scene" in "a matter of months, or years."[44] (One of Mrs. Duniway's favorite metaphors to explain her opposition to prohibition was that covering an "abscess . . . with a rigid prohibition plaster" would cause "the virus thus confined [to] burrow deeper and yet deeper into the body of the man, and would ultimately rot him to death.")[45]

Duniway made no secret of her resentment at having to care for Ben without physical or financial help. She knew nothing about nursing, and complaints filled her letters:

> I am doing everything I can to help me to grow into a sweet, intellectual old age, but it's up-hill work, under the circumstances. Your father . . . has quite recovered from his late sciatica, and seems the same as for forty years. He reads the *Oregonian*, his only occupation from morning till night.
>
> My years are *wasting!* I have no time for literary work; no chance to condense or collate thoughts—much less put them to paper. . . . I feel that some change for me is inevitable, if it is only to the insane asylum.

Her children were not sympathetic: "When I tell him (Wilkie) that it is *hard* that I should be left *alone* in my declining years to endure the environment which *my love for my children alone nerved me to endure for nearly half a century,* he says 'there is nothing unusual the matter,' etc. and changes the subject. . . ." She sent Ben to visit "his people" for a month in the summer of 1895. Then Ralph and his new wife Kate took him in. Duniway exclaimed, alluding to the hated "trust" agreement, "I simply *cannot* retain my reason under the conditions of the past year. I don't feel unkindly to him, . . . but it is not my duty to simply wash dishes forever in his atmosphere, and divide dole, *and I won't.*" But Kate gave up as soon as Father fell sick again. Throughout the winter and spring of 1896, with recovered appetite but failing mind, Ben sat "'ever, forever,' in the corner, in a hot room, as of yore, watching me struggle to support him in complacency and contentment. If there isn't freedom for me in the next life there ought to be; that's all! *Certes,* I've failed to secure it in this."[46]

Ben Duniway became more and more of a burden, falling in the basement—where his wife found him half-conscious and had to carry him upstairs herself—disappearing all night after a visit to Harvey Scott, losing all awareness of time and place. Sixty-two-year-old Abigail Scott Duniway, without any nurses or housekeepers to help her and no money to hire them because of her sons' "hard times," dosed Ben with castor oil, the nineteenth-century cure-all. "The care of him, when his bowels finally acted, was equal to that of a dozen babies."[47]

It was not just the current illness which upset Abigail Duniway; it was the intensification of a lifelong problem, the culmination of personal and marital sorrow which had never been resolved. "At times," said Duniway, "my heart goes out to him with an overweening sympathy, because of his incomplete existence, and I find myself wondering if such as he will have another chance, in a new life upon the earth, in some future generation!"[48] She herself, however, could not believe in such a new life; Ben's wasted existence and slow dying filled her with despair for her own and a loneliness which could not be assuaged. Even the most "saintly" and domestic of women would have been sorely tried by the circumstances of the forty-three-year-long Duniway marriage. Abigail Duniway was neither.

The lassitude and "contentment" which Duniway so often complained of in Ben's character, along with the loquaciousness of his younger years and the long silences of his last year, suggest the probability that Ben Duniway's doctors had followed standard medical practice for the back injury he sustained in 1861. Medical historians now know that "chronic pain in the mid-19th century was a likely prelude to opium addiction." Opium was the foundation of such widely used patent medicines as laudanum, and it was also "extolled . . . uncritically" by all the leading British and American medical textbooks. The United States Army surgeon general drank it mixed with wine at every meal, for example, and Sigmund Freud used it as a general tonic and cure for alcoholism. Addiction, when it was recognized at all, was generally considered evidence of weak character rather than inevitable—putting patients into a double bind with their disgusted relatives. It was believed that sudden withdrawal could lead to death, though cocaine was sometimes recommended as a cure. Purgation with a cathartic was used to "neutralize" the system.[49] Whether or not Ben Duniway was such a tragic victim of the inadequacies of nineteenth-century medicine (which can never be determined, of course), his sciatic pain alone would have been severely disabling.

Abigail Duniway was certainly aware of opium usage. Opiates and drugged whiskey frequently appear in her novels—as a remedy for fever, as a cause of the near death of a heroine's brother (she recognizes it by the odor of opium), as a means of control administered with a hypodermic needle by the evil "Dr. McClurge." The invalidism of Margaret Rudson's mother is caused by drugs originally administered by a doctor and continued for comfort. The mother's suffering is such that her daughter gives her a lethal dose of cocaine to enable her to "slip away peacefully to death."[50] The *New Northwest* reprinted an article describing the miseries of opium addiction "among nearly all classes, and its effect upon mind and body . . . generally disastrous." But, when a Portland minister called for an opium ban in 1880, Duniway claimed whiskey was even more dangerous. Her argument against total prohibition was that whiskey would always be available to those who wanted it, by the use of medical prescriptions—as was also the case with drugs. After listening to a sermon entitled "The Opium Fiend" in 1893, she told Clyde, it "ought to warn physicians against prescribing sedatives in their practice."[51]

Benjamin Charles Duniway died on 4 August 1896. Clyde had come home that summer for the first time in several years, so the whole family was together to share the sorrow of losing "poor old father." In the spring there had been some sort of family upheaval, during which Mother Duniway "unbosomed" herself in a letter which Clyde destroyed. There remain only various censored letters and a cryptic note from Hubert alluding to "the difficulty you mention. [possibly Clyde's matrimonial rejection] . . . [W]e must endeavor to arrange it so there will be no chance for the matter to ever be brought up."[52] While Clyde was home Willis had a "terrible quarrel" with his mother, "both paying each other in kind." Clyde remembered that "After Willis left he had to lock her in and get her in tears like a child to break the feud. It was over some business deal in which each thought the other had the better."[53] Whatever else went wrong will never be known, except for Wilkie's letter to Clyde just after he left:

> Dear brother, your visit was not productive of much happiness to you, I fear, as the family skeleton was exposed to your gaze in a manner that could not have been possible if you had been away; but trials come to us all, and, though the one we boys have gone through was a severe one, and one whose presence seemed wholly unnecessary, yet we must make the best of it and try to believe that all things have their use and purpose. It was hard and it is hard, but I am trying to put it to one side as much as possible, and I believe you are philosopher enough to do the same. The loss of poor old father was in the order of nature; we all felt badly, but under the circumstances could not mourn deeply.[54]

During the following years Abigail Duniway was frequently ill with "la grippe" and "bilious" attacks. She had such spells all her life, especially after emotional or physical strain, but the winter of 1897 was particularly bad. Nevertheless, after recovering from Ben Duniway's death, Abigail was able to turn her full attention back to the issue of woman suffrage as the new century approached. Though "robbed" and "misunderstood," she was determined to complete her life's work before she died. At sixty-four, she felt there was not much time left.

CHAPTER 12

Freedom at Last

"I'm ready to go."

In a speech delivered in Grand Rapids, Michigan, to the national convention of the NAWSA in 1899, Abigail Scott Duniway employed her typical rhetoric to tell the assembled women "How to Win the Ballot."

> God made the sexes to match each other. Show me a woman who doesn't like men, and I will show you a sour-souled, vinegar-visaged specimen of unfortunate femininity, who owes the world an apology for living in it at all; and the very best thing she could do for her country, provided she had a country, would be to steal away and die, in the company of the man who doesn't like women. . . . A home without women in it, is only half a government. Man without a woman is like one-half of a pair of dislocated shears. Woman without man is like the other half of the same disabled implement. Male and female created He them, saith the Higher Law, and to them God gave dominion "over every living thing upon the earth"—except each other.

The scissors analogy, drawn from Benjamin Franklin's *Poor Richard* sayings, was used in many nineteenth-century discourses on the nature of womanhood and marriage. It was a well-known fact, however (though possibly not to Duniway herself), that NAWSA's Anna Howard Shaw hated men and had, like many other "New Women" of her era, deliberately chosen never to marry. Duniway's speech went on to discuss tactics:

> If you wish to convince a man that your opinion is logical and just, you have conquered the outer citadel of his resentment when he throws back his head and opens his mouth to laugh. . . . Your next step must be to impress upon all men the fact that we are not intending to interfere, in any way, with their rights; and all we ask is to be allowed to decide, for ourselves, also as to what our rights should be.

It was "the advent of good women in the border territories" that changed the riotous conditions of public life, Duniway continued, anticipating some modern analysts of women's role in the history of the West. The ballot would neither destroy the home nor revolutionize society, as women had proved "by their conduct, as voters, in Wyoming, Colorado, Utah,

206

and Idaho." These states had all passed suffrage for women without any prohibitionist agitation. "Your ideal, hysterical reformer, whose aim in life is to put men in leading strings, like little children," said Duniway, "doesn't hail from any state where women vote."[1]

Temperance-prohibitionists, who had by then become the major force in the woman suffrage movement, listened without conviction as Duniway told them about woman's "greatest blunder" during "the last two decades."

> Whenever she demands the ballot, not simply because it is her right to possess it, but because by its use, she expects to reconstruct the genus man by law, on a basis of her own choosing, she only succeeds in driving nails into the closed coffin lid of her own and other women's liberties.

To the assembled reformers, now predominantly Protestant, middle-class, nativist, evangelical, and antisocialist conservatives, she proclaimed,

> Catholics have just as good right to their religious opinions as Protestants. Republicans have just as good right to their political bias as Democrats, and Socialists have just as good a right to their reformatory fancies as Prohibitionists.

Thus, any attempt by national or state suffrage associations to become champions of a particular "ism" would alienate opponents and rally only those who agreed. "We need all the votes we can get from all parties to win," declared Duniway. Her speech concluded with the confident assertion that Oregon in 1900 would ratify an equal suffrage amendment "as the most fitting accompaniment to the dawn of the 20th century."[2]

If only she had been right about that election, the new wave of prohibitionist-suffragists might have forgiven Abigail Scott Duniway and allowed her the credit in history which she deserved. But financial interests, hard money advocates, antiprohibitionists, liquor interests—and Harvey Scott's *Oregonian*—could not overlook the threat of woman suffrage, despite Duniway's assurances. The strength of the WCTU and the opposition to her among other women was obvious. Men like Harvey Scott, who aspired to become a senator or even vice-president within the corrupt political milieu of the time, could not afford to let her win. (Scott's bid for senator was defeated in the legislature in 1903, and he did not obtain the vice-presidential nomination in 1905.)[3]

The election of 1900 was a crucial test of Abigail Duniway's "still hunt" method. This involved an emphasis on persuasion of influential voters through personal contacts and educational publicity rather than a mass appeal through a public campaign which would stir up opposition. As Frances Gotshall praised it in 1899 in a report to the national organization, by "dispelling prejudice and opposition" Mrs. Duniway "left the Legislators free to act, without instructions from their constituents." Unknown to others, Duniway also wrote personal letters to journalists and leaders of the liquor industry, assuring them that the majority of women did not favor prohibition and urging the justice of female suffrage. Suspicious of any workers who might connect her cause to prohibition, as in 1884, Duniway refused all help from national organizers except $100 for printing expenses. As she later reported,

> I received no less than 40 appeals from Eastern women, urging an immediate organization of a "hurrah campaign." Each applicant expected employment at a good salary, expenses included, to be guaranteed by our Executive Committee, not one of whom was receiving or expecting a penny for her long years of devotion to the work which had made a "campaign" possible. But, as there was no money to hire speakers (and none were wanted) I, at least, felt for the first time in my life like saying, "Blessed be poverty."[4]

The vote was extremely close—only two thousand short of victory: 28,402 No to 26,265 Yes, with a negative plurality in Portland of 3,473. The heartbreaker revealed another "villain." Harvey Scott's *Portland Oregonian* suddenly launched a massive editorial campaign against the amendment two weeks before the election, the only opposing paper out of 229 in Oregon. Scott himself was "out of town" and unable to fulfill the promise of support he had given his sister the previous February. At that time, when the relatives all gathered for a birthday dinner, there had been "a regular old-time Scott turn at extravagant expressions, and heat and anger on his part" about woman suffrage. Harvey had been "in an awful state of mind, and abused Aunt Kate some, and mother and her boys very badly." But when Abigail went to see him again, "he made a most abject apology, . . . told her he had been worried by a multitude of things . . . and was almost beside himself; hoped that 'sister, you will forgive me'; . . . acknowledged he had been wrong to oppose woman suffrage, and would not do so any more." Wilkie reported to Clyde that his mother now thought her victory assured.[5]

Harvey's betrayal enraged Abigail Scott Duniway. Using what she considered her most potent weapons—ridicule and sarcasm—she accused Harvey of the most despicable crimes in her book—mental incompetence and family disloyalty:

> My poor, Dear Brother. . . . The most charitable construction the many loyal women of your acquaintance can put upon your conduct toward the many brainy women of your own household, every one of whom is a suffragist, is that the cheap male sycophants who suck their sustenance from your editorial seats, (which they are not big enough to fill,) have flattered you till

you are insane on the sex question. The women everywhere must be apprised of this.

. . . I now understand the full meaning of Mr. Pittock's (your good partner's) words to me last summer, when [he] said that what you needed, most of all, was mental rest, for your dyspepsia and rheumatism.

The bitterness I have felt toward you because of your brutal treatment of your family during this season of trial is all dispelled before this new peril. . . . Your faithful sister *Jenny*

Once a hopeless drudge on a Hardscrabble farm, now known as Abigail Scott Duniway of the United States

She also wrote a scorching political pamphlet which Susan B. Anthony persuaded her to modify before its publication.[6]

Unfortunately, Duniway's mockery was the weapon of a powerless woman; men alone held the financial keys to political control—and they did not hesitate to use them. When the chips were down, editor Harvey Scott owed more to them than to his sisters. Abigail Scott Duniway understood such pressure, but she was unwilling to believe that her own brother and sons—who always maintained the appearance of absolute rectitude—could ever be connected to the hated whiskey interests. The extent of political corruption which afflicted Portland, Oregon, and most other urban areas in 1900 had not yet been revealed to most Americans. Abigail Duniway probably knew more about politics than other women because of her family connections and long experience, but her own opposition to prohibition did not blind opponents to the strength of the WCTU reform movement. As NAWSA's President Carrie Chapman Catt later admitted, "Had there been no prohibition movement in the United States, the women would have been enfranchised two generations before they were."[7]

Abigail Duniway's sons shared neither the sense of total dedication to her cause nor the sense of total devastation in its defeat. In 1900 she felt close to the end of her life; they were sorry for her loss as one might be sorry for the loser of a tennis game. Wilkie wrote Clyde that "Mother's active animosity against Uncle Harv has given place to a determined but rather good-natured opposition, which becomes her. . . . [A]nd he has ordered his family not to call on mother any more. How's that for smallness?"[8] Ralph suggested that Clyde invite her to visit him in California, where "she might get a hold on herself; stop worrying over the past; lose her bitterness; and get interested in something else." He wanted her to become "reasonably content . . . and stop crying down her own people and posing as a martyr." He thought that if she could only take up the Oregon suffrage movement "in a hopeful, pleasant way, that would be good for her, but she is so old, and weak, and so wrought up over the way she has been treated, that she cannot take hold of it in a way that will do her any good, but it will do her harm." He considered her "a problem and how to solve it I do not know. . . . Something for her to eat, wear and sleep is not sufficient."[9] Such patronizing concern must have been almost as disturbing to Duniway as the defeat itself.

But Ralph was right about her physical condition. For the past decade Abigail Duniway had been having more and more infections which were slow to heal, episodes of "biliousness" and rheumatism, and, of course, the great weight gain which shows in her photographs. She spoke increasingly of the late summer "cornginer" [angina?] which had plagued her "ever since Ralph's birth" in 1869, and of her "chronic infirmity" of the bladder, which "will go with me to the crematorium unless I submit to surgery." Her doctor said it was "probably too late" for surgery and that she "must simply avoid lifting, or other exhausting work, and use a local remedy." She visited mineral water springs, as she had been doing for thirty years, hoping "these waters will heal, or at least modify" the "abrasions" caused by the "artificial aids" she wore for her fallen uterus. Such establishments were the best sources of gynecological treatment in the nineteenth century. In 1903, when she finally did go to California to visit Clyde and his new wife, a long-standing ear infection forced her into the hospital for a mastoidectomy. She almost died, and after the long recovery, remained deaf in one ear.[10]

Despite the bad health and discouragement, in 1904 she began planning for another suffrage referendum. Oregon's Initiative and Referendum Amendment, passed in 1902, meant that the long process of submitting an amendment to the legislature was no longer necessary. Because of her illness, nothing had been done in time for a 1904 vote, but there were two years to prepare for 1906. A grand Lewis and Clark Exposition was being planned in Portland as a centennial celebration in the summer of 1905. It even included an Abigail Scott Duniway Day arranged by her brother. (They had "made up" during her illness.) This was the year that Duniway published an entirely new version of her first novel, now called *From the West to the West*, extolling manifest destiny and the civilization of Oregon. As president of OSWSA, Mrs. Duniway invited the national association to hold its annual convention in Portland. She hoped "to 'show off' the national association before an Oregon audience, after which it was expected that they would return to their homes, glad to continue co-operating with us, under our direction."[11]

But other suffragists had different ideas. One of the leaders among them was Clara Colby, editor of the *Woman's Tribune*, which she had brought to Oregon in 1904 from Washington and previously from Nebraska. Colby wanted support from OSWSA but Duniway refused. As she explained to Clyde,

We will ignore her as far as possible—not to be rude. She thinks we are going to *win*, hence this visitation. . . . She announced that we could blame *her* if we were defeated, and she could bear it. It is hard to be patient with people who for mercenary considerations will scuttle your ships. I consider her coming into Oregon with her paper at this crisis a heinous crime.[12]

Colby's "little suffrage paper" had been successfully published ever since 1883, including a daily edition of 12,500 copies in 1888. She was well known in the national suffrage movement, a product of Wisconsin and Nebraska, a friend of Elizabeth Cady Stanton—with equally radical views on the Bible and female subordination, and a member along with Duniway of the committee which prepared the merger of NWSA and AWSA in 1889. But she was an ardent prohibitionist with close ties to the WCTU. Duniway's antipathy was long-standing. In her controversial speech to NWSA in 1889 she had singled out Mrs. Clara B. Colby specifically with other "self-imported Eastern Suffragists" as the cause of woman suffrage's "ruin" in Washington State in 1888. Duniway's bitterness was unmitigated when she later identified Colby as one of the ambitious newcomers to Oregon who had "attached themselves to the National Officers" before the 1906 campaign, claiming "'that Mrs. Duniway was injuring the cause.'" Colby was the candidate who tried to engineer a coup against Duniway as president of OSWSA after the 1906 defeat.[13]

The NAWSA convention deliberately snubbed Mrs. Duniway in the 1905 proceedings. Even though she was the Oregon association's president, she was not even included on the program. She found an opportunity anyway to stride to the podium and recite her "Centennial Ode." At this time coolheaded, diplomatic Carrie Chapman Catt had resigned her NAWSA presidency to care for her dying husband, so it was the opinionated Anna Howard Shaw and others who led the national organization. Anxious to take advantage of the promising prospects for an Oregon victory, "they held a supposedly secret conclave with a few of [Duniway's] ambitious eleventh-hour opponents and decided to 'take the Duniway bull by the horns.'" Duniway resigned from the 1906 campaign in anger when the secret leaked. She "retreated to the rear of their procession and carried their banner on the tips of her little horns."[14]

Duniway claimed that all suffrage association records were lost or destroyed in the 1905 change of leadership. Rancor was rampant, though it did not become public until after the election. The politico-social atmosphere in Oregon at the time was filled with turmoil. Not only were prominent politicians like Senators Fulton and Mitchell, longtime supporters of Duniway, being indicted for land fraud in a flurry of muckraking exposés; there was also a highly charged evangelical revival taking place in Portland. This followed an emotional Local Option Amendment controversy in 1904 during which Portland's Presbyterian minister accused Scott's *Oregonian* of helping "to fasten gambling and prostitution on the city of Portland." The *Pacific Baptist* called it the "greatest moral conflict that has ever agitated the state of Oregon." An eloquent young Baptist minister, J. Whitcomb Brougher, was later asked to offer prayers at an evening session of the NAWSA convention, attacked Mayor George Williams, former United States attorney general and Scott's closest friend, with sermons called "The Mayor of Sodom," "Our City's Crimes and Criminals," and "What Shall It Profit a City to License Crime?"[15]

Under national organization control WCTU women wearing white ribbons for prohibition were the primary campaigners in that disastrous and expensive suffrage campaign of 1906. After Susan B. Anthony's death in March, Anna Howard Shaw and others hurried to Oregon to make their work a symbolic tribute to Anthony. Mrs. Duniway was ignored and slandered, her methods ridiculed. Sarah Evans, one of her Woman's Club opponents who was part of the national coterie, later wrote in the *History of Woman Suffrage*, "Dr. Shaw, while keeping her finger on the pulse of all the work, was speaking to great crowds constantly," which "aroused the corrupt influences in politics and the upper and lower classes of anti-suffragists as never before and they jointly employed Ferdinand Reed, an experienced politician, at a high salary" to organize the defeat. It looks as if "radicalization" rather than victory was at least the unspoken motive of women like Mrs. Evans—just as Duniway claimed. Anna Shaw's lack of political acumen is revealed by her explanation of the Oregon defeat in 1906; she said a rainstorm and an earthquake in California diverted minds from the election.[16]

Carrie Chapman Catt later documented the carefully enforced opposition of the Brewer's and Wholesale Liquor Dealers' Association of Oregon. It sent a circular to every retail liquor seller in the state, enclosing ballot tickets showing how to vote, asking each retailer to get twenty-five votes among his employees and other businessmen, and *to return a numbered post card to the Association* to indicate compliance.[17] Though the scheme was discovered and publicized at the time, the financial pressure obviously paid off. Similar corrupt practices were used against suffrage referendums throughout the country. It was Duniway's awareness of such methods which caused her to insist that women should not stir up fear of prohibition in the first place. She also considered total prohibitionism a form of religious fanaticism for which all women should not be blamed.

The campaign cost over $25,000 and left OSWSA in debt, but Anna Howard Shaw and the national board never forgave Duniway for the defeat or for blaming *them* for the defeat. For the next six years, they withheld all financial support from OSWSA. Despite OSWSA's continued payment of affiliate dues the national insisted that it repudiate Mrs. Duniway, which it would not. Instead, they sent money to a committee of the Portland Woman's Club which included Mrs. Colby and Mrs. Evans. Some national suffragists helped privately, however. Laura Clay of Kentucky, who had come to admire Abigail Duniway as she worked on the 1906 campaign, sent large personal contributions. (She was forced off the national board in 1910.) Many Oregon suffragists remained loyal to Duniway and angry at the tactics of her opponents. Charges and countercharges appeared in the papers during the following years—at the same time that the national organization's autocratic and ineffective leadership was disturbing many dedicated longtime suffragists.[18]

Numerous letters among the Duniway Papers reveal the personal animosity between Duniway and Shaw—each absolutely convinced of her own righteousness. For example, Duniway wrote Shaw on 18 September 1906 saying, "we shall soon have everything in as good working order as you found it," now that she was "re-launching the ship." "Every scratch I get from the WCTU cat, and its abettors," she continued,

> is welcomed as a necessary part of my very strenuous labors. I only worry now about one *fool friend*. Mrs. C. A. Colby is that *fool*. Haven't you some place on earth to put the old tramp where there is no campaign pending? But for her system of "butting in" the women of Washington would have been re-freed by its State constitutional convention; and, but for her, the two old cats who got on our State Board last year would not have cut any figure in the Oregon campaign. I know what I'm about, and I know better than you, or any one else can learn, from your view-point, what it is that "disgusts men"! You and your ex-officers and agents are evidently working for *organization, glory* and *salary*. I am working for *success*, and you ought to know, by this time, that we can only get success by the votes of men.

In response to a Duniway letter of 27 May 1907 to the "National President," still complaining about the 1906 debacle, Secretary Kate Gordon replied on 7 June 1907 that she wished "to personally resent the tone of your letter to our President, as well as . . . the manner in which you express your opinion of the National's handling of affairs. . . . I must confess that your lack of dignity reflects sadly upon you as the leader of the State." She now agreed that "the only thing that could be done for Oregon was 'to leave her severely alone.'"

Duniway requested $2,000 to be used at the Oregon society's discretion to pay for a petition campaign in 1908. The national refused. Nevertheless, after the legislature turned down a joint resolution for a suffrage amendment, she herself took out a loan for $500, and petitions were successfully gathered to put the matter to a vote in 1908. Another

dismal defeat. Meanwhile, Shaw and others claimed Duniway was stealing suffrage funds for her own use. That fall Mrs. Duniway began another petition campaign for the 1910 election—this time with a new
wording—"No citizen who is a taxpayer shall be denied the right to vote
on account of sex." The idea had been suggested by "a sagacious leading
editor" and Oregon's governor, as a halfway step which would also make
people think about taxation without representation. Due to a printing
error, the words "white male" which still defined voters in the Oregon
constitution were eliminated from the amendment, giving it a much
more sweeping significance and making its title, Tax-Paying Suffrage
Amendment, inaccurate. This caused widespread confusion—opposition by socialists and non-tax-paying men as well as antisuffragists. The
WCTU withheld support because they felt the false title would cause the
law to be declared unconstitutional. The case was hopeless even before
the election. Mrs. Duniway was convinced that someone had deliberately
sabotaged the printing while her son Willis, the state printer, was gone
for three months recovering from a heart attack.[19]

The situation was very different in 1912. Washington, led by Emma
Smith DeVoe, a close friend of Duniway, had obtained the suffrage in
1910, California in 1911. DeVoe had successfully refused the help of
national organizers when they held their convention that year in Seattle.
She shared Duniway's views about how to campaign for suffrage. De-
Voe's letters refer disdainfully to "Anner Pshaw," and she later explained to Connecticut's suffrage association president Hepburn,

> It is a matter of history that their "co-operation" has been a great hin-
> derence in nearly every state where the National has participated, which
> implies dictation. Their contortions at the Seattle National convention dur-
> ing our Washington campaign, are too ridiculous to relate. Their turning us
> out of that convention for our refusal to permit them to ruin our prospects,
> proved a most fortunate occurrence because it left us free to conduct our
> own campaign, which resulted in the greatest victory ever gained, for we
> carried EVERY COUNTY IN THE STATE.[20]

By 1912 Oregon's way was prepared and public support much stronger.
Furthermore, Harvey Scott's sudden death in 1910 brought an end to
Oregonian opposition.

With the help of loyal supporters, especially Viola Coe, who had been
president or acting president of OSWSA ever since 1905, and Dr. Marie
Equi of the College Women's Club, Duniway obtained petitions and
submitted the amendment in January 1912. But she became deathly ill
that February, suffering from pneumonia and then blood poisoning in
her leg, which required two incisions (without anesthesia) to drain the
infection. Her sons were sure she could not survive—but she did. She

insisted she could not afford to die until suffrage was achieved. By spring she was able to direct the campaign from her bed, with yellow equal suffrage banners on her house and publicity from her pen. Others, however, carried out well-organized precinct work, rallies, and even the first-prize-winning Rose Festival Parade float. Frequent emphasis on the aged Mrs. Duniway's illness and long years of dedication to the cause provided sentimental publicity. A huge banquet in October, just before the election, honoring the seventy-eighth birthday of Abigail Scott Duniway, crippled by arthritis in a wheelchair, helped consummate the campaign.[21]

Above all, squabbling between opposing factions was held to a minimum. Just before Duniway's near-fatal illness, she had learned that a committee of the Woman's Club, led by active Democrat Sarah Evans, was trying to organize an executive coordinating committee superceding Duniway's, with "anonymously donated" funds which turned out to be from Anna Howard Shaw. Marie Equi squelched it and held onto OSWSA leadership. She also wrote a fourteen-page letter to Shaw—remarkable in its forceful and threatening rhetoric. "If the amendment is defeated this time," she said, "it will be by your campaign committee, stirring up strife." "Can you show any better record for Suffrage than Mrs. Duniway?" she asked, as she discussed the injustice of giving NAWSA funds to the Woman's Club instead of to OSWSA.

> Why tell a dying old captain to help *herself?* . . . [Y]ou would rather blame the Mother of Suffrage—all right go ahead, and I'll tell you again, it was a combination of circumstances. You won't be able to blame Mrs. Duniway this time, if we are defeated. . . . [I]t will be a case of poor management, with a campaign committee [from the Woman's Club] who will not be interfered with, who can work in secret as much as they please, spend "Eastern money" how they please, and run the campaign just as they please, but they will not talk about that old lady any more where I can ever hear of it—and if they attack me, I'm able to take care of myself.

Anna Shaw, said Equi, was a woman who had "let her personal rancour and bias hold her for six long years" and "would not or could not be reasonable where Mrs. Duniway was concerned." Referring to the 1905–06 campaign, she went on:

> Your "harmonizers" would go to Mrs. Duniway and tell her the disagreeable things you had said of her, and then would tell you disagreeable things that she had said of you. . . . [T]hen the merry war was on. . . . I wasn't fighting anyone, and heard both sides from your people, because at that time I was only entertaining the different members of your association, and did not even know Mrs. Duniway well enough to hold any converse with her; therefore, if I had any prejudice, it would have been in favor of you,

especially as I thought you a wonder—one of God's Elect—and *you know it*. . . .

    Evans is a traitor—do you get this? clearly? She has bitten the hand of one, who has not only made her in Suffrage, but in the Womans Club. Get one unanimous opinion from the club, and you will find that Mrs. Evans is heartily disliked.

National organizers, said Equi, "were told all sorts of dirty things about Mrs. Duniway; who told them—Evans. . . . Then Mrs. Evans would go to Mrs. Duniway, hold her by the hand, and speak of friendship—God, it makes me sick." Anna Shaw had not won any state in which she had campaigned and had been kept out of Washington and California for fear that her "brilliant, sarcastic speech . . . would lose the cause." Now Sarah Evans "holds your sack and she hasn't as much use for you as Mrs. Duniway once had—I've heard her talk. . . . Sarah is known to be slippery, and she has slipped one over on you, and has done this through your ill feeling. . . . I would like to shake you; you have a brain; for God's sake come to and use it." In summation, Sarah Evans had told Marie Equi all about Shaw's scheme to overthrow "Mrs. D."

> I may yet tell it all, to a yearning reporter, over my signature and, remember, I have witnesses. They must keep hands off Mrs. D in the future, and they must have their instructions to this effect from you; otherwise, I will forget the CAUSE and remember only, there is a woman sick, not only in body but in heart, a woman too old to be wearied and annoyed by heartless women who are filled with political greed.[22]

Oregon voters approved woman suffrage in 1912 by a very small majority. But it was Sarah Evans who wrote the negative *History of Woman Suffrage* account—claiming that Oregon's record number of suffrage defeats was caused by Mrs. Duniway's antagonistic methods and "arbitrary personal decisions that proved to be errors in judgment."[23] The excess expenditures which Evans deplored were mostly incurred in the 1906 campaign! Most Oregonians recognized instead the energy expenditure of Mrs. Duniway herself. Governor West asked her to write and sign the equal suffrage proclamation. She became the first registered woman voter in Multnomah County. Her life's work was finally done.

    Abigail Scott Duniway, however, had not stopped fighting. Asked by the registrar whether she should be listed as "retired," she replied, "No, I am not retired yet. . . . I am still working to the best of my ability to help bring equal suffrage to every part of the United States."[24] She turned her attentions to the National Council of Women Voters founded by Emma Smith DeVoe after Washington women became voters. Duniway had represented Oregon at the stormy organizational meeting in Tacoma, Washington, in 1911, then became honorary president and continued to advise DeVoe and contribute money for her work in the next few years. DeVoe was as proud of the West as Duniway was. She even admonished "the non-voting suffragists of the East [to] cease publishing their bickerings and jealousies and concentrate their energies on the vital issue, woman suffrage, and show a disposition to give praise to the woman who has succeeded wherein they have failed." She told Abigail Duniway that when a "young lady asked me who I thought should receive the votes for one of the six most useful women . . . I said Mrs. Duniway. Then I explained to her the folly of looking always to the East for gray matter."[25]

By this time, most western voting women were backing Alice Paul's Congressional Union, which was working for a federal suffrage amendment, even though NAWSA had repudiated Paul for refusing to obey the national board's directions. As one woman wrote to Margaret S. Roberts, Idaho's foremost suffragist, in 1914:

> Miss Shaw was worse this year than ever before, and turned and spat upon her hostesses even more venomously than before. She is extremely jealous of the Congressional Union, and openly declares she will "smash" them— after they entertained the convention *at her request* & at an expense of over $2000. She is positively the limit of boorishness & jealousy. . . . [T]he Rev. Anna would rend them limb from limb. But they go calmly on, for they are working for suffrage & not for personal glory.[26]

Emma DeVoe told Margaret Roberts, when she accepted a position on the Congressional Union's advisory board, that "We must put more *love* into our work, but with Miss Shaw at the head of the National it seems that hate is the dominant factor." In 1913, at the State Federation of Women's Clubs convention in Mt. Hood, Abigail Scott Duniway publicly repeated an earlier threat to Shaw that if she "again set foot in Oregon" Mrs. Duniway would make her "face the legal consequences" for the lies she had told and for "confiscating" the 1912 suffrage campaign funds.[27]

The National Council of Women Voters was well established by the time a national suffrage amendment was finally ratified in 1920, but East–West antagonism was ultimately destructive. Carrie Chapman Catt, who returned to the NAWSA presidency in 1916, arbitrarily organized a National League of Women Voters without regard for the circumstances of western women. Idaho's Margaret Roberts, unable to attend the planning meeting because of lack of travel money, protested the "new organization taking over the name of the National Council of Women Voters. This is a Western Organization and one that it took time and money to organize. As you know we are incorporated. Why cannot all the voters come into this organization?" She got nowhere. The council, which had affiliated with NAWSA, was swallowed up and virtually ignored in further suffrage history. Eleanor Flexner's definitive *Century of Struggle* called it "an abortive attempt." DeVoe and Roberts and other westerners were too far from new centers of power in the industrialized East.[28]

In 1914, Abigail Scott Duniway published her autobiography, *Path Breaking*. It was mostly a revision and compendium of her past writings. And it was, like everything else Duniway wrote, primarily intended to be a polemical document. A prohibition amendment was at issue in Oregon in 1914. Duniway was determined to prevent such a "fanatic, church-state coalition" from affecting the nationwide battle for suffrage. A resultant storm of fury came from prohibitionists, accusing Duniway of selling out to whiskey, "permitting your influence to be exploited for the benefit of this appalling source of misery and crime . . . dishonoring your declining years and . . . us also." Indeed, the enmity was so great that when she sent a copy of her book to Portland suffragist Elizabeth Eggert, the woman returned it with bitter denunciation and a refusal to read it. (Duniway replied, *"And Thou, Too, Brutus!"*)[29] One had to have a fighting temperament to endure such rejection.

Despite Duniway's efforts, prohibition did pass in Oregon in 1914. Fear of the tremendous increase in rootless immigrants and unemployed laborers led by the controversial Industrial Workers of the World was now rampant in Oregon. Portland's population had more than doubled since 1900, while the state's had increased by 70 percent. The freethinking old pioneers of Duniway's generation were almost gone. Soon the First World War would make Oregon even more class conscious and paranoid. Among those arrested and jailed for sedition because of pacifist–socialist beliefs was Duniway's strong-minded friend Dr. Marie Equi.[30] One can be sure that political antagonisms had much to do with the squabbles and judgments of the previous decade.

Fortunately, Abigail Scott Duniway did not have to endure any more battles. In 1915, shortly before her eighty-first birthday, she finally succumbed to an infected toe which refused to heal. Possibly she inherited a diabetic tendency which was never diagnosed, though she and Wilkie both had suspected it for some time.[31] Typical of the misunderstanding that followed her throughout life was the legend that she died because she had tried to treat the infection herself. In fact, it was a recurrence of the infection she had suffered in 1912, and Duniway obtained the best doctors in Portland to treat it. But without modern antibiotics the aged body could no longer sustain the active mind and fighting spirit. After weeks of suffering, and the amputation of two toes, Mrs. Duniway finally whispered, "I'm ready to go."[32]

Abigail Scott Duniway's opposition to prohibition, along with her free-thinking, proto-populist philosophy, were major factors in the burgeoning and almost-successful woman's rights movement in the Pacific

Northwest until approximately 1890. She represented a particular seg-
ment of midwest and western early pioneers among whom women were
welcome co-civilizers. They were independent farmers and small businessmen who also opposed slavery, "border ruffians," and monopoly
capitalists threatening their dignity and their way of life. Such men were
reluctant to accept Duniway's ideas about sex and family limitation, but
her political, economic, and social orientation matched their own. Her
salty language, freewheeling humor and sarcasm, religious skepticism
and iconoclasm echoed her milieu and well represented the many other
"strongminded women" of the American frontier.

Abigail Scott Duniway did exactly what she set out to do. She expressed both in words and action the reality and the autonomous possibilities of the nineteenth-century frontier woman. Increasingly circum-
scribed and deliberately hindered by the laws, customs, and political
machinations of men, such women were finally imprisoned within the
society and the corporate financial world of the Gilded Age. The doctrine of women's sphere and moral superiority which had developed
among the religious, business, and mercantile leaders of the East and the
plantation owners of the South was also adopted among women themselves to enforce piety and conformity upon dissenters. Transportation
and communication, along with cutthroat competition and industrialization, disrupted and displaced the self-sufficiency of the small farm and
its culture, creating an urbanized middle class and an eastern "establishment" which no longer valued the crudeness of frontier pioneers or the
egalitarianism of frontier living.

Abigail Scott Duniway made herself a conscious spokesperson for a
way of life and for a kind of woman who could build the ideal world of
the future. She once told *New Northwest* readers: "We have never liked
the business of talking of self, but when one person is, and has been a
representative of all phases of honorable existence in a new country, and
that person is in a position to add a mite to the history of such country,
by submitting personal experiences for public consideration, it is, perhaps, false delicacy that withholds the publication of important facts."[33]
Duniway freely chose to risk enmity and to stand, when necessary for
her cause, alone. Recognizing the paradoxes in her own life, she grieved
for failures and resented her opponents. But she also rallied her indomitable spirit and continued to fight for what she believed. She might have
won the short-term battle for acceptance and respectability by giving in
on prohibition and trying to avoid controversy. Instead she remained on
her pioneer path, which could be vindicated finally only by the course of
history. The frontier spirit she represented thus lives as a legacy for all
women, and for all Americans.

APPENDIX 1

GENEALOGY OF ABIGAIL JANE SCOTT AND BENJAMIN CHARLES DUNIWAY

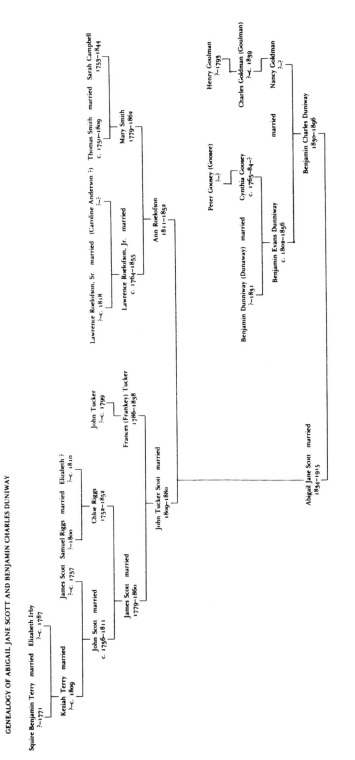

APPENDIX 2

BROTHERS AND SISTERS OF ABIGAIL SCOTT DUNIWAY

James Lawrence Scott
   Born 28 Nov. 1831, Groveland, Illinois
   Died 17 March 1833, Groveland, Illinois
Mary Frances Scott
   Born 19 May 1833, Groveland, Illinois
   Died 9 Sept. 1930, Lafayette, Oregon
   Married Amos Cook, 16 Aug. 1853
Abigail Jane Scott
   Born 22 Oct. 1834, Groveland, Illinois
   Died 11 Oct. 1915, Portland, Oregon
   Married Benjamin Charles Duniway, 2 Aug. 1853
Margaret Ann Scott
   Born 27 Oct. 1836, Groveland, Illinois
   Died 24 Sept. 1865, Tillamook, Oregon
   Married George Fearnside, 4 April 1854
Harvey Whitefield Scott
   Born 1 Feb. 1838, Groveland, Illinois
   Died 7 Aug. 1910, Baltimore, Maryland (after surgery)
   Married Elizabeth Nicklin, 31 October 1865; Margaret McChesney, 28 June
      1876
Catherine Amanda Scott
   Born 30 Nov. 1839, Groveland, Illinois
   Died 27 May 1913, Portland, Oregon
   Married John R. Coburn, 23 June 1857
Harriet Louisa Scott
   Born 9 March 1841, Groveland, Illinois
   Died 2 Jan. 1930, Seattle, Washington
   Married William R. McCord, 25 Nov. 1856; Isaac A. Palmer, c. 1875
John Henry Scott
   Born 1 Oct. 1843, Groveland, Illinois
   Died 1 May 1862, Forest Grove, Oregon
Edward Scott
   Born 13 March 1845, Groveland, Illinois
   Died 10 April 1845, Groveland, Illinois
Sarah Maria Scott
   Born 22 April 1847, Groveland, Illinois
   Died 24 Nov. 1901, Portland, Oregon
   Married James Monroe Kelty, 23 June 1869
William Neill Scott
   Born 4 Dec. 1848, Groveland, Illinois
   Died 27 Aug., 1852, Oregon Trail—Blue Mountains

222

Alice Scott
  Born 8 Sept. 1851, Groveland, Illinois
  Died 8 Sept. 1851, Groveland, Illinois
Rhoda Ellen Scott
  Born 4 Nov. 1855, Olympia, Washington
  Died 26 Aug. 1943, Oregon City, Oregon
  Married DeWitt Clinton Latourette, c. 1880
Ward Beecher Scott
  Born 26 Sept. 1863, Forest Grove, Oregon
  Died 17 Sept. 1895, Forest Grove, Oregon

APPENDIX 3

CHILDREN OF ABIGAIL SCOTT DUNIWAY
AND BENJAMIN CHARLES DUNIWAY

Clara Belle Duniway
  Born 26 May 1854, near Needy, Clackamas County, Oregon
  Died 21 Jan. 1886, Portland, Oregon
  Married Don H. Stearns, December 1876
Willis Scott Duniway
  Born 2 Feb. 1856, near Needy, Clackamas County, Oregon
  Died 5 Aug. 1913, Portland, Oregon
  Married Mary Alice MacCormac, 25 Dec. 1894
Hubert Ray Duniway
  Born 24 March 1859, near Lafayette, Yamhill County, Oregon
  Died 28 Nov. 1938, New York, N.Y.
  Married Ida Lesley, 1878 (deceased, 1883); Cora Parsons, 1884 (divorced, 1906); Eleanora Allen, 29 April 1910
Wilkie Collins Duniway
  Born 13 Feb. 1861, near Lafayette, Yamhill County, Oregon
  Died 30 May 1927, Portland, Oregon
  Married Wilhemina Barck, 17 May 1894
Clyde Augustus Duniway
  Born 2 Nov. 1866, Albany, Oregon
  Died 24 Dec. 1944, Stanford, California
  Married Caroline Cushing, 11 June 1901
Ralph Roelofson Duniway
  Born 7 Nov. 1869, Albany, Oregon
  Died 7 Dec. 1920, Portland, Oregon
  Married Kate Schermerhorn, 20 Sept. 1894

Notes

INTRODUCTION

1. ASD, *From the West to the West: Across the Plains to Oregon,* p. 147.
2. Flexner, *Century of Struggle,* p. 159; ASD, "Introduction" to *Path Breaking* (Schocken reprint), pp. xi–xii. See *History of Woman Suffrage,* vol. 6, pp. 538–48, entry written by Sarah A. Evans, one of ASD's prime enemies—see chap. 12 above.
3. See Aileen S. Kraditor, *The Ideas of the Woman Suffrage Movement,* pp. 39, 55–56, and passim; *Up From the Pedestal,* pp. 16, 18. Other recent books on the subject of woman suffrage in America are listed in the Bibliography. See also Daniel J. Boorstin, *The Lost World of Thomas Jefferson,* pp. 187, 190–91; Chilton Williamson, *American Suffrage: From Property to Democracy, 1760–1860,* p. 279 and passim.
4. Oswald West, "Reminiscences," *Ore. Hist. Q.* 50 (Dec. 1949).

CHAPTER 1. A FRONTIER CHILDHOOD

1. ASD, *Path Breaking,* p. 3; "Personal Reminiscences of a Pioneer," p. 449, pamphlet in Duniway Papers. All genealogical information in this chapter is from David Duniway's genealogical file.
2. ASD, "Narrative," in Harvey Scott, *History of the Oregon Country,* vol. 3, p. 246. Letter from Catherine Scott Coburn to ASD, 12 Oct. 1912, ASD Scrapbook II, Duniway Papers.
3. ASD, "Personal Reminiscences," p. 449. Cf. R. Carlyle Buley, *The Old Northwest: Pioneer Period, 1815–1840,* vol. 1, p. 310; Eliza Woodson Farnham, *Life in Prairie Land,* p. 85; and anonymous compilation, *History of Tazewell County, Illinois,* pp. 218, 331–32.
4. James Scott Papers in Duniway Collection, including sheriff's memorandum book, deeds, letters from postmaster general, etc.; *Tazewell County,* pp. 240, 205–07, 475–76, 486, 662, 665, 668, 461; ASD, "Personal Reminiscences," p. 449.
5. *Tazewell County,* pp. 215, 196, 263–65, 476.
6. "Personal Reminiscences," p. 450; *Path Breaking,* p. 7.
7. *Path Breaking,* pp. 5–6.
8. Letter to Barbara Booth, 11 April 1914, p. 3, spec. coll., U. Oregon Library, Eugene, Oregon; *Path Breaking,* p. 10.
9. *Path Breaking,* p. 7; *Judith Reid: A Plain Story of a Plain Woman,* chap. 1, *NNW,* 12 May 1871.
10. *Judith Reid,* chap. 2, 19 May 1871. See Johannes Meintjes, *Olive Schreiner:*

Portrait of a South African Woman (Capetown: Hugh Keartland, 1965), pp. 7–8, for a comparable episode at the same age of seven in the life of Schreiner—which she too later incorporated into her novels.

11. *NNW*, 11 June 1875; 12 Jan. 1877; 12 May 1876. *From the West to the West*, p. 26. The image is from Jonathan Edwards's "Sinners in the Hands of an Angry God," still influential and repeated one hundred years after he used it.
12. Neill Johnson, "Autobiography," p. 18, MS in Duniway Papers. *From the West to the West*, p. 227; *NNW*, 12 May 1876.
13. *Laban McShane: A Frontier Story*, chap. I, *NNW*, 13 Sept. 1883.
14. *Dr. Spock Talks with Mothers: Growth and Guidance* (Greenwich, Conn.: Fawcett Crest, 1961), pp. 61–62.
15. In *History of Woman Suffrage*, vol. 3, p. 768.
16. E.g., in *NNW: Ellen Dowd*, chap. 1, 5 Jan. 1872; *Judith Reid*, chaps. 1–5, 12 May to 2 June 1871; *Amie and Henry Lee*, chap. 1, 29 May 1874.
17. *Judith Reid*, chap. 5, *NNW*, 2 June 1871.
18. *Ellen Dowd*, chap. 1, *NNW*, 5 Jan. 1872.
19. *Path Breaking*, p. 8.
20. "John Tucker Scott," *Oregon Native Son*, vol. 1 (July 1899), p. 174, in U. Oregon Library. Alfred Holman, "Introduction," in Scott, *Oregon Country*, vol. 1, p. 8. Cf. *From the West to the West, pp. 19, 73.*
21. *NNW*, 29 Jan. 1875; 29 Jan. 1880.
22. *Path Breaking*, p. 8.
23. Ibid., p. 3; Letter to Barbara Booth, pp. 1–2; J. L. Johnson, "Overland to Oregon in 1851," MS.
24. *Democracy in America*, vol. 1, ed. Phillips Bradley, p. 328. See also Ray Allen Billington, *America's Frontier Heritage*, pp. 80ff.
25. Letter from J. T. Scott to James Scott, 4 April 1852, mentions *Ill. Journal*. Receipts in James Scott Papers, 5 Oct. 1843, 12 Sept. 1843, 11 Dec. 1839. The *Register* was edited by S. H. Davis, possibly a relative; H. K. W. Davis was a partner later. See Wm. Scott, *Newspapers and Periodicals of Illinois, 1814–1879*, pp. 276, 278, 4, 305, 321, lxii. Marshall Turley, who married Tucker Scott's sister, owned a printing press—letter from Louvisa S. Turley to James Scott, 28 Feb. 1856. ASD, "Women in Journalism," MS speech in Duniway Papers.
26. Editorial, *NNW*, 30 June 1871. *Tazewell County*, p. 462, says Benjamin and Rebecca (Whittier) Greeley, from New Hampshire, settled in 1836 on the same section as James Scott and Neill Johnson.
27. See Sidney Ditzion, *Marriage, Morals and Sex in America*, pp. 110, 137–38, 142–43, 145, 146, 148, 152. Debate between Greeley and Owen in Horace Greeley, *Recollections of a Busy Life*, pp. 570–618; see also pp. 103–04, 150.
28. See Lee Nash, "Refining a Frontier: The Cultural Interests and Activities of Harvey Scott," or Nash's articles: "Scott of the *Oregonian:* The Editor as Historian," pp. 197–232; "Harvey Scott's 'Cure for Drones': An Oregon Alternative to Public Higher Schools," pp. 70–79. Scott described his youth and education in *Oregon Country*, vol. 3, pp. 131ff.
29. Greeley, *Hints Toward Reforms*, pp. 47.

30. Ibid., pp. 144–45. *NNW*, 16 Feb. 1877.
31. ASD, "Personal Reminiscences," p. 450; letter to Barbara Booth, pp. 2–3; in *History of Woman Suffrage*, vol. 3, p. 768; J. L. Johnson, "Overland to Oregon," p. 9. *NNW*, 25 Aug. 1884, identifies Parker.

CHAPTER 2. "SOUTHRONS" AND YANKEES

1. Numerous letters in James Scott Papers, plus his sheriff's tax list.
2. Quoted by Fred Lockley, *Oregon Sunday Journal*, 22 June 1913, clipping in ASD Scrapbook II. Buley, *Old Northwest*, vol. 2, p. 246.
3. Scott, *Oregon Country*, vol. 1, p. 7. Genealogical evidence from family papers and David Duniway research, summarized in my dissertation, "Abigail Scott Duniway of Oregon: Woman and Suffragist of the American Frontier," chap. 1 and Appendices. Following information from Duniway files.
4. Benjamin Terry Will in James Scott Papers; estate appraisal, J. Scott, Halifax Co., Va., 19 May 1758, contents listed, total £60.19. William Waller Hening, ed., *The Statutes at Large* (N.Y., 1809–23), 7, pp. 220, 307. Undated letter from Aunt Rhoda Scott Richardson, included with letter to Clyde, 16 Sept. 1913. Letters to Clyde from Amasa Scott, Craftsbury, Vt., 14 Oct. and 20 Dec. 1893. For background, cf. Richard Hofstadter, *America at 1750*, pp. 33–35 and passim; Richard A. Bartlett, *The New Country*, p. 68; Aubrey C. Land, "Economic Base and Social Structure: The Northern Chesapeake in the Eighteenth Century."
5. "Historical Documentation Map of Surry County, No. Carolina" (Jamestown, N.C.: The Custom House, 1979) shows Scott/Murphey/Riggs locations.
6. Letter from Aunt Rhoda; inventory of John Scott Estate, 1811; Duniway files; James Scott Papers, including lawsuit documents 1804–08 and sheriff's records. ASD to Clyde, 10 Feb. 1913, mentions Lucy Hanks relationship.
7. Cf. Moynihan, "Abigail Scott Duniway of Oregon," chap. 1, pp. 33–34; *Tazewell County*, p. 475; *Path Breaking*, p. 3; letters in James Scott Papers. Niels Henry Sonne, *Liberal Kentucky: 1780–1828*, p. 13. Cf. T. Scott Miyakawa, *Protestants and Pioneers*, pp. 45, 49; Arthur K. Moore, *The Frontier Mind*.
8. *Tazewell County*, pp. 240–41, 219, 564. Letters to James Scott from Lindsey Scott, 18 June 1836, from Allen Daugherty, 3 Sept. 1829, 1 June 1831. Alfred Brunson, "A Prairie Fire and a Claim Association," in *Prairie State*, Paul M. Angle, ed., p. 164.
9. Cf. David Brion Davis, *The Problem of Slavery in the Age of Revolution*, pp. 46–47, 201–03; William B. Allen, *A History of Kentucky*, p. 178; Thomas Ford, *A History of Illinois*, pp. 54–55; Merton Lynn Dillon, "The Anti-Slavery Movement in Illinois: 1824–1835," in *The Old Northwest: Studies in Regional History, 1787–1910*, ed. Harry N. Scheiber, pp. 297, 311. See also Eugene H. Berwanger, *The Frontier Against Slavery*. John Tucker will in James Scott Papers.
10. "Memoirs of Mrs. Mary Rolofson Gamble," p. 5, Duniway Papers. Cf. *Tazewell County*, pp. 475–76.

11. Letter from Joel Knight, in *Missouri Cumberland Presbyterian,* clipping reprinted in Wylie Wayne Rolofson, "The Rolofson Family Story," photostated typescript in Duniway Papers, p. 10. Letter from Margaret Scott to Lawrence Roelofson, 1 April 1853.

12. "Memoirs of Mrs. Gamble, p. 2; "The Roelofson Family Story," p. 13; Hiram A. Hunter, ed., "A Narrative of the Captivity and Sufferings of Isaac Knight from Indian Barbarity" (Evansville: Journal Office, 1829), typescript copy, Duniway Papers, from original in Darlington Library, U. of Pittsburgh.

13. Ibid., pp. 3–15.

14. Paul Wallace Gates, "Tenants of the Log Cabin," in *Landlords and Tenants on the Prairie Frontier,* pp. 16, 13, 14. "Roelofson Family Story," p. 5, See also *Henderson: A Guide to Audubon's Home Town in Kentucky,* pp. 15–27.

15. Family tradition, from David Duniway. Cf. B. W. McDonnold, *History of the Cumberland Presbyterian Church,* p. 40. Sydney Ahlstrom, *A Religious History of the American People,* pp. 431–36; Robert V. Foster, "A Sketch of the Cumberland Presbyterian Church," *American Church History,* p. 261.

16. Davis, *Problem of Slavery,* p. 203; Ahlstrom, *Religious History,* p. 433.

17. "Rolofson Family Story," p. 10; Foster, "Sketch of the Cumberland Presbyterian Church," p. 294. See Ahlstrom, *Religious History,* pp. 444–45; McDonnold, *Cumberland Presbyterian Church,* pp. 9, 13, 15–17, 44.

18. McDonnold, *Cumberland Presbyterian Church,* p. 173. Duniway genealogical files: 28 Dec. 1849, 5 Oct. 1850. "Memoirs of Mrs. Gamble," p. 2. Letters of Margaret Scott to Lawrence Roelofson, 1 April 1853. Johnson, "Autobiography," p. 20.

19. Scott, *Oregon Country,* vol. 1, p. 253; *Tazewell County,* p. 58.

20. From William Cullen Bryant, *Prose Writings* (N.Y., 1884), reprinted in *Prairie State,* p. 108. *Tazewell County,* pp. 475, 706.

21. *Tazewell County,* pp. 653, 248–50, 535. Farnham, *Life in Prairie Land,* p. 155. Johnson, "Autobiography," p. 19. Descriptions of the town are in Abner D. Jones, *Illinois and the West,* pp. 72–74; Edward Ellsworth, *Illinois in 1837,* p. 106.

22. James Scott Papers. Johnson, "Autobiography," p. 20; *Tazewell County,* pp. 652–53.

23. Contemporary descriptions of the 1830 boom can be found in Ford, *History of Illinois,* p. 181; Frederick Gerhard, *Illinois As It Is,* pp. 82–83. See also Bernard Bailyn et al., *The Great Republic: A History of the American People* (Boston: Little, Brown and Co., 1977), pp. 477–83; Buley, *Old Northwest,* vol. 1, p. 229. The journal of accounts for June 1836 to March 1837 of the Caffee-Scott Company is in the R. Edwin Browne Collection in Independence, Missouri. ASD, "Personal Reminiscences," p. 449. A drawing of the house and surrounding farm is in Scott, *Oregon Country,* vol. 3, facing p. 240. Duniway genealogical files: G. W. Turley to James Scott, 16 Dec. 1836; bond of T. J. Farnham to John Caffee and Lindsey Scott, 28 Jan. 1837.

24. Ford, *History of Illinois,* pp. 178–79; Gerhard, *Illinois As It Is,* pp. 81–89. Letters in James Scott Papers: Matthew Tucker to J. T. Scott 24 June 1837; James H. Tucker to James Scott, 9 April 1838, 22 June 1838. Farnham's

court suit was on 2 April 1838, settlement, 13 April 1838, articles of dissolution, 5 Sept. 1838. Duniway genealogical files: James Tucker to James Scott, 9 April 1838; suit, 2 April 1838. See also Farnham, *Life in Prairie Land*, pp. 210–11.

25. Lindsey Scott to J. T. Scott, 13 Nov. 1838, James Scott Papers. Farnham, *Life in Prairie Land*, p. 259, pp. 256ff. *Path Breaking*, p. 7. *Tazewell County*, pp. 568, 566, 331–32; Buley, *Old Northwest*, vol. 1, chap. 5.
26. Duniway genealogical files: Allen S. Daugherty to James Scott, 3 Sept. 1829, 1 June 1831; a cousin at St. Joseph's College, Ky., to Lindsey, 30 March 1830—all expressing sympathy for Lindsey's disease. Lindsey to James Scott, 18 June 1838; to John T. Scott, 31 Aug. 1838, 13 Nov. 1838, 18 Nov. 1838 all include description of symptoms. James H. Tucker to John T. Scott, 14 March 1839, Hezekiah Davis to John T. Scott, 4 Jan. 1839; A. L. Morrison to J. T. Scott, 15 Jan. 1839; coroner and jury verdict, 30 Jan. 1839; John Fondey, M.D., to Dr. Asa Lee Davison, 25 Feb. 1839; A. L. Davison to John T. Scott, 11 June 1839; news clipping from *Canton Herald*, 2 Feb. 1839. ASD deplored this family scandal, wishing the evidence had been destroyed rather than saved.
27. Filed in April, completed 11 June 1842, Duniway genealogical file. *Path Breaking*, pp. 5–6. Letter to Clyde, 22 June 1914. Cf. *Captain Gray's Company*, pp. 9, 15.
28. Ahlstrom, *Religious History*, p. 400. See also George Willis Cooke, *Unitarianism in America*, pp. 349, 227, 368. On p. 151, Cooke says that in 1836 the church found Tremont one of its most promising locations. See also, Daniel Walker Howe, The Unitarian Conscience, p. 305. Jones, in *Illinois and the West*, p. 74. Farnham, *Life in Prairie Land*, pp. 156–57.
29. *NNW*, 15 Sept. 1876; Letitia Capell, "Biography of Abigail Scott Duniway," p. 11, quoting Harvey Scott's son Leslie. Elijah Brown married Tucker Scott's sister and took over the Scott farm when he left for Oregon.
30. Roelofson Clan Papers, Oregon State Library, Salem, Oregon; "Autobiography," p. 20.
31. *Captain Gray's Company*, p. 38. J. L. Johnson, "Overland to Oregon," p. 3. Letters in James Scott Papers.
32. ASD, *Amie and Henry Lee*, chap. 2, *NNW*, 5 June 1874. Farnham, *Life in Prairie Land*, pp. 63, 334. *Captain Gray's Company*, p. 57. Cf. Buley, *Old Northwest*, vol. 1, pp. 364–65.
33. Jones, *Illinois and the West*, p. 75. John Allen Krout, *The Origins of Prohibition*, pp. 86, 87, 121. Also pp. 90, 92, 114, 169, 173.
34. Krout, *Origins of Prohibition*, pp. 175, 204, 208, 210–213. Cf. Carl Sandburg, *Abraham Lincoln*, pp. 73–74.
35. *Tazewell County*, pp. 563, 314–20. Scott, *Newspapers of Illinois*, pp. lxvi, 278, 336. The *Register's* successor was silenced, like Lovejoy's, by the burning of its office and press in 1850.
36. ASD, *NNW*, 30 June 1871. See Buley, *Old Northwest*, vol. 2, pp. 620, 467–68; Theodore Clarke Smith, *The Liberty and Free Soil Parties in the Northwest*, pp. 4–5, 19. On p. 327 Smith refers to "Southern anti-slavery Scotchmen from North Carolina and Virginia."

37. Gerhard, *Illinois As It Is*, p. 87; Buley, *Old Northwest*, vol. 2, p. 246. Sandburg, *Abraham Lincoln*, p. 49. The proclamation, printed in the *Sangamon Journal*, was widely disseminated by the post–Civil War women's movement. A copy is in the Duniway Papers.
38. Accounts, 29 Sept. 1840 to Jan. 1841, James Scott Papers. *Tazewell County*, p. 146; Sandburg, *Abraham Lincoln*, p. 77.
39. *Path Breaking*, pp. 8, 4. James Scott Papers.

CHAPTER 3. OVERLAND TO OREGON

1. *Path Breaking*, p. 4.
2. See Buley, *Old Northwest*, vol. 2, pp. 44ff; Billington, *Westward Expansion*, pp. 105, 242, 249, 283; William Vipond Pooley, "Settlement of Illinois," p. 370; Jones, *Illinois and the West*, pp. 31–34.
3. *Life in Prairie Land*, pp. 328–29. Cf. Henry Nash Smith, *Virgin Land*, pp. 215, 218, 223.
4. Stuart B. Mockford, ed., "Jason Lee's Peoria Speech," pp. 19–26; Joseph Schafer, "Harvey W. Scott, Historian," p. 192. Copies of magazine in U. of Oregon Library, Eugene, Oregon.
5. T. J. Farnham, *Travels in the Great Western Prairies*, vol. 2, p. 315. See Caroline C. Dobbs, *Men of Champoeg*, pp. 98–103; Fred Lockley, "Impressions and Observations of the Journal Man," 21 and 22 March 1925, clippings in Duniway Papers.
6. Schafer, "Harvey W. Scott, Historian," p. 193. See Oscar Osburn Winthur, *The Old Oregon Country*, p. 99: After the first "Great Migration" of 1843, which brought about 1,000 settlers, the population of the Willamette Valley was about 1,500. By 1849, when the first governor was appointed, there were 9,083 people, and in 1850, 13,294. Capell, "Biography of ASD," p. 15, says Scott owned Pratt's *Guide*, 1848; Palmer's *Journal*, 1847; Hastings' *Emigrants' Guide*, 1845; Colton's maps; Fremont's Expedition *Report*, 1843; Charles Preuss' Oregon Trail Map, 1846.
7. Scott, *Oregon Country*, vol. 1, p. 49.
8. *Path Breaking*, p. 3. Ill. state archives, 30 June 1850, as reported to Clyde Duniway, 14 Aug. 1925, show Scott's farm being worth $4,000, tools $100, livestock $680. He had 80 acres improved and 120 unimproved, from which he harvested 1,800 bushels corn, 30 wheat, 20 potatoes, 50 lbs. wool, $100 of fruit, 25 tons hay, $100 in slaughtered animals, 250 lbs. butter and $20 other "home manufactures."
9. Sandburg, *Abraham Lincoln*, p. 104. See also Justin Turner and Linda Turner, *Mary Todd Lincoln: Her Life and Letters* (Knopf: N.Y., 1972), pp. 39–40. I am indebted to Kathryn Kish Sklar for this reference.
10. Three hundred and twenty acres was half a square mile. Wives got their shares only if they were married within one year of their husband's arrival. See Dorothy O. Johansen and Charles M. Gates, *Empire of the Columbia*, p. 231.
11. Johnson, "Autobiography," pp. 22–23: "The main reason of the Scheme

falling through was: there was not such a body of land to be found in Oregon," and "no two of the members of the colony settled nigher each other than 15 or 20 miles." J. L. Johnson, "Overland to Oregon," pp. 8–9. Scott, *Oregon Country*, vol. 3, p. 325.

12. *Captain Gray's Company*, p. 18. See E. Earl Newsom, ed., *David Newsom, The Western Observer, 1805–1882*, p. 45, letter to *Ill. Journal*, 2 Oct. 1852: "No man can charge me with deceiving him in regard to the character of that journey. Mr. Thurston, M. C. did, representing it as a pleasure trip, and that emigrants had no need of money after crossing the Missouri river." Of his own crossing, 28 Nov. 1851 (pp. 28–30): "My experience has been *dear* bought. May others profit by it. . . . But I have seen the elephant, and my traveling propensities are cured. My expenses and losses since I left . . . are $2,375. . . . This is a journey to try a man's soul and strength, and purse. . . . Men of families, with limited means, should never attempt this journey. Old persons or invalids should stay in the States." Apparently Tucker Scott did not see that letter. On diseases, see Buley, *Old Northwest*, vol. 1, pp. 247ff; Moynihan, "Children and Young People on the Overland Trail," p. 280.

13. "Narrative," in Scott, *Oregon Country*, vol. 3, pp. 240, 238.

14. Landes eventually bought the Scott farm, where Duniway visited in the 1880s, reporting in the *NNW* with a sentimental comment about the old romance. *Tazewell County*, p. 480; David Duniway interview *From the West to the West*, p. 16. Elijah Brown was the actual brother-in-law who took over Scott's farm and the care of "the old folks." No railroads came to Tazewell County until the 1860s, though they were chartered as early as 1835. *Tazewell County*, p. 732.

15. David Duniway interview, Feb. 1976.

16. See Roderick Nash, *Wilderness and the American Mind*, p. 46; Smith, *Virgin Land*.

17. Letter from J. T. Scott to *Tazewell County Mirror*, 13 June 1852—clipping in ASD's "Journal of a Trip to Oregon." Figures included 11,340 men, 2,065 women, 2,874 children. See also Scott's letter to James Scott, 28 May 1852, Browne Papers. Scott, *Oregon Country*, vol. 3, p. 226, gives later figures, including 18,765 men, 4,270 women, and 5,590 children. See John D. Unruh, Jr., *The Plains Across*, p. 120, for total emigration figures—70,000 to Oregon, California, and Utah by trail in 1852.

18. Scott, *Oregon Country*, vol. 3, p. 240; Harriet Scott Palmer, "Crossing Over the Great Plains by Ox-Wagons," (c, 1926), p. 2, Duniway Papers.

19. See Scott, *Oregon Country*, vol. 3, pp. 232–33, 237; David Duniway notes.

20. *From the West to the West*, p. 55. ASD's "Journal of a Trip to Oregon," MS in Duniway Papers, is hereinafter cited by date of entry from typescript copy prepared by David Duniway. Clyde Duniway cited Alice Duniway about ASD leaving out details. Tucker Scott and Maggie made a copy of the journal, sent it back to James Scott, who then sent it to Marshall Turley to be printed. He said it was "to much out of date . . . [to] pay expenses"—letters from L. S. Turley to James Scott, 28 Feb. [1856?], Edwin Browne Papers. In 1976, Ed Browne, descendant of Polly Scott and Elijah Brown, followed the journal's route from Missouri to Oregon. Knowing nothing of the Duniways,

he inquired at the Oregon Historical Society for information on ASD. He met David Duniway and discovered the identical journal and an unknown relative. Letter to me from David Duniway, 24 Sept. 1977.

21. Letter from Aunt Etty (Harriet) to Clyde Duniway, 24 March 1925, Duniway Papers. See also Scott, *Oregon Country*, vol. 3, pp. 246, 234.

22. Scott, *Oregon Country*, vol. 3, p. 241.

23. Palmer, "Crossing the Great Plains," p. 2.

24. Tucker Scott to James Scott, 9 June 1852; Palmer, "Crossing the Great Plains," pp. 2–3.

25. See Moynihan, "Children on the Overland Trail," p. 283.

26. Letter with "Journal of a Trip to Oregon." Cf. Nash, *Wilderness and the American Mind*, chap. 4.

27. This was probably Thomson's "Lobelia No. 6," a vegetable concoction based on the botanic theory of medicine. It was well known on the frontier. See Buley, *Old Northwest*, vol. 1, pp. 249, 284.

28. Unruh, *Plains Across*, p. 122.

29. Scott, *Oregon Country*, vol. 3, pp. 272–74.

30. Palmer, "Crossing the Great Plains," p. 3; *Path Breaking*, pp. 8–9.

31. A. J. Scott to James Scott, 18 July 1852.

32. *From the West to the West*, p. 119; *Path Breaking*, p. 297.

33. Scott, *Oregon Country*, vol. 3, p. 274; Palmer, "Crossing the Great Plains," pp. 3–4.

34. Palmer, "Crossing the Great Plains," pp. 8–9; Scott, *Oregon Country*, vol. 3, p. 292.

35. Scott, *Oregon Country*, vol. 3, p. 242; Clyde Duniway notes.

36. Palmer, "Crossing the Great Plains," pp. 4–5.

37. Scott, *Oregon Country*, vol. 3, p. 243.

38. Ibid., pp. 305, 310; Palmer, "Crossing the Great Plains," p. 6.

39. Palmer, "Crossing the Great Plains," p. 7.

40. Catherine Scott Coburn, in Scott, *Oregon Country*, vol. 3, p. 244.

41. Lockley, "Impressions and Observations," 21 March 1925; Clyde Duniway notes.

42. Scott, *Oregon Country*, vol. 3, p. 247.

43. Ibid., pp. 245, 247.

44. Palmer, "Crossing the Great Plains," p. 8.

45. William J. Cuddy, in Scott, *Oregon Country*, vol. 3, p. 325.

CHAPTER 4. THE FARMER'S WIFE

1. Frances Fuller Victor, *All Over Oregon and Washington*, p. 167. Figures from Hubert Bancroft [F. F. Victor], *History of Oregon and Washington, 1848–1888*, vol. 2, p. 259; letter to James Scott, 7 June 1853, p. 3. Unruh, *Plains Across*, p. 120, estimates 3,600 in 1851 and 10,000 in 1852.

2. Harriet Scott to James Scott, 26 Nov. 1852; to Augusta Brown, 26 Nov. 1852. Illinois was called the "Sucker State"; wet Oregonians became "Webfoots."

3. Quoted by Fred Lockley, *Oregon Sunday Journal*, 22 June 1913, ASD Scrapbook II, Duniway Papers.

4. Printed 20 March 1853, clipping with ASD's "Journal of a Trip to Oregon" in Duniway Papers. See William Bowen, "The Oregon Frontiersman: A Demographic View," in *The Western Shore*, ed. Thomas Vaughan, pp. 183–84, showing that 66 percent of the population in 1850 was southern and only 493 out of 9,682 immigrants were from New England. Midwesterners were a distinct but significant minority.

5. Letter from Margaret Scott to "My Dear Grandfather," 1 April 1853. Mary Frances Scott Cook, interview with Fred Lockley, "Impressions and Observations," 21 March 1925, news clipping in Duniway Papers.

6. Letter from John Tucker Scott to James Scott, 29 March 1853, Browne Papers.

7. See Krout, *The Origins of Prohibition*, pp. 144, 210, 303.

8. Both letters in Browne Papers, as are all the letters cited regarding this case. Copies in Duniway Papers.

9. Letters from Harriet Scott Palmer to Wilkie Duniway, 11 April 1924; Margaret to James Scott, 26 Sept. 1854; ASD to James Scott, 24 Sept. 1854.

10. J. T. Scott to James Scott, 10 April 1854; ASD to James Scott, 24 Sept 1854; Ruth Stroller, ed., *Old Yamhill: The Early History of its Towns and Cities*, p. 37. See n. 43 on Bailey.

11. Harvey Scott, *Oregon Country*, vol. 2, p. 32. See also Kenneth Scott Latourette's autobiography *Beyond the Ranges*. According to David Duniway, National Archives, Indian War Claim 5961 for Ruth Stevenson Scott, lists marriage on 27 Nov. 1854.

12. Scott, "Retrospect of Pioneer Beginnings," *Oregon Country*, vol. 2, p. 29. His return trek is in *Oregon Country*, vol. 3, p. 133.

13. *Path Breaking*, p. 9; David Duniway, letter to me, Sept. 1980, p. 4, on the Riggs relationship; Scott, *Oregon Country*, vol. 3, pp. 178, 248, and fn. 1. Chloe Boone Curry's schoolhouse is pictured in *Oregon Country*, vol. 2, facing p. 180. A flood in 1884 changed the course of the Rickreall River and left Eola stranded.

14. ASD to Barbara Booth, 11 April 1914, p. 3, Special Collections, U. of Oregon. See Robert Horace Down, *A History of the Silverton Country*, pp. 190, 192, 195, 211; David Tyack, "The Tribe and the Common School," pp. 13–23; Marianne Hunsaker D'Arcy, "Some Early Oregon Schools," in *Souvenir of Western Women*, ed. Mary Douthit, pp. 55ff.

15. Bowen, "The Oregon Frontiersman, pp. 189–90, forgets that the early marriage process continued for several years after 1850. See also Bancroft, *History of Oregon*, vol. 2, p. 38. W. A. Goulder, *Reminiscences: Incidents in the Life of a Pioneer in Oregon and Idaho*, p. 169, tells of a father urging a young man to marry his daughter while the boy insisted she was too young. The new husband sent his wife to school for 3 years after the marriage.

16. *NNW*, 24 Sept. 1875. A simoon is a violent, hot sandstorm of Asian and African deserts. The phrase was often used by westerners in the nineteenth century.

17. *NNW*, 19 Jan. 1872. See D. C. Bloomer, *Life and Writings of Amelia Bloomer*,

pp. 13,37. Also letter to Henry C. Wright, c. 1845, in Gerda Lerner, ed., *The Female Experience*, p. 425.

18. Microfilm of U.S. Bureau of Land Management plat book of Oregon Donation Land Claims in Oregon State Archives, and *Index to Oregon Donation Land Claims*, published by Genealogical Forum of Portland, Ore. See also Down, *Silverton Country*, pp. 166, 76.

19. Scott, *Oregon Country*, vol. 2, p. 86, vol.3, p. 249, vol. 5, p. 255. Fred Lockley, *Oregon Sunday Journal*, 22 June 1913, clipping in Duniway Papers. See also Down, *Silverton Country*, pp. 133, 171, 121; *NNW*, 9 April 1875. Helen Krebs Smith, *The Presumptuous Dreamers*, vol. 1, pp. 32, 39, 44, cites other land holdings from Clackamas County tax records.

20. "Personal Reminiscences," p. 451; see also *Path Breaking*, pp. 9–10.

21. *Portland Evening Telegram*, 16 April 1910, clipping in Duniway Papers. Lockley, *Oregon Sunday Journal*, 22 June 1913, ASD Scrapbook II.

22. See, e.g., *Captain Gray's Company*, p. 282; *NNW*, 9 Sept. 1880.

23. *NNW*, 12 March 1875.

24. "Narrative," in Scott, *Oregon Country*, vol. 3, p. 248.

25. *Path Breaking*, pp. 49–50. *Captain Gray's Company*, p. 279.

26. *NNW*, 8 Jan. 1875.

27. "Narrative," in Scott, *Oregon Country*, vol. 3, p. 249. Also *Path Breaking*, p. 282; *NNW*, 22 Jan. 1875; letter from ASD to James Scott in Illinois [1855?], Duniway Papers. Cf. "John's Promise," *NNW*, 14 Nov. 1873.

28. Letter from Harriet Scott to "Pa," 8 June [1856].

29. Letter from ASD to Alice (Mrs. Willis) Duniway, 1 Feb. 1914. See Helen Olson Halvorsen and Lorraine Fletcher, "Nineteenth Century Midwife: Some Recollections," pp. 39–49.

30. *NNW*, 5 May 1871.

31. Letter, dated "Cottage Home June 8th A D 1855" but obviously 1856 because of its reference to Willis, pasted in back of ASD's "Journal of a Trip to Oregon."

32. D. Newsom, *Western Observer*, letter of 5 Oct. 1855, p. 61. Also, letters of 15 Aug. 1853, 12 June, 15 July, 29 Oct. 1854. Bancroft, *History of Oregon*, vol. 2, p. 337. Harriet to Wilkie Duniway, 11 April 1924. *Path Breaking*, p. 4, mistakenly dates the fire in 1855.

33. Clyde Duniway notes; Down, *Silverton Country*, pp. 121, 192, 231, 41; Smith, *Presumptuous Dreamers*, pp. 43–44.

34. *Argus*, 12 Sept. 1857. The *Path Breaking* version, pp. 284–85, is not the same as the iambic pentameter original.

35. *Argus*, 16 Jan. 1858, 3 July 1858.

36. See Alfred Powers, *History of Oregon Literature*, pp. 204–07; Fred Lockley, *Oregon's Yesterdays*, p. 308; Larsell, *The Doctor in Oregon*, p. 301; quotation from Joseph Gaston, *Portland, Oregon*, vol. 1, pp. 666, 494. Down, *Silverton Country*, pp. 155, 157, 170–77; Robert Carlton Clark, *History of the Willamette Valley, Oregon*, pp. 414–17.

37. Down, *Silverton Country*, pp. 239, 177–78, 130–31.

38. See Robert W. Johannsen, *Frontier Politics and the Sectional Conflict*, pp. 59, 79, 124, 150–51. Central Oregon was the "Douglas belt," and northern

counties, with more New Englanders and urbanites, voted for Lincoln. See also, Bowen, "Oregon Frontiersman," in *Western Shore*, pp. 183–84.

39. *Argus*, 21 April, 21 July, 25 Aug., 8 Sept., 3 Nov., 1855; 8 March 1856; 4 April 1857; 19 Jan. 1856.

40. Reported in *Salem Statesman*, 17 Sept., 22 Sept. 1857, in Smith, *Presumptuous Dreamers*, pp. 48–50. Gaston, *Portland, Oregon*, vol. 1, pp. 10–16.

41. D. Newsom, in *Western Observer*, "Letter to *Ill. Journal*," Jan. 1857, p. 66; "Letter to *Oregon Statesman*," 21 Dec. 1857. *Argus*, April 1857 issues. Thomas C. McClintock, "Seth Lewelling, William S. U'Ren and the Birth of the Oregon Progressive Movement," pp. 197ff. Neill Johnson, "Cause and Cure of Disease in Fruit Trees," *Argus*, 18 Sept. 1858. He gave a keg of apples to editor Adams, noted in 7 Aug. 1858 issue. Joseph Gaston, *Portland, Oregon*, vol. 1, pp. 351–55.

42. *Captain Gray's Company*, pp. 281, 308, 310. Letter from ASD to Clyde, 31 Jan. 1893, mentions "long ago" reading of *Martin Chuzzlewit, Little Dorrit*, and *Nicholas Nickolby [sic]*. Dickens's books were serialized in *Harper's Monthly* in the 1850s.

43. Margaret Jewett Bailey, *The Grains, or, Passages in the Life of Ruth Rover, With Occasional Pictures of Oregon, Natural and Moral*. The only extant copy of this book is in the Beinecke Library, Yale U. See Powers, *History of Oregon Literature*, pp. 213–14; Sidney Warren, *Farthest Frontier*, p. 246.

CHAPTER 5. STEPPING FORTH

1. Bishop Berkeley, "The Course of Empire," *Argus*, 20 Nov. 1858.

2. *Captain Gray's Company*, pp. iii, iv.

3. Ibid., pp. 104, 272. See Ann Douglas, *The Feminization of American Culture*, pp. 227ff.

4. *Captain Gray's Company*, pp. 272, 320.

5. Ibid., p. 65.

6. Ibid., pp. 281, 204, 209, 79, 97, 99, 323.

7. *Argus*, 21 July, 25 Aug., 8 Sept., 3 Nov. 1855; 8 March 1856; 4 April 1857. Larsell, *Doctor in Oregon*, pp. 207, 301; Powers, *History of Oregon Literature*, pp. 204, 207; Lockley, *Oregon's Yesterdays*, p. 308.

8. G. Thomas Edwards, "Dr. Ada M. Weed: Northwest Reformer," pp. 5–40. Trall's books were *Home Treatment for Sexual Abuses, The Hydropathic Encyclopedia, The Illustrated Family Gymnasium, The New Hydropathic Cook-Book. The Health and Diseases of Women* came out in 1862.

9. Edwards, "Dr. Ada M. Weed," p. 19.

10. *Statesman*, 10 May 1859, in Smith, *Presumptuous Dreamers*, p. 69.

11. J. L. Johnson, "Overland to Oregon," pp. 37–38, 41, 42, 45, 75.

12. *Captain Gray's Company*, pp. 20, 57, 183–87, 216, 331–32.

13. *Argus*, 18 and 25 Dec. 1858; 1 Jan. 1859. D. Newsom, letter to *Ill. State Journal*, 14 Feb. 1859, in *Western Observer*, p. 88: thirty couples were divorced; the requests of ten others were too late for action.

14. *Argus*, 22 Jan. 1859.

15. Ibid., 23 April 1859. Hubert Ray Duniway was born 24 March 1859.
16. Ibid., 14 May, 21 May, 4 June, 25 June, 23 July 1859. Also 16 April.
17. See George A. Belknap, *Oregon Imprints, 1848–1870*, p. 17. Louvisa Turley to James Scott, 1 Jan. 1860, 14 Nov. 1858; J. T. Scott to A. J. Davis, 24 April 1859, Browne Papers. Smith, *Presumptuous Dreamers*, pp. 68–70.
18. *Argus*, 28 May 1859.
19. Editorial, *NNW*, 5 May 1871; Introduction, *From the West to the West.*
20. *Path Breaking*, pp. 13–14.
21. Arthur L. Throckmorton, *Oregon Argonauts*, p. 210; D. Newsom, letters to *Oregon Farmer*, 5 March 1860, 8 Feb. 1859, to *Ill. State Journal*, 14 June, 29 Aug., 7 Nov. 1859, all in *Western Observer*, pp. 114, 86, 103, 105, 109–10; Smith, *Presumptuous Dreamers*, p. 76, from Yamhill Co. Land Records.
22. *Oregon Farmer*, 18 Oct. 1860; *Path Breaking*, p. 10.
23. *Oregon Farmer*, August 1859, 21 Sept. 1859, 24 Dec. 1859, 6 July 1860. Other letters 6 Feb. 1860, 26 March 1860, 21 April 1860, 5 June 1860. ASD, "How I Became a Literary Woman," Duniway Papers.
24. See D. Newsom, *Western Observer*, p. 86; *Argus*, 14 Aug. 1858.
25. *Oregon Farmer*, 5 Oct. 1860.
26. Ibid., 21 July 1860.
27. Ibid., 22 Aug. 1860.
28. Ibid., 18 Sept. 1860. See also the letter from Arator accusing Amigo of bigotry and impudence.
29. Ibid., 7 Dec. 1859, 26 March 1860.
30. *NNW*, 26 May 1871. Cf. Catherine Scott Coburn in Scott, *Oregon Country*, vol. 1, p. 317, describing a similar incident in 1854!
31. E.g., in *Oregon Farmer*, "Embellishments of a Country Home," 15 Feb. 1861; "Boy's Talk" series, 15 Feb.–15 April 1861; articles on husbands' making wills for protection of wife's interests and on kitchen planning, 15 Aug., 15 Sept. 1861; numerous stories in 1862. ASD, Editorial, *NNW*, 5 May 1871: "We have written and published during the past twelve years, enough of poems, sketches, criticisms, letters, etc., etc., to fill half a dozen volumes."
32. *Oregon Farmer*, "My Farm Don't Pay," 1 April 1861; "Farmer's Wife," 15 June 1861—cf. "A Dialogue for the Times," ibid., p. 1; *Captain Gray's Company*, p. 170. Ben went to the mines in the summer of 1862, Harvey Scott in 1863, Neill Johnson from 1861–63: Scott, *Oregon Country*, vol. 3, p. 77; Johnson, "Autobiography," p. 26. Cf. Goulder, *Reminiscences*, pp. 210–14.
33. *Path Breaking*, pp. 28–29.
34. Scott, *Oregon Country*, vol. 5, p. 136, 305–06. Also Bancroft, *History of Oregon*, vol. 2, pp. 482–83.
35. *Oregon Farmer*, 4 Jan. 1862.
36. Ibid. Cf. D. Newsom letter, same issue, *Western Observer*, p. 162.
37. *Oregon Farmer*, 1 Feb. 1862.
38. Ibid., 1 April 1862; letter from Martha Caffee to Thomas Roelofson, 1867.
39. *Oregon Farmer*, 15 May 1862.
40. Letter from ASD to "My Dear Husband," 4 May 1862. Cf. Scott, *Oregon Country*, vol. 3, pp. 140–41.
41. *Path Breaking*, pp. 14–15.

42. Gaston, *Portland, Oregon*, vol. 1, p. 355; *Path Breaking*, pp. 16, 13.

43. *Judith Reid*, chap. 14, *NNW*, 4 Aug. 1871. A similar incident occurs in *Her Lot*, chap. 26, 26 July 1878.

44. *Path Breaking*, p. 16.

45. *Path Breaking*, p. 17.

46. ASD, *NNW*, 9 April 1875. Scott, *Oregon Country*, vol. 1, pp. 129, 181; vol. 2, p. 17. ASD, *NNW*, 5 May 1871. *Oregonian*, 31 Aug. 1864, in Smith, *Presumptuous Dreamers*, p. 92.

47. Quoted in Smith, *Presumptuous Dreamers*, pp. 102–04.

48. Smith, *Presumptuous Dreamers*, p. 107, from County Deed Records. See Victor, *All Over Oregon and Washington*, pp. 176–77. The population was 2,000 in 1871.

49. *Path Breaking*, p. 19. Cf. advertisement, *Albany States' Rights Democrat*, 24 Nov. 1866, in Smith, *Presumptuous Dreamers*, p. 107.

50. David Duniway interview, including Robert Stevenson Testimony; letter to me, 29 July 1977 and 10 May 1982, citing 1870 census figures. Machine described by Johnson relatives, remembering one their parents bought. Letter from Isaac Ball in *Oregon Farmer*, March 1859, p. 114, describes similar contraption, made with old whiskey or molasses barrel and a crank to turn it. An R. G. Dun & Co. credit report on Mrs. Duniway, 14 Nov. 1869, said she and her husband "together are worth probably $1500 to $2,000" and are "respectable people, making an honest living tho' of slim financial strength." Oregon vol. 5, p. 22, R. G. Dun & Co. Collection, Baker Library, Harvard University Graduate School of Business Administration. This citation was kindly brought to my attention by Prof. Mary Lee Spence of the University of Illinois, and is quoted by permission of Dun & Bradstreet.

51. Scott, *Oregon Country*, vol. 1, pp. 6, 12. Shattuck was Pacific University's first professor of ancient languages, a member of the 1857 constitutional convention, an Oregon Supreme Court judge from 1862 to 1867 and 1874 to 1878, and a member of Portland's city council and school board (vol. 2, p. 280). Nash, "Refining a Frontier," and "Scott of the *Oregonian*." Also, on his prodigious memory, Alfred Holman, in Scott, *Oregon Country*, vol. 1, pp. 26–27, and elsewhere; Gaston, *Portland, Oregon*, vol. 1, p. 506.

52. *NNW*, 5 May 1871.

53. Holman, in Scott, *Oregon Country*, vol. 1, p. 29.

54. *Amie and Henry Lee*, chaps. 16, 18, 18 Sept. and 30 Oct. 1874. Cf. Ann Douglas Wood, " 'Scribbling Women' and Fanny Fern."

55. ASD, "How I Became a Literary Woman."

56. Chap. 26 (serialized as *Her Lot, NNW*, 1878). See *One Woman's Sphere*, chap. 20, 22 Oct. 1875, 3 Sept. 1875.

57. *Path Breaking*, pp. 28, 22.

58. Ibid., p. 23.

59. Ibid., pp. 23–24.

60. David Duniway and Duniway genealogical file. Annie Fearnside became a typesetter for *NNW* and then a schoolteacher—*NNW*, 9 July 1875, 10 May 1878. Picture in Duniway Papers. Victor, *All Over Oregon and Washington*, p. 226.

61. *Oregonian*, 18 July 1868, p. 3, col. 2. Letter to editor, *NNW*, 7 Sept. 1877. Unfortunately, all Catherine Coburn's correspondence was burned by her daughters (Smith, *Presumptuous Dreamers*, p. 248 fn. 92). See Gaston, *Portland, Oregon*, vol. 1, p. 606.

62. Letters to Clyde, 2 Nov. 1902, 2 Aug. 1900, 9 Jan 1901. See also 18 May 1902, 25 Sept. and 27 Oct. 1903. Duniway liked "good Saxon patronymics" (see *One Woman's Sphere*, chap. 7, *NNW*, 16 July 1875). See Richard W. and Dorothy C. Wertz, *Lying-In: A History of Childbirth in America*, p. 110, and illustration, p. 103, of an elaborate "uterine supporter" which may have been what Duniway wore. For the prevalence of such problems see Gerda Lerner, *The Grimké Sisters from South Carolina*, p. 290; Catherine Beecher, *Letters to the People on Health and Happiness*, pp. 7–13, 121–30; William Alcott, *The Young Woman's Book of Health*, pp. 243–49; Linda Gordon, *Woman's Body, Woman's Right*, p. 24.

63. *NNW*, 5 May 1871. Perhaps this was a typographical error for 300.

64. Letters to Clyde, 29 April 1894, 17 Nov. 1897.

65. *Path Breaking*, p. 40.

CHAPTER 6. CIRCUIT RIDER IN THE CAUSE OF WOMEN

1. *Path Breaking*, p. 40.

2. See Sandra Myres, *Westering Women*, chap. 8, for an excellent summary of suffrage developments in western states. ASD mentions *Revolution* in "Women in Journalism," MS speech 1897, Scrapbook II.

3. Elisabeth Anthony Dexter, *Colonial Women of Affairs*, pp. 37, 102, 111, 188, and *passim;* pp. 185, 190 refer to the postrevolutionary "mania for codifying . . . all done by men" and to growing wealth and industrialization. Mary R. Beard, *Woman as Force in History*, pp. 88–155, stresses the development of equity law to circumvent common law and protect female property rights, but considers neither the extent to which frontier lawyers followed Blackstonian formulations nor their influence on the whole legal structure, e.g., Oregon's George Williams, who became United States attorney general under Grant. Norma Basch, "Amphibious Women: Exceptions to Married Women's Common Law Disabilities in New York, 1815–1848"; Randy Sue Rabinowitz, "The Married Women's Property Acts in New York: A Legal History." Both reveal the limitations of equity law as a protection for women and cite it in fact as a cause of further erosion of their autonomy.

4. *Oregon Herald*, quoted in *NNW*, 8 Nov. 1872. David Duniway says colored woman was Mrs. Beatty. Flexner, *Century of Struggle*, pp. 164–70; *History of Woman Suffrage*, vol. 3, p. 768; ASD, "Editorial Correspondence," *NNW*, 29 April 1886.

5. *Path Breaking*, p. 40; Gaston, *Portland, Oregon*, vol. 1, p. 333; H. K. Smith, *Presumptuous Dreamers*, pp. 142, 253 fn. 148.

6. *Path Breaking*, p. 67; *History of Woman Suffrage*, vol. 3, p. 769; *Oregonian*, 16 Jan. 1871, reprinted in H. K. Smith, *Presumptuous Dreamers*, p. 144; Gayle R. Bandow, "'In Pursuit of a Purpose,'" pp. 24, 79–80, says only three issues from 1871 remain in the Bancroft Library.

7. *Path Breaking*, pp. 67, 206.

8. "Eminent Women I Have Met," MS speech *ca.* 1900 in Scrapbook II, Duniway Papers. Edward T. James et al., eds. *Notable American Women, 1607–1950*, vol. 1 (Cambridge, Mass.: Belknap Press, Harvard, 1971), pp. 223–25.

9. *Oregonian*, 16 Jan. 1871—quoted in Smith, *Presumptuous Dreamers*, p. 144; *Path Breaking*, p. 68.

10. *Oregonian*, 25 Jan. 1871—quoted in Smith, *Presumptuous Dreamers*, p. 145.

11. Capell, "Biography of Abigail Scott Duniway," pp. 47, 51–52; Bandow, "'In Pursuit of a Purpose,'" p. 32. A large ad for Mrs. Duniway's millinery store appeared in all early issues of the *NNW*, along with a fashion news column which was discontinued after the stores were sold.

12. "Personal Reminiscences," p. 457; also letter to Clyde, 10 Oct. 1894; *Path Breaking*, p. 20.

13. *NNW*, 12 June 1874. The charge was made by Timothy Davenport, a Silverton area Republican who was among the earliest supporters of woman suffrage. But in 1874 Duniway was supporting John Mitchell's faction in the splintering Republican party; Davenport was one of the reformists.

14. See e.g., Editorial, *NNW*, 11 Oct. 1872, 25 Sept. 1874, 24 Dec. 1875. David Duniway, "Abigail Scott Duniway, Path Breaker," in *With Her Own Wings*, p. 204; Clyde Duniway, "My Memories of Abigail Scott Duniway."

15. Path Breaking, p. 31; Warren, *Farthest Frontier*, pp. 131–37; Bowen, "The Oregon Frontiersman," pp. 192ff.; Nash, "Refining a Frontier," p. 69; Marie Lazenby, "Down-Easters Out West," pp. 9, 13, 21; Victor, in *All Over Oregon and Washington*, p. 153, said Portland had thirty businessmen whose annual incomes ranged between $5,000 and $50,000—ten of them over $16,000.

16. ASD, "Temperance and Woman's Rights," *NNW*, 18 Aug. 1871, reported 149 liquor dealers in Portland. See also Gaston, *Portland, Oregon*, vol. 1, pp. 632–33; Warren, *Farthest Frontier*, p. 137; Malcolm Clark, Jr., "The Second Hundred Years," in *Western Shore*, p. 289.

17. *NNW*, 5 May 1871.

18. Ibid., 4 March 1880.

19. Editorial, *NNW*, 10 July 1879.

20. Bethenia Owens-Adair, *Some of Her Life Experiences*, pp. 80, 83. See other testimonial letters in Duniway Papers.

21. Bandow, "'In Pursuit of a Purpose,'" p. 33.

22. *NNW*, 16 Dec. 1886. See Winthur, *The Old Oregon Country*, esp. p. 275. ASD, "The Stage-Driver's Story," pp. 85–90.

23. Clippings in ASD file, Ore. Hist. Soc., Portland, Ore.

24. *Path Breaking*, pp. 43–47; Ida Husted Harper, *The Life and Work of Susan B. Anthony*, vol. 1, pp. 391, 395–96. The trip and its significance are analyzed by Jean M. Ward, "The Emergence of a Mentor-Protégé Relationship."

25. Harper, *Susan B. Anthony*, vol. 1, p. 397. See also *NNW*, 8 Sept. 1871.

26. *NNW*, 17 Nov. 1871. Gaston, *Portland, Oregon*, vol. 1, p. 508; Scott, *Oregon Country*, vol. 1, pp. 73, 276–78; *Daily Oregon Bulletin*, 20 Oct. 25, 8 Nov. 1871.

27. *NNW*, 6 Oct. 1871.

28. Ibid.; Ward, "Mentor-Protégé Relationship," p. 36; *Path Breaking*, p. 46.

29. "Editorial Correspondence," *NNW*, 22 Oct., 20 Oct. 1875; Anthony quoted by Ward, "Mentor Protégé Relationship," pp. 38–39.
30. Harper, *Susan B. Anthony*, vol. 1, p. 399; *NNW*, 17 Nov., 3 Nov. 1871.
31. *Path Breaking*, p. 45; *NNW*, 17 Nov. 1871. Letters from Anthony, 4 Nov., 16 Nov. 1871, in Harper, *Susan B. Anthony*, vol. 1, pp. 399–400; to *NNW*, 1 Dec. 1871. *History of Woman Suffrage*, vol. 3, p. 769.
32. *Path Breaking*, p. 48.
33. Sunday *Oregonian*, 28 Feb. 1886, from back of lecture brochure, ASD Scrapbook II, Duniway Papers.
34. See Robert D. Clark, "From Genesis to Darwin: The Metamorphosis of Thomas Condon," in *Western Shore*, pp. 198–234. Condon discovered the ancestor of the horse.
35. "Editorial Correspondence," *NNW*, 20 Nov. 1874.
36. *Edna and John*, chap. 9, *NNW*, 29 Dec. 1876.
37. Introduction to *Blanche Le Clerq* MS, Duniway Papers; introduction to *Mrs. Hardine's Will*, *NNW*, 13 Nov. 1879.
38. *NNW*, 8 Dec. 1871, 21 Feb. 1873, 16 and 30 Jan. 1874, 13 Feb. 1874, 15 May 1874.
39. "Editorial Correspondence,"*NNW*, 30 Nov., 7 Dec. 1877; 24 Dec. 1875; 17 and 31 Dec. 1875; 18 Sept. 1874; 12 Feb. 1875. Also 25 June 1875.
40. "Editorial Correspondence," *NNW*, 30 Nov. 1877.
41. Ibid.; *Path Breaking*, pp. 86–87.
42. *Path Breaking*, pp. 86–87.
43. Introduction to *Martha Marblehead*, *NNW*, 15 June 1877; letter to editor, *NNW*, 7 Sept. 1877.
44. "Editorial Correspondence," *NNW*, 30 Nov. 1877.
45. "Editorial Correspondence," *NNW*, 30 July, 20 Aug. 1875. See also 5 April 1883 on Seattle real estate; 25 Aug. 1881—lots at $25 and a block for $150 in Seaview, Wash.; 24 Dec. 1875.
46. "Editorial Correspondence," *NNW*, 19 Aug. 1886.
47. "Editorial Correspondence," *NNW*, 27 Aug. 1875, 22 Sept. 1881. See also 10 July 1879, 24 June 1880.
48. "Editorial Correspondence," *NNW*, 14 June 1883. The wedding occurred 18 Nov. 1880 and included a *charivari* in the eastern Oregon village of Mitchell, not far from Spanish Gulch. A poignant story in the 16 Sept. 1880 issue described the mother–son encounter.
49. "Editorial Correspondence," *NNW*, 2 July 1875; 9 April 1872, 23 June 1881.
50. "Editorial Correspondence," *NNW*, 2 Oct. 1874. She was reporting on the Oregon legislature in Salem.
51. "Editorial Correspondence," *NNW*, 8 Dec. 1881.
52. Ibid., 24 April 1874.
53. Ibid., 6 Aug. 1875.
54. Ibid., 27 Nov. 1874.
55. Ibid., 30 Nov. 1877.
56. Ibid., 17 Nov. 1881.
57. Ibid., "Editorial Correspondence," 18 Sept. 1874.
58. *One Woman's Sphere*, chap. 20, *NNW*, 22 Oct. 1875.

59. Ibid., chap. 3, 18 June 1875.
60. "Editorial Correspondence," *NNW*, 25 June 1875, 27 Aug. 1875.
61. Ibid., 15 Sept. 1881. See also 20 May 1880, 11 Nov. 1880.
62. Ibid., 31 July 1874.
63. Ibid., 9 March 1877.

CHAPTER 7. TO LOOSE THE BONDS

1. *Edna and John*, chap. 9, *NNW*, 29 Dec. 1876; *One Woman's Sphere*, chap. 3, *NNW*, 18 June 1875; *Mrs. Hardine's Will*, chap. 28, 27 May 1880.
2. See Bowen, "The Oregon Frontiersman," pp. 191–92.
3. See Russell Trall, *Hydropathic Encyclopedia*, vol. 2, pp. 493–99, or Augustus Kinsley Gardner, *Conjugal Sins* (1870) and *Our Children* (1872), as cited in G. J. Barker-Benfield, *The Horrors of the Half-known Life*, pp. 253, 295–97. Also selected documents in Nancy Cott, ed., *Root of Bitterness*, pp. 263–308; William Leach, *True Love and Perfect Union*, pp. 81ff., especially pp. 87–89, 375; Lerner, *The Female Experience*, pp. 89–97—an unpublished essay on marriage by Sarah Grimké, written 1852–57; Andrew Sinclair, *The Better Half: The Emancipation of the American Woman*, chap. 11; Gordon, *Woman's Body, Woman's Right*, pp. 95–185; Charles E. Rosenberg, "Sexuality, Class and Role in Nineteenth-Century America," p. 139; David J. Pivar, *Purity Crusade*, p. 151.
4. "Editorial Correspondence," *NNW*, 3 May 1883.
5. Flexner, *Century of Struggle*, pp. 153–54; Page Smith, *Daughters of the Promised Land*, pp. 143–57; Arlene Kisner, ed., *The Lives and Writings of the Notorious Victoria Woodhull and Her Sister Tennessee Claflin* includes, pp. 3–9, an excerpt from Theodore Tilton's biography of Woodhull published in 1871.
6. Kisner, *The Notorious Victoria Woodhull*, pp. 11, 28.
7. Ibid., p. 27.
8. Cooke, letter to ed., *NNW*, 2 June 1871; ASD, "Editorial," 18 Aug. 1871.
9. *NNW*, 21 June 1872; 2 March 1882.
10. *Judith Reid*, chap. 13, *NNW*, 28 July 1871.
11. Ibid., chap. 30, 8 Dec. 1871.
12. Yours Truly, *NNW*, 25 May 1877, took sharp aim at a visiting lecturer on female physiology for not knowing what he was talking about—including the use of the word "mensuration" instead of "menstruation." When another woman defended the lecturer, Duniway agreed that such lectures were valuable, but only if they were accurate. See also Elizabeth Cady Stanton, *Eighty Years and More*, p. 290.
13. "Equality of Difference in Sex," *NNW*, 13 Jan. 1881; *One Woman's Sphere*, chap. 16, 17 Sept. 1875; *Judith Reid*, chap. 32, 22 Dec. 1871; *The Happy Home*, chap. 11, 29 Jan. 1875. See also Pivar, *Purity Crusade*, pp. 151, 155–56; Rosenberg, "Sexuality, Class and Role," pp. 135, 137, 139, 141–43.
14. *NNW*, 9 June 1871. *One Woman's Sphere*, chap. 5, *NNW*, 2 July 1875; chap. 11, 13 Aug. 1875.
15. *Madge Morrison: The Mollala Maid and Matron*, chap. XV, *NNW*, 4 March

1876. Lerner, *The Female Experience*, p. 425, documents a similar real-life incident in 1845.

16. *Margaret Rudson; A Pioneer Story*, MSS revised in 1914 from an earlier story, box 47, Duniway Papers, chaps. 12, 13, 16, 35. The theme of marriage as a business relationship occurs many times in ASD's writings, the first as early as one of the Xenittie letters, *Argus*, 11 Jan. 1859.

17. *Ethel Graeme's Destiny*, chap. 15, p. 80, galley proof copy in Duniway Papers as revised in 1881 from *Her Lot; or, How She Was Protected*, NNW, 1878.

18. 12 May 1871. Miller was a cause célèbre in Portland at the time, a gifted poet in her own right who was left destitute by her fame-seeking husband. Duniway published some of her work but most of it was lost. Possibly the book Mrs. Miller was selling was Noyes's *History of American Socialisms*, (Lippincott, 1870; repr. Dover, 1966). This included excerpts from Noyes's *Bible Communism* (1848) and the *Hand-Book* of the Oneida Community. See Dover ed., pp. 623–40, esp. p. 633.

19. Letter to Clyde, 26 Dec. 1892. Besant had collaborated in reprinting Dr. Charles Knowlton's *Fruits of Philosophy* in a low-priced pamphlet for English working-class readers. The resultant trial made her famous. See Roger Manvell, *The Trial of Annie Besant and Charles Bradlaugh*, p. 59.

20. Letter to Clyde, 7 Jan. 1893. Karezza was based on Noyes's method of male continence; see Raymond Lee Muncy, *Sex and Marriage in Utopian Communities*, pp. 33, 160–96. Duniway thought Teed was out to "put money in his purse" by forming "Unities" to practice his "celibate doctrines" all over the country.

21. *NNW*, 19 May 1871; "Temperance and Woman's Rights," *NNW*, 18 Aug. 1871.

22. *NNW*, 9 April 1872 and 5 Feb. 1880; *Dux*, chap. 7, 23 Oct. 1884; *Amie and Henry Lee*, chap. 21, 16 Oct. 1874.

23. *Path Breaking*, pp. 63–64.

24. "Editorial Correspondence," *NNW*, 26 April 1872. Abby Kelley was one of the first and best-known women orators for abolition, upon whose attempt to speak at a meeting of the Conn. Anti-slavery Society in 1840 the chairman threatened to resign because of the "outrage on decency." See P. Smith, *Daughters of the Promised Land*, p. 125.

25. "Ante-Natal Murder," *NNW*, 3 Jan. 1873, 21 Nov. 1873, 17 June 1886, 9 Jan. 1879.

26. *Dux: A Maiden Who Dared*, chap. 7, *NNW*, 23 Oct. 1884; chap. 26, 5 March 1885.

27. *The Happy Home*, chap. 11, *NNW*, 29 Jan. 1875. *Dux*, chap. 7, 23 Oct. 1884.

28. *Path Breaking*, pp. 59–60, 82; Owens-Adair, *Some of Her Life Experiences*, p. 80.

29. *NNW*, 2 June 1871.

30. *Edna and John*, chaps. 4, 6, *NNW*, 27 Oct., 24 Nov. 1876.

31. *NNW*, 2 June 1871.

32. *NNW*, 24 Sept. 1875.

33. *The Happy Home; or, The Husband's Triumph*, chap. 13, 12 Feb. 1875.

34. *NNW*, 19 July 1883.

35. *Mrs. Hardine's Will*, chap. 28, *NNW*, 27 May 1880.
36. *Captain Gray's Company*, p. 204; Editorial, *NNW*, 25 Sept. 1874.
37. Clyde Duniway, "My Memories of Abigail Scott Duniway."
38. See, e.g., letters to Clyde, 22 April 1893 and 12 Feb. 1893; Clyde Duniway, "My Memories of Abigail Scott Duniway," p. 6.
39. "Editorial Correspondence," *NNW*, 11 Dec. 1874.
40. *NNW*, 6 Oct. 1871.
41. *NNW*, 16 Dec. 1880.
42. *Path Breaking*, pp. 93, 97; also *NNW*, 10 July 1884.
43. *NNW*, 24 March 1881.
44. See *Path Breaking*, p. 33. Also, *NNW*, 26 Jan., 2 Feb., 9 March 1882. According to the Ore. Hist. Soc. (3 Aug. 1977 letter of Gordon Manning to me), there are no extant copies of the 22 Jan. or 15 Jan. 1882 *Sunday Welcome* in which the slander appeared.
45. *NNW*, 8 Jan. 1875; David Duniway interview; "Report of the Convention," *NNW*, 19 Feb. 1880.
46. Hubert to Clyde, 9 May 1895. Letters from ASD to Clyde, 10 Feb. 1890 and [7 Nov. 1892].
47. *Ethel Graeme's Destiny*, chaps. 14, 15.
48. Ibid., chaps. 15, 26.
49. "Editorial Correspondence," *NNW*, 7 Aug. 1874, 13 Aug. 1875.
50. Editorial, *NNW*, 28 March 1873; Clyde Duniway notes.
51. *Madge Morrison*, chap. 7, *NNW*, 28 Jan. 1876.
52. *Edna and John, A Romance of Idaho Flat*, chap. 18, *NNW*, 20 April 1877.
53. Clyde Duniway notes. "Editorial Correspondence," *NNW*, June 1876–March 1877, describes the trip; 16 Feb. 1877 mentions the illness.
54. *Ellen Dowd, The Farmer's Wife*, chap. 7, *NNW*, 16 Feb. 1872. See also *Judith Reid* (1871), *The Happy Home* (1874–75), *One Woman's Sphere* (1875), *Madge Morrison* (1875–76), and the early chaps. of *Edna and John* (1876).
55. *Edna and John*, chap. 22, 18 May 1877.
56. See "Yours Truly," *NNW*, 30 March, 11 May 1877; ad, 16 Feb. 1877; Gaston, *Portland, Oregon*, vol. 1, p. 503.
57. Gaston, *Portland, Oregon*, vol. 1, pp. 503, 354; Clyde Duniway Notes.
58. *DeLauncey Curse*, chap. vol. 1, *NNW*, 10 Sept. 1885.
59. "Letter from the Fireside," 4, *NNW*, 28 Jan. 1886. *NNW*, 13 Jan. 1887.
60. Letters from ASD to Clyde, 31 Dec. 1893; Wilkie to Clyde, 1 March 1894; ASD to Clyde, 27 March 1894.
61. Clyde Duniway notes; David Duniway interview. The baby is buried in Forest Grove as the adopted son of B. C. and A. J. Duniway.
62. *Fact, Fate and Fancy*, chaps. 14–18, *NNW*, 26 Dec. 1878 to 23 Jan. 1879 (this was exactly when Ida and Hubert returned from San Francisco); chap. 30, 24 April 1879; *Mrs. Hardine's Will*, chap. 28, 27 May 1880.
63. Letter to Clyde, 24 Nov. 1893. In a 15 Dec. 1892 letter she refers to another "young lady" as "the only one [Willis] has ever come in contact with who inspires him in the right way," and 3 Sept. 1893, he has "several others on his string."

64. Letter to Clyde, 13 Sept. 1893. Letters from Willis to Alice and Alice to Willis, Willis Duniway file, Duniway Papers.
65. See, e.g., Susan Brownmiller, *Against Our Will: Men, Women and Rape.*

CHAPTER 8. OF PRAYER AND PROHIBITION

1. See Ahlstrom, *Religious History of the American People*, pp. 733, 745; Douglas, *The Feminization of American Culture;* Daniel Calhoun, *The Intelligence of a People.*
2. Norman H. Clark, *The Dry Years*, is an indispensable study of this movement in the Pacific Northwest. Ruth Bordin, *Woman and Temperance*, is the best recent national study.
3. *NNW*, 6, 13, 27 March 1874.
4. "Editorial Correspondence, *NNW*, 17 April 1874.
5. *Path Breaking*, p. 32. Son of the renowned Rev. Wm. G. Eliot of St. Louis, who founded the Western Unitarian Conference in 1852, T. L. Eliot's nephew was poet T. S. Eliot. The first Unitarian church was organized in Portland in 1866.
6. Letter to Clyde, 22 April 1893; John Frederick Scheck, "Transplanting a Tradition," pp. 90–93, 104–05. See also Scheck, "Thomas Lamb Eliot and His Vision of an Enlightened Community," in *Western Shore*, pp. 235–69; Clark, *Willamette Valley*, pp. 662–63; George Willis Cooke, *Unitarianism in America*, p. 368; Stow Persons, *Free Religion: An American Faith.* Howe, *The Unitarian Conscience*, p. 382 fn. 98, points out that one-third of 540 late-nineteenth-century reformers were reared as Unitarians.
7. *Path Breaking*, p. 12.
8. In a letter to Clyde, 4 Oct. 1898, Duniway mentioned attending a seance which included such notable public figures as Sen. Mitchell, Gov. William Thayer, and Ralph Duniway's law partner. Mr. and Mrs. Seth Lewelling and William U'Ren also experimented with Duniway in such events. See McClintock, "Seth Lewelling, William S. U'Ren and the Birth of the Oregon Progressive Movement," p. 201. The eminent Lester Frank Ward predicted in 1870 that "Spiritualism would one day become the prevailing faith of America": Persons, *Free Religion*, p. 103. Clyde Duniway, "My Memories of Abigail Scott Duniway," p. 9., named the medium.
9. *NNW*, 22 Aug. 1873. She described a camp meeting on 4 Sept. 1874, and on 3 July 1874 she reported joining a seance but "nothing came of it." On 19 Aug. 1880, she approved "test seances" to test the truth of spiritualism.
10. *Path Breaking*, p. 279. Clyde Duniway notes, photograph in Duniway Papers.
11. *From the West to the West*, pp. 181, 183.
12. *NNW*, 26 Aug. 1880. ASD answered the charge of blasphemy 9 Sept. 1880.
13. *NNW*, 7 April 1881.
14. "Editorial Correspondence," *NNW*, 7 Oct. 1886.
15. Scott, *NNW*, 6 Aug. 1875. Other essays appeared 25 June, 2 July, 16 July 1875. See Nash, "Refining a Frontier," pp. 338–78. Annie Everest's essays appeared 27 April, and 25 May 1882.

16. "Editorial Correspondence," *NNW*, 12 Jan. 1877. Quotes on Moody from Ahlstrom, *Religious History*, pp. 765, 766. *NNW*, 28 Aug. 1884, identifies Mrs. Ingersoll.

17. *NNW*, 30 June 1871.

18. "Editorial Correspondence," *NNW*, 20 Oct. 1876.

19. The double signature on the note seems to indicate that Lowrance or his wife or both felt unusually threatened by Duniway. One wonders if there had been some romance between him and his young parishioner which accounted for the mutual hatred they now felt—and for the free love charge. Many of Duniway's early serial novels include a character—a tutor, a singing master, or a potential preacher—who entices the young innocent heroine into a duplicitous marriage and then leaves her to suffer through the rest of the novel's tragedies—e.g., *Judith Reid, Ellen Dowd*. Duniway was related to Judge Parks of Lincoln, Ill., so there may have been political as well as moral overtones to the dispute. See *NNW*, 12 Jan. 1877.

20. *NNW*, 20 Oct. 1876.

21. *NNW*, 12 Sept. 1878.

22. *NNW*, 17 April 1874. Historian Joseph R. Gusfield has pointed out that in the 1870s the WCTU was primarily an upper-class phenomenon, while suffragism was a concern of the middle and lower classes. A few years later the situation was reversed. Cited in Clark, *The Dry Years*, pp. 68–69. For a description of the whole campaign, see Malcolm H. Clark, Jr., "The War on the Webfoot Saloon," or Frances Fuller Victor, "Women's War on Whiskey," in Annie Wittenmyer, *History of the Woman's Temperance Crusade*, pp. 699–716. Cf. Bordin, *Woman and Temperance*, pp. 8–11, 31–33.

23. *NNW*, 27 March 1874. See also, Gaston, *Portland, Oregon*, vol. 1, pp. 415–17, 431.

24. *Path Breaking*, pp. 69, 70.

25. Ibid., pp. 71–72.

26. *NNW*, 26 May 1871.

27. *Path Breaking*, pp. 62–63.

28. Ibid., pp. 64–65.

29. Reprinted in *NNW*, 7 March 1873. See also ASD's *History of Woman Suffrage* account, vol. 3, pp. 771–73; letter from Belle Cooke to *NNW*, 28 March 1873. Mrs. Thornton, who ran an exclusive academy in Oregon City (Gaston, *Portland*, vol. 1, p. 658), might have been offended years earlier by *Captain Gray's Company*.

30. Scott, *Oregon Country*, vol. 4, p. 73, calls Pennoyer a "Northern Democrat, with Southern principles." Vol. 1, pp. 273–78, describes Brown.

31. *NNW*, 19 May 1871.

32. ASD, "Temperance and Woman's Rights," *NNW*, 18 Aug. 1871; Gaston, *Portland, Oregon*, vol. 1, pp. 632–33; Clark, "The Second Hundred Years," in *Western Shore*, p. 288; Nash, "Refining a Frontier," pp. 91–92, 412–25.

33. See Kraditor, *Ideas of the Woman Suffrage Movement*, p. 44 fn. 1.

34. See Mill, *Utilitarianism, Liberty, and Representative Government*, pp. 196, 206, 210–11, as cited and discussed in Ross Evans Paulson, *Woman Suffrage and Prohibition*.

35. "Temperance Suffragists," *NNW*, 29 July 1880.
36. *NNW*, 2 June 1871.
37. *NNW*, 17 April 1874.
38. *NNW*, 21 June 1883.
39. Editorial, *NNW*, 10 June 1886.
40. "The Temperance Problem," *NNW*, 8 July 1886.
41. "The Temperance Problem, No. 3," 22 July 1886.
42. "The Temperance Problem, No. 2," 15 July 1886; ibid., No. 3, 22 July 1886. See also *Path Breaking*, p. 100.
43. "The Temperance Problem, No. 4," 29 July 1886.
44. Ibid.
45. See *Her Lot*, chap. 4, *NNW*, 22 Feb. 1878; *Laban McShane*, chap. 19, 17 Jan. 1884; chap. 20, 24 Jan. 1884. In the latter she calls it the Hahnemann method. David F. Musto, *The American Disease*, p. 3, says opiates were used to cure morphine and alcohol addiction. *Newsweek*, 23 Nov. 1981, p. 76, cites a similar cure still used today in Russia.
46. "The Temperance Problem, No. 4," 29 July 1886.
47. "The Temperance Problem, No. 6, 12 Aug. 1886.
48. Reprinted in "Editorial Correspondence," *NNW*, 30 Sept. 1886.
49. "Editorial Correspondence," 30 Dec. 1886. On 23 Dec. 1886 she referred to the "less than half a dozen would-be leading suffragists in Oregon" who were envious of her position and wanted to take her place. *Path Breaking*, pp. 82–83 identifies them.

CHAPTER 9. DETHRONING THE IDOL GOLD

1. Letter to Clyde, 31 Dec. 1893.
2. According to Alfred Holman, in Scott, *Oregon Country*, vol. 1, pp. 73–74.
3. "Equality of Difference in Sex," *NNW*, 13 Jan. 1881. Cf. *Path Breaking*, p. 157.
4. *NNW*, 16 Sept. 1880.
5. "Report of the Convention," *NNW*, 19 Feb. 1880. Ledger, Duniway file, Ore. Hist. Soc.
6. *NNW*, 20 Oct. 1881, 16 Sept. 1880, 14 Oct. 1880.
7. *Dux: A Maiden Who Dared*, chaps. 9, 10, 15, 18, 19, *NNW*, 6, 13 Nov., 18 Dec. 1884, 8, 15 Jan. 1885. Chap. 18 also includes an analysis of Judge Matthew Deady's commentary on the Constitution, and a peroration against the recent Supreme Court decision against the civil rights of Negroes.
8. "Is Prohibition Wise?" in *Path Breaking*, p. 191. For the justice–expediency distinction, see Kraditor, *Up From the Pedestal*, p. 18; also her *Ideas of the Woman Suffrage Movement*.
9. "Equality of Difference in Sex," *NNW*, 13 Jan. 1881. For a synopsis of scientific theories about women in the nineteenth century, see Cynthia Russett, "The Arrested Female: Recapitulation Defines Woman." See also, e.g., *NNW*, 24 March 1881, 26 Jan. 1882; ASD, *The Coming Century*, 2 Nov. 1891 (box 32, Duniway Papers).

10. "How to Win the Ballot," *Path Breaking*, p. 157; *NNW*, 30 July 1875; 12 Sept. 1878. See also 21 Nov. 1873, 22 Jan. 1880, 5 Oct. 1882; *Edna and John*, chaps. 1, 2, 11, *NNW*, 29 Sept. and 6 Oct. 1876, 19 Jan. 1877.

11. *Dux*, chap. 18, *NNW*, 8 Jan. 1885. See also *Path Breaking*, p. 120.

12. *NNW*, 8 Jan. 1875; report of OSWSA convention, *NNW*, 14 Feb. 1884; chap. 6 above.

13. *NNW*, 29 Aug. 1873. See also *NNW*, 8 Jan. 1880.

14. *NNW*, 22 June 1882.

15. *NNW*, 17 June 1886.

16. Margaret Fuller, *Woman in the Nineteenth Century*, pp. 320–34. Stanton, *Eighty Years and More*, pp. 145–46.

17. "Judd and John Mundane," *NNW*, 25 Feb. 1886; "Editorial Correspondence," 3 June 1886.

18. "Editorial Correspondence," *NNW*, 8 July 1880, 15 July 1880.

19. J. D. Cleaver, curator of collections, Ore. Hist. Soc., showed it to me in Feb. 1976. I had found a clipping in Duniway Papers about ASD's contribution of a quilt which she had begun to make after Ralph's birth in 1869. She told Clyde, 5 Dec. 1900, that a group of women had raised money to buy it. I wondered why it was not among the many quilts on display at the bicentennial exhibit of the Ore. Hist. Soc. When it was brought out of the archives and unrolled in Mr. Cleaver's office, we all understood why. Entitled "Grandmother's Flower Garden," the bright red coverlet has a flounce of violently contrasting magenta. The stitching is so large and uneven that one can see why she also gave up being a milliner. Thus, for the historian, one artifact is worth 1,000 words!

20. Letter to Clyde, 31 Dec. 1893.

21. See Morton J. Horwitz, *The Transformation of American Law: 1780–1860*, pp. xv, xvi, 265. Cf. chap. 6, n. 3, above.

22. *Captain Gray's Company*, pp. 8–9, 15, 27.

23. "Editorial Correspondence," *NNW*, 5 April 1883.

24. *NNW*, 5 May 1871. Long quotes from the petition appear with Duniway's answers on the front page of the paper. See Madeline Vinton Dahlgren, *Thoughts on Female Suffrage, and in Vindication of Woman's True Rights*.

25. Gaston, *Portland, Oregon*, vol. 1, pp. 22–27. *NNW*, 5 May 1871; see Cynthia D. Kinnard, "'Think of Such Narrowness of Vision!'—Political Anti-Feminism, from Antisuffrage to the 'Stop ERA' Movement."

26. Greeley, *Hints Toward Reforms*, pp. 21, 23, 47, 49, 134, 27, 31, 38, 40.

27. *NNW*, 26 Jan. 1872.

28. *NNW*, 6 Nov. 1874, reprinted from W. S. Cameron's recording in Reed's Opera House, Salem, on 5 Oct. 1871.

29. See Henry George, Jr., *The Life of Henry George*, pp. 200–27. Only 1000 copies of the pamphlet were sold and it got no public recognition—p. 235. Henry Nash Smith, *Virgin Land*, pp. 123–29. George N. Belknap, "Still More Addenda to Belknap's *Oregon Imprints*," p. 207.

30. Quoted by Alfred Holman, introduction, Scott, *Oregon Country* vol. 1, p. 95. Nash, "Refining a Frontier," p. 91. Billington, *Westward Expansion*, p. 638,

See Gaston, *Portland, Oregon*, vol. 1, pp. 559 ff. See also Scott, *Oregon Country*, vol. 1, pp. 346–48.

31. *Path Breaking*, p. 20; letter to Clyde, 10 Oct. 1894.

32. *NNW*, 19 May 1871.

33. Peirce, "Cooperative Housekeeping," *Atlantic Monthly*, 22–23 (Nov.–March 1868–69). See Dolores Hayden, "Two Utopian Feminists and Their Campaigns for Kitchenless Houses," "Melusina Fay Peirce and Cooperative Housekeeping," and *A "Grand Domestic Revolution": Feminism, Socialism and the American Home, 1870–1930*, pp. 51, 60, 67, 77–78, 80, 115. See also Robert V. Hine, *Community on the American Frontier*, chap. 9, "Cooperative Colonies."

34. *NNW*, 31 Dec. 1875, 3 Feb. 1881. *Laban McShane*, chap. 4, *NNW*, 4 Oct. 1883. Hayden, *"Grand Domestic Revolution,"* p. 89. See Peirce, *Cooperative Housekeeping: How Not to Do It and How to Do It.* ASD's lecture topic mentioned 31 Dec. 1875.

35. "Editorial Correspondence," *NNW*, 27 Sept. 1883.

36. *Dux: A Maiden Who Dared*, chap. 23, *NNW*, Feb. 12, 1885.

37. "Editorial Correspondence," *NNW*, 16 Dec. 1880.

38. "Editorial Correspondence," *NNW*, 3 July 1884.

39. *NNW*, "Editorial Correspondence," 25 March–3 June 1886. Record book, Duniway Papers. Rodman Paul, ed., *A Victorian Gentlewoman in the Far West*, pp. 265–75, 326–29. Wm. E. Smythe, *The Conquest of Arid America*, was an apostle of irrigation systems as the key to America's development—but irrigation came twenty years later and was based upon the ideas of men like Arthur Foote.

40. *NNW*, 2 Sept. 1886.

41. *Margaret Rudson*, chaps. 32, 25.

42. Letters to Clyde, 1 June 1894, 19 Jan. 1894, 29 Jan. 1894.

43. See Hayden, *"Grand Domestic Revolution,"* pp. 137, 148, 150.

44. Editorial, *NNW*, 17 June 1880.

45. ASD, letter to Clyde, 22 Feb. 1886, transcribed by David Duniway, says, "The Sound riots interrupted all my plans" and refers to "all the news." *NNW*, 18 Feb., 25 Feb. 1886.

46. Alfred Holman, in Scott, *Oregon Country*, vol. 1, p. 63. The quote was from an 1893 *Oregonian* editorial. Leslie McKay Roberts, "Suffragist of the New West," p. 158. Ralph to Clyde, 30 Oct. 1896.

47. "Editorial Correspondence," *NNW*, 11 March 1880.

48. *NNW*, 22 April 1880.

49. Letters to Clyde, 31 Dec. 1893, 29 Oct. 1896.

50. Letter to Clyde, 3 Sept. 1893.

51. Letter to Clyde, 13 Sept. 1893; David Duniway interview, Feb. 1976.

52. "Letters from the Fireside," no. 2, *NNW*, 14 Jan. 1886. See Matthew Josephson, *The Robber Barons*.

53. Lawrence Goodwyn, *The Populist Movement*, pp. 8–19, 99. See also Norman Pollack, *The Populist Response to Industrial America*.

54. "Editorial Correspondence," *NNW*, 13 Dec. 1883.

55. See *NNW*, 20 Nov. 1884.
56. 30 Oct. 1884, 6 and 13 Nov. 1884.
57. E.g., "Editorial Correspondence," *NNW*, 15 Jan. 1885. 6 Nov. 1884. See also 30 Oct. 1884 and elsewhere.
58. *NNW*, 29 April 1886.
59. Letter to Clyde, 8 Dec. 1894.

CHAPTER 10. THE CESSPOOL OF POLITICS

1. Clarence B. Bagley, "Pioneer Papers of Puget Sound," p. 369.
2. Scott, *Oregon Country*, vol. 4, p. 33; Johansen and Gates, *Empire of the Columbia*, pp. 328–29. Joanna L. Stratton, *Pioneer Women*, pp. 136, 241, mentions Anthony.
3. Henry Pittock, *Oregonian* publisher and later a millionaire—his mansion at the top of the city is now a museum—was near bankruptcy in 1872 and had to sell temporarily to Sen. Corbett. Scott bought Ben Holladay's *Bulletin* and edited it for eighteen months in opposition to the *Oregonian*. In 1877, after almost six years as customs collector and marriage to a Pennsylvania lady whose father had just discovered oil on his land, Scott bought back his interest in the *Oregonian* and edited it for the rest of his life. See Nash, "Refining a Frontier," pp. 34–35.
4. Gaston, *Portland, Oregon*, vol. 1, p. 632–33.
5. "Open letter to voters," *NNW*, 13 Sept. 1883. Letter to Clyde, 6 Oct. 1897.
6. Editorial, *NNW*, 30 June 1871.
7. *Path Breaking*, p. 77.
8. "Editorial Correspondence," *NNW*, 21 June 1872.
9. "Repentance and Restitution," *NNW*, 20 June 1873; Earl Pomeroy, *The Pacific Slope*, p. 137. Gaston, *Portland, Oregon*, vol. 1, pp. 559–62.
10. "Bossism," *NNW*, 28 July 1881. Adams became collector of customs at Astoria in 1861. Harvey Scott was customs collector from 1870 to 1876. Simeon Francis became surveyor general of Washington Territory under Lincoln.
11. Editorial, *NNW*, 28 March 1873. Bandow, "In Pursuit of a Purpose," p. 38.
12. Editorial, *NNW*, 27 Feb. 1874.
13. "Yours Truly," *NNW*, 13 Feb. 1874.
14. *NNW*, 20 Feb. 1874.
15. "Letter to the editor," *NNW*, 13 Feb. 1874. Roberts, "Suffragist of the New West," pp. 59–60; Loughary's papers are in the Oregon State Library. *NNW*, 25 Nov. 1880, says Loughary had ten children and was also a nurse-midwife.
16. See *NNW*, 9 July 1875; Robert E. Cowan et al., *The Forgotten Characters of Old San Francisco* (San Francisco: Ward Ritchie Press, 1938), p. viii. *NNW*, 4 Dec. 1874.
17. *NNW*, 11 Dec. 1874.
18. *Amie and Henry Lee*, chap. 8, *NNW*, 17 July 1874.
19. *NNW*, 23 Aug. 1878. The founding is recorded in *NNW*, 10 and 26 Jan. 1877. See also *Path Breaking*, pp. 94–95. Report of last meeting, *NNW*, 7 June 1883.

20. *NNW*, 26 Feb. 1880.
21. Editorial, *NNW*, 1 May 1879.
22. "Editorial Correspondence," *NNW*, 10 July 1879.
23. Ibid., 17 July 1879.
24. *NNW*, 8 July 1880. See esp. *Path Breaking*, pp. 84–85.
25. "Letter to the editor," from Corwin, *NNW*, 11 Nov. 1880. Duniway's similar comments are in *NNW*, 1 April, 8 July, 4 Nov. 1880, 24 March 1881, 26 June 1884. On 16 Sept. 1880, she reported that the state's Democratic governor would sign a suffrage bill if the Republican legislature passed it.
26. See Martha Frances Montague, "Woman Suffrage Movement in Oregon," pp. 35, 40. *Path Breaking*, p. 61, erroneously says the property rights bill was passed in 1874. See Beard, *Women as Force in History*, pp. 170–76. Wayne E. Fuller, "School District 37: Prairie Community," pp. 419–32.
27. *NNW*, 16 Sept. 1880. 21 and 28 Oct. 1880.
28. "Letter to the editor," *NNW*, 25 Nov. 1880. 7 Oct. 1880; *Path Breaking*, p. 193.
29. *NNW*, 16 Nov. 1882.
30. Capell, "Biography of Abigail Scott Duniway," p. 51, quoting Judge Henry McGinn in 1915.
31. *NNW*, 31 March 1881. Details of the case occur throughout *NNW* during 1881 and culminate in the 26 Jan. 1882 issue. See chap. 7 above.
32. Harvey Scott, *History of Portland, Oregon*, p. 420. Gaston, *Portland, Oregon*, vol. 1, p. 501, is unusually vague about the paper. Neither mentions the resultant court case.
33. Details of the *Northwest News* and its running battle with the Duniways appear in *NNW*, 19 April 1883, 9 Aug. 1883, 24 Jan., 28 Feb. 1884, and elsewhere. The threat was in *NNW*, 5 Oct. 1882; final ruling, 26 June 1884. Scott, *History of Portland*, p. 337, identifies Stott as judge, 1880–84, with a "meager salary."
34. Reported in *NNW*, 29 May 1884, 1 Sept. 1884, 12 June 1884. See Clark, *History of the Willamette Valley*, p. 716; Roberts, "Suffragist of the New West," p. 84; *Path Breaking*, p. 193.
35. Gaston, *Portland, Oregon*, vol. 1, p. 562, explains how "purchased voters" were rewarded by "spotters" at the polls or "herded up . . . like cattle at the round-ups . . . and sold . . . at so much per head." *NNW*, 19 June 1884, reports bribery by notorious ward leaders, the Wolf brothers. 12 June 1884 includes reference to an *Oregonian* allegation of illegal voting and various frauds. See also her dispute with antisuffrage Asahel Bush, 3 July 1884.
36. *History of Woman Suffrage*, vol. 3, p. 776. See also *NNW*, 5 June 1884, Willard's visit, *NNW*, 21 January 1883.
37. *Path Breaking*, p. 193; *NNW*, 19 June 1884. "After the Defeat," *NNW*, 5 June 1884. *NNW*, 6 March–24 April 1884, describes the NWSA trip. On Leavitt, see Bordin, *Woman and Temperance*, pp. 38, 88.
38. 10 July, 21 June, 24 July 1884.
39. *NNW*, 5 June 1884. The picture is now in the Ore. Hist. Soc. Key obtained by David Duniway from Library of Congress for 292 faces, 17 women.
40. "Letter to Editor," *NNW*, 25 Sept. 1884. See chap. 12 above.

41. See T. A. Larson, "The Woman Suffrage Movement in Washington," p. 52. Larson notes that eight Republicans voted against her in 1873. However, there was a split in the Republican party that year.
42. "Editorial Correspondence," *NNW*, 1 Nov., 18 Oct. 1883.
43. "Editorial Correspondence," *NNW*, 8 Nov. 1883. ASD explained her reasoning in numerous places, including a speech reported in the *Palouse Gazette Supplement*, 18 June 1886, clipping in Duniway Papers, Scrapbook II. On Tacoma vs. Portland, see D. W. Meinig, *The Great Columbia Plain*, pp. 260–70.
44. Larson, "Woman Suffrage Movement in Washington," p. 53, accepts the testimony of opponents that Duniway caused all the antagonism because she "mocked and ridiculed unreconstructed editors and legislators." While there is truth to that, one must also look at the political and financial background of both the newspapers and the legislators, several of whom were former neighbors or personal friends of Duniway.
45. Reprinted from the *Standard* in *NNW*, 15 Nov. 1883. *NNW*, 10 Nov. 1881 mentions friendship with Murphy and 8 July 1886 his connection with the *Argus*. See Clark, *The Dry Years*, p. 33 and elsewhere, on Murphy.
46. "Editorial Correspondence," *NNW*, 17 June 1886.
47. See Gaston, *Portland, Oregon*, vol. 1, pp. 334–35; Ezra Meeker, *The Busy Life of Eighty-Five Years*, pp. 225–29; John E. Caswell, "The Prohibition Movement in Oregon," p. 79; *NNW*, 25 June 1875.
48. "Editorial Correspondence," 25 March 1886. See also *Palouse Gazette Supplement*, 18 June 1886, Duniway Papers; *Path Breaking*, pp. 197–99.
49. *NNW*, 25 March 1886.
50. *Path Breaking*, p. 198.
51. *Path Breaking*, pp. 201–03.
52. "Editorials," *NNW*, 27 June 1873, 30 Jan. 1874.
53. See Clark, *The Dry Years*, p. 37; Larson, "Woman Suffrage Movement in Washington," p. 54.
54. Duniway Publishing Co. account books in Ore. Hist. Soc. library, vols. 1, 2, 4, 8, 10. See also Bandow, "In Pursuit of a Purpose," pp. 44, 48.
55. See quitclaim deed from Harvey Scott and wife to W. S. Duniway, 25 Aug. 1886, for lot 6, division 3 of Riverview addition to Albina in Multnomah Co., warranty deed for same lot to Willis from John and Mary Muir on 9 May 1882, Willis Duniway Papers. Scott may have been holding the property as collateral for a mortgage.
56. *NNW*, 20 Oct. 1881. Thompson is first of 110 charter members listed in Duniway Pub. Co. book, vol. 1, p. 4, Ore. Hist. Soc. Cf. *NNW*, 19 Feb. 1880, 19 Oct. 1882, 23 Dec. 1886; *Path Breaking*, pp. 82–83.
57. Gaston, *Portland, Oregon*, vol. 1, p. 588.
58. Duniway genealogical file; letters from Wilkie to Clyde, 1 March 1894; Hubert to Clyde, 20 Aug. 1888. Brower & Thompson incorporated 17 April 1890, bankrupt 1895. Thompson's husband (Ore. Hist. Soc. files) was a contractor who died in 1861. (Perhaps a relative helped Hubert?) Letter from Harvey Scott to Gov. Lord, 15 June 1894.

CHAPTER 11. I'VE BEEN ROBBED

1. Details of the land claims, payments, family contributions and expenses are in Duniway Publishing Co. ledgers and papers. See also Wilkie to Willis, 16 Dec. 1895, listing deeds and locations.
2. Clyde Duniway, "My Memories of Abigail Scott Duniway," p. 11.
3. Letters to Clyde, 14 and 17 May 1892; letter from Wilkie to Clyde, 30 June 1900; Ralph to Clyde, 14 Jan. 1893.
4. Letter to Clyde [? Nov. 1892] enclosed with Hubert to Clyde, 20 Nov. 1892. Clyde Duniway, "My Memories of Abigail Scott Duniway," p. 13. Ralph to Clyde, 30 July 1893, said, "Yesterday was the worst day in the financial history of Portland." See Bailyn, *Great Republic*, pp. 835, 881–83.
5. Hubert to Clyde, 20 Nov., 6 Dec. 1892. ASD to Clyde, 15 Dec., 20 Nov. 1892.
6. Willis to Clyde, 25 Dec. 1892. Hubert to Clyde, 25 Dec. 1892.
7. E.g., Ralph to Clyde, 7 and 28 April 1895, 7 May 1895, 27 Feb. 1896, 7 April 1896 (on "the situation here"), 21 April 1896; ASD to Clyde, 24 Nov. 1893 (on management of the ranch), 16 and 26 Jan. 1896, 6 and 19 April 1896, 18 and 26 Oct. 1896. One whole letter from his mother in which she "unbosomed" herself (mentioned in her letter to him on 17 May 1896) is missing. Hubert to Clyde, 4 June 1896. David Duniway, letter to me 29 July 1977, is of the opinion that "the censored portions relate to something about himself [i.e., Clyde] that he did not want me to know. I can guess, but the nature of the censored passages is unprovable."
8. Ralph to Clyde, 7 April 1895, 15 Sept. 1895, 23 Oct. 1895.
9. Hubert to Clyde, 20 May 1899. Trust agreements in Duniway Papers, 3 Jan. 1893, amended 23 May 1895, 11 Aug. 1896, 29 Feb. 1904, 17 Jan. 1914. David Duniway, letter to me, 31 Oct. 1978:

> Since Dad and his brothers, eventually, only Dad and Wilkie contributed on a regular basis to their mother's support, it was a 'pious fraud'. She thought she was being supported by her own investments. The two men did get title to the 5th and Clay property, and the house that was built in the garden as a rental about 1904, did help pay, but it was Dad's property in Vancouver, which provided his funds, at least in the first years.

10. Ralph to Clyde, 9 July 1893; ASD to Clyde, 3 Sept. 1893.
11. 19 Jan. 1896. Hubert to Clyde, 9 May 1895; Clyde Duniway notes.
12. 31 Oct. 1893; 16 Dec. 1893.
13. Letters to Clyde, 9 Aug. 1894—last four words in large, heavy handwriting; 9 Sept. 1894.
14. Letters to Clyde, 15 Aug. 1894, 26 March 1896, 24 Nov. 1895, 23 Dec. 1893.
15. Manuscripts in Duniway Papers; letter to Clyde, 22 Aug. 1892.
16. Wilkie to Clyde, 17 May 1909.
17. See *Path Breaking*, pp. 133–43, 189–200; other speeches among her papers. Letter from ASD to Clyde, 29 July 1894, includes an unidentified news-

paper clipping of 21 July about the strike speech. Also 23 Aug., 30 Sept. 1894.

18. *Path Breaking*, p. 203. ASD to Clyde, 21 May 1893, 5 Feb. 1895; 2 and 22 Feb. 1895, 26 Oct. 1896. Catt to ASD, 14 March 1895, in Duniway Papers, box 32.

19. James W. Montgomery, *Liberated Woman, A Life of May Arkwright Hutton*, p. 48. T. A. Larson, "Idaho's Role in America's Woman Suffrage Crusade," p. 6; "Woman Suffrage Movement in Washington," pp. 58–61.

20. ASD to Clyde, 18 Nov. 1896, 22 Dec. 1896.

21. T. A. Larson, "Woman's Rights in Idaho," p. 4; *Path Breaking*, pp. 210–12.

22. Railroad lawyer John Mitchell had capitulated to the gold standard advocates, so wealthy mine-owner Jonathan Bourne engineered a legislators' boycott to prevent a quorum from electing Mitchell to the Senate. See Pomeroy, *The Pacific Slope*, p. 198. Also see letters from ASD to Mitchell, 3 and 10 Feb. 1897, from Duniway Papers, in my dissertation, pp. 645–47.

23. *Path Breaking*, pp. 213, 111, 122, 107.

24. Letters to Clyde, 14 Nov. 1895, 18 March 1896.

25. Letter to Clyde, 16 Jan. 1896.

26. *Path Breaking*, pp. 111, 213.

27. See McClintock, "Seth Lewelling, William S. U'ren and the Birth of the Oregon Progressive Movement," p. 201; Pomeroy, *The Pacific Slope*, pp. 196–99.

28. Letters to Clyde, 10 Nov. 1892, 25 Jan. 1893. See also 23 Dec. 1893.

29. Letters to Clyde, 3 May 1893, 12 Feb. 1893, 31 Jan. 1893, 21 July 1899, and numerous others. Earl to ASD, Jan. 1903.

30. Letters from Ralph to Clyde, 6 Nov. 1892; Wilkie to Clyde, 1 March 1894.

31. Letters to Clyde, 13 Sept. 1893, 8 Dec. 1894.

32. Wilkie to Clyde, 17 Aug. 1906; ASD to Willis, 6 Feb. 1909; ASD to Clyde, 16 Feb. 1907; Ralph to Clyde, 7 Nov. 1912; Clyde Duniway notes; David Duniway, May 1982.

33. Letters in Duniway Papers; Ore. Hist. Soc. files; Smith, *Presumptuous Dreamers*, p. ix.

34. Hubert to Clyde, 24 July 1894.

35. Ralph to Clyde, 18 Dec. 1892, 21 Aug. 1904, 20 Nov. 1892, 6 Oct. 1897, 27 April 1898. Hubert to Clyde, 24 April 1896. Ralph to Clyde, 23 Nov. 1896; Kate to Clyde, 2 Jan. 1897; Ralph to Clyde, 11 May 1901.

36. Letter to Clyde, 6 April 1896. Willis to Clyde, 23 Nov. 1896; Wilkie to Clyde, 21 Oct. 1896.

37. Letter to Clyde, 5 Sept. 1896; Ralph wrote Clyde, 17 Sept. 1896, that the mistake was in Hubert's accounts. Wilkie to Clyde, 15 May 1907.

38. Hubert to Clyde, 15 Jan. 1901, 15 April 1901, 14 July 1901, 8 Feb. 1903, 1 Jan. 1905, 21 Feb. 1905, 8 April 1906, 31 Aug. 1906, 20 March 1907. Clyde Duniway's notes.

39. Letter to Clyde, 9 Aug. 1910.

40. Ore. Hist. Soc. files on Ruth Duniway Kerby. David Duniway interview, Feb. 1976.

41. News clipping published 27 July 1892, included with ASD letter to Clyde, 25

Jan. 1893; David Duniway. Josephson, *Robber Barons*, pp. 268–71; pp. 260–64 describe Frick. Clyde Duniway, "My Memories of Abigail Scott Duniway," pp. 12, 13.

42. Letter from ASD to Clyde, 29 April 1894, including clipping; *History of Woman Suffrage*, vol. 4, p. 739. Letter to Clyde, 14 Jan. 1894.

43. Ralph to Clyde, 19 Jan. 1896.

44. David Duniway, letter to me, 30 July 1977, from his father's testimony. As quoted with the italics to Clyde by ASD, 24 March 1895. Other symptoms are mentioned in numerous letters.

45. *Path Breaking*, p. 100. See also "The Temperance Problem, No. 3," *NNW*, 22 July 1886; Editorial, *NNW*, 29 Oct. 1875.

46. Letters to Clyde, 28 July 1895, 18 March 1896, 5 Oct. 1895, 16 Feb. 1896.

47. Letter to Clyde, 19 April 1896; see also other letters of 1896.

48. Letter to Clyde, 26 March 1896.

49. Letter to me from David Musto, 10 Jan. 1978. Musto points out that no one can tell from this distance in time and the scant evidence whether Ben Duniway was actually addicted. Musto, *The American Disease*, pp. 69–72, 7, 77, 11, 14, 18, 26, 89. See also Larsell, *The Doctor in Oregon*, pp. 139, 153.

50. *The Happy Home*, chap. 9, *NNW*, 22 Jan. 1875; *Laban McShane*, chaps. 19, 20, *NNW*, 17 and 24 Jan. 1884; *Judge Dunson's Secret*, chap. 9, *NNW*, 10 May 1883; *Margaret Rudson*, MS chaps. 1–2. See also *Dux* chap. 7, *NNW*, 23 Oct. 1884; *Fact, Fate and Fancy*, chap. 30, *NNW*, 24 April 1879.

51. 17 Dec. 1875, 12 Feb. 1880; letter to Clyde, 18 Feb. 1893.

52. See n. 7; Hubert to Clyde, 4 June 1896.

53. David Duniway notes, from his father's testimony. Clyde had not been home for a visit since 1890, so it must have been that summer.

54. 30 Aug. 1896.

CHAPTER 12. FREEDOM AT LAST

1. *Path Breaking*, pp. 156–59, 160–62.

2. Ibid., pp. 163, 165, 167, 168. See Franklin, "On Early Marriages," in *The Wise and Witty Sayings of Poor Richard* (Dublin. Repr. ed., 1802).

3. Warren, *Farthest Frontier,*, p. 207; ASD to Clyde, 9 June 1904, on vice-presidency, "And he'll succeed, too, if Mitchell doesn't block the game." Mitchell was indicted the next year for land fraud.

4. In *Path Breaking*, pp. 154, 116–17.

5. Wilkie to Clyde, 7 Feb. 1900; Montague, "Woman Suffrage Movement in Oregon," pp. 78–79; *Oregonian* editorials from 22 May to 5 June 1900.

6. Letter, ASD to Harvey, 9 June 1900, and pamphlet, Duniway Papers.

7. See Clark, "The Second Hundred Years," *Western Shore*, p. 289; Catt and Shuler, *Woman Suffrage and Politics*, p. 279.

8. 7 July 1900.

9. Ralph to Clyde, 10 July 1900.

10. See esp. letters to Clyde, 25 Sept. 1903, 16 May and 5 Sept. 1904, 27 Oct. 1903, 9 Jan. 1901, 2 Aug. 1900, 22 Aug. 1900. Cf. Kathryn Kish Sklar, *Catherine Beecher*, pp. 206–09, 318.

11. *Path Breaking*, pp. 226–27.
12. Letter to Clyde, 2 Oct. 1904.
13. See *Notable American Women*, vol. 1, pp. 355–57; *Path Breaking*, pp. 195, 225, 229.
14. *Path Breaking*, p. 227. Cf. Anthony letter of 1884 quoted in chap. 10 above.
15. Ibid., pp. 83–84; Lee Nash, "Refining a Frontier," pp. 412–17; Scott, *Oregon Country*, vol. 1, p. 346.
16. *History of Woman Suffrage*, vol. 6, p. 543; Anna Howard Shaw, *Story of a Pioneer*, p. 292.
17. Catt and Shuler, *Woman Suffrage and Politics*, pp. 124–25.
18. See, e.g., letters from ASD to Anna Shaw, Kate Gordon, Laura Clay; newspaper clippings, etc. in Duniway Papers. Also leaflet copy of Alice Henry, "The National American Woman Suffrage Association: A Nineteenth Century Constitution and Twentieth Century Needs," from *Life and Labor*, Feb. 1912; letters from ASD to Laura Clay, 26 Feb., 30 May, 5 June, 24 Nov., 1908, 29 Oct. 1912, Clay Collection. See also Paul E. Fuller, *Laura Clay and the Woman's Rights Movement*, pp. 97–101, 118–20, 123–27.
19. Letter to Clyde, 8 May 1908; *Path Breaking*, p. 179; Roberts, "Suffragists of the New West," pp. 199–202.
20. Letter from DeVoe to Hepburn, 10 Feb. 1914, copy in Duniway Papers. Letters to ASD, 3 March and 12 Feb. 1914. See also letter to ASD, 15 Sept. 1909, Duniway Papers, Scrapbook II. DeVoe, in *History of Woman Suffrage*, vol. 6, pp. 676–82.
21. ASD to Laura Clay, 29 Oct. 1912, Clay Collection. Letters to Clyde from Hubert, 10 March 1912; from Wilkie, 5, 13, 15, 16, 18 March 1912.
22. Undated copy of 1912 letter in Duniway Papers.
23. *History of Woman Suffrage*, vol. 6, p. 545, 548. There was a majority of 4,161 out of 118,369 votes.
24. Clipping from *Morning Oregonian*, 15 Feb. 1913, Duniway Papers.
25. Clippings in Duniway Papers; *Path Breaking*, pp. 244–49; letters from DeVoe to ASD, 12 Feb., 3 March, 7 July 1914; DeVoe to Hepburn, 10 Feb. 1914.
26. Cora Smith King to Roberts, 28 Jan. 1914, Roberts Papers.
27. DeVoe to Roberts, 8 April 1915 in ibid. ASD to Shaw, 2 Oct. 1906. ASD to Clyde, 9 Oct. 1913 with clipping from *Oregonian*, 7 Oct. 1913. Ralph to Clyde, 10 Oct. 1913, deplored his mother's "intemperate outbreak . . . against Anna Shaw."
28. See Roberts to Catt, 27 Feb. 1919 and other letters between them in folder 4, Roberts Papers; Flexner, *Century of Struggle*, p. 302; Larsen, "Idaho's Role in America's Woman Suffrage Crusade," pp. 6–10.
29. Eggert to ASD, 1 Oct. 1914; ASD to Eggert, 2 Oct. 1914, Duniway Papers.
30. See Clark, "Second Hundred Years," *Western Shore*, pp. 298–300.
31. See ASD to Clyde, 4 May 1913. Bilious attacks several times a year, always after emotional upheavals, referred to in ASD's *NNW* "Editorial Correspondence" and in many letters; frequent slow-healing infections; great weight gain after forty; unusually large babies. One newspaper obituary for John Tucker Scott says he died of diabetes. The condition of Uncle Lindsey Scott

was certainly pathological, as suspected by his own doctor; see chap. 2, n. 26, above. Grandmother Frances Tucker Scott's early death after years of "dropsy" is suspicious. (See chap. 2 above.) Abigail's Aunt Louvisa Turley, Tucker Scott's sister, had a long history of bilious illness and serious eye trouble (letters in James Scott Papers and Edwin Browne collection). Wilkie Duniway's eye disease and then blindness, which came on him right after the emotional upset of being fired in 1915, is also indicative. Willis Duniway's heart problems and Clara's "consumption" after childbirth, plus the heart problems of grandchildren make one wonder. See Sigmund Stephen Miller, ed., *Symptoms: The Complete Home Medical Encyclopedia* (N.Y.: Thomas Y. Crowell Co., 1976), pp. 480–83.

32. Quoted in Ralph to Clyde 5 Oct. 1915. See also 18, 21, 23, 30 Sept. 1915, and telegram 6 Oct. 1915.
33. 22 Jan. 1875.

Bibliography of
Works Consulted

MANUSCRIPTS

David C. Duniway Collection, Salem, Oregon
    Abigail Scott Duniway, letters to Clyde Duniway, 1890–1915, and "Journal of a Trip to Oregon," 1852
    Duniway business ledgers, deeds, etc. from 1887
    Duniway Scrapbooks with news clippings, MS speeches, letters to and from Duniway, letters-to-editors, 1880–1915
    Clyde Duniway notes and "My Memories of Abigail Scott Duniway"
    Willis, Hubert, Wilkie, and Ralph Duniway, letters
    Duniway genealogical file, compiled by David Duniway, with miscellaneous related material
    Edwin Browne Collection, photostated copies of Scott family letters
    James Scott Papers, letters and documents, 1769–1862
    Scott and Roelofson family memoirs, pamphlets, pictures, news clippings
    Neill Johnson, "Autobiography"

Laura Clay Collection, Margaret I. King Library, U. of Kentucky, Lexington, Ky.
Margaret Roberts Papers, Schlesinger Library, Radcliffe College, Cambridge, Mass.
New Northwest, 1871–87, Smith College Library, Northampton, Mass., on microfilm
Oregon City Argus, 1855–60, Oregon Historical Society, Portland, Oregon, on microfilm
Oregon Farmer, 1859–62, Oregon Historical Society, Portland, Oregon, on microfilm
Oregon Historical Society, file on A. S. Duniway, including ledgers of Duniway Publishing Co. and Oregon State Woman Suffrage Asso., 1871–87

PUBLICATIONS BY ABIGAIL SCOTT DUNIWAY

Captain Gray's Company, or Crossing the Plains and Living in Oregon. Portland, Oregon: S. J. McCormick, 1859.
David and Anna Matson. N.Y.: S. R. Wells & Co., 1876.
From the West to the West: Across the Plains to Oregon. Chicago: A. C. McClurg, 1905.
"Journal of a Trip to Oregon." Edited by David Duniway. Glendale, Calif.: Arthur B. Clark Co. Forthcoming. MS in Duniway Papers

My Musings. Portland, Oregon: Duniway Publishing Co., 1875.

Path Breaking: An Autobiographical History of the Equal Suffrage Movement in Pacific Coast States. 2d ed. Portland, Ore.: James, Kerns & Abbott, 1914. Reprint. N.Y.: Schocken Books, 1971.

"The Stage-Driver's Story." *Phrenological Journal* (Aug. 1879): 85–90.

Serialized novels in *New Northwest:*

Judith Reid; A Plain Story of a Plain Woman 12 May 1871–22 Dec. 1871

Ellen Dowd, The Farmer's Wife (in two parts) 5 Jan. 1872–26 Sept. 1873

Amie and Henry Lee: or, The Spheres of the Sexes 29 May 1874–13 Nov. 1874

The Happy Home: or, The Husband's Triumph 20 Nov. 1874–14 May 1875

One Woman's Sphere; or, The Mystery of Eagle Cove 4 June 1875–3 Dec. 1875

Madge Morrison, The Mollala Maid and Matron 10 Dec. 1875–28 July 1876

Edna and John: A Romance of Idaho Flat 29 Sept. 1876–15 June 1877

Martha Marblehead: The Maid and Matron of Chehalem 29 June 1877–8 Feb. 1878

Her Lot; or, How She Was Protected retitled and slightly revised in Duniway Papers as *Ethel Graeme's Destiny: A Story of Real Life* 1 Feb. 1878–19 Sept. 1878

Fact, Fate and Fancy; or, More Ways of Living than One 26 Sept. 1878–15 May 1879

Mrs. Hardine's Will 20 Nov. 1879–26 Aug. 1880

The Mystery of Castle Rock, A Story of the Pacific Northwest 2 March 1882–7 Sept. 1882

Judge Dunson's Secret: An Oregon Story 15 March 1883–6 Sept. 1883

Laban McShane: A Frontier Story 3 Jan. 1884–6 March 1884

Dux: A Maiden Who Dared 11 Sept. 1884–5 March 1885

The DeLauncey Curse; or, the Law of Heredity—A Tale of Three Generations 10 Sept. 1885–4 March 1886

Blanche LeClerq: A Tale of the Mountain Mines 2 Sept. 1886–24 Feb. 1887

SOURCES ON ABIGAIL SCOTT DUNIWAY

Bandow, Gayle R. "'In Pursuit of a Purpose': Abigail Scott Duniway and the *New Northwest*." M.S. thesis, University of Oregon, June 1973.

Capell, Letitia. "Biography of Abigail Scott Duniway." M.A. thesis, University of Oregon, 1934.

Montague, Martha Frances. "Woman Suffrage Movement in Oregon." M.A. thesis, University of Oregon, 1930.

Morrison, Dorothy Nafus. *Ladies Were Not Expected: Abigail Scott Duniway and Women's Rights*. New York: Atheneum, 1977.

Moynihan, Ruth Barnes. "Abigail Scott Duniway of Oregon: Woman and Suffragist of the American Frontier." 2 vols. Ph.D. diss., Yale University, 1979.

Richey, Elinor. "The Unsinkable Abigail." *American Heritage*, 26 (Feb. 1975).

Roberts, Leslie McKay. "Suffragist of the New West: Abigail Scott Duniway and the Development of the Oregon Woman Suffrage Movement." B.A. thesis, Reed College, 1969.

Ross, Nancy W. *Westward the Women*. New York: Alfred A. Knopf, 1944.

Smith, Helen Krebs. *The Presumptuous Dreamers, A Sociological History of the Life and Times of Abigail Scott Duniway.* Vol. 1, *1834–1871.* Lake Oswego, Ore.: Smith, Smith and Smith Publishing Co., 1974.

Ward, Jean M., and Jeannie McKnight. "Abigail Jane Scott Duniway." Research paper for Wilderness Woman Project, April 1978.

Ward, Jean M. "The Emergence of a Mentor-Protégé Relationship: The 1871 Pacific Northwest Speaking Tour of Susan B. Anthony and Abigail S. Duniway." Paper delivered at Northwest Women's Heritage Conference, University of Washington, 1–3 April 1982.

———. "Abigail Scott Duniway: Oregon's Pioneer Feminist." *Old Stuff* 2 (Winter 1977). Reprinted from *Scribe* 5 (July 1976).

PRIMARY SOURCES

Alcott, William. *The Young Woman's Book of Health.* New York: Miller, Orton, and Mulligan, 1855.

Angle, Paul M., ed. *Prairie State: Impressions of Illinois, 1673–1967, By Travelers and Other Observers.* Chicago: University of Chicago Press, 1968.

Bailey, Margaret Jewett. *The Grains, or, Passages in the Life of Ruth Rover, with Occasional Pictures of Oregon, Natural and Moral.* Portland, Ore.: Carter and Austin, Printers, 1854.

Beecher, Catherine. *Letters to the People on Health and Happiness.* New York: Harper & Bros., 1855.

Bloomer, D. C., ed. *Life and Writings of Amelia Bloomer.* 1895. Reprint. New York: Schocken, 1975.

Cartwright, Peter. *Autobiography.* New York: Abingdon Press, 1956.

Dahlgren, Madeline Vinton. *Thoughts on Female Suffrage, and in Vindication of Woman's True Rights.* Washington, D.C.: Blanchard and Mohun, 1871.

Ellsworth, Edward. *Illinois in 1837, A Sketch Descriptive of the Situation, Boundaries, Face of the Country, Prominent Districts, Prairies, Rivers . . . of the State of Illinois.* Philadelphia: S. Augustus Mitchell, and Grigg and Elliot, 1837.

Farnham, Eliza Woodson. *Life in Prairie Land.* New York: Harper, 1846.

Farnham, Thomas Jefferson. *Travels in the Great Western Prairies, The Anahuac and Rocky Mountains, and in the Oregon Territory.* 2 vols. Poughkeepsie, N.Y.: Kelley and Lossing, 1841; London: Richard Bentley, 1843.

Ford, Thomas. *A History of Illinois.* Chicago: S.C. Griggs and Co., 1854.

Fuller, Margaret. *Woman in the Nineteenth Century.* Boston: J. P. Jewett & Co., 1855.

Gerhard, Frederick. *Illinois As It Is.* Chicago: Keen & Lee, 1857.

Goulder, W. A. *Reminiscences: Incidents in the Life of a Pioneer in Oregon and Idaho.* Boise, Idaho: Timothy Regan, 1909.

Greeley, Horace. *Hints toward Reforms, in Lectures, Addresses and Other Writings.* New York: Harper and Bros., 1850.

———. *Recollections of a Busy Life.* New York: J. B. Ford and Co., 1868.

Halvorsen, Helen Olson, and Lorraine Fletcher. "Nineteenth Century Midwife: Some Recollections." *Oregon Historical Quarterly* 70 (March 1969): 39–49.

Henry, Alice. "The National American Woman Suffrage Association: A Nineteenth Century Constitution and Twentieth Century Needs." *Life and Labor* (Feb. 1912).

History of Tazewell County, Illinois. Chicago: Charles C. Chapman and Co., 1879.

History of Woman Suffrage. Vols. 1–3. Edited by Elizabeth Cady Stanton, Susan B. Anthony, and Matilda Joslyn Gage. Rochester, N.Y.: Charles Mann, 1881, 1882, 1886. Vol. 4. Edited by Susan B. Anthony and Ida Husted Harper. Indianapolis: The Hollenbeck Press, 1902. Vols. 5–6. Edited by Ida Husted Harper. New York: J. J. Little and Ives, 1922.

Johnson, J. L. "Overland to Oregon in 1851." MS. Collection of Western Americana, Yale University Library, New Haven, Ct.

Jones, Abner D. *Illinois and the West, with a Township Map, Containing the Latest Surveys and Improvements.* Boston: Weeks, Jordan and Co., 1838.

Kisner, Arlene, ed. *The Lives and Writings of the Notorious Victoria Woodhull and Her Sister Tennessee Claflin.* Washington, N.J.: Times Change Press, 1972.

Latourette, Kenneth Scott. *Beyond the Ranges: An Autobiography.* Grand Rapids, Mich.: Wm. B. Eerdmans Publishing Co., 1967.

Meeker, Ezra. *The Busy Life of Eighty-Five Years.* Seattle, Wash.: [The Author], 1916.

Newsom, E. Earl, ed. *David Newsom: The Western Observer, 1805–1882.* Portland, Ore.: Oregon Historical Society, 1972.

Owens-Adair, Bethenia. *Some of Her Life Experiences.* Portland, Ore.: Mann and Beach [1914?].

Peirce, Melusina Fay. "Cooperative Housekeeping." *Atlantic Monthly* 22–23 (Nov.–March, 1868–69).

––––––. *Cooperative Housekeeping: How Not to Do It and How to Do It, A Study in Sociology.* Boston: James R. Osgood, 1884.

Shaw, Anna Howard. *The Story of a Pioneer.* New York: Harper and Bros., 1915.

Stanton, Elizabeth Cady. *Eighty Years and More: Reminiscences, 1815–1897.* New York: T. Fisher Unwin, 1898. Reprint. New York: Schocken, 1971.

Tocqueville, Alexis de. *Democracy in America.* Edited by Phillips Bradley. New York: Vintage Books, 1945.

West, Oswald. "Reminiscences." *Oregon Historical Quarterly* 50 (Dec. 1949).

Wittenmyer, Annie. *History of the Woman's Temperance Crusade.* Boston: James H. Earle, 1882.

SECONDARY SOURCES

Abernethy, Thomas Perkins. *Three Virginia Frontiers.* Baton Rouge, La.: Louisiana State University Press, 1940.

Ahlstrom, Sydney. *A Religious History of the American People.* New Haven: Yale University Press, 1972.

Allen, William B. *A History of Kentucky, Embracing Gleanings, Reminiscences, Antiquities, Natural Curiosities, Statistics, and Biographical Sketches.* Louisville, Ky.: Bradley and Gilbert, 1872.

Bagley, Clarence B. "Pioneer Papers of Puget Sound." *Oregon Historical Quarterly* 4 (1903).

Bailyn, Bernard, et al. *The Great Republic*. Boston: Little, Brown and Co., 1977.

Bancroft, Hubert Howe [Frances Fuller Victor]. *History of Oregon and Washington, 1848–1888*. San Francisco: The History Co., 1888.

Barker-Benfield, G. J. *The Horrors of the Half-known Life: Male Attitudes Toward Women and Sexuality in Nineteenth-Century America*. New York: Harper and Row, 1976.

Bartlett, Richard A. *The New Country: A Social History of the American Frontier, 1776–1890*. New York: Oxford University Press, 1974.

Basch, Norma. "Amphibious Women: Exceptions to Married Women's Common Law Disabilities in New York, 1815–1848." Paper delivered at Fifth Berkshire Conference on the History of Women, Vassar College, 16–18 June 1981.

Beard, Mary R. *Woman as Force in History: A Study in Traditions and Realities*. Collier edition. New York: Macmillan, 1946.

Belknap, George A. *Oregon Imprints, 1845–1870*. Eugene: University of Oregon Press, 1968.

————. "Still More Addenda to Belknap's *Oregon Imprints*." *Oregon Historical Quarterly* 82 (Summer 1981).

Berwanger, Eugene H. *The Frontier Against Slavery: Western Anti-Negro Prejudice and the Slavery Extension Controversy*. Urbana: University of Illinois Press, 1967.

Billington, Ray Allen. *America's Frontier Heritage*. New York: Holt, Rinehart and Winston, 1966.

————. *Far Western Frontier: 1830–1860*. New York: Harper and Bros., 1956.

————. *Westward Expansion: A History of the American Frontier*. 4th ed. New York: Macmillan, 1974.

Boorstin, Daniel J. *The Lost World of Thomas Jefferson*. Boston: Beacon Press, 1948.

Bordin, Ruth. *Woman and Temperance: The Quest for Power and Liberty, 1873–1900*. Philadelphia: Temple University Press, 1981.

Brownmiller, Susan. *Against Our Will: Men, Women and Rape*. New York: Simon and Schuster, 1975.

Buley, R. Carlyle. *The Old Northwest: Pioneer Period, 1815–1840*. 2 vols. Indianapolis: Indiana Historical Society, 1950.

Calhoun, Daniel. *The Intelligence of a People*. Princeton, N.J.: Princeton University Press, 1973.

Caswell, John E. "The Prohibition Movement in Oregon." *Oregon Historical Quarterly* 40 (1939).

Catt, Carrie Chapman, and Nettie Shuler. *Woman Suffrage and Politics: The Inner Story of the Suffrage Movement*. New York: Charles Scribner's Sons, 1923.

Clark, Malcolm H., Jr. "The War on the Webfoot Saloon." *Oregon Historical Quarterly* 58 (1957).

Clark, Norman H. *The Dry Years: Prohibition and Social Change in Washington*. Seattle: University of Washington Press, 1965.

————. *Mill Town: A Social History of Everett, Washington, from Its Earliest Beginnings on the Shores of Puget Sound to the Tragic and Infamous Event Known as the Everett Massacre*. Seattle: University of Washington Press, 1970.

Clark, Robert Carlton. *History of the Willamette Valley, Oregon.* Chicago: S. J. Clarke Publishing Co., 1927.

Cooke, George Willis. *Unitarianism in America.* Boston: American Unitarian Asso., 1902.

Cott, Nancy, ed. *Root of Bitterness: Documents of the Social History of American Women.* New York: Dutton, 1972.

Cummings, Richard Osborn. *The American and His Food: A History of Food Habits in the United States.* Chicago: University of Chicago Press, 1941.

Davis, David Brion. *The Problem of Slavery in the Age of Revolution.* Ithaca, N.Y.: Cornell University Press, 1975.

Dexter, Elisabeth Anthony. *Colonial Women of Affairs.* Boston: Houghton Mifflin, 1924.

Dillon, Merton Lynn. "The Anti-Slavery Movement in Illinois: 1824–1835." In *The Old Northwest: Studies in Regional History, 1787–1910,* edited by Harry N. Scheiber. Lincoln: University of Nebraska Press, 1969.

Ditzion, Sidney. *Marriage, Morals and Sex in America: A History of Ideas.* New York: Bookman Assoc., 1953.

Dobbs, Caroline C. *Men of Champoeg.* Portland, Ore.: Metropolitan Press, 1932.

Douglas, Ann. *The Feminization of American Culture.* New York: Alfred A. Knopf, 1977.

Douthit, Mary Osborn, ed. *Souvenir of Western Women.* Portland, Ore.: Anderson and Duniway Co., 1905.

Down, Robert Horace. *A History of the Silverton Country.* Portland, Ore.: Berncliff Press, 1926.

DuBois, Ellen C. *Feminism and Suffrage: The Emergence of an Independent Women's Movement in America, Eighteen Forty-Eight to Eighteen Sixty-Nine.* Ithaca, N.Y.: Cornell University Press, 1978.

Duniway, Clyde. "The Development of Freedom of the Press in Massachusetts." 1906. Reprint. New York: Burt Franklin, 1969.

Edwards, G. Thomas. "Dr. Ada M. Weed: Northwest Reformer." *Oregon Historical Quarterly* 78 (March 1977).

Ellis, David M., ed. *The Frontier in American Development: Essays in Honor of Paul Wallace Gates.* Ithaca, N.Y.: Cornell University Press, 1969.

Faragher, John Mack. *Women and Men on the Overland Trail.* New Haven and London: Yale University Press, 1979.

Faragher, John Mack, and Christine Stansell. "Women and Their Families on the Overland Trail to California and Oregon, 1842–1867." *Feminist Studies* 2 (1975).

Flexner, Eleanor. *Century of Struggle: The Woman's Rights Movement in the United States.* Cambridge, Mass.: Harvard University Press, 1959.

Foster, Robert V. "A Sketch of the Cumberland Presbyterian Church." In *American Church History.* New York: Christian Literature Co., 1894.

Fuller, Paul E. *Laura Clay and the Woman's Rights Movement.* Lexington: University of Kentucky Press, 1975.

Fuller, Wayne E. "School District 37: Prairie Community." *Western Historical Quarterly* 12 (Oct. 1981).

Gaston, Joseph. *Portland, Oregon: Its History and Builders.* Vol. 1. Chicago and Portland: S. J. Clarke Publishing Co., 1911.

Gates, Paul Wallace. *Landlords and Tenants on the Prairie Frontier: Studies in American Land Policy.* Ithaca N.Y.: Cornell University Press, 1973.

————. "The Homestead Law in an Incongruous Land System." *American Historical Review* 41 (July 1936).

George, Henry, Jr. *The Life of Henry George.* New York: Doubleday and McClure Co., 1900.

Goodwyn, Lawrence. *The Populist Movement: A Short History of the Agrarian Revolt in America.* New York: Oxford University Press, 1978.

Gordon, Linda. *Woman's Body, Woman's Right: A Social History of Birth Control in America.* New York: Grossman Publishers, 1976.

Grimes, Allan P. *The Puritan Ethic and Woman Suffrage.* New York: Oxford Univeristy Press, 1967.

Hampsten, Elizabeth. *"Read This Only to Yourself": Private Writings of Midwestern Women, 1880–1910.* Bloomington: Indiana University Press, 1982.

Harper, Ida Husted. *The Life and Work of Susan B. Anthony.* 2 vols. Indianapolis and Kansas City: Bowen-Merrill Co., 1899.

Hayden, Dolores. *A "Grand Domestic Revolution": Feminism, Socialism and the American Home, 1870–1930.* Cambridge, Mass.: MIT Press, 1981.

————. "Melusina Fay Peirce and Cooperative Housekeeping." *International Journal of Urban and Regional Research* 2 (1978).

————. "Two Utopian Feminists and Their Campaigns for Kitchenless Houses." *Signs* 4 (Winter 1979).

Henderson: A Guide to Audubon's Home Town in Kentucky. Compiled by Workers of the Writers' Program of the Works Projects Administration in the State of Kentucky, American Guide Series. Northport, N.Y.: Bacon, Percy and Daggett, 1941.

Hine, Robert V. *Community on the American Frontier.* Norman: University of Oklahoma Press, 1980.

Hofstadter, Richard. *America at 1750: A Social Portrait.* New York: Alfred A. Knopf, 1971.

Horwitz, Morton J. *The Transformation of American Law: 1780–1860.* Cambridge, Mass.: Harvard University Press, 1977.

Howe, Daniel Walker. *The Unitarian Conscience: Harvard Moral Philosophy, 1805–1861.* Cambridge: Harvard University Press, 1970.

James, Edward T., et al. *Notable American Women, 1607–1950: A Biographical Dictionary.* Cambridge, Mass.: The Belknap Press, Harvard University Press, 1971.

Jeffrey, Julie Roy. *Frontier Women: The Trans-Mississippi West, 1840–1880.* New York: Hill and Wang, 1979.

Johannsen, Robert W. *Frontier Politics and the Sectional Conflict: The Pacific Northwest on the Eve of the Civil War.* Seattle: University of Washington Press, 1955.

Johansen, Dorothy O., and Charles M. Gates. *Empire of the Columbia.* 2d ed. New York: Harper and Row, 1967.

Josephson, Matthew. *The Robber Barons: The Great American Capitalists, 1861–1901.* New York: Harcourt, Brace and World, 1962.

Kessler, Lauren. "Fringe Group Access to the Mainstream Press: The Fight for Women's Political Equality and the Oregon Press, 1884–1912." Paper presented at Pacific Northwest Historians Conference, Walla Walla, Wash., April 1980.

———. "Harvey Scott, Sam Jackson and the 1906 Campaign for Woman Suffrage in Oregon: A Study of Newspaper Bias." Paper presented to Association for Education in Journalism, History Division Conference, Berkeley, Calif., March 1980.

Kinnard, Cynthia D. "'Think of Such Narrowness of Vision!'—Political Anti-Feminism, from Antisuffrage to the 'Stop ERA' Movement." Paper presented at the Society for Values in Higher Education Conference, St. Mary's College, South Bend, Ind., Aug. 1976.

Kraditor, Aileen S. *The Ideas of the Woman Suffrage Movement: 1890–1920.* New York: Columbia University Press, 1965; Doubleday & Co., Inc., Anchor reprint, 1971.

———. *Up From the Pedestal: Selected Writings in the History of American Feminism.* Chicago: Quadrangle, 1968.

Krout, John Allen. *The Origins of Prohibition.* New York: Alfred A. Knopf, 1925.

Land, Aubrey C. "Economic Base and Social Structure: The Northern Chesapeake in the Eighteenth Century." *Journal of Economic History* 25 (1965).

Larsell, O. *The Doctor in Oregon: A Medical History.* Portland, Ore.: Binfords & Mort, 1947.

Larson, T. A. "Dolls, Vassals, and Drudges—Pioneer Women in the West." *Western Historical Quarterly* 3 (Jan. 1972).

———. "Idaho's Role in America's Woman Suffrage Crusade." *Idaho Yesterdays* 18 (Spring 1974).

———. "The Woman Suffrage Movement in Washington." *Pacific Northwest Quarterly* 67 (April 1976).

———. "Woman Suffrage in Western America." *Utah Historical Quarterly* 38 (Winter 1970).

———. "Woman's Rights in Idaho." *Idaho Yesterdays* 16 (Spring 1972).

Lazenby, Marie. "Down-Easters Out West." Armitage Prize Essay, *Reed College Bulletin* 25 (April 1947).

Leach, William. *True Love and Perfect Union: The Feminist Reform of Sex and Society.* New York: Basic Books, 1980.

Lerner, Gerda, ed. *The Female Experience.* New York: Schocken, 1979.

———. *The Grimké Sisters from South Carolina: Rebels Against Slavery.* Boston: Houghton Mifflin Co., 1967.

———. *The Majority Finds Its Past: Placing Women in History.* New York and Oxford: Oxford University Press, 1979.

Lockley, Fred. *Oregon's Yesterdays.* New York: Knickerbocker Press, 1928.

Manvell, Roger. *The Trial of Annie Besant and Charles Bradlaugh.* New York: Horizon Press, 1976.

McClintock, Thomas C. "Seth Lewelling, William W. U'Ren and the Birth of the Oregon Progressive Movement." *Oregon Historical Quarterly* 68 (Sept. 1967).

McDonnold, Benjamin Wilburn. *History of the Cumberland Presbyterian Church.*

Nashville: Board of Publications of the Cumberland Presbyterian Church, 1888.

Meinig, D. W. *The Great Columbia Plain: A Historical Geography, 1805–1910.* Seattle: University of Washington Press, 1968.

Miyakawa, T. Scott. *Protestants and Pioneers: Individualism and Conformity on the American Frontier.* Chicago: University of Chicago Press, 1964.

Mockford, Stuart B., ed. "Jason Lee's Peoria Speech." *Oregon Historical Quarterly* 59 (1958).

Montgomery, James. *Liberated Woman: A Life of May Arkwright Hutton.* Spokane, Wash.: Gingko House Publishers, 1974.

Moore, Arthur K. *The Frontier Mind: A Cultural Analysis of the Kentucky Frontiersmen.* Lexington: University of Kentucky Press, 1957.

Morgan, David. *Suffragists and Democrats: The Politics of Woman Suffrage in America.* East Lansing: Michigan State University Press, 1972.

Moynihan, Ruth Barnes. "Children and Young People on the Overland Trail." *Western Historical Quarterly* 6 (July 1975).

Muncy, Raymond Lee. *Sex and Marriage in Utopian Communities: Nineteenth Century America.* Baltimore: Penguin, 1974.

Musto, David F. *The American Disease: Origins of Narcotic Control.* New Haven and London: Yale University Press, 1973.

Myres, Sandra. *Westering Women.* Albuquerque: University of New Mexico Press, 1982.

Nash, Lee. "Harvey Scott's 'Cure for Drones': An Oregon Alternative to Public Higher Schools." *Pacific Northwest Quarterly* 64 (April 1973).

———. "Refining a Frontier: The Cultural Interests and Activities of Harvey Scott." Ph.D. diss., University of Oregon, 1961.

———. "Scott of the *Oregonian:* The Editor as Historian." *Oregon Historical Quarterly* 70 (Sept. 1969).

Nash, Roderick. *Wilderness and the American Mind.* Rev. ed. New Haven and London: Yale University Press, 1973.

O'Neill, William L. *Everyone Was Brave: The Rise and Fall of Feminism in America.* Chicago: Quadrangle, 1969.

Papachristou, Judith. *Women Together.* New York: Alfred A. Knopf, *Ms.* Book, 1976.

Paul, Rodman, ed. *A Victorian Gentlewoman in the Far West: The Reminiscences of Mary Hallock Foote.* San Marino, Calif.: Huntington Library, 1972.

Paulson, Ross Evans. *Woman Suffrage and Prohibition: A Comparative Study of Equality and Social Control.* Glenview, Ill.: Scott, Foresman and Co., 1973.

Persons, Stow. *Free Religion: An American Faith.* New Haven: Yale University Press, 1947.

Pivar, David J. *Purity Crusade: Sexual Morality and Social Control, 1868–1900.* Westport, Conn.: Greenwood Press, 1973.

Pollack, Norman. *The Populist Response to Industrial America.* Cambridge Mass.: Harvard University Press, 1962.

Pomeroy, Earl. *The Pacific Slope; A History of California, Oregon, Washington, Idaho, Utah, & Nevada.* New York: Alfred A. Knopf, 1965. Reprint. Seattle: University of Washington Press, 1973.

Pooley, William Vipond. "The Settlement of Illinois from 1830 to 1850." *Bulletin of the University of Wisconsin Historical Series*, no. 1. Madison, Wis.: 1908.

Potter, David M. "American Women and American Character." In *American Character and Culture: Some Twentieth Century Perspectives*, edited by John A. Hague. Deland, Fla.: Edward Everetts Press, 1964.

Powers, Alfred. *History of Oregon Literature*. Portland, Ore.: Metropolitan Press, 1935.

Rabinowitz, Randy Sue. "The Married Women's Property Acts in New York: A Legal History." Paper delivered at Fifth Berkshire Conference on the History of Women, Vassar College, June 1981.

Riley, Glenda. *Frontierswomen: The Iowa Experience*. Ames: Iowa State University Press, 1981.

Rosenberg, Charles E. "Sexuality, Class and Role in Nineteenth-Century America." *American Quarterly* 125 (May 1973).

Russett, Cynthia. "The Arrested Female: Recapitulation Defines Woman." Paper delivered at the Fifth Berkshire Conference on the History of Women, Vassar College, June 1981.

Ryan, Mary P. *Womanhood in America: From Colonial Times to Present*. 2d ed. New York: Franklin Watts, New Viewpoints, 1979.

Sandburg, Carl. *Abraham Lincoln: The Prairie Years and the War Years*. New York: Harcourt, Brace and World, 1954.

Schafer, Joseph. "Harvey W. Scott, Historian." *Oregon Historical Quarterly* 34 (Sept. 1933).

Scheck, John Frederick. "Transplanting a Tradition: Thomas Lamb Eliot and the Unitarian Conscience in the Pacific Northwest, 1865–1905." Ph.D. diss., University of Oregon, 1969.

Scott, Anne Firor, and Andrew M. Scott. *One Half the People: The Fight for Woman Suffrage*. Philadelphia: J. B. Lippincott Co., 1975.

Scott, Francis William. *Newspapers and Periodicals of Illinois, 1814–1879*. Springfield: Illinois Historical Library, 1910.

Scott, Harvey. *History of the Oregon Country*. 6 vols. Compiled by Leslie M. Scott. Cambridge, Mass.: Riverside Press, 1924.

———. *History of Portland, Oregon*. Syracuse: D. Mason and Co., 1890.

Sinclair, Andrew. *The Emancipation of the American Woman*. New York: Harper Colophon, 1965. Published in England as *The Better Half*. London: Jonathan Cape, 1966.

Sklar, Kathryn Kish. *Catherine Beecher: A Study in American Domesticity*. New Haven and London: Yale University Press, 1973.

Smith, Helen Krebs., ed. *With Her Own Wings: Historical Sketches, Reminiscences, and Anecdotes of Pioneer Women*. Portland, Ore.: Beattie and Co., 1948.

Smith, Henry Nash. *Virgin Land: The American West as Symbol and Myth*. Rev. ed. Cambridge, Mass.: Harvard University Press, 1973.

Smith, Page. *Daughters of the Promised Land: Women in American History*. Boston: Little, Brown and Co., 1970.

Smith, Theodore Clarke. *The Liberty and Free Soil Parties in the Northwest*. New York: Longmans, Green, and Co., 1897.

Smythe, William E. *The Conquest of Arid America*. New York: Macmillan, 1905.

Sonne, Niels Henry. *Liberal Kentucky: 1780–1828*. Lexington; University of Kentucky Press, 1968.

Stoeltje, Beverly J. "A Helpmate for Man Indeed: The Image of the Frontier Woman." *Journal of American Folklore* 88 (Jan.–March 1975).

Stratton, Joanna L. *Pioneer Women: Voices from the Kansas Frontier*. New York: Simon and Schuster, 1981.

Stroller, Ruth, ed. *Old Yamhill: The Early History of its Towns and Cities*. Lafayette, Ore.: Yamhill County Historical Society, 1976.

Throckmorton, Arthur L. *Oregon Argonauts: Merchant Adventurers on the Western Frontier*. Portland, Ore.: Oregon Historical Society, 1961.

Turner, Frederick Jackson. *Frontier and Section: Selected Essays*. Edited by Ray Allen Billington. Englewood Cliffs, N.J.: Prentice-Hall, 1961.

Tyack, David. "The Tribe and the Common School: The District School in Ashland, Oregon in the 1860s." *The Call Number*, University of Oregon Library Publication 27 (Spring 1966).

Unruh, John D., Jr. *The Plains Across: The Overland Emigrants and the Trans-Mississippi West, 1840–1860*. Urbana: University of Illinois Press, 1979.

Vaughan, Thomas, ed. *The Western Shore: Oregon Country Essays Honoring the American Revolution*. Portland, Ore.: Oregon Historical Society, 1976.

Victor, Frances Fuller. *All Over Oregon and Washington*. San Francisco: John H. Carmany, 1872.

———. *See* Bancroft, Hubert Howe

Warren, Sidney. *Farthest Frontier: The Pacific Northwest*. New York: Macmillan, 1949.

Welter, Barbara. *Dimity Convictions: The American Woman in the Nineteenth Century*. Athens: Ohio University Press, 1976.

Wertz, Richard W., and Dorothy C. Wertz. *Lying-In: A History of Childbirth in America*. New York: Schocken, 1979.

Williamson, Chilton. *American Suffrage: From Property to Democracy, 1760–1860*. Princeton, N.J.: Princeton University Press, 1960.

Winthur, Oscar Osburn. *The Great Northwest*. 2d ed. New York: Alfred A. Knopf, 1950.

———. *The Old Oregon Country: A History of Frontier Trade, Transportation, and Travel*. Stanford, Calif.: Stanford University Press, 1950.

Wood, Ann Douglas. "The 'Scribbling Women' and Fanny Fern: Why Women Wrote." *American Quarterly* 23 (Spring 1971).

INDEX

Abolition. *See* Antislavery activity

Abortion, 108, 115

Adams, William L., 59, 60, 90, 97, 174, 249n10

Agrarianism, 65, 154, 163

Alcoholism: cures for, 14, 145, 204, 246n45; of Lindsey Scott, 20–21; of uncles, 22, 28, 41, 73; and women, 118; as disease, 141

American Woman Suffrage Association, 86, 92

Anthony, Susan B., 8, 84, 85, 91, 171, 173, 182, 186, 194, 209, 212; traveling with ASD, 92–95, 109, 119, 185; reading *NNW*, 99

Antislavery activity: of Scott family, 12, 14–15, 23, 32; in Oregon, 59

Antisuffrage argument, 88, 94, 114, 117, 120, 150, 155–56, 164, 176, 207; and Mrs. J. Blakesley Frost, 93, 94; religious opposition, 114, 131, 132, 134–36; and prohibition, 181, 212

Anti-woman's rights: 69–70, 72; religious opposition, 93–94; Democratic opposition, 119. *See also* Democrats

Astoria, Oregon, 99–100

Bailey, Margaret Jewett, 47, 61

Baker, Edward B., 24, 70–71, 98, 133, 171, 174

Baptists, 14, 21, 138, 146, 212

Birth control: by self-restraint, 64, 69, 70, 108, 110–12, 113; Bradwell's advice, 86; knowledge of, 108; contraceptives, 113; and Annie Besant and Cyrus Teed, 113

Boone, Daniel, 13, 16, 50, 52

Bradwell, Myra, 86

Brown, Beriah, 93, 140

Bush, Asahel, 59, 64, 67, 198

Catt, Carrie Chapman, 194, 209, 211, 217

Centennial Exposition, 91

Childbirth: fictional rendition of, 7; Ann Scott's, 8, 28; Miranda Goudy's, 29. *See also* Duniway, Abigail Scott

Clackamas County, 53, 59

Class differences: Yankees vs. southerners, 18, 21, 22, 23, 26, 139; in Oregon and Pacific Northwest, 44, 62, 89, 108, 171; depicted in novels, 65; East vs. West, 86, 96, 138, 155, 195, 217; rich vs. poor, 155, 156, 164, 185, 194

Clay, Laura, 213

Coburn, Catherine Scott, 1, 3, 6, 29, 30, 31, 38, 39, 41, 43, 142–43; death of husband, 81; as secretary of State Suffrage Assn., 96; as *NNW* editor, 175; vital statistics, 222

Coe, Viola, 214

Colby, Clara, 210–11, 213

Collins, Col. John, 85

Columbian Exposition of 1893, 194

Cook, Amos, 27, 43, 44

Cook, Fanny Scott, 1, 6, 11, 29, 37, 39, 40, 74; marriage of, 46; suffrage activity, 96; vital statistics, 222

Cooperative associations, 68, 69, 156, 160, 162, 163; ASD's Idaho scheme, 163, 193

Cooperative housekeeping, 159–61

Corruption, 89, 140–41, 172, 173, 180–81, 186, 209, 211, 212, 250n35

Cumberland Presbyterians, 1, 2, 4–5, 10, 11, 17–18, 21, 24, 138; in Oregon, 28, 59

Dalton, Martha, 84

Democrats: in Illinois, 12, 23, 24; in Oregon, 59, 77, 93, 119, 139–41, 171, 176, 177, 181; vs. Republicans, 146; in Washington, 183. *See also* Antisuffrage argument; Secessionists

DeVoe, Emma Smith, 214, 216–17

Disease: on Illinois frontier, 1, 20, 28; of Frances Tucker Scott, 9; of Lindsey Scott, 20; of Ann Scott, 28, 31; cholera epidemic, 30; on Oregon Trail, 30, 34,

suffrage, 139, 143–46, 207; and breweries, 184–86. *See also* Women's Christian Temperance Union
Temperance Alliance, 114, 139, 174, 176, 177
Thompson, Mary, 147, 149, 187
Train, George Francis, 158
Tremont, Illinois, 19, 21, 23; and A. Lincoln, 24

Unions, 68, 163, 165–66, 168–69, 194
Unitarianism: in Tremont, Illinois, 21; in Oregon, 132
Utilitarianism, 90

Victor, Frances Fuller, 91
Villard, Henry, 161, 169, 184
Voluntary motherhood. *See* Birth control

Walla Walla, Washington, 93–94, 121, 185–86
Weed, Ada and Gideon, 64
West, Oswald, xv, 216
Whigs, 9, 10, 12, 23, 24, 59, 148
Willard, Frances, 142, 181
Williams, George, 60, 140, 212
Woman's Club, 154, 196, 213, 215
Woman's rights, 10, 65–66; associated

with Republicans, 59, 60, 64; and property, 60, 75, 80; in Pacific Northwest, 90, 178, 218–19; ASD's views of, 107, 158; domestic implications, 107, 129; financial autonomy, 148–49, 161. *See also* Anti-woman's rights
Woman suffrage: early views and debate, 66, 84–85, 146; ASD's commitment to, 82, 84, 85, 90, 126, 138–39, 207; and prohibitionists, 139, 141, 142, 144, 149–50, 207; and temperance, 139, 142, 143, 184–86; in Washington, 169, 182–84, 214; in Oregon, 178, 179, 195, 197; Oregon campaign of 1884, 178–82; of 1900, 207–08; of 1906, 210–12, 215–16; of 1908, 213; of 1910, 214; of 1912, 214–16. *See also* Anti-suffrage argument; Idaho
Women's Christian Temperance Union, 91, 131–32, 138, 142, 146, 181, 211, 212; and ASD, 184, 214
Women's work: on farms, 54, 56, 61, 66, 68, 69, 71, 74; in Oregon City woolen mills, 152
Woodhull, Victoria, 108–10, 133

Yankees, 18–19, 21, 22, 23, 27, 65, 86, 89

Printed in the United States
141157LV00002B/29/A

9 780300 034783

Made in the USA
Monee, IL
09 November 2021